MEXICO
The Remaking of an Economy

SECOND EDITION

Nora Lustig

Brookings Institution Press
Washington, D.C.

Library of Congress Cataloging-in-Publication data

Lustig, Nora.
    Mexico, the remaking of an economy / Nora Lustig. — 2d ed.
       p.   cm.
    Includes bibliographical references (p.) and index.
    ISBN 0-8157-7582-2 (cloth). — ISBN 0-8157-7301-3 (pbk.)
    1. Mexico—Economic policy—1970–2. Mexico—Economic
conditions—1982-   I. Title.
HC135.L87   1998
338.972–DC21   98-26072
                                                                  CIP

987654321

The paper used in this publication meets minimum requirements
of the American National Standard for Information Sciences—
Permanence of Paper for Printed Library Materials:
ANSI Z39.48-1984.

Typeset in Palatino

Composition by Harlowe Typography
Cottage City, Maryland

Printed by R. R. Donnelley & Sons
Harrisonburg, Virginia

For Antonio, Carlos Javier, Liliana,

my mother, and in memory of my father

Foreword

In mid-1982 Mexico was in a deep economic crisis. The country was saddled with a large foreign debt, world interest rates were high, commercial banks had stopped lending to the third world, and the price of oil was dropping. With rampant inflation, increasing capital flight, and chaos in the financial and foreign exchange markets, conditions at home were no better. To confront internal imbalances and accommodate adverse external conditions, Mexico adjusted its spending and sought new ways to foster growth. The crisis and adjustment imposed great hardship on the Mexican population, but in contrast to many countries in the region, Mexico adapted to the new situation without serious political or social disruptions.

Between 1982 and 1991, the Mexican economy underwent a profound change. Careful macroeconomic management replaced chronic fiscal imbalances, external trade was liberalized, markets were deregulated, and ownership restrictions removed. Even so, improvement in the Mexican economy took much longer than many—-including the Mexican government and the International Monetary Fund—-had expected. In 1988, after several failed attempts, inflation was brought under control, and starting in 1989 per capita output growth was positive for three consecutive years.

The first edition of this book, represented by chapters one through four, constitutes one of the first comprehensive studies of Mexico's adjustment and economic reform. Nora Lustig analyzes Mexico's economic evolution from the outset of the debt crisis in 1982 until the sweeping reforms began to bear fruit in the early 1990s. She examines the country's outward-oriented development strategy and its search for greater economic integration with the United States and Canada under the North American Free Trade Agreement.

Since the first edition was published in 1992, the Mexican economy has alternately raised and dashed hopes for its future. In the early 1990s, Mexico was considered a "model reformer," following the changes made in the wake of the 1982 debt crisis. The new policy prescription, outward oriented and private sector based, was a turnaround from the inward-looking interventionist strategy pursued before the mid-1980s. However, declining economic indicators culminated in a financial crisis of devastating proportions at the end of 1994. Nevertheless, subsequent domestic policy reforms, particularly in banking and finance, combined with an international rescue package, have put the Mexican economy back on the road to recovery. Growth rates in 1996 and 1997 have reenforced this optimistic view.

In this second edition of *Mexico: The Remaking of an Economy*, with new chapters five through nine and some updates to the earlier chapters, Nora Lustig expands on her previous analysis. She discusses the peso crisis of 1994 and the ensuing rescue package, and she details the reactions of the international financial community and its motives for offering support. Finally, she shows how recent economic events have filtered through to the microeconomy, highlighting the negative effects on poverty and inequality.

Many persons who provided information and documentation were colleagues of Nora Lustig in Mexico, employees of the U.S. and Mexican governments in Mexico, at the Mexican Embassy in the United States, or in the private sector. Though the author must thank them as a group rather than individually, this in no way diminishes her gratitude to them. Without their help, neither edition of this book could have been written.

Many scholars shared their expertise with the author and provided useful comments on her manuscript. The author is particularly grateful to Carlos Bazdresch, Susan Benda, Barry Bosworth, Mario Dehesa, Rudiger Dornbusch, Raúl Feliz, Albert Fishlow, Michael Gavin, Manuel Guitian, Mauricio González, Richard Haass, Peter Hakim, Steve Herzenberg, Alain Ize, Steve Kamin, Claudio Loser, Roberto Marino, Antonio Martin del Campo, Darryl McLeod, Carlos Paredes, Jaime Ros, John Steinbruner, Lance Taylor, and Sidney Weintraub. For their insightful suggestions on chapter 3, the author thanks Harold Alderman, Clifford Gaddy, Sam Morley, Per Pinstrup-Andersen, and

George Rossmiller. Aisha Williams and César Bouillon helped prepare the final tables and documentation of the second edition, and Janet Herrlinger helped in the typing and the preparation for the publication of the second edition.

Finally, the author greatly appreciates the help of staff members at Brookings. Arianna Legovini and Rebecca Harris provided valuable research assistance to the first and second edition, respectively; Tom Arend, Christian Ende, and Myles Nienstadt, helped to find documentation and to prepare the tables of the first edition. Catherine Kreyche, Caroline Lalire, and Patricia Dewey edited the manuscript of the first edition, and Theresa Walker edited the second edition. Annette D. Leak, Louise Skillings, and Ann Ziegler typed the various drafts of the first edition. Jay Smith and Adrianne Goins verified the factual content of the first edition, aided by Z. Selin Hur. Maya Dragicevic verified the second edition. The index was prepared by Julia Petrakis and Bruce Tracy.

During much of the time she was writing the first edition of this book, the author was first on sabbatical and later on leave from El Colegio de Mexico. The author is grateful for the Colegio's support.

Brookings gratefully acknowledges the financial support of the John D. And Catherine T. MacArthur Foundation for the first edition and the support of the Carnegie Corporation of New York and the John D. and Catherine T. MacArthur Foundation for the second edition.

The views expressed in this study are those of the author and should not be ascribed to any of the persons or organizations mentioned above, or to the trustees, officers, or other staff members of the Brookings Institution.

MICHAEL H. ARMACOST
President

July 1998
Washington, D.C.

Contents

PART 2   The *Re*-Remaking of an Economy

Tables

Figures

Preface to the Second Edition

The first edition of this book was published at the height of "Mexico-optimism." In 1992, most analysts and observers viewed Mexico as a model reformer among developing nations, a country that would soon reap the benefits of having chosen the right path. Although I did not share the same degree of optimism proclaimed by others, the first edition of this book was upbeat about Mexico's economic prospects. Two years later, however, nearly everything went awry.

At the end of 1994, Mexico was on the verge of a financial collapse. To avoid the collapse, the International Monetary Fund and the United States had to arrange an international financial rescue package of unprecedented magnitude. The package, however, did not prevent a major contraction in Mexico's output. In 1995, instead of the prosperity anticipated in the aftermath of the North American Free Trade Agreement (NAFTA), Mexico faced its worst recession since the Great Depression. Even before the crisis of 1995, Mexico's economic performance was lackluster. The growth in output had been positive since 1989, but it declined to the point that per capita output growth was negative in 1993. Especially disturbing was the fact that poverty in the poorest states was on the rise—government efforts notwithstanding—and inequality remained very high.

For the critics of reform, the cause of Mexico's disappointing performance and the 1994 financial crisis is to be found in the market-oriented reforms introduced by the Mexican government since the mid-1980s. Instead of fostering growth—it is argued—reforms such as trade liberalization ended up choking large productive sectors that were not ready to compete in the international arena, thereby weakening the economy and its potential for growth. In its extreme version, such a view would contend that both Mexico's slow growth and the 1994 crisis illustrate how "neoliberal" economic policies are bound to fail and, therefore, should be rolled back.

For the reform minded, Mexico's worse-than-expected performance is explained by the fact that the reforms did not go far enough. Rigidities imposed by existing labor legislation, centralized public finances, the preservation of state ownership in such areas as the petroleum sector and railroad transportation, and the slowness of the process to give land ownership titles to previous *ejidatarios*, are some leading examples of the incompleteness of reforms.

In reality, the answer is more complex than simply choosing between the supporters of reform or critics of the neoliberal model. The main purpose of this new edition is to examine precisely what factors explain Mexico's lackluster performance and the peso crisis. In addition to contributing to the understanding of a traumatic experience in Mexico's recent economic history, this analysis is meant to yield helpful insights for other reforming economies around the globe.

Abbreviations and Acronyms

CEPAL	Comisión Económica para América Latina y el Caribe (Economic Commission for Latin America and the Caribbean)
CFE	Comisión Federal de Electricidad (Federal Commission of Electricity)
CONAPO	Consejo Nacional de Población (National Council of Population)
CONASUPO	Comisión Nacional de Subsistencias Populares (National Commission of Popular Subsistence)
COPLAMAR	Coordinación General del Plan Nacional de Zonas Deprimidas y Grupos Marginados (General Coordination of the National Plan for Depressed Zones and Marginal Groups)
EFF	extended fund facility
FDI	foreign direct investment
FERRONALES	Ferrocarriles Nacionales (National Railways)
FICORCA	Fideicomiso para la Cobertura contra el Riesgo Cambiario (Trust Fund for the Coverage of Exchange Rate Risks)
FTA	free trade agreement
GATT	General Agreement on Tariffs and Trade
GSP	Generalized System of Preferences
IMSS	Instituto Mexicano del Seguro Social (Mexican Institute of Social Security)
INCO	Instituto Nacional del Consumidor (National Consumers Institute)
INEGI	Instituto Nacional de Estadística, Geografía e Informática (National Institute of Statistics, Geography, and Informatics)
ISSSTE	Instituto de Salud y Seguridad Social para Trabajadores del Estado (Health and Social Security Institute for State Employees)
LIBOR	London interbank offer rate
NAFINSA	Nacional Financiera, S.A. (National Financing Institution)

NAFTA	North American Free Trade Agreement
OECD	Organization for Economic Cooperation and Development
ORP	official reference price
PASE	Pacto de Solidaridad Económica (Economic Solidarity Pact)
PECE	Pacto para la Estabilidad y el Crecimiento Económico (Pact for Economic Stability and Growth)
PEMEX	Petróleos Mexicanos (Mexican Petroleum Company)
PIRE	Programa Inmediato de Reordenación Económica (Program of Immediate Economic Reorganization)
PRI	Partido Revolucionario Institucional (Institutional Revolutionary Party)
PRONASOL	Programa Nacional de Solidaridad (National Program of Solidarity)
PSBR	public sector borrowing requirement
SDR	special drawing rights
TELMEX	Teléfonos de México
TIFT	Understanding Regarding Trade and Investment Facilitation Talks
USITC	U.S. International Trade Commission

PART I

The Remaking of an Economy

Introduction

IN WHAT SENSE is the Mexican economy being "remade"? Mexico has not been subject to physical destruction by nature or by war. Nor is it a country whose productive structure was the result of decades of central planning. In this sense the remaking of Mexico is less dramatic than, for example, that of Germany after World War II or of Eastern Europe and the former Soviet Union in the 1990s. What has been happening in Mexico is different.

During the 1980s Mexico experienced what Latin American social scientists call a change in its "development model." Gone is the import-substitution industrialization model that characterized Mexico since the 1930s. Instead, Mexico has become an open economy in which the state's intervention is limited by a new legal and institutional framework. Under the new model, the tendency is for the market to replace regulation, private ownership to replace public ownership, and competition, including that from foreign goods and investors, to replace protection. Nothing illustrates the change in strategy more vividly than the pursuit of a free trade agreement with the United States, first mentioned by Salinas in June 1990,[1] and the constitutional reform of land distribution and the *ejido* system adopted at the end of 1991.[2]

What prompted this change in development strategy? Mexico had taken a risk in the 1970s by borrowing heavily in world capital markets and indulging in overexpansive policies, and then paid dearly when oil prices fell and world interest rates rose. Adjustment to the new circumstances required a policy that would increase net exports, generating foreign exchange to service the external debt. Because the government, not the private sector, owed most of the external debt, fiscal policy also had to change in order to increase revenues and cut

1

noninterest expenditures. The restoration of growth required changes that would build confidence and encourage private capital inflows by means other than commercial bank loans, which were no longer available. Finally, to make the economy more flexible and competitive in a global context, the rules that governed the flow of goods and investment had to change.

Mexico's Adjustment and Recovery: A Summary

In mid-1982 Mexico was in a deep economic crisis. The international environment was adverse to a Mexico saddled with foreign debt. World interest rates were high, the price of oil, Mexico's main export, was falling, and commercial banks had stopped lending. This unfavorable international environment exacerbated the consequences of domestic imbalances and contributed to rampant inflation, capital flight, and chaos in the financial and foreign exchange markets. To confront the internal imbalances and accommodate the adverse external conditions, Mexico was compelled to adjust its expenditures, reorient its output, and find new ways to foster growth.

In the early 1990s Mexico gained recognition as a country successfully managing economic adjustment and reform. Inflation slowed, flight capital was returning, domestic and foreign investment was rising, and per capita output began to grow. The path to recovery, however, had been far from smooth. Well into the late 1980s, analysts wondered why Mexico's recovery was so slow despite the sound macroeconomic policies and structural reforms it had instituted. The slow recovery imposed high social costs on the Mexican population, as per capita real disposable income fell on average by 5 percent a year between 1983 and 1988.[3]

For some six years the Mexican government focused economic policy on restoring stability, particularly on lowering the rate of inflation and keeping the loss of international reserves in check. It finally succeeded in 1988, when inflation decreased from monthly averages close to 10 percent at the beginning of the year to about 1 percent by year's end.[4] However, growth did not follow.

Only a combination of more decisive external support and a shift in Mexico's development strategy managed to produce a turnaround. The changes regarding the role of the state in economic matters and the country's economic interaction with the rest of the world are particularly striking. Reforms sought to reduce state intervention and regulation so as to open new investment opportunities, build business confidence, and create a more flexible and efficient incentive structure. These reforms have called for substantial modifications in the legal and institutional frameworks of the economy that will shape the country for decades to come.

Mexico's experience in the 1980s presents an interesting case study of how a country coped with the debt crisis and managed to recover from its effects. The case of Mexico also provides several important lessons regarding stabilization and reform. This book attempts to analyze Mexico's policies and performance in the 1980s by addressing the following questions: What caused the 1982 debt crisis, and why was economic recovery so difficult to achieve? What explains Mexico's ultimately successful recovery, and will it be sustainable? What have the social costs of adjustment been, and who has borne the greatest share? Finally, what are the salient characteristics of the new development strategy, particularly in the reforms of the public sector and the foreign trade and investment regimes? The period under analysis extends from the 1978–81 oil boom and the 1982 debt crisis until mid-1991, when the negotiation of a North American Free Trade Agreement (NAFTA) began.[5]

In chapter 1, I argue that macroeconomic mismanagement, not the cumulative effect of thirty years of inward-oriented industrialization, was the root of the 1982 crisis.[6] In the late 1970s, on the mistaken assumption that the rise in world oil prices and the availability of cheap external credit would continue, the Mexican government engaged in a spending spree. The resulting fiscal deficit increased inflation rates and the trade deficit. The fiscal and external gaps were filled with external borrowing. In 1981, when the price of oil began to fall and external credit became more expensive and of a shorter maturity, the Mexican government failed to implement fiscal and relative price adjustments to adapt to the new, less favorable conditions. Fear of an imminent devaluation of the peso fueled capital flight, and a large nominal devaluation followed in early 1982.[7]

As inconsistent policies were pursued, the macroeconomic environment became increasingly chaotic.[8] Capital flight continued, and as reserves were depleted and no more credit was available to service debt payments, in August 1982 the Mexican government had to declare an involuntary moratorium on its debt, triggering a debt crisis that soon acquired global proportions.[9] Tensions between the private sector and the government peaked in September 1982, when the government announced the nationalization of the banking system.[10] When Miguel de la Madrid's government came to power in December 1982, it confronted the unenviable task of restoring economic stability in the face of a hostile domestic private sector and reluctant external creditors.

Chapter 2 closely analyzes the economic policies pursued to restore economic stability and growth from 1983 onward. Here I address the question of why recovery began to occur only in 1989, and at a modest rate, despite Mexico's record as a "model" debtor and the substantial progress in fiscal adjustment and structural reform achieved during the previous years.

In other Latin American countries the political resistance of different social groups expressed in massive strikes or threats of coups added to the climate of economic instability and made the necessary adjustment more difficult. However, Mexico's difficulties cannot be blamed on the political resistance of wage earners or other social groups to absorbing the costs of adjustment. In Mexico, policymakers enjoyed remarkable freedom to act during six years of economic hardship. There were no serious wage conflicts, threats from the military, peasant uprisings, or active guerrilla movements.

Economic, not political, difficulties were at the heart of Mexico's slow recovery. Three explanations for the slow recovery have been put forward.[11] Some analysts blame the adverse external conditions—low oil prices, high interest rates, and scarce external credit—that prevailed during most of the decade.[12] Others claim that structural reforms, such as trade liberalization, deregulation, and public enterprise privatization, were not introduced early enough.[13] Yet a third group argues that the slow recovery resulted primarily from an overzealous economic policy that cut government spending and private credit too deeply.[14]

I argue that the main explanation for Mexico's slow economic recovery lies in the adverse external conditions—that is, scarce external credit, unfavorable terms of trade, and high real world interest rates—that prevailed since 1982.[15] These adverse external conditions resulted in net resource transfers to the rest of the world large enough to preclude effective stabilization and renewed growth.[16] These transfers increased inflationary pressures and impeded a "bounce back" of the Mexican economy after what should have been a two-year, rather than an eight-year, adjustment period.[17] The negative resource transfers were large because the effect of the reduction in external credit and of higher interest payments was compounded by capital flight, which after 1983 was itself a result, to a large extent, of the adverse external conditions.

For many reasons the large accumulated external debt, combined with adverse external conditions, had a negative effect on growth.[18] First, the prevailing conditions deterred private investment. The Mexican government contracted most of the external debt under the assumption that oil prices would remain high (or even increase) and that external interest rates would decrease to previous low levels. The government's budget constraint, that is, that the present value of the future flow of net government revenues must equal zero, was drastically altered when oil prices declined and interest rates remained high. The initial stock of debt was no longer payable under the previous conditions unless both the revenue and expenditure sides of the public accounts were radically changed. Moreover, if the required fiscal changes were insufficient or difficult to put into practice, the government would have to resort to inflationary financing by printing money. The private sector's perception that the government would be forced to impose higher taxes or resort to inflationary financing explains its reluctance to invest in Mexico and the recurrent bouts of capital flight. This shifting of domestic savings abroad further slowed recovery and reduced the prospects for growth. Whenever the government tried to deter capital flight with high real domestic interest rates, private investment and growth were also negatively affected.

Second, lower oil prices, higher real interest rates, and external credit rationing, all of which implied drastic adjustments in the fiscal noninterest (or primary) budget, further impeded recovery. These constraints triggered a much larger relative cut in public investment than in current government expenditures because the Mexican government had to act quickly, and found it politically and administratively easier to cut investment. Lower public investment, however, may translate into bottlenecks in infrastructure that can limit future output growth.

Third among the debt's negative effects was the series of devaluations of the Mexican currency from 1982 onward. With a heavy debt burden and adverse external conditions, Mexico had to devalue its peso in order to help generate the necessary balance-of-trade surplus. Although devaluation was inevitable, particularly if the government was to service the external debt, its impact, at least in the short run, fueled inflation and precluded recovery.[19] The depressed real wages caused by the devaluation translated into economic recession rather than rapid restructuring.[20] A devaluation also had a negative effect on private investment because it increased the debt burden of the private sector's dollar-denominated debt and the cost of noncompetitive imports.[21]

The adverse external conditions also partly explain why it was so difficult to reduce inflation.[22] On the one hand, avoiding a balance-of-payments crisis required a high real exchange rate, which implied successive nominal devaluations, while price stability required a stable nominal exchange rate.[23] On the other hand, the cut in the fiscal deficit required for lower inflation rates became more difficult to achieve, since falling oil prices meant lower revenues for PEMEX, the state-owned oil monopoly, and thus for the government, while interest payments on external and domestic debt rose.

Given the sizable social costs (discussed in chapter 3) incurred during the slow recovery, one wonders whether the situation could have been different. Two sets of questions arise. One set concerns domestic policymaking; the other involves actions taken by, or against, the outside world.

Given the limited autonomy imposed by the adverse external environment, could different policies have met the same balance-of-payments and inflation targets without sacrificing as much in growth and real wages? One of the tasks of chapter 2 is to analyze if and how domestic policies could have been better—in particular, if and how the pursuit of stabilization could have achieved similar results in slowing inflation and yet have been less costly in foregone output and wage losses.

The results obtained from the stabilization program implemented in 1988, known as the Economic Solidarity Pact, showed that incomes policy can yield remarkable outcomes when combined with fiscal adjustment.[24] Incomes policy helped bring inflation down to the lowest levels at smaller costs in terms of output losses and wage reduction. Why was incomes policy not tried earlier? First, it is possible that economic conditions—the availability of foreign currency reserves, in particular—were not ripe before 1987. Second, for a few years Mexican policymakers, like most mainstream economists, mistrusted incomes policy because of its interventionist quality.

Of course, better alternatives are always easier to find with hindsight. Given the depth of the crisis and the extent of the adjustment required, it is unclear to what degree stabilization policies could have been fine-tuned at the time. The government had to correct previous fiscal imbalances and serve a bulky external debt, while the availability of net foreign revenues and credit was drastically reduced. This was by no means an easy task.

Was it a good idea to intensify trade liberalization in 1988 as part of the Economic Solidarity Pact? In chapter 2, I argue that the intensification of trade liberalization may have been ineffective in its short-term impact on domestic inflation and may have added to the overall climate of uncertainty. For example, the huge surge in imports that followed trade liberalization added to the uncertainty surrounding the sustainability of the fixed exchange rate and encouraged some capital flight (see table 2-4). However, trade liberalization, especially when combined with the initiative to form a North American free trade area, helped jump-start the economy by attracting investment to the export sector. Trade liberalization could also prove helpful to medium- and long-term goals, including keeping domestic prices of tradable goods in line with international prices, introducing more structural flexibility and efficiency, and opening new investment opportunities. In hindsight the Economic Solidarity Pact may have provided a good policy setup to announce an acceleration of trade liberalization, because reserves were high and the anti-inflation objective made the measure appear justifiable.

Should trade liberalization and the divestiture of public enterprises have been started early in 1983 and proceeded more quickly? There are three—not mutually exclusive but distinct—interpretations of how structural reforms could have helped speed recovery. First, some argue that structural reforms would have removed the inefficiencies associated with the previous inward-oriented, state-led development strategy, which some analysts saw as the reason for Mexico's crisis in the first place.[25] Second, reforms could have helped recover the confidence of the business sector by showing the government's commitment to market-oriented reforms. Third, reforms may have stimulated capital repatriation and foreign investment by generating new opportunities for business.[26]

However, many of the gains in efficiency from structural reform are usually medium term. For example, the divestiture of public enterprises by law may require public outlays to compensate laid-off employees, and in the short run, the costs of privatization may outstrip the benefits. Or worse, even when the net short-run effect is positive, hasty structural decisions may prove detrimental in the medium term. For example, selling public enterprises in the midst of a crisis may have resulted in severe underpricing. Privatization requires time and financial and administrative resources to avoid bad deals.

Furthermore, to have engaged in trade liberalization in 1983, when confidence in the government and foreign currency reserves were low and inflation was still high, might have been destabilizing. Yet the immediate adoption of some reforms in 1983, such as the reprivatization of the recently nationalized banks, would have promoted the business sector's confidence. Such a move, however, may have been politically unpalatable for reasons discussed in chapter 2. It is very difficult to gauge whether the effects of front-loading structural reforms would have been predominantly positive or negative in the short run.

If the main source of economic difficulties was the adverse external environment, was there an alternative to absorbing the external shocks internally? Should the Mexican government have suspended payments on its external debt? Should the international community have been more flexible in providing finance and establishing debt schedules?

One obvious alternative to absorbing the external shocks internally was to suspend payments on the foreign debt. In chapter 2, I argue that a unilateral suspension of payments on the external debt would have been risky. Although the Mexican government would have enjoyed an immediate direct benefit, it is unclear whether the indirect effects would have been positive or negative; that is, whether retaliation by commercial banks or capital flight from a skeptical private sector would have eaten up the self-attained debt relief. Results in Latin American countries that chose to suspend payments are mixed.[27] Costa Rica, for example, obtained a sustained benefit from the extra resources provided by a moratorium, but other countries, such as Peru, did not.

Could Mexico have replicated Costa Rica's experience? A successful moratorium would have required the government to implement a credible macroeconomic program, win the confidence of the Mexican private sector to stave off capital flight, and gain the support of the U.S. government to "neutralize" commercial banks and maintain access to other sources of credit and foreign investment. Although the first condition was met in several instances between 1982 and 1987, the second and third were not. On the other hand, since the political resistance to absorbing adjustment internally was low, paying the debt became the least risky alternative. One question that remains is why the Mexican government was unable to gain enough domestic and external support to declare a moratorium.[28]

A better and quicker response from international agencies and creditor governments would have made a difference. International financial institutions and the governments of industrialized countries underestimated the magnitude of the adjustment required as well as the sluggish pace of economic recovery. As a result, official financing was insufficient and tied to performance criteria based on too short a time span.[29] Creditor country governments delayed in making commercial banks accept reasonable forms of debt or debt service reduction.[30] In retrospect it seems clear that effective management of the debt crisis and subsequent shocks required an earlier combination of debt reduction and longer-term official lending.[31] International agencies should not have required that a country be up-to-date in its debt servicing with commercial banks as a precondition for access to official funds, because this left countries with little option but to accept the conditions of their de facto cartelized creditor banks.

The international agencies and creditor governments were effective in protecting the large money-center banks from serious financial crisis.[32] The debt strategy ruled out a potential failure in international capital markets by ensuring an "involuntary" flow of lending from commercial banks so that debtor countries could meet debt service obligations. At the same time, the banks had an opportunity to move to more secure reserve positions and diversify their portfolios. The official management of the crisis, however, meant ultimately that creditors and creditor countries fared better than debtor countries. Without the backing of multilateral agencies and industrial governments, bankers would probably have been in worse shape.[33] Latin American countries could have done in the early 1980s what they did during the 1930s, when, except for Argentina and Cuba, they declared moratoria on debt service.[34]

Some may wonder why, if Mexico was eventually able to pull itself out of the crisis, the international community should have responded differently. If the required adjustment could have been smaller, thanks to more timely financing or debt relief, recovery would have occurred sooner, and the social costs would have been lower. As discussed in chapter 3, in the 1980s real incomes fell, poverty rose, and social indicators deteriorated. Some of this damage, such as the contraction in investment in physical and human capital, may produce lasting effects. Had the burden-sharing of the overborrowing and overlending of the late 1970s been different, some of these costs could have been avoided.

As of 1988, although Mexico had inflation under control and the preconditions for recovery were in place, the economy remained stagnant. It is true that Mexico could count on the robust industrial base and entrepreneurial capacity developed in the post–World War II period. Fiscal and monetary discipline had been attained, and runaway inflation had been checked. Relative price adjustment, particularly the reduction in real wages, had been achieved, and structural reform in the public sector and the trade regime was moving ahead.

However, all these preconditions turned out to be insufficient to attract flight capital and foreign investment on the scale required for recovery. A prompt and sustainable recovery required a turnaround in the flow of net resource transfers; that is, higher external credits, lower external debt payments, capital repatriation, higher foreign investment, or some combination thereof. A decisive turnaround in the flow of external resources demanded additional efforts by the government. The first initiative was to seek a reduction in the stock and service of the external debt. In mid-1989 Mexico signed an agreement in principle with its commercial banks to reduce its medium- and long-term debt under the so-called Brady Plan. (The details of the agreement are discussed in the appendix.) The debt agreement, however, was not enough. A few months after its announcement, it had yet to generate the "virtuous circle" of sustained larger capital inflows, lower domestic interest rates, and output growth that some had expected. To drive recovery, other fundamental measures were required.

Two important events took place in the first part of 1990: the decision to reprivatize the banks and the revelation of Mexico's interest in a free trade agreement with the United States.[35] These announcements were followed by immediate capital inflows, which increased in subsequent months. The selling of several public enterprises (including some of the banks), the prospects of greater integration with the U.S. market, and attractive returns in the stock exchange translated into a jump in capital repatriation and foreign investment.[36] The recovery was in place. In 1991, for the first time since 1981, gross domestic product (GDP) per capita growth rates were positive for three consecutive years, and the outlook was good.

The outside world also played a role in Mexico's recovery. In early 1989 the U.S. government's attitude toward Mexico became more favorable. Mexico was no longer seen as a corrupt and unreliable country that created migratory, environmental, and narcotics-trafficking problems for the United States. Instead, Mexico was seen as providing the United States with opportunities for economic and political partnership. This new attitude opened the way for the debt reduction agreement subsequently signed between Mexico and its foreign commercial creditors. It also opened the way to negotiations on a North American Free Trade Agreement between Canada, Mexico, and the United States, concluded in August 1992. Last but not least, U.S. support was instrumental in the decision of international agencies to increase their support for Mexico. In 1989 the International Monetary Fund (IMF) signed an extended fund facility, the World Bank pledged to lend about U.S.$2 billion a year from 1989 to 1992, and the Inter-American Development Bank (IDB) increased its lending.

Is the recovery Mexico enjoyed between 1989 and 1991 sustainable? In step with the larger capital inflows in 1990 and 1991, the current account of the balance of payments has quickly deteriorated. Exports continue to grow, albeit at a slower pace, while imports are surging. The expansion of imports may be, to some extent, a one-time phenomenon. Consumers are buying durables that before the liberalization of trade could only be smuggled into the country. More important, producers are importing capital goods to increase their productive capacity. Thus the current account deficit may shrink in the future, as these immediate effects disappear and investment generates the anticipated improvements in productivity and net exports.

This process, however, may take a few years. In the meantime, will capital inflows be sufficient to finance the deterioration of the current account? If expectations about Mexico's future continue to be as optimistic as those prevailing in 1991, capital inflows may remain high for years to come. The prospect of a North American Free Trade Agreement certainly makes investing in Mexico attractive, and capital may continue to arrive in large sums. If so, the Mexican economy could grow at relatively high rates, and Mexico could even become the economic miracle of the 1990s. If expectations change, capital inflows slow, and inflation is not reduced to close to world levels, however, Mexican policymakers will have to curb demand and introduce additional institutional reforms to encourage capital inflows.[37] In such a scenario, growth may slow, at least until new investment brings about the expected productivity gains.

The Mexican experience teaches several important lessons. Regarding stabilization, it underscores the need to correct macroeconomic, particularly fiscal, imbalances once and for all. At the same time, the Mexican experience illustrates the advantages of incomes policy and the potential risks of liberalizing trade before price and financial stability are in place. It also shows how economic recovery relies on introducing institutional changes that increase business confidence and open new, profitable opportunities for private investment.

In some respects, however, Mexico's case is probably difficult to replicate. Two conditions were paramount to Mexico's successful adjustment: the acquiescence of its labor force in the face of drastic cutbacks in wages, and the unique cohesion and control of the Mexican state. Both can be attributed to Mexico's singular political system dominated by one party, the Institutional Revolutionary Party (PRI), which has governed the country for almost seventy years.[38] Thus the Mexican case is in many respects a unique example of how adjustment costs can be absorbed internally without serious political or economic disruption.

A Note on Method

This book seeks to describe and interpret Mexico's economic experience during the 1980s. The methodology is eclectic. The causes and implications of many events are subject to different, often conflicting, interpretations. Unfortunately, in many instances a testing of counterfactual postulates is neither feasible nor available. Nor can there be an econometric analysis of the main hypotheses. More often than not the analysis must be speculative, based on inferences from economic theory, other experiences, or common sense. I have tried to include the results of existing econometric analysis whenever possible, such as in analyzing the contribution of price and wage controls to curbing inflation. Even in those instances the results should be taken with caution, econometrics notwithstanding.

The data presented in the book come primarily from official statistics. I have tried to use the same source for each concept and include the definitions in the corresponding notes. Only the data for the estimates of poverty and household income distribution in chapter 3 required elaboration.

Chapter One

The Genesis of the 1982 Crisis

B ETWEEN 1950 and 1970 the Mexican economy performed
remarkably well. During this period Mexico generated per
capita annual growth rates of 3 to 4 percent with an annual inflation
rate of about 3 percent.[1] During these "golden years" Mexico's economy was industrialized and modernized. Yet changes in government
policy in the 1970s made Mexico's economy more vulnerable to external events, which ultimately precipitated a severe economic crisis in
1982.

The Golden Years of "Stabilizing Development"

Mexico followed a decidedly inward-looking development path
throughout the post–World War II period.[2] Rapid industrialization
in the 1950s and 1960s occurred within an economic environment
protected by trade barriers. The proportion of imports subject to licensing requirements increased from 28 percent in 1956 to more than 60
percent on average in the 1960s and about 70 percent on average
in the 1970s.[3] The contribution of import substitution and domestic
demand, as against external demand, to overall manufacturing growth
from 1950 to 1960 confirms the inward character of Mexico's industrial
growth, especially when contrasted with such outward-oriented economies as Korea and Taiwan in the 1960s (table 1-1).

Changes in the composition of output reflect the industry-centered
nature of Mexico's development. In 1950 industry accounted for 21.5
percent of total output, rising to 24 percent in 1960 and 29.4 percent in
1970. Meanwhile, the share of agriculture and other primary activities
declined, while services remained relatively constant (table 1-2). Industrial development was accompanied by urban growth. The urban

TABLE 1-1. *Average Annual Growth Rates and Sources of Changes in Total Gross Manufacturing Production in Mexico, Korea, and Taiwan, Selected Periods, 1950–75*[a]
Percent

Country and years	Average annual growth rate	Sources of change				
		Domestic demand expansion	Export expansion	Import substitution	Changes in input-output coefficients	Total
Korea						
1955–63	10.4	57.3	11.5	42.2	−11.0	100.0
1963–70	18.9	70.1	30.4	−0.6	0.1	100.0
1970–73	23.8	39.0	61.6	−2.5	1.8	100.0
Taiwan						
1956–61	11.2	34.8	27.5	25.4	12.3	100.0
1961–66	16.6	49.2	44.5	1.7	4.6	100.0
1966–71	21.1	34.9	57.0	3.8	4.3	100.0
Mexico[b]						
1950–60	7.0	71.8	3.0	10.9	14.4	100.0
1960–70	8.6	86.1	4.0	11.0	−1.0	100.0
1970–75	7.2	81.5	7.7	2.6	8.2	100.0

Source: Excerpted from Kemal Dervis, Jaime de Melo, and Sherman Robinson, *General Equilibrium Models for Development Policy*, World Bank Research Publication (Cambridge University Press, 1982), table 4.3, p. 106.

a. For a description of the methodology see source. The average annual growth rates in this table differ from those in table 1-4, perhaps because the authors describe these figures as preliminary. Figures are rounded.

b. Preliminary results.

population, those living in towns with more than 2,500 inhabitants, grew from 42.6 percent in 1950 to 58.7 percent of total population in 1970.[4] Employment simultaneously shifted from agriculture to the service and industrial sectors (table 1-3).

Population growth was high from 1950 through the 1970s, reaching a yearly rate of almost 3.5 percent.[5] Despite the rapid growth in industrial employment, it was not high enough to accommodate the expanding urban labor force. The service sector became the "cushion" sector where surplus urban labor found a livelihood, albeit at low productivity and income.

Confidence on the part of the financial and business sectors charac-

TABLE 1-2. *Percentage Distribution of Gross Domestic Product, by Sector, Selected Years, 1950–85*[a]

Year	Agriculture[b]	Mining[c]	Industry[d]	Services[e]	Total
1950	19.1	5.1	21.5	54.4	100.0
1960	15.7	4.9	24.0	55.3	100.0
1970	11.5	4.8	29.4	54.5	100.0
1980	8.1	3.2	29.2	59.4	100.0
1985	8.4	3.6	27.7	60.3	100.0

Sources: Figures for 1950, 1960, and 1970 are based on data from the Banco de México (1977, 1979), published in Nora Lustig, *Distribución del ingreso y crecimiento en México: Un análisis de ideas estructuralistas* (Mexico City: Colegio de México, 1981). The figures for 1980 are from Instituto Nacional de Estadística, Geografía e Informática (INEGI), *Sistema de cuentas nacionales de México 1980–1986*, tomo 1: *Resumen general* (Mexico City, 1988), p. 194. The figures for 1985 are from INEGI, *Sistema de cuentas nacionales de México 1985–1988*, tomo 1: *Resumen general* (Mexico City, 1990), p. 118.

a. There might be differences in the definition of data included in each sector between 1950 and 1960–85 figures. Thus they are not strictly comparable. Figures are rounded.

b. Includes agriculture, cattle raising, forestry, and fishing.

c. Includes oil extraction.

d. Includes manufacturing, construction, electricity, and petrochemicals.

e. Includes commerce, transportation, communications, government, and financial and personal services.

terized the "stabilizing development" (*desarrollo estabilizador*) period, as the years between 1954 and the late 1960s were called in Mexican circles.[6] The prudent macroeconomic policies followed by successive governments resulted in capital inflows from abroad, which translated into savings spent domestically instead of returning abroad as flight capital.[7] In addition, capital inflows differed from those of the 1970s; direct investment was higher and external borrowing lower, as was true for Latin America as a whole.

Until the late 1960s, relatively sound fiscal and monetary policies and the absence of major external shocks and wage indexation mechanisms explained low inflation rates. Given low inflation and the general "pro-business" economic environment, the fixed exchange rate policy, with the values of the dollar set at 12.50 pesos in 1954, was both credible and feasible.[8] In the first half of the 1970s, however, fiscal mismanagement resulted in increasing inflation and, ultimately, a balance-of-payments crisis in mid-1976 that ended the fixed exchange rate regime.

TABLE 1-3. *Percentage Distribution of the Economically Active Population, by Type of Activity, 1950, 1960, 1970*

Sector	1950	1960	1970
Agriculture[a]	58.3	54.2	39.4
Industry[b]	16.0	19.0	23.0
Services[c]	21.5	26.1	31.9
Unspecified	4.3	0.7	5.8

Source: INEGI, *Estadísticas históricas de México*, tomo 1 (Mexico City, August 1985), table 6.1, p. 251. Figures are rounded.

a. Includes agriculture, cattle raising, fishing, and forestry.

b. Includes mining, oil industry, manufacturing, construction, and electricity.

c. Includes commerce, transportation, other services, and government.

Mexico's good economic performance ended in the mid-1970s for two reasons. First, because higher public spending was not accompanied by higher government revenues, the fiscal deficit rose and with it the current account deficit and inflation (table 1-4). Second, the leftist rhetoric and actions by President Luis Echeverría provoked a negative reaction in the business community and eroded the confidence of investors.[9]

The economic inefficiency associated with an inward-looking development also has been often mentioned as one of the primary causes of the 1976 economic crisis. This, however, is not necessarily true. Certainly the positive effect of Mexican protectionism had probably run its course.[10] But if macroeconomic policies had continued to be sound, structural inefficiencies would presumably not have resulted in a crisis like that of 1976. More likely, structural inefficiencies would have been evident in declining growth rates.

Macroeconomic Imbalances and the 1976 Balance-of-Payments Crisis

In the early 1970s the government's response to a slowdown in growth partially triggered by the oil shock of 1973 was expanding public expenditures and increasing state intervention. These policies, however, were more than a way to respond to economic sluggishness. They signaled a fundamental change in the emphasis the government would place on the business sector's demands and the latter's role in

TABLE 1-4. *Leading Economic Indicators, 1956–76*
Percent

Item	1956–72	1973–76
Gross domestic product		
(rate of increase)	6.7	6.1
Inflation rate[a]	3.1	16.7
Public deficit/GDP[b]	2.5	8.0
Current account/GDP	−2.5	−4.1

Source: José L. Alberro and Jorge E. Cambiaso, "Características del ajuste de la economía mexicana," paper prepared for a project, Políticas Macroeconómicas de Ajuste en América Latina, HOL/85/543 (December 1986), table 1, p. 41.
a. Based on the national consumer price index starting from 1969; for previous years, the wholesale price index was used.
b. Information starting from 1965.

the economy.[11] The belief at the time was that a country in which the state controlled a larger share of investment, owned more "strategic" sectors (energy, steel, and so on), and regulated more of the price-setting mechanism would be more prosperous, more equitable, and less vulnerable to the political pressures of the business sector at home and abroad.

Echeverría's government viewed greater state intervention as the best way to relieve social tensions that erupted during bloody 1968 riots and subsequent student unrest. The government was also concerned about guerrilla activity in the countryside. In response to these political and social pressures the government stepped up public spending, including its social spending, and attempted to strengthen the government's control of the economy by increasing the number of state enterprises and regulations.[12]

Echeverría hoped that an active state, through an increase in expenditures and public investment, could clear bottlenecks and improve living standards. Thus this period saw a large investment in infrastructure projects and an expansion in educational and public health services. But it also saw a lot of waste. The macroeconomic result was a rising fiscal deficit, financed by borrowing in world capital markets.

The policy mix of financing a rising fiscal deficit by external borrowing while maintaining a fixed exchange rate became unsustainable.

Public finances became increasingly fragile, and eventually the disequilibrium in the external accounts became unmanageable. The numbers are revealing. The fiscal deficit, that is, the consolidated public sector borrowing requirement (PSBR), rose from 2.5 percent of GDP in 1971 to 10 percent in 1975.[13] During the same period the deficit in the current account of the balance of payments jumped from U.S.$0.9 billion to U.S.$4.4 billion.[14] The foreign public debt rose from U.S.$6.7 billion to U.S.$15.7 billion.[15] Finally, the inflation rate, Mexico's pride in the previous two decades, reached chronic two-digit levels, rising from 3.4 percent in 1969 to an average of 17.0 percent in 1973–75.[16]

The government-expenditure-led growth broke down in 1976. The private sector, worried about the course of economic policy and antagonized by the state's expansionism and Echeverría's leftist rhetoric and actions, resorted to capital flight. Capital flight was used as a way to protect wealth against an expected currency devaluation and also as a political weapon against Echeverría's attacks on the private sector, such as the land expropriation in the Yaqui Valley in 1976. For a time the government stuck to the 1954 exchange rate, financing capital flight through additional borrowing and reserves.[17] But the Central Bank's reserves were soon exhausted. In August 1976, for the first time in twenty-two years, the peso was "allowed to float" in the foreign exchange market. An almost 40 percent devaluation of the peso against the dollar followed.[18] The economy was in crisis: output fell sharply and inflation accelerated. For the first time in almost twenty years, the Mexican government turned to the IMF for financial relief, and an extended fund facility was signed in late 1976.

Domestic factors, however, were not the only cause of the 1976 crisis. External shocks, especially the worldwide recession following the 1973 oil price increases, took their toll (at the time Mexico was a net importer of oil). According to one author's estimates, external factors contributed to approximately two-thirds of the balance-of-payments disequilibrium in 1975.[19]

Powerful political enemies emerged in response to President Echeverría's policies to combat Mexico's pressing political and social problems. In trying to solve these problems, Echeverría's government jettisoned a history of prudent macroeconomic management and stability. It was a sad finale for this government, which, despite good intentions, failed to deliver on its promises of sustained economic development. Contrary to expectations, Mexico became more vulnerable to exogenous events and thoroughly failed to meet its goal of a self-reliant, sustained, and "shared" development.[20]

The Oil Boom and the Onset of the 1982 Crisis

The recession that followed the 1976 crisis was short lived. Massive oil discoveries prompted the lifting of external constraint and triggered a dramatic policy change. Instead of adjusting to scarcity, the government now had to "administer the abundance," a phrase often used by José López Portillo, president between December 1, 1976, and November 30, 1982. The widely shared official view was that Mexico would be able to grow at unprecedentedly high rates from 1978 onward. Unfortunately, the opportunity provided by oil revenues was largely overestimated and the revenues misused.

The stated goal of López Portillo's government was to foster Mexico's economic growth and self-reliance through promotion of an active and dominant public sector. Contrary to government expectations, subsequent events showed that the country's economy actually became more vulnerable. As a consequence of policies followed during the oil boom, the government was ultimately less capable of implementing economic and political initiatives.

López Portillo confirmed the discovery of massive oil reserves shortly after becoming president and decided to use the reserves to foster Mexico's growth.[21] As a tradable good under the control of PEMEX (the state-run oil company), oil was expected to relieve the economy from both foreign exchange and fiscal constraints. At the prospect of higher revenues, the public and private sectors went on an investment spree beginning in 1978, which was accelerated by an oil price rise and new oil discoveries in 1979.[22]

This "public-expenditure-led growth" produced impressive results in aggregate output, investment, and employment during the four years of the oil boom.[23] Total GDP grew at an annual average of 8.4 percent, total investment increased by 16.2 percent a year, and urban employment expanded at 5.7 percent a year between 1978 and 1981 (table 1-5).[24]

Behind this optimistic picture, however, some cracks appeared.[25] As in most resource-based export booms, the domestic currency became increasingly overvalued.[26] High expectations of future public revenues fomented a rising fiscal deficit. The overvalued exchange rate, coupled with a large fiscal deficit, resulted in a growing balance-of-payments disequilibrium. During the first two years of the boom, however, the size of the imbalance was not cause for alarm. True, the fiscal deficit equaled 7.5 percent of GDP in 1980 (table 1-5). But the situation was not out of control because the deficit could have been largely corrected by changing part of the subsidies scheme, for example, by charging a higher price on the domestic gasoline, which at the time was much lower than gasoline prices abroad.

The problem became more acute as the price of oil continued its rapid rise in 1980.[27] Mexican policymakers misread this signal by assuming it was a permanent increase, and the spending spree accelerated during the second half of 1980 and the beginning of 1981. By the end of 1981 the fiscal deficit had swollen to 14.1 percent of GDP (table 1-5). Forecasts that misinterpreted the future behavior of some crucial variables provoked the spending spree. For instance, the international price of oil was expected to remain high, or even increase. Also, external interest rates were expected to fall in real terms. In both cases, exactly the opposite occurred.

It should be noted that Mexico was not alone in erroneously forecasting oil prices. For example, the 1980 *World Development Report* forecasted the price per barrel of oil in constant 1980 dollars at U.S.$35.10 in 1985 and U.S.$40.85 in 1990 (a nominal price of U.S.$78.30).[28] These numbers were higher still in the 1981 *World Development Report*: the 1990 forecast for the price of a barrel of oil in constant 1980 dollars was U.S.$42.0. According to the report, "real petroleum prices are likely to increase at some 3 percent a year in the 1980s, or 10 percent a year in nominal terms."[29] Had the price of oil followed this pattern, it is unlikely that Mexico would have experienced the 1982 crisis at all.

The growing public deficit was partly financed by borrowing abroad, especially from commercial banks that competed to grant loans to the public and private sectors in Mexico. Initially the rise in external borrowing seemed within reasonable limits. Between 1978 and 1980 total foreign public debt increased from U.S.$26.3 billion to U.S.$33.8 billion (table 1-5). The ratio of total external debt to GDP, however, declined from 35.8 percent in 1977 to 31.3 percent in 1980.[30] Analysts tend to agree that the size of the foreign debt up to the end of 1980 did not generate an untenable situation.[31] Fueled by expansionary

TABLE 1-5. *Economic Performance, 1976–81*

Item	1976	1977	1978	1979	1980	1981	Average 1976–77	Average 1978–81	Average 1976–81
Gross domestic product (annual percent change)[a]	4.2	3.4	8.2	9.2	8.3	7.9	3.8	8.4	6.9
GDP per capita (annual percent change)[a]	1.2	0.5	5.2	6.1	5.0	5.5	0.8	5.5	3.9
Gross fixed investment (annual percent change)[b]	0.4	−6.7	15.2	20.2	14.9	14.7	−3.2	16.2	9.4
Urban open unemployment rate (percent)[c]	6.8	8.1	6.8	5.7	4.6	4.2	7.5	5.3	6.0
Consumer prices (annual percent change), annual average (1978 = 100)[d]	15.8	29.1	17.5	18.2	26.3	27.9	22.4	22.5	22.5
Fiscal deficit to GDP (percent)[e]	9.9	6.7	6.7	7.6	7.5	14.1	8.3	9.0	8.7
Total external debt (billions of U.S. dollars)[f]	27.5	30.9	34.6	40.3	50.7	74.9	29.2	50.1	43.1

a. Banco de México, *Indicadores económicos* (Mexico City, August 1987), p. II-H-2. The figures used for the calculations are denominated in millions of 1970 pesos. The difference between the numbers in this table and those in table 2-4 is due to the weights used to calculate the 1970 and 1980 GDP deflators.

b. Ibid., table II-H-9, p. II-H-15. The difference between the numbers in this table and those in table 2.4 is due to the weights used to calculate the 1970 and 1980 GDP deflators.

c. For 1976 and 1977, Secretaría del Trabajo y Previsión Social, *Programa nacional de empleo, 1980–82*, vol. 1 (Mexico City, 1982), table 21, p. 65. For 1978–81, Jaime Ros, "Mexico from the Oil Boom to the Debt Crisis: An Analysis of Policy Responses to External Shocks, 1978–85," in Rosemary Thorp and Laurence Whitehead, eds., *Latin American Debt and the Adjustment Crisis* (University of Pittsburg Press, 1987), table 1. The 1976 and 1977 figures are the average of the period 1976–77.

d. For 1976, Banco de México, *Indicadores económicos* (Mexico City, March 1988), table III-2, p. III-2. For 1977–81, Banco de México, *Indicadores económicos: Resumen* (Mexico City, February 1992), p. f.

e. For 1976–78, World Bank, *Mexico: Recent Economic Developments and Prospects*, (Washington, 1984), table 5.1.1, p. 114. For 1979–81, Macro Asesoría Económica, *Realidad económica de México, 1991* (Mexico City, 1991) table 20.1, p. 539. The "fiscal deficit" is the "public sector borrowing requirement."

f. For 1976, E. Zedillo Ponce de León, "Mexico's Recent Balance of Payments Experience and Prospects for Growth," *World Development*, vol. 14 (August 1986), p. 963. For 1977–81, José Angel Gurría, "La política de deuda externa de México 1982–1990," Mexico City, January 1991, anexo 1, p. 26.

TABLE 1-5 *(continued)*

Item	1976	1977	1978	1979	1980	1981	Average		
							1976–77	1978–81	1976–81
Total public debt (billions of U.S. dollars)[g]	20.8	22.9	26.3	29.8	33.8	53.0	21.9	35.7	31.1
Nominal U.S. prime rate (percent)[h]	6.8	6.8	9.1	12.7	15.3	18.9	6.8	14.0	11.6
Export oil prices average (U.S. dollars per barrel)[i]	. . .	. . .	13.3	19.6	31.3	33.2	. . .	24.3	. . .
Share of oil exports in total exports (percent)[j]	15.4	22.3	30.7	45.1	67.3	72.5	18.9	53.9	42.2
Real exchange rate (free) (1970 = 100)[k]	103.3	129.4	124.0	120.5	107.8	90.8	116.4	110.8	112.6
Balance of trade (billions of U.S. dollars)[l]	−2.6	−1.1	−1.8	−3.2	−3.4	−3.8	−1.9	−3.0	−2.6
Current account balance (billions of U.S. dollars)[m]	−3.7	−1.6	−2.7	−4.9	−10.7	−16.1	−2.6	−8.6	−6.6
Capital flight (billions of U.S. dollars)[n]	3.0	0.9	0.1	0.02	−0.3	11.6	2.0	2.9	2.6

g. For 1976, Zedillo, "Mexico's Recent Balance of Payments Experience," table 3, p. 967. For 1977–81, Gurría, "La política de deuda externa," anexo 1, p. 26.

h. Robert Devlin, *Debt and Crisis in Latin America: The Supply Side of the Story* (Princeton University, 1989), p. 50.

i. Macro Asesoría Económica, *Realidad económica de México, 1991*, table 21.1, p. 555. The figure for 1978 is calculated as the ratio of oil export revenues (US$1.774 billion) from PEMEX, *Anuario estadístico 1987* (Instituto Mexicano del Petróleo, Mexico City), p. 117; and number of barrels (133,247 thousand) from DIEMEX-WHARTON, *Mexican Project, vol. 2, July 1982* (Wharton Econometrics Forecasting Associates, June 1982), table 5.01, p. 7 of the Historical Statistics appendix.

j. Banco de México, *Indicadores económicos* (August 1987), table IV-H-5, p. IV-H-45.

k. Banco de México, *Indicadores económicos* (February 1992), table IV-17, p. IV-22.

l. Banco de México, *Indicadores económicos* (August 1987), p. IV-H-45.

m. Ibid., pp. IV-H-27 to IV-H-32.

n. José Angel Gurría and Sergio Fadl, "Efectos de la política económica en la fuga de capitales: La experiencia de México, 1970–1989," unpublished paper, table 1.

government policies, the problem remained the upward climb of the debt. The public sector was not alone in terms of its optimistic expectations. Between 1978 and 1980 the stock of private foreign debt increased from U.S.$7.2 billion to U.S.$16.9 billion.[32]

The expansionary policies financed by external credit exacerbated the usual outcomes of a natural resource–based export boom.[33] A well-known effect of a windfall is that part of the increased domestic aggregate demand generates inflationary pressures in the nontradable sector and consequently an appreciation in the exchange rate.[34] This is detrimental for nonresource-based exports and results in an "unwarranted" import desubstitution. This occurred in Mexico as nonoil exports performed poorly and industrial growth lagged behind overall growth. Because this process was accompanied by a growing fiscal deficit, the demand for imports increased further. The increased demand for imports in turn aggravated the trade deficit, which rose from U.S.$1.8 billion in 1978 to U.S.$3.4 billion in 1980 (table 1-5).

As a result of the poor performance of the nonoil trade balance, the external account became even more dependent on oil exports, which reached 72.5 percent of total exports of goods and services in 1981 (see table 2-2). Thus the foreign exchange revenues became more sensitive to fluctuations in oil prices. Higher interest rates, on the other hand, required more foreign earnings devoted to servicing the debt. In 1981, with lower oil prices and higher interest rates, the current account reached an unprecedented deficit equal to U.S.$16.1 billion, which was financed to a large extent with more indebtedness (table 1-5).

In mid-1981, with oil prices sliding, the economic situation began to unravel. Unfortunately, the government did not move fast enough to correct the imbalance and calm fears. An attempt to reduce the budget deficit failed. Policymakers could not reach a consensus on whether to realign the exchange rate or impose import and capital controls. When a convincing shift in policy did not follow the oil price decline of mid-1981, capital flight accelerated sharply, reaching U.S.$11.6 billion for that year (table 1-5).[35] For a few months the government responded by sustaining the value of the peso through continued and increasingly short-term external borrowing. This process contributed to the development of Mexico's "debt overhang," which would make adjustment so much more difficult in the future.[36]

In early 1982 international oil prices continued their downward trend begun in 1981, while capital flight remained high. In addition, during the next twelve months, nearly half the country's foreign debt required repayment or refinancing. This aggravated the effect of the already threatening external conditions. By mid-February 1982 maintaining the peso through borrowing was no longer possible. A devaluation of the peso followed. By March the exchange rate had changed from 26.35 (in January 1982) to more than 45.46 pesos to the dollar.[37]

What followed in 1982 has been called a disorderly adjustment because the policies pursued were inconsistent.[38] Initially, the government adopted a fiscal contraction-cum-devaluation package that involved cuts in real public investment, cuts in subsidies on basic foodstuffs, an increase in energy prices, and an 80 percent nominal devaluation of the peso. However, in April "emergency increases" in wages were recommended that included a 30 percent rise in the minimum wage and smaller increases for higher wage levels. This recommendation to increase wages ran counter to the purported goal of maintaining a realistic fixed exchange rate and stable prices, thus exacerbating capital flight.[39]

In August, as foreign reserves reached a record low, the government announced a freeze, followed by a forced conversion at below-market rates, of dollar-denominated bank accounts. The freeze angered the middle class, the principal holders of these accounts, and contributed to the further erosion of government credibility, which in turn further boosted capital flight. The once cordial relationship between the López Portillo government and the private sector became ever more strained. The happy days of what the government had called the alliance for production were gone, and the business sector's confidence in the government crumbled altogether soon thereafter.

Also in August, continuous capital flight and the interruption of the flow of commercial lending led to new and dramatic devaluations, as well as a ninety-day suspension on foreign debt payments of the principal.[40] These events signaled the beginning of the international debt crisis. The days of a "bullish" lender's market for Mexico and other third world debtors ended; any new borrowing would be hard to obtain.[41]

The government's response to the crisis materialized in measures aimed at forcing an end to the foreign exchange drain. On September 1, 1982, full exchange controls of capital flows were adopted, and the Mexican banking system was nationalized, a measure that infuriated the Mexican financial sector.[42] The business sector's distrust and resentment toward the government had been pushed to the limit only three months before a new president, Miguel de la Madrid, was to take office.

Large devaluations of the peso, chaos in the financial markets, and a slowdown in economic activity characterized 1982. Output contracted by 0.6 percent, inflation rose to 98.8 percent, and foreign currency reserves fell to U.S.$1.8 billion, about one month's worth of 1982 total imports of merchandise and nonfactor services (see tables 2-1 and 2-4).

Concluding Remarks

• Why did the López Portillo government not see the dangers of engaging in expansionary policies financed with foreign borrowing? Had the 1976 crisis not served as a good example of the dire consequences of such a strategy? Given the prospects of the world oil market, the López Portillo government did not consider the 1975–76 period the proper analogy. This turned out to be a serious mistake and the 1976 crisis recurred in 1982 on a grander and more durable scale. Four years of high output growth were followed by six years of failed attempts to lower inflation and restore economic growth.

Most analysts agree that the Mexican crisis was the result of expansionary government policies that resulted in higher inflation and a growing balance-of-payments disequilibrium.[43] Although they agree that the government should have followed a less expansionary path, they differ strongly over which policies should have been followed. Some have argued in favor of using fiscal and relative price adjustments,[44] while others have supported a combination of price, capital, exchange rate, and import controls to curb inflation and keep the trade balance in check.[45]

In fact, the disagreement between these two approaches was evident throughout the López Portillo presidency. Discussion initially centered on trade policy. Some members of the economic cabinet supported the elimination of import restrictions and a movement toward free trade. Others, however, believing that this would destroy Mexico's industrial base and have a negative impact on growth, opposed trade liberalization. When international prices began to fall in mid-1981, no consensus existed on how to restore price stability and correct the balance-of-trade disequilibrium. One group urged fiscal moderation and exchange rate depreciation, whereas another insisted on import and price controls.

In retrospect, had the government followed a less expansionary fiscal policy in 1980 and early 1981, the effects of the external shocks would have been milder. The most serious mistake, however, was the government's inaction in the face of a decline in oil prices in mid-1981, reflecting in part the erroneous assumption that oil prices would soon recover. Much of this inaction had to do with the differences within López Portillo's economic cabinet, a diversity of opinion the president himself encouraged. Yet opinions were so fundamentally opposed that debate led to a stalemate in the decisionmaking process just when the situation required prompt action. The economy became mired in the worst possible situation: there was complete free convertibility of the currency, with an increasingly overvalued exchange rate and a large fiscal deficit. Not surprisingly, capital flight was rampant.[46]

Despite the general consensus that the 1982 crisis was largely caused by macroeconomic mismanagement, some counterfactual exercises illustrate that adoption of the required fiscal adjustment earlier in 1981 would not have occurred without costs, reflected in higher inflation and lower output.[47] The perception that the decline in oil prices was temporary and the awareness of the costs implied by fiscal adjustment may be a good explanation for why the government refrained from taking action in 1981. Subsequent events showed that the costs associated with an earlier adjustment would have been lower. Postponing adjustment turned out to be a big mistake.

The oil boom did not produce the desired dramatic transformation of the economy and permanent improvement in living standards. On the contrary, it was followed by crisis and increased poverty. Mexicans paid dearly for their government's disregard for careful macroeconomic management and efficiency in the allocation and administration of resources. Ironically, Echeverría's and López Portillo's governments, both so keen on defending Mexico's economic independence and raising the quality of life of the Mexican people, followed policies that ultimately subverted these goals.

The incoming administration of President de la Madrid had the unenviable task of having to correct large fiscal imbalances and to respond to external problems while faced with a hostile private sector, unsympathetic creditor banks, and international institutions inexperienced in managing a global crisis such as the debt crisis that started in 1982. Chapter 2 analyzes how stability and economic recovery were eventually achieved despite the adverse external conditions. It focuses on Mexico's adjustment to falling oil prices and the drastic decline in external credit in the 1980s and on how conditions to jump-start the economy were restored.

Chapter Two

From Crisis to Recovery

MIGUEL DE LA MADRID HURTADO took office in December 1982. In his cabinet, policymaking enjoyed a greater degree of consensus than it had in the López Portillo administration. There was broad agreement regarding the causes of the crisis and the measures required to overcome it and restore a growing, stable economy.[1] In the short run, cabinet members agreed that price and financial stability needed to be reestablished. Medium-range goals included increasing the competitiveness of the Mexican economy, relying more on internal than on external savings, and promoting the deregulation and decentralization of economic life.

The consensus view on the underlying cause of the 1982 crisis held that runaway inflation and balance-of-payments disequilibrium resulted from a large fiscal deficit and the misalignment of relative prices, in particular the exchange rate. Falling oil prices and higher world interest rates had triggered the crisis but lay beyond the control of policymakers. Capital flight was reviewed as a consequence of bad domestic policy rather than as a cause of the crisis. The government expected that, once order in the fiscal accounts was restored, the value of the currency was adjusted, and external debt payments were restructured, inflation would subside, external capital inflows would resume, and growth would follow. The process, however, turned out to be far more difficult than expected.

A group of de la Madrid's policymakers also saw the crisis as the result of the past inward-looking development strategy followed during the post–World War II period. In their view this strategy had fostered an inefficient allocation of resources and introduced unnecessary supply rigidities. In addition, as a consequence of the state's interventionist role in the economy, business and financial leaders

28

became increasingly distrustful. However, the importance given to the economy's incentive system and institutional framework as causes of the crisis and to the need for structural reform was not shared with equal fervor by all members of de la Madrid's cabinet. Thus, during the first two years of his term, structural reform was slow.

After the failure of the first stabilization attempt in mid-1985, structural reform began in earnest. It accelerated in 1988 with the implementation of a stabilization package, known as the Pact, which was at last successful. Between 1989 and 1991, under the Salinas administration, economic reform reached those areas that used to be considered "untouchable." Striking examples of bold reform included the reprivatization of the banks, the pursuit of a free-trade agreement with the United States, and, foremost, the privatization of the *ejido* land tenure system.

The First Attempt at Stabilization, 1983–85

In December 1982 de la Madrid announced his first stabilization package, the Programa Inmediato de Reordenación Económica (Program of Immediate Economic Reorganization), known as the PIRE.[2] The program was conceived in two stages: a "shock treatment" in 1983 followed by "gradualist" policies in 1984–85. De la Madrid's economic team believed that price and financial stability would be restored through a drastic reduction in the government's deficit and an initial large devaluation of the peso. Fiscal austerity would curb inflation and, coupled with the devaluation, would generate the required surplus in the trade account.[3] For the corrective measures to be effective, however, indexation of the nominal wages had to be preempted. To make this possible, the government decided to adjust the minimum wage and the wages of public employees to expected inflation instead of to past price increases. This wage adjustment procedure was to prevent an automatic increase in labor costs that would have fueled inflation.

The program received IMF support and financing and the government signed an extended fund facility (EFF) with the IMF in late 1982.[4] The agreement would allow Mexico to draw approximately U.S.$3.7 billion in separate installments from January 1983 to December 1985.[5] As we will see later, however, the agreement was interrupted in mid-1985 because of Mexico's noncompliance with specified targets.

The "shock treatment" began with a large devaluation of the "free" and "controlled" exchange rates (of 113 and 95 percent, respectively),

TABLE 2-1. *Fiscal Adjustment and Real Exchange Rate, 1980–91*

Item	1980	1981	1982	1983	1984	1985	1986	1987	1988	1989	1990	1991	Average 1983–88	1983–85	1986–87	1988–90
Fiscal adjustment																
Primary government surplus (percent of GDP)[a,b]	–3.0	–8.0	–2.5	4.0	4.8	3.9	2.5	5.7	8.4	8.3	8.0	5.5	4.9	4.2	4.1	8.2
Public sector borrowing requirement (PSBR) (percent of GDP)[b]	7.5	14.1	16.9	8.6	8.5	9.6	15.9	16.0	12.5	5.6	3.9	1.5	11.9	8.9	16.0	7.3
Exchange rate realignment																
Real exchange rate (controlled) (1970 = 100)[c]	107.8	90.8	124.2	135.2	110.9	106.8	155.9	169.8	140.3	127.5	123.4[d]	118.5[d]	...	...	...	...
Percent rate of devaluation	–10.5	–15.8	36.8	8.9	–18.0	–3.7	46.0	8.9	–17.4	–9.1	–3.2	–4.0	4.1	–4.3	27.4	–9.9

a. The primary surplus excludes interest payments (on internal and external debt).
b. Banco de México, *The Mexican Economy 1996* (Mexico City, 1996), p. 294, table 31.
c. For 1980–90, Banco de México, *Indicadores económicos* (Mexico City, February 1992), table IV-17, p. IV-22 (annual averages). The figure for 1991 is the January–November average. A lower (higher) index indicates a real appreciation (depreciation). For 1982 onward the index is for the controlled exchange rate.
d. Preliminary figures.

both announced in December 1982.[6] The program envisioned an increase in tax and nontax revenues and a cut in public expenditures, so that by the end of 1983 the fiscal deficit, or public sector borrowing requirement, would be almost half of its record level of 16.9 percent of GDP in 1982 (table 2-1). The government and the IMF expected that these measures would result in the reduction of the inflation rate from about 100 percent in 1982 to 55 percent in 1983 (table 2-3) and a U.S.$2 billion drop in the current account deficit.[7] Output growth for 1983 was expected to be zero. As we shall see, the actual outcome was quite different.

With debt service running at 62.2 percent of export revenues in 1982, the U.S.$92.4 billion foreign debt required prompt attention (table 2-2). From the beginning, de la Madrid's government made it clear that it was willing to seek a solution with the international community to meet its debt service payments. It dismissed unilateral actions, as well as the creation of a "Debtors' Club" with the other large debtors in Latin America. De la Madrid replaced the previous administration's "involuntary" suspension of payments in mid-1982 with a record of compliance with debt obligations, albeit with several reschedulings of payments.

Because of the number of short-term loans taken during 1981 and early 1982, there was lumpiness in the payments from 1983 to 1985. The first round of negotiations focused on rescheduling the principal due over the rest of the decade. In December 1982 the Mexican government requested that commercial banks reschedule the payments of U.S.$23,150 million in amortizations for the period between August 23, 1982, and December 3, 1984. Negotiations were completed in August 1983.[8]

In addition, the Mexican government borrowed U.S.$5 billion from commercial banks and U.S.$2 billion from the Paris Club. New loans were used primarily to make interest payments on the previous outstanding debt. The interest bill for 1983–85 was U.S.$10.7 billion a year (table 2-2). Private external debt was also subject to a restructuring exercise. About U.S.$12 billion of the U.S.$23 billion of this debt was also rescheduled to eight years, with a four-year grace period, and covered for exchange rate risk by a government program.[9]

The 1983 restructuring exercise substantially reduced the payments of principal due for 1983–84.[10] Starting in 1985, however, the refinancing requirements were larger than they would have been in its ab-

TABLE 2-2. *Debt Burden, External Shocks, and Net Resource Transfers,*
1980–90

Item	1980	1981	1982	1983	1984	1985
Debt burden						
Total external debt (billions of U.S. dollars)[a]	50.7	74.9	92.4	93.8	96.7	96.6
Public sector external debt (billions of U.S. dollars)[a]	33.8	53.0	59.7	66.6	69.4	72.1
Interest payments (billions of U.S. dollars)[b]	6.1	9.5	12.2	10.1	11.7	10.2
Ratio of external debt to GDP (percent)[a,c]	26.0	29.9	54.2	63.0	55.0	52.4
Debt service ratio (percent)[d]	42.4	49.4	62.2	50.4	42.8	43.8
Magnitude of the external shocks						
Export oil prices, average (U.S. dollars per barrel)[e]	31.3	33.2	28.7	26.3	26.8	25.3
Share of oil exports in total exports (percent)[f]	67.3	72.5	77.6	71.8	68.6	68.2
U.S. prime rate, nominal (percent)[g]	15.3	18.9	14.9	10.8	12.0	9.9
Terms of trade, adjusted for interest rate movements (1970 = 100)[h]	112.8	126.8	86.1	69.4	70.8	72.4
Net resource transfers to GDP (percent)[i]	n.a.	n.a.	6.3	7.6	6.8	6.9

a. For 1980 to 1988, growth rates calculated from José Angel Gurría, "La política de deuda externa de México, 1982–1990," anexo 1, p. 26. (Mexico, January 1991). For 1989 to 1990, Banco de México, *The Mexican Economy 1996* (Mexico City, 1996), table 53, p. 318.

b. The figures for 1980 to 1988 are from the Banco de México as cited by Macro Asesoría Económica, "Realidad Económica de México: 1991" (Mexico, 1990), p. 563. The figures for 1989 to 1995 are from Banco de México, *The Mexican Economy 1996*, table 43, p. 308.

c. The figures for GDP in U.S.$ from 1980 to 1988 are from World Bank, "Mexico in Transition: Towards a New Role for the Public Sector," Report 8770-ME (Washington, D.C., May 22, 1991) table A3, p. 138. The figures for GDP in U.S.$ from 1989 to 1990 are from Banco de México, *The Mexican Economy 1996*, table 5, p. 264.

d. The 1980 and 1981 figures for merchandise exports, factor and nonfactor services, amortizations and interest payments are from Macro Asesoría Económica "Realidad Económica de México: 1991" (Mexico, 1990) tables 21.5, 21.6, pp. 563, 567. Debt service ratio figures for 1982 to 1984 are from the Banco de México, *The Mexican Economy 1989* (Mexico, 1989) p. 150; and for 1985 to 1988 from *The Mexican Economy 1990* (Mexico, 1990). The figures for 1989 and 1990 are from Banco de México, *The Mexican Economy 1996*,

TABLE 2-2. *(continued)*

						Average		
1986	1987	1988	1989	1990	1983–88	1983–85	1986–87	1988–90
101.0	107.5	100.4	95.3	104.3	99.3	95.7	104.3	100.0
75.4	81.4	81.0	76.1	77.8	74.3	69.4	78.4	78.3
8.3	8.1	8.6	9.3	9.0	9.5	10.7	8.2	9.0
77.7	76.5	58.1	46.1	42.7	63.8	56.8	77.1	49.0
48.6	42.8	43.4	23.5	88.1	45.3	45.7	45.7	51.6
11.9	16.0	12.2	15.6	19.2	19.8	26.2	14.0	15.7
39.3	41.8	32.6	22.4	24.8	53.7	69.5	40.6	26.6
8.3	8.2	9.3	10.9	10.0	9.8	10.9	8.3	10.1
52.9	67.0	60.5	64.5	67.9	65.5	70.9	60.0	64.3
4.2	2.9	6.8	1.2	0.4	5.9[j]	7.1	3.6	2.8

table 43, p. 308, and table 54, p. 319 (Mexico, 1996). The ratio is calculated as 'interest payments plus amortizations' divided by exports of 'goods and services.'

e. The figures for 1980 through 1984 are from Macro Asesoría Económica, "Realidad Económica de México 1991" (Mexico, 1990), p. 555. The figures for 1985 through 1990 are from Ernesto Zedillo, "Primer Informe de Gobierno, Anexo" (Mexico, 1995), p. 107. Price given is a weighted average of Mexico's oil export mix.

f. The figures for 1980 to 1984 are from Banco de México, "Indicadores Economicos," (Mexico, August 1987), pp. IV-H-45. The figures for 1985 to 1988 are from Banco de México, *The Mexican Economy 1991* (Mexico, 1991), table 38, p. 216. The figures for 1989 and 1990 are calculated from Banco de México, *The Mexican Economy 1996* (Mexico, 1996), table 43, p. 308, which uses a new methodology for calculating exports. Therefore, figures are not strictly comparable with previous years.

g. U.S. President, *Economic Report of the President 1996* (Washington, 1996), table B-69, p. 360.

h. Terms of trade adjusted for international interest rates. Source: Banco de México, *The Mexican Economy 1994* (Mexico, 1994), table 29, p. 239.

i. A negative sign means a positive net inflow. Gurría, "La política de deuda externa," p. 10.

j. Preliminary.

sence. Despite the restructuring of debt payments, the net resource transfers remained above 7 percent of GDP between 1983 and 1985 (table 2-2). High net resource transfers, indicating negative net external inflows, were partly a consequence of continuing capital flight (table 2-4).

The goals of the second phase—the "gradualist" phase—of the stabilization program included a slower but steady deceleration of inflation, further improvement of the trade surplus, and resumption of the historical growth rates. Gradualism meant that no new drastic fiscal and exchange rate measures would be taken. To decelerate inflation the government planned to maintain a grip on the fiscal deficit and set the so-called key prices—the exchange rate, the minimum wage, and the prices of goods and services sold by the public sector—according to the program's inflation target. The government expected that if inflation subsided and fiscal and relative price corrections were sustained, growth would follow.

The Failure of the First Stabilization Program

When first announced, the program was expected to result in zero output growth in 1983, followed by a gradual recovery. Output growth was to return to its historical rate of 6 percent a year by 1985, and inflation was to fall to 18 percent a year by December 1985 (table 2-3). What happened, however, was quite different. The 1983 downturn was much larger than expected; the desired reduction in inflation was not achieved; and, needless to say, historical growth rates were not restored.

Table 2-3 provides a comparison of goals and outcomes. In 1983 the growth rate of output was -4.2 percent rather than the targeted zero growth, while inflation equaled 81 percent instead of the expected 55 percent. In contrast, the PIRE "overachieved" the current account goal—that is, the surplus was higher than the target. The fiscal deficit (as a percentage of GDP) was the only variable on target.[11]

In early 1984 there was a moderate economic recovery that continued until mid-1985, when Mexico faced another balance-of-payments crisis. The government responded with a step-wise devaluation of the peso and the announcement of cuts in the fiscal deficit and domestic credit. Once again, growth slowed and inflation accelerated.

The very circumstances that triggered the mild recovery of 1984

TABLE 2-3. *Targets and Actual Performance of the First Stabilization Program, 1983–85*

Item	1982	1983	1984	1985
Inflation (December–December consumer prices) (percent)				
Original IMF projections[a]	. . .	55.0	30.0	18.0
Revised targets (government)[b]	. . .	. . .	40.0	35.0
Actual performance	98.8	80.8	59.2	63.7
PSBR[c] (percent of GDP)				
Original IMF projections[a]	. . .	8.5	5.5	3.5
Revised target (government)[b]	. . .	8.5	5.5–6.5	5.1–5.6
Actual performance	16.9	8.6	8.5	9.6
Current account balance				
Original IMF projections, (percent of GDP)[a]	. . .	−2.2	−1.8	−1.2
Actual performance (percent of GDP)	−3.6	3.6	2.4	0.7
Revised targets (government) (billions of U.S. dollars)[b]	. . .	. . .	0.0–0.5	1.0–2.0
Actual performance (billions of U.S. dollars)	−6.2	5.4	4.2	1.2
Real GDP growth (percent)				
Original IMF projections[a]	. . .	0.0	3.0	6.0
Revised targets (government)[b]	. . .	. . .	0.0–1.0	3.0–4.0
Actual performance	−0.6	−4.2	3.6	2.6

Source: IMF and government targets are original projections published in Nora Lustig and Jaime Ros, *Mexico,* WIDER Country Study 7 (Helsinki: World Institute for Development Economics Research of the United Nations University, March 1987), table 3, p. 67. Actual performance from tables II.1, II.4.

a. Late 1982.

b. Annual targets contained in Presidencia de la República, "Criterios generales de política económica." This document is sent to Congress in November–December of each year and presents the budget along with the main objectives of economic policy for the coming year.

c. Public sector borrowing requirement.

contributed in part to its demise, as well. In particular, the government's relaxation of its fiscal stance and the appreciation of the exchange rate backfired. Both contributed to rapid deterioration of the trade surplus starting in mid-1984.[12] Imports surged and the growth of nonoil exports slowed.[13] This deterioration was exacerbated by worsening terms of trade for goods exported by Mexico. In 1985 oil export revenues dropped 11 percent as a result of falling world oil prices.[14]

The strategy chosen to combat inflation and reduce it to desired levels also failed. From mid-1983 to late 1984, inflation fell.[15] But by early 1985 inflation reached a new plateau, running in the first three months at a rate similar to that of late 1984.[16] Pegging the increases of key prices alone to expected inflation was not enough to curb inflation once and for all. Other prices continued to rise by inertia and as a result of the program's lack of credibility.

The relaxation of the fiscal deficit and the rapid deterioration of the external trade balance further undermined credibility. Given Mexico's debt obligations, the public perceived that the trade account's deterioration was not sustainable and that a devaluation of the peso was inevitable. In addition, because Mexico did not comply with its targets, the IMF suspended financing for the country around mid-1985. All of these circumstances, taken together, sparked another run on the peso, which resulted in the balance-of-payments crisis of mid-1985.

Why did the first stabilization program fail, and why did the targets and expectations of the goverment and the IMF prove unrealistic? Several reasons have been advanced. Some authors emphasize that the policies followed to combat inflation and reduce the disequilibrium in the balance of payments were inadequate.[17] Others, while not disagreeing with that interpretation, stress that the program also failed in part because fundamental reforms, such as trade liberalization and privatization, were absent.[18]

Subsequent events in Mexico and other countries suggest that the measures included in the PIRE are not sufficient to bring inflation down. The measures were based on the assumption that a reduction in the nominal fiscal deficit, combined with a large initial currency devaluation followed by a pegged exchange rate, would suffice to stop inflation and restore a balance-of-payments equilibrium.[19] But the amount of short-run tension created between reducing the fiscal deficit and "getting the prices right" (including the exchange rate), on the one hand, and controlling inflation, on the other, was underestimated. Even though wages were not fully indexed to past inflation, the devaluation of the currency and the rise in public prices resulted in other price increases, thereby fueling inflation.

The fact that inflation did not come down as fast as expected in 1983 and that the fiscal targets (as a proportion of GDP) were set in nominal terms had a greater contractionary effect than anticipated. The direct contractionary effect of the devaluation was also higher than expected, and this explains part of the sharp fall in output.[20] The 1983 overshooting was unfortunate, not only because of the forgone output during that year, but because it gave rise to a false sense of optimism. Government officials believed that the worst was over and that policy measures could be geared toward gradually curbing inflation and stimulating economic recovery. In retrospect, this interpretation was wrong, and Mexico faced a balance-of-payments crisis again in mid-1985.

In hindsight, the program clearly underestimated the limitations imposed by the large accumulated debt and the extent to which the external environment would remain adverse in terms of oil prices and access to external credit. Given the size of the external "shocks," the adjustment process in Mexico required a change in the size and composition of Mexico's physical capital, a delay in the servicing of its debt, and an improvement in its access to external credit, none of which the outside world was willing to provide.[21] As one author put it: "The early demise of the 1984 recovery revealed the vulnerability of the economy to external shocks. As soon as the external environment turned less favorable and the economy began to grow, the balance of payments—and the general climate of expectations—deteriorated rapidly. This episode also uncovered the true dimensions of the debt overhang and the difficulties of implementing stabilization policies in a context of falling terms of trade, and, more generally, of changing relative prices."[22]

Should structural reforms such as trade liberalization and privatization have been introduced as early as 1983? Would these reforms have prevented the failure of the PIRE? The impact of trade liberalization on inflation in the short run is far from evident, and to engage in trade liberalization when the international reserve position was shaky and foreign financing was scarce may have been unwise, though trade liberalization could be "sold" to the World Bank in exchange for badly needed structural adjustment loans. However, some "structural" measures might have improved the business-government relationship and prevented further capital flight. A good example is the reprivatization of the banking system.[23] Reprivatizing the banks early could have helped the government mend fences with the private sector and deter capital flight.

However, reprivatizing the banks in 1983 would have involved risks. First, many members of de la Madrid's government had approved, and even applauded, López Portillo's nationalization of the banks a few months before de la Madrid took office.[24] Such a quick change of mind may not have been taken seriously and, therefore, may not have substantially strengthened credibility. Second, de la Madrid had to place himself in the center of the political spectrum. The government had agreed to a tough IMF program and to sustaining payments on the external debt. If, in addition to these "unpopular" decisions, the banks were returned to the private sector, the government could have been accused of giving in completely to pressures from the right and could have lost support from the leadership in the more moderate forces, especially those linked to the labor sector.

It should be mentioned that the first adjustment program failed despite the downward flexibility of real wages. Between 1983 and 1985 real wages drastically declined. Regardless of the indicator used, the cumulative contraction was well above 30 percent (table 2-4). Surprisingly, wage cuts did not lead to massive strikes or widespread political discontent. The prevailing flexibility of real wages gave the Mexican government uncommon freedom to act. It also placed the bulk of the adjustment costs internally.

Policymakers in other large debtor countries in Latin America did not enjoy the same flexibility. Wage resistance in Argentina and Brazil, for example, was much stronger during this period (though wages did fall by more subsequently).[25] The governments of Argentina and Brazil were compelled to distribute the burden of adjustment between their own population and external creditors, the commercial banks in particular.[26]

Mexico absorbed the full cost of adjustment internally. But, despite notable cuts in the fiscal deficit and drastic declines in real wages, the effort failed. Neither price stability nor historical growth rates were restored (table 2-4). Even worse, the PIRE ended with another balance-of-payments crisis in mid-1985.

From the 1986 Oil Shock to the 1987 Run on the Peso

The balance-of-payments crisis in mid-1985 led again to the implementation of harsh stabilization measures. Both fiscal and monetary policy turned contractionary, and the controlled exchange rate was devalued. In contrast with the 1983 program, the stabilization measures were accompanied by an acceleration in trade liberalization signaling the beginning of the structural reform process. In July 1985 import licensing requirements were substantially reduced and the proportion of imports not subject to licensing increased from 16.4 percent in December 1984 to 64.1 percent in July 1985 (table 5-2). Before the decree, the aim had been to liberalize up to 35–45 percent of total imports by December 1985. The acceleration of liberalization was accompanied by a tariff increase to compensate slightly for the reduction of license requirements. The trade-weighted average tariff rose from 23.5 percent in June to 28.5 percent by December.[27] The new emphasis on trade liberalization signaled the beginning of what would eventually become a fundamental change in development strategy.[28]

The initial impact of the program was a deceleration in output growth. These were difficult times in Mexico. No new IMF funding was available after the interruption of the program in mid-1985 caused by Mexico's inability to comply with the fiscal targets. The devastating earthquake that hit Mexico City in September 1985 further demoralized the country.[29] Policymakers hoped that the measures undertaken in mid-1985 would bear fruit the following year. With the sharp fall in world oil prices in 1986, however, such hopes soon disappeared.

The price of oil fell from an average of U.S.$25.5 a barrel in 1985 to U.S.$12.0 a barrel in 1986 (table 2-2).[30] Despite the rapid expansion of nonoil exports in 1983 and 1984 of 32.5 percent and 20.7 percent a year, respectively, the share of oil to total exports was still as high as 68.2 percent in 1985 (tables 2-4 and 2-2). In addition, revenues from oil represented about 26.2 percent of total government revenues.[31] The Mexican economy was still extremely vulnerable to fluctuations in oil prices, and the reduction of Mexico's dependence on oil revenues became a major target.

For most of the year the 1986 oil shock had to be absorbed internally, since no additional external funding was made available. The loss in foreign exchange revenues was U.S.$8.5 billion, equivalent to 6.7 percent of GDP, 48 percent of total export receipts, and 26.2 percent

TABLE 2-4. *Indicators of Economic Performance, 1981–91*
Annual percent change unless otherwise specified

Item	1981	1982	1983	1984	1985	1986
Output and income						
Gross domestic product[a]	8.8	–0.6	–4.2	3.6	2.6	–3.8
GDP per capita[a,b]	5.9	–3.0	–6.3	1.5	0.6	–5.5
Disposable income per capita[a,c,d]	3.4	–5.4	–14.2	–1.0	1.9	–15.3
Inflation						
Consumer prices[d]						
Annual average	27.9	58.9	101.9	65.4	57.7	86.2
December–December	28.7	98.8	80.8	59.2	63.7	105.7
Private Demand						
Investment[e]	13.9	–17.3	–24.2	9.0	12.2	–10.4
Consumption[f]	7.4	–2.5	–5.4	3.3	3.6	–2.8
Wages						
Wages quoted by industrial survey[g]	5.0	0.1	–24.1	–6.8	1.1	–6.9
Minimum wage[h]	1.0	–0.1	–21.9	–9.0	–1.2	–10.5
Average real remuneration in						
manufacturing[d,i]	3.8	0.7	–22.8	–7.1	–2.8	–5.9
External Sector						
Imports[j]	17.7	–37.9	–33.8	17.8	11.0	–7.6
Exports[l]	11.6	21.8	14.2	5.8	–4.5	4.5
Nonoil exports[m]	–0.1	–2.4	46.3	28.1	–4.0	22.9
Balance of trade (billions						
of U.S. dollars)[n]	–3.8	6.8	13.8	12.9	8.5	4.6
Current account balance						
Billions of U.S. dollars[o]	–16.1	–6.2	5.4	4.2	1.2	–1.7
Billions of U.S. dollars[p]	...	...	...	...	...	...
Gross international reserves,						
end of period (billions						
of U.S. dollars)[q]	5.0	1.8	4.9	8.1	5.8	6.8
Capital flight (billions of U.S. dollars)[r]	11.6	6.5	2.7	1.6	0.7	–2.2
Average interest rate on						
one-month CETES (percent)[s]						
Nominal	...	...	56.6	48.6	60.2	86.7
Real	...	...	–3.8	1.2	9.9	12.3

n.a. Not available.

a. For 1980–84, Instituto Nacional de Estadística, Geografía e Informática (INEGI), *Sistema de cuentas nacionales de México 1980–1986*, tomo 1: *Resumen general* (Mexico City, 1988), table 91, p. 194. For 1985, INEGI, *Sistema de cuentas nacionales de México, 1985–1988*, tomo 1: *Resumen general* (Mexico City, 1990), table 79, p. 118. For 1986–87, INEGI, *Sistema de cuentas nacionales de México, 1986–1989*, tomo 3: *Cuenta de producción* (Mexico City, 1991). For 1988–89, revised figures from INEGI, unpublished document.

TABLE 2-4. *(continued)*

1987	1988	1989	1990	1991	Average 1983–88	Average 1983–85	Average 1986–87	Average 1988–90
1.7	1.3	3.3	4.5	3.6	0.2	0.6	–1.0	3.0
–0.1	–0.5	1.5	2.4	1.9	–1.8	–1.5	2.9	0.9
5.0	–5.4	7.9	6.3	n.a.	–5.1	–4.7	–5.7	2.8
131.8	114.2	20.0	26.7	22.7	92.9	75.0	109.0	53.6
159.2	51.7	19.7	29.9	18.8	86.7	67.9	132.5	33.8
6.4	10.2	7.5	13.6	13.0	–0.3	–2.5	–2.2	10.3
–0.1	1.8	6.8	5.7	4.9	0.1	0.4	–1.3	4.9
–6.5	–0.5	8.9	n.a.	n.a.	–7.7	–10.6	–6.7	n.a
–6.3	–12.7	–6.6	–9.1	–4.5	–10.5	–11.1	–8.4	–9.5
–1.9	–1.3	9.0	2.9^k	4.9^k	–7.3	–11.3	–3.9	3.4
5.1	36.7	21.3	19.7	16.8	1.4	–4.7	–4.1	25.7
19.5	5.8	2.3	3.6	4.6	5.5	4.7	6.6	3.9
15.5	16.2	2.4	7.7	5.8	19.5	13.2	32.1	8.6
8.4	1.7	–0.7	–3.0^k	–11.2^k	8.3	11.7	6.5	–0.7
4.0	–2.4	–5.4	...	...	1.8	3.6	1.2	...
...	...	–5.8	–7.5	–14.6	...	...	...	...
13.7	6.6	6.9	10.2	17.5	7.7	6.3	10.3	7.8
0.3	1.1	–2.9	n.a.	n.a.	0.7	1.7	–1.0	n.a.
96.0	69.2	45.0	35.6	19.3	68.7	55.1	91.3	49.3
–2.9	29.2	29.9	17.3	4.4	7.1	2.3	4.4	25.6

For 1990–91, Banco de México, *The Mexican Economy 1996* (Mexico, 1996), table 7, p. 266.

b. The yearly population levels are calculated using data from Consejo Nacional de Población (CONAPO), Mexico.

c. Nominal figures for 1980–84, INEGI, *Sistema de cuentas nacionales de México, 1980–1986*, table 2, p. 28. Nominal figure for 1985, INEGI, *Sistema de cuentas nacionales de México, 1985–1988*, table 2, p. 27. Nominal figures for 1986–89, INEGI, *Sistema de cuen-*

TABLE 2-4. *(notes continued)*

tas nacionales de México, 1986–1989. Real figures are derived using the consumer price index (1980 = 100) from Banco de México, *The Mexican Economy 1991* (Mexico City, 1991), table 28, p. 204.

d. For 1980 to 1984 Banco de México, *Indicadores económicos; Resumen* (Mexico City, February 1992). For 1985 to 1991, Banco de México, *The Mexican Economy 1996* (Mexico, 1996), table 7, p. 266.

e. For 1981–85, Macro Asesoría Económica, *Realidad económica de México 1991* (Mexico City, 1991), cuadro 19.1, p. 457; for 1986–88, Macro Asesoría Económica, *Realidad económica de México 1995*, cuadro 24.1, p. 301; for 1989–95, Banco de México, *The Mexican Economy 1996*, table 6, p. 265.

f. For 1981–85, Macro Asesoría Económica, *Realidad económica de México 1991*, cuadro 19.1, p. 457; for 1986–88, Macro Asesoría Económica, *Realidad económica de México 1995*, cuadro 24.1, p. 301; and for 1989–95, Banco de México, *The Mexican Economy 1996*, table 6, p. 265.

g. *Compendio de indicadores de empleo y salarios* (Mexico City: Comisión Nacional de los Salarios Mínimos, 1991).

h. For 1980–86, *Salarios compendio estadístico* (Mexico City: Comisión Nacional de los Salarios Mínimos, December 1986), table 5A, pp. 25–27. For 1987–90, Banco de México, *Informe anual*, p. 119 (1987), p. 136 (1988), p. 138 (1989), p. 139 (1990). For 1991, *GEA Laboral* (Mexico City: January 20, 1992), p. 27.

i. For 1981–90 nominal figures, Banco de México, *Indicadores económicos* (February 1992), table III-25, p. III-39. For 1991, Macro Asesoría Económica, *Macro perspectivas* (April–June 1992), year 5, p. 26.

j. Data obtained electronically from INEGI, "Sistema de cuentas nacionales de México oferta y demanda global a precios de 1980" (http://dgenesyp.inegi.gob.mx/).

k. Preliminary figures.

l. Data obtained electronically from INEGI, *Sistema de cuentas nacionales*.

m. Data obtained electronically from INEGI, *Sistema de cuentas nacionales, sector externo, exportaciones petroleras y no petroleras.*

n. For 1980–1988, Macro Asesoría Económica, *Realidad económica de México 1991* (Mexico City, 1991), table 21.1, p. 553. For 1990, Banco de México, *The Mexican Economy 1991*, table 38, p. 216. Preliminary figure for 1991, *GEA Económico*, p. 22. The balance of trade is the difference between merchandise exports and merchandise imports.

o. Macro Asesoría Económica, *Realidad económica de México 1991* (Mexico, 1990), table 21.5, p. 563.

p. The difference between this entry and the results in Macro Asesoría Económica, note o, given through 1989 is a change in the estimated "transfers" (remittances) by Mexicans residing abroad. Strictly speaking these figures are not comparable with those for previous years. For 1989 to 1991, Banco de México, *The Mexican Economy 1996*, table 43, p. 308.

q. For 1981 to 1988, Banco de México, *The Mexican Economy 1991* (Mexico City, 1991), table 43, p. 309.

r. José Angel Gurría and Sergio Fadl, *Efectos de la política económica en la fuga de capitales: La experiencia de México, 1970–1989* (Mexico City, 1990), table 1. The 1989 figure is preliminary. The estimate of capital flight excludes interest earned on foreign private capital; thus, it is a lower boundary.

s. For 1981 to 1989, Centro de analisis e investigación económica, *The Mexican Economy: A Monthly Report* (Mexico, 1996), table 43, p. 309. The 1990 and 1991 figures are from Grupo de Economistas y Asociados (Mexico City).

of public sector revenues.[32] One author provides a detailed account of how insensitive the multilaterals (the IMF and the World Bank) and the U.S. government were to Mexico's plight during this period.[33] Though because of the earthquake the IMF provided emergency assistance of about U.S.$300 million in early 1986, Mexico was not able to draw funds under a new agreement with the IMF until mid-November of that year.[34] The International Bank for Reconstruction and Development (IBRD) disbursed a loan of U.S. $400 million for earthquake rehabilitation and reconstruction in 1986.[35]

In early 1986 there were rumors that Mexico would declare a unilateral moratorium on its external debt.[36] In fact, the Mexican authorities had put together a plan to suspend all payments on debt service and replace them with deposits in domestic currency kept in the Central Bank.[37] U.S. officials, however, were able to convince the Mexican government that such a strategy would backfire and committed themselves to making new financing available to Mexico.[38] However, as will be seen, the financing did not come until the end of the year.

The 1986 oil shock provided an opportunity to consider a different approach to the management of the external debt, including a unilateral suspension of payments. Because of the 1985 earthquake international sympathy toward Mexico was running high. In addition, real wages had fallen dramatically since 1983 (table 2-4). More important, the Mexican government had shown its commitment to outward-oriented reforms and sound macroeconomic policies. Did the Mexican government miss a golden opportunity to reduce its debt burden by suspending payments on external debt?

A unilateral suspension of payments would have meant rising tensions with the international financial institutions, the U.S. government, and, of course, the commercial banks. The key question is whether Mexico could have generated the support of the Mexican business community so that any extra savings in foreign exchange resulting from the suspension would not vanish in capital flight. It is unclear whether or not this support was forthcoming. In any event, the Mexican authorities decided not to take the risk.

Given the size of the oil shock and the lack of external financial support, the Mexican government concentrated on two objectives. In the short run it focused on protecting the balance of payments and avoiding a depletion of reserves in foreign currency. In the medium run the objective was simple: reduce Mexico's dependence on world oil prices. Oil revenues would have to make up a smaller share of the required higher export and fiscal revenues. A depreciated peso would help achieve both goals. A higher rate of depreciation, however, translated into higher inflation.

As the rate of daily nominal depreciations increased, the real controlled exchange rate of the peso depreciated 46 percent during 1986 (table 2-1). The depreciation of the controlled exchange rate was so large that by the end of 1986 the controlled and free exchange rates were on par.[39] As expected, inflation, measured in December–December rates, accelerated from 63.7 percent in 1985 to 105.7 percent in 1986 (table 2-4). Nonetheless, inflation was kept well below the level of nominal devaluation. This was the result of a combination of the existing downward flexibility of real wages, a tightening of credit policies, and further cuts in public spending.

In terms of the traditional measure, the public deficit rose despite fiscal cuts of noninterest expenditures. However, the jump in the public sector borrowing requirement (PSBR) from 9.6 percent of GDP in 1985 to 15.9 percent in 1986 was, finally, no longer considered an adequate indicator of the government's efforts or of the pressure on real resources (table 2-1). By then it was accepted that a large PSBR ratio was a result of inflation, not its cause. The legacy of the 1983 overkill was that other fiscal indicators should be used to judge efforts and performance. Two measures used since are the operational budget (the fiscal deficit adjusted for inflation), which measures the pressure on resources, and the primary balance, which measures the government's fiscal efforts because it excludes items "beyond its control," such as interest payments on domestic and external debt. In 1986 these two measures worsened, but, given the reduction in world oil prices, their deterioration was much smaller than that reflected in the PSBR.

In 1986, GDP fell by 3.8 percent (table 2-4). Given the magnitude of the oil shock and the lack of additional external credit, this contraction was not surprising. In fact, one can argue that Mexican authorities were able to handle the shock with policies that successfully protected Mexico's balance of payments and international reserves. The trade surplus was U.S.$4.6 billion—in spite of the lower price and volume of oil exports. Moreover, gross foreign currency reserves rose by about U.S.$1 billion, ending the year at U.S.$6.8 billion (table 2-4).[40] Once again the bulk of the adjustment costs was absorbed internally. In

1986 real wages dropped between 6 and 11 percent, depending on the indicator (table 2-4).

The strategy of making the dollar increasingly more expensive also contributed to the medium-term objective of reducing Mexico's reliance on oil exports. The structure of exports underwent a remarkable change. The proportion of oil export revenue in total export revenue was reduced from 68.2 percent in 1985 to 39.3 percent in 1986 (table 2-2). This reduction was the result of the lower price of oil, which had dropped from U.S.$25.5 a barrel in 1985 to U.S.$12.0 in 1986 (table 2-2), and a 41 percent rise in nonoil exports in 1986 (table 2-4). This shift in the composition of exports, which has been sustained over time, made the Mexican economy less vulnerable to variations in oil prices.

In the official view, the evolution observed in 1986 was proof that it was better to use exchange rate policy, instead of import restrictions, to deal with a balance-of-payments crisis.[41] It was argued that import restrictions discourage exports by making the importables used as inputs in the production of exports more expensive, whereas exchange rate depreciation stimulates exports while reducing imports.

Some comments are in order. An exchange rate depreciation makes importables indiscriminately more expensive, but the use of import licensing may keep some of the importables (for example, intermediate inputs) at lower relative prices. Perhaps more important, one fundamental condition must exist to accomplish a significant real devaluation without falling into runaway inflation or a deep recession: the economy must have a low degree of indexation. In particular, real wages must be flexible downward, without frequent nominal wage adjustments. This was certainly characteristic of Mexico, but other countries in and outside the region did not share such a degree of flexibility in wage bargaining. Import restrictions may also be less costly than devaluation in terms of inflation, output, and wage losses in the short run.[42] However, to raise import restrictions would have given the private sector the wrong signal. The Mexican authorities were keen on convincing the business community of its commitment to outward-oriented reform. Higher import restrictions would have meant continuing to play by the rules that prevailed during the era of import-substitution and inward-oriented development.

In hindsight, a period of undervaluation of the domestic currency may have been what was needed to encourage a shift in product orientation from domestic to foreign markets. An "expensive" dollar for a sustained period makes export ventures attractive (it is equivalent to an export subsidy). It also reduced the dislocation costs of import liberalization: the protection afforded by an undervalued exchange rate de facto gave firms time to adjust to more open markets.

A higher inflation plateau, nonetheless, was the cost of trying to keep the real exchange rate fixed, and, to a large extent, higher inflation undermined the benefits outlined above. In addition, an undervalued exchange rate provided exporters and domestic producers with artificially high profits and protection at the expense of wages. Finally, because in Mexico the contractionary effects of devaluation have always offset the expansionary impact (at least in the short run), a depreciating exchange rate was inconsistent with economic recovery. To refocus on the goals of price stability and economic recovery, it was necessary to slow down the nominal depreciation of the peso. That most likely would have resulted in a real appreciation of the peso, which, to be sustainable during the transition to a new equilibrium growth path, required additional external resources.

As mentioned, the 1983 debt rescheduling exercise raised the need for external financing from 1985 onward. Thus the Mexican government worked on a second rescheduling beginning in mid-1984. This exercise was concluded in 1985 and affected about U.S.$48 billion of the external debt: the U.S.$20 billion due between 1985 and 1990, the more than U.S.$23 billion that had been restructured in the 1983 exercise, and the U.S.$5 billion of new loans obtained in 1983.[43] This rescheduling exercise resulted in a smoother distribution of the payments for the principal due.[44] After the drop in oil prices, however, Mexico's external financing needed to rise further.

Faced with the threat of a unilateral moratorium by Mexico, the commercial banks reluctantly agreed to cooperate with the U.S. initiative known as the Baker Plan.[45] In fact, Mexico became the "pilot case" of the plan. Toward the end of 1986 the banks agreed to lend U.S.$6 billion of "new" money and reschedule payments on past debt. About 83 percent of the U.S.$52.2 billion of principal due was rescheduled over a twenty-year period with seven years of grace, and the interest rate premium was reduced from 1.12 percentage points to 0.8125 over LIBOR. Private debt was also rescheduled: about U.S.$9.7 billion was converted into twenty-year loans with a seven-year grace period.[46]

In a conceptual breakthrough, the agreement signed with the banks also included approximately U.S.$1.7 billion in contingency financing, should the growth rate during the first quarter of 1987 be less than anticipated. The message was clear: the Mexican government would do what was necessary to stick to its stabilization and reform goals; however, should economic recovery not follow, the banks would need to assume that this was a problem resulting from insufficient financing.

Official financing was also made available.[47] In September 1986 the government signed a new standby agreement with the IMF for U.S.$1.7 billion, to be disbursed in quarterly installments. For the first time in its history, the IMF agreed to include a contingency financing clause in the agreement. The Mexican government convinced IMF authorities that, should the price of oil fall below U.S.$9 a barrel, additional funds for up to U.S.$720 million were to be made available. In addition, for the first time an IMF agreement included the possibility of an automatic relaxation of the fiscal targets should the actual growth rate fall below a specified level. The World Bank made commitments to contribute U.S.$2.3 billion in net lending during 1986-87, the first of several structural and sectoral adjustment loans Mexico received from the World Bank.[48] Altogether, private and official funds amounted to U.S.$12.5 billion, a sum the government estimated was required for both exchange rate stability and moderate growth.[49] The accumulation of new loans and rescheduling from official sources gave rise to a complex web of cross-conditionality between official creditors and commercial banks and within both. Official lending from the World Bank was given in support of Mexico's structural reform, which thereby would be accelerated.[50]

In 1987, with more external financing available (table 2-5) the focus of macroeconomic policy shifted away from balance-of-payments protection to price stability and economic recovery. With these objectives in mind, the daily rate of peso depreciation was slowed. Fiscal discipline was simultaneously pushed further, which, together with the higher price of oil, resulted in a significant increase in the primary surplus of the public sector: from 1.6 percent of GDP in 1986 to 4.7 percent in 1987 (table 2-1).

New loans, slightly higher oil prices, and the performance of nonoil exports resulted in a current account surplus in 1987. The surplus amounted to U.S.$4.0 billion, while the level of gross foreign currency

TABLE 2-5. *Net Public Indebtedness, Net IMF Disbursements, and Interest Payments, 1982–90*
Millions of dollars

Item	1982	1983	1984	1985	1986	1987	1988	1989	1990[a]
Total net debt	7,429	5,087	2,613	763	73	2,961	-825	-1,190	2,168
Disbursement	11,196	8,774	6,231	4,817	11,197	9,535	8,434	4,908	7,687
Amortization	3,767	3,687	3,618	4,054	11,124	6,574	9,259	6,098	5,518
Long-run debt	8,337	4,622	2,461	708	249	3,726	-1,142	-1,065	1,685
Disbursements	11,196	6,832	4,814	3,572	10,184	8,569	7,165	3,608	5,539
Amortization	2,859	2,210	2,354	2,864	9,522	3,289	8,307	4,673	3,854
Commercial Banks	5,975	4,537	2,884	860	-399	4,410	-2,970	-1,986	110
Disbursements[b]	7,770	5,209	3,075	1,287	253	4,782	1,176	44	430
Amortization	1,795	673	191	427	652	373	5,125	2,031	320
Bilateral	486	281	55	318	676	1,442	733	346	743
Disbursements	853	781	619	1,005	1,802	2,666	1,770	1,749	2,243
Amortization	367	501	564	687	1,126	1,223	1,037	1,403	1,500
Suppliers	4	216	-119	1	-9	-31	-12	24	91
Disbursements	46	319	143	65	53	34	21	50	123
Amortization	42	104	262	64	62	65	33	27	32
IDB[c] and World Bank	1,147	178	603	711	913	393	697	701	706
Disbursements	1,375	505	979	1,166	1,446	1,086	1,642	1,615	1,772
Amortization	229	327	376	455	533	694	945	914	1,066

Bonds	725	−588	−473	−488	−519	−934	1,389	−149	35
Disbursements	1,151	17	0	49	0	1	2,556	150	971
Amortization	426	606	473	537	519	935	1,167	299	936
Short-run debt	−908	465	152	55	−176	−764	316	−125	483
Disbursements	0	1,942	1,417	1,246	1,013	966	1,268	1,300	2,147
Amortization	908	1,477	1,264	1,190	1,189	1,730	952	1,425	1,664
Credit Commodity Corporation	145	1,254	−59	−370	−445	−23	217	159	−53
Disbursements	145	1,309	742	260	157	272	532	491	396
Amortization	0	54	801	630	602	295	315	332	449
Total	**7,574**	**4,279**	**2,969**	**205**	**−44**	**2,938**	**−608**	**−1,031**	**2,115**
Disbursements	**11,341**	**10,579**	**7,388**	**5,077**	**11,354**	**9,806**	**8,966**	**5,399**	**8,083**
Amortization	**3,767**	**6,299**	**4,419**	**4,685**	**11,726**	**6,868**	**9,574**	**6,430**	**5,967**
IMF	201	1,003	1,204	296	616	320	−69	303	731
Disbursements	201	1,003	1,204	296	741	600	350	943	1,608
Amortization	0	0	0	0	125	280	419	640	877
Interest payments	12,203	10,103	11,716	10,156	8,342	8,097	8,639	9,377	9,018

Sources: Secretaría de Hacienda y Crédito Público; interest payments from table 2-2.

a. Excludes the guarantees pledged under the debt agreement with commercial banks signed in February 1990. Preliminary figures.

b. Excludes the resources retroactive to mid-1989 included in the debt agreement.

c. Inter-American Development Bank.

reserves rose to an unprecedented U.S.$13.7 billion (table 2-4). During the second quarter economic activity began recovering, albeit at a slow pace, and resulted in a year-end growth rate of 1.7 percent (table 2-4). Inflation, however, continued to be high in 1987: between 7 and 8 percent a month from January to November. The continuing depreciation of the peso, though at a slower rate, was quickly translated into higher inflation, fiscal efforts notwithstanding.[51]

Managing the oil shock of 1986 and the pursuit of an accelerated restructuring of exports resulted in a higher inflation plateau. During 1986 and part of 1987 the Mexican authorities "overdevalued" the peso (table 2-1). This policy was undertaken partly to avoid the previous mistake of allowing the exchange rate to appreciate too quickly and end up with another balance-of-payments crisis. However, trying to keep the real exchange rate steady translated into higher inflation and a greater degree of indexation of other prices in the economy. Devaluation did buy short-term external adjustment, but at a cost of stabilization. A consequence of the exchange rate policy of 1986 was the accumulation of a large amount of gross reserves in the Central Bank (table 2-4) and the change in the profitability of export activities. These set the stage for the implementation of the new anti-inflation measures and gave a push to the outward-oriented development strategy.

However, that the economic situation was still precarious was shown by the run on the peso that followed the crash of the stock exchange in October 1987. This "speculative" attack on the currency was surprising, because the country had unprecedented levels of foreign reserves and the macroeconomic and structural policies were all in the "right direction." Mexican policymakers saw in the high inflation rate the cause of the volatility of expectations. This convinced them to make fighting inflation a top priority once again, but this time a new policy prescription would be tried. In December 1987 the government announced the Economic Solidarity Pact, known later as "the Pact," which promised to reduce monthly inflation to about 2 percent by the end of the following year.[52]

The Implementation of the Economic Solidarity Pact

The Pact was jointly signed by the government and formal representatives of labor, agricultural producers, and the business sector. Its basic components were further cuts in the fiscal deficit, tighter monetary policy, trade liberalization, and, for the first time since the crisis erupted in 1982, a comprehensive incomes policy.[53]

When the Pact was initially announced the minimum wage, the controlled exchange rate, and public prices were to be adjusted upward in December 1987, then kept fixed through the end of February. Beginning in March these prices would be increased each month in line with expected levels of inflation.[54] The measures announced at the end of February 1988, however, were quite different.[55] They amounted to a de facto freeze on prices and wages. The government agreed to keep the exchange rate and public prices frozen during March and allowed minimum wages to rise only 3 percent and then kept them fixed.[56] The private sector, in turn, committed itself to not raising prices. During 1988 the Pact was renewed four times.

The Pact had three ingredients. First, there was a demand management component, that is, the fiscal primary surplus was increased and the supply of credit contracted. Second, the government implemented incomes policies to break the inertial inflation and stabilize expectations. Lastly, there was a program of structural reform that featured an acceleration of trade liberalization (discussed in chapter 5) and the divestiture of public enterprises (discussed in chapter 4).[57]

The Pact produced immediate good results. During the second semester of 1988 average inflation was 1.2 percent a month, far lower than the 9 percent registered during the same period in 1987.[58] In 1988 real GDP grew at 1.3 percent, nonoil exports at 15.2 percent, and private investment at 10.9 percent (table 2-4). The Pact clearly fared better than the more orthodox stabilization program of 1983. The reduction in inflation was much larger, growth was positive, and real wages fell by considerably less than in 1983, though they also started out at a lower level than in 1983 (table 2-4). There is, however, one fundamental difference. The Pact was launched when foreign reserves were high (estimated at about U.S.$13.7 billion), even increasing to U.S.$16 billion shortly afterward.[59] The reserves allowed the government to sustain a fixed nominal exchange rate while import tariffs were reduced and demand and output could experience a slight expansion. A year later, in March 1989, foreign reserves were estimated at about U.S.$6 billion. That is, the "cost" of the policy package, measured in terms of loss in reserves, was about U.S.$10 billion. In a way, foreign reserves in Mexico played the role that U.S. financial support had played in the Israeli stabilization program. Because Mexico had no access to further sources of finance, short of a moratorium, it had to use its own "savings."

Why did the Pact work, and why had a similar program not been tried earlier? The unprecedented drop in the inflation rate should be attributed to the fact that the Pact added the use of incomes policy to fiscal and monetary discipline. According to one econometric exercise the contribution made by incomes policy to the reduction of inflation was significantly large.[60] In the past, Mexican authorities were reluctant to use any sort of generalized price-and-wage control mechanism. Some opposed it because they were not convinced of its theoretical soundness. Other policymakers were leery of using price controls for more pragmatic reasons. Memories of the failed Plan Austral in Argentina and Plan Cruzado in Brazil, which used incomes policy as their centerpiece, were too fresh. Incomes policy implied an investment in government credibility, which may have been too dear to risk at a time when confidence in the government's ability was particularly low. For several years the Mexican government may have considered itself too discredited vis-à-vis the private sector to implement a price freeze.

However, to those who were reluctant to use incomes policy, it became clear that fiscal and monetary discipline by itself would not suffice. Moreover, there was the positive example of Israel, which had curbed inflation using a package combining fiscal austerity and incomes policy. Lastly, a number of conditions made the decision less risky in 1988 than before. First, though Mexico could not count on additional external finance as Israel had, the Banco de México held record levels of foreign reserves.[61] This would make fixing the exchange rate a more credible policy, and reserves could be partially used to finance the expected deterioration in the balance of trade. Second, the required additional fiscal adjustment was feasible because most of the work had already been done. Third, the peso was undervalued so that the inevitable exchange rate appreciation following a freeze could be less damaging and less complicated to manage. Fourth, although the popularity of de la Madrid's government was not high, the Mexican state had the institutional clout and authority to make implementing an incomes policy easier than in other countries. Its corporatist character provided the government with adequate interlocutors to implement such a policy, and the long experience of the

Mexican state in price regulation could be applied to the new circumstances. Also, the fact that a comprehensive incomes policy had not been tried in the past, before the fiscal adjustment was in place, would make the measure more credible.

In a way all four conditions had been present since late 1986, but Mexican policymakers still believed that fiscal austerity with a reduction in the rate of depreciation of the peso would suffice to bring inflation down. It took the unexpected exchange rate debacle in November 1987 and the jump in inflation that followed to set the change.[62] However, the time for a Pact-like program had been ripe at least since the last quarter of 1986. An overcautious approach to policymaking may have delayed recovery and caused more income losses than necessary on the already hard-hit population (see chapter 3).

The acceleration of trade liberalization announced as part of the Pact became perhaps the most controversial measure of the package. The maximum tariff was lowered from 40 percent to 20 percent, official import prices were eliminated, and import permits were removed from all items except parts of agriculture, automobiles, and pharmaceuticals.[63] Trade liberalization combined with an appreciating exchange rate resulted in a considerable worsening of the trade balance. This deterioration made the policy of keeping the value of the peso fixed, and trade liberalization itself, less credible and further stalled capital repatriation. So although trade liberalization was a way to increase credibility with the business and international communities by showing Mexico's commitment to reforms, because it was not clear whether trade liberalization–cum–a fixed exchange rate was sustainable, the measure may have created difficulties in the short run.

To prevent capital from leaving the country, domestic real interest rates had to be high enough to compensate for the perceived exchange rate risk. For nearly two years real domestic interest rates remained close to 30 percent a year (table 2-4).[64] These high domestic interest rates significantly increased the burden of servicing the domestic debt. In 1988 domestic debt was about 18.5 percent of GDP, and real interest payments on domestic debt took about 8 percent of GDP.[65] This put pressure on the fiscal accounts, thereby endangering the stabilization efforts. Hence it became necessary to be tougher on noninterest expenditures and government revenues.[66] It also entailed large transfers of resources to the private sector, especially to the upper-income echelons (table 3-12).

An obvious question, then, is whether it was a good idea to engage in trade liberalization when it was known that an exchange rate appreciation would be inevitable.[67] The argument given in favor of trade liberalization was the potential contribution to lowering inflation by making external prices work as a "ceiling." Based on an analysis for several manufacturing sectors, one study does not find strong evidence that in the short run trade liberalization had a significant impact on curbing markups.[68] But leaving aside short-run costs and benefits, if the long-term goal was to move toward free trade, the climate provided by the Pact was politically conducive to accelerating liberalization. Record high reserves and an initially undervalued exchange rate were solid preconditions. Nonetheless, it might have been wiser to have delayed a full-fledged trade liberalization until after inflation was under control.[69] That might have permitted a more rational use of foreign exchange reserves and resulted in lower domestic interest rates.[70]

The success of the Pact relied on the prevailing initial conditions as well as on the characteristics of its implementation. Three conditions were particularly crucial: the fiscal deficit under control, strong external accounts, and the fact that relative prices were allowed to realign before the wage and price freeze was launched.[71]

As for its implementation, several features are worth mentioning. First, the Pact included a large dose of strict, orthodox measures, such as fiscal deficit cuts and credit tightening; second, the form in which the program was implemented differed greatly from its analogues in Argentina and Brazil. Decisions were concerted rather than forced by decree.[72] Wary of the bad reputation of price and wage freezes, the government never used the words "freeze" or "heterodox" in its jargon. In addition, the government did not make any open-ended commitments to keep the (controlled) exchange rate or public prices fixed. In principle, the policy was subject to revision each time the parties met to discuss the Pact. This was a precaution to preserve government credibility in the event conditions were not sustainable.[73] Finally, the government devised from the start a mechanism—a commission made up of high-ranking officials from the government itself and representatives from labor, agriculture, and business—to monitor the evolution of the Pact on a weekly basis. This quickly alerted policymakers to supply shortfalls and noncompliant participants. [74]

The Pursuit of Economic Recovery

The Pact brought inflation under control, but economic recovery remained elusive. It would soon be evident that fiscal discipline and structural reforms could be necessary conditions for growth but were by no means sufficient. Fiscal discipline was essential to recover and maintain price and financial stability, but a "cooled down" economy would not encourage private investment.[75]

The Mexican government could not lead recovery with expansionary policies because that would fuel inflation and erode hard-won private sector confidence. Likewise, the private sector was not going to lead the recovery because it feared a failure or reversal of the policies. The challenge faced by the Salinas administration when it came to power in December 1988 was to end this impasse.[76]

After taking office, Carlos Salinas de Gortari announced the Pact for Economic Stability and Growth (PECE). The program underscored the government's commitment to growth without sacrificing price stability. Recovery was hindered by the large negative transfer of domestic resources, which Mexico had produced year after year since the crisis erupted in mid-1982. Between 1983 and 1988 the amount of net resources transferred abroad equaled 5.9 percent of GDP a year (table 2-2).[77] This had been preceded by eleven years of positive transfers totaling U.S.$15 billion in real terms.[78] This transfer of resources was not the result of a healthy economy in which people chose to spend less than they earned, as in Germany, Japan, and Korea, but was the by-product of stagflation and low wages.

The priority had to be reversing the trend in resource transfers so that Mexico would not be forced to produce large trade surpluses to finance debt service and capital flight. High real domestic interest rates could only be a temporary solution to capital flight because of their negative effect on the fiscal stance and economic growth. The solution to capital flight had to come from measures that were sustainable.

To reverse the trend in resource transfers, it was essential to concentrate efforts on three fronts: reduction of the burden of debt servicing, encouragement of capital repatriation, and attraction of new foreign investment. Convincing the private sector at home and abroad that the Mexican economy was viable and worthy of confidence was the challenge ahead. In the process, the U.S. government needed to be convinced of this too, because without U.S. support neither official financing nor debt reduction was possible.

After four rescheduling exercises, several debt-for-equity swaps, and a zero-coupon debt discount operation, the external debt continued to be a major obstacle to recovery, or so it was perceived by potential investors.[79] Policymakers believed that a debt-reduction agreement with commercial banks was essential to reduce net resource transfers and enhance the business sector's confidence. The Mexican government's decisiveness was an important factor in persuading the U.S. government to launch the so-called Brady Plan, the new debt strategy in which debt and debt service reduction would play a fundamental part.[80] The Brady Plan was announced on March 10, 1989. Then, as happened in the past, Mexico became the first country to sign a debt agreement with the commercial banks under the new plan. It signed the agreement in principle with the advisory committee representing the banks in July 1989 and the final agreement in February 1990.[81]

The direct savings in cash flow derived from the agreement were not impressive. Based on the interest rates prevailing in 1990, they were estimated to equal about U.S.$1 billion a year for the first five years,[82] or close to 10 percent of total interest payments. Government officials, as well as economists and observers, were confident that the indirect effect of the agreement would boost the private sector's confidence, encourage capital repatriation, and, therefore, produce lower domestic interest rates and encourage economic growth.[83]

When that did not happen quickly enough, other alternatives had to be pursued. By early 1990 trade and public sector reforms were proceeding swiftly (see chapters 4 and 5). However, these had not produced a step-wise change in badly needed capital inflows. Mexico's recovery was dependent on foreign savings to finance the excess of imports over exports associated with higher levels of economic activity. There was a need for policies that would, so to speak, "shake up" expectations. And such policies, two in particular, were produced.

First, in early May 1990 the government formally announced it planned to reprivatize the banks. This had an immediate impact on expectations, and capital inflows speeded up. As a result of this inflow, nominal domestic interest rates on twenty-eight day Treasury bonds (CETES) dropped 14 percentage points from March to June 1990, when they equaled 32.4 percent.[84] This decline was a turning point in the behavior of domestic real interest rates, which had been over 40 percent for much of the previous year.[85] More important, this change in the behavior of interest rates signaled the long-awaited increase in private sector confidence.

The other break-through announcement was in August 1990, when Salinas made explicit Mexico's intent to seek a free trade agreement with the United States. This initiative gave a large boost to business confidence because (as argued in chapter 5) it made the reversal of reform in Mexico more unlikely and opened new investment opportunities. As a consequence of heightened creditworthiness, capital continued to flow in and domestic interest rates fell even further. The interest rate on 28-day Treasury certificates dropped another 6.4 percentage points from June to December 1990, when it reached the level of 26 percent.[86] Altogether, average real interest rates fell from 29.9 percent in 1989 to 8.4 percent in 1990 (table 2-4).

Capital inflows are a combination of capital repatriation, foreign loans, and foreign investment. Balance-of-payments accounts do not give figures for capital repatriation. Data from other sources, however, indicate that capital repatriation has been high. The Secretariat of Finance and Public Credit, for example, estimated that capital repatriation during 1990 reached U.S.$4.3 billion.[87]

Altogether (net) capital inflows have been rising rapidly. They were equal to U.S.$3 billion in 1989 and to U.S.$9.7 billion in 1990. For the January–July period, capital inflows increased from U.S.$4.7 billion in 1990 to U.S $12.2 billion in 1991. Some estimates put the total figure of capital inflows from January to September 1991 in the realm of U.S.$15 billion.[88] In 1991 foreign investment was roughly equal to U.S.$10 billion, and it is interesting to note a sharp change in its composition. Direct foreign investment itself did not increase between 1990 and 1991, but portfolio investment was five times larger in 1991.[89] This speaks well of Mexico's creditworthiness and the greater sophistication of its financial markets. The worrisome side of it is that a large portion of the portfolio investment is not of a long-run nature (ten years or more), which reflects the investors' cautiousness vis-à-vis Mexico's future. However, another sign of optimism is that there has been an increase in foreign lending, particularly to Mexico's private sector.

Official support from the outside world has also played its part in financing Mexico's recovery. For example, in May 1989 the IMF approved an EFF U.S.$4.1 billion, to be disbursed in quarterly tranches until February 1992. The World Bank gave a loan for close to U.S.$2 billion in 1989 and committed itself to lend on average similar amounts between 1990 and 1992.[90] Both institutions and Japan contributed to front-load their disbursements to put together the guarantees for the Brady-type agreement with commercial banks (see appendix).

The contribution from the United States has been more intangible but nonetheless important. The U.S. government's support was essential to get access to official credit sources. The greatest support was exercised during the negotiations of the Brady-type debt agreement. Without the United States government "arm twisting" commercial banks, it is unlikely that an agreement would have been reached as quickly. Another crucial contribution has been the U.S. government's positive response to negotiating a North American Free Trade Agreement.

By 1991 it seemed that Mexico was finally turning the corner. The long years of austerity seemed to have reached an end. The reforms and price stability had finally generated enough private confidence to produce a turnaround. In 1991 inflation closed at 18.8 percent, and the growth rate of GDP was estimated at 3.6 percent (table 2-4).

On the question of whether the recovery is sustainable, there are two areas of concern. One is the inflation rate. Though inflation is under control, Mexico still has some way to go to reach world inflation rates. In the meantime the exchange rate will undergo further appreciation, which has a negative effect on net exports and could produce a reversal of expectations.

A second source of concern is the current account of the balance of payments, the trade balance in particular.[91] The recovery implied an upsurge of imports of 17 percent in 1991. The bad news is that although nonoil exports increased at the rate of 12.8 percent during the same period and total exports at 5.5 percent, the disparity in the growth rates of imports and exports led to a balance-of-trade deficit equal to U.S.$11.2 billion in 1991 (table 2-4). This deficit was financed by the inflows of capital discussed above, which were large enough not only to close the gap but also to increase foreign reserves. The good news is that the highest increase is to be found in capital goods imports (24.8 percent) and the lowest in consumer goods imports (10.6 percent).[92] Thus the upsurge in imports is in part a response to the expansion of productive capacity in anticipation of Mexico's positive outlook.

With a sound fiscal stance, lower inflation rates, rising foreign reserves, and low real domestic interest rates, the situation seems to be on firm ground. The current large imbalance in the trade account may well be a one-time phenomenon in the sense that it is the result of the modernization of the productive plant that will soon render its fruits in the form of higher net exports. If the current expansion pays off in higher productivity growth in the future, the disequilibrium will disappear and so will the real appreciation of the exchange rate. The crucial element is whether this expected rise in the productivity of investment will be attained and the capital inflows will be forthcoming at the required rate during the transition period. If that is the case, the Mexican recovery is not only sustainable but shall soon show higher growth rates of output. But should capital flow at a slower pace, the expansion of the economy will be contained.[93]

Concluding Remarks

In retrospect, Mexico's experience suggests a number of lessons. First, restrictive fiscal and monetary policies are essential to restoring price stability and balance-of-payments equilibrium. However, they are not sufficient even when wages and other key prices are not indexed. Orthodox macroeconomic policies can work best when accompanied by the setting of some nominal anchors. In the case of Mexico, nominal anchors were set during the Pact via a carefully managed incomes policy that affected the exchange rate, wages, and prices.

Second, regarding the impact on stabilization, import liberalization works in two contrary ways. On the one hand, import prices may work as a ceiling for the domestic price of tradables. But on the other, import liberalization can be a destabilizing force if liberalization results in a sharply worsened balance of trade causing nervous asset holders, fearing a devaluation, to transfer capital abroad. If that happens quickly and in large amounts a devaluation will become a self-fulfilling prophecy, and the stabilization effort will be defeated.[94] Mexico avoided such an outcome by keeping domestic real interest rates high, putting a burden on the fiscal stance, and using up a good portion of its foreign currency reserves.

Third, many of Mexico's difficulties in reaping the benefits of good policymaking arose from the relatively scarce and always uncertain availability of foreign financing. The required recurrent negotiation rounds with commercial banks and the short time spans attached to official financing, especially from the IMF, created additional pressures in an environment in which expectations were already extremely high and the required restructuring large. A different international management of the debt crisis could have resulted in a different distribution of adjustment costs, in which creditors, especially commercial banks, would have had to pay their share for "irresponsible" lending policies and creditor governments would have had to pay for their previous lack of adequate supervision. In Mexico the costs were borne internally, especially by those who could not resort to capital flight to protect themselves.

Last but not least, fiscal austerity, real wage reduction, and compliance with the menu of reforms suggested by Bretton Woods institutions may not be sufficient to spark economic recovery. The Mexican case shows that, to convert stabilization into sustained growth, innovative institutional change is necessary. In Mexico this sort of change was expressed in the government's decision to seek a free trade agreement with the United States. This initiative, together with the reprivatization of the banks, contributed to a turnaround in business expectations. As a consequence, private investment and capital inflows rose and made recovery possible.

Chapter Three

The Social Costs of Adjustment

THE PROCESS OF adjustment that followed the 1982 balance-of-payments crisis produced considerable economic hardship for the Mexican people. To the extent that the fall in living standards reflected the fact that the previous expansionary policies were unsustainable, some may argue that the costs of adjustment were inevitable, since people had been living "beyond their means." However, as was argued in chapter 2, adverse external conditions, such as an additional worsening of the terms of trade and lack of adequate external credit, caused the recovery in Mexico to be slow and living standards to fall even further. Despite the large internal efforts to restore equilibrium, good policy and austerity went unrewarded for a long time.

Adjustment, Living Standards, and Income Distribution

Following a standard theoretical distinction, an adjustment process can be separated into two kinds of mechanisms: (a) those directed at expenditure reduction and (b) those directed at expenditure switching from tradable goods to those that cannot be traded in world markets. When a country faces a long-lasting external shock in its terms of trade and external credit becomes so tight that a previous expansionary policy is unsustainable, these two mechanisms come into play to restore equilibrium both in the domestic market and in the balance of payments.[1] These mechanisms will come into play in either an "orderly" manner by explicit policy decisions, or in a "disorderly" manner by inflation, or, more likely, in some combination of both.[2]

Switching policies is supposed to increase output of tradables and reduce their consumption. Expenditure reduction policies are supposed to reduce consumption of both tradables and nontradables. The most commonly used switching device is a nominal devaluation of the domestic currency, and the standard expenditure reduction is a cutback in the fiscal deficit. Both mechanisms will affect real incomes and their distribution between wages and profits. Moreover, if switching and expenditure-reduction mechanisms have a contractionary effect on the economy, as they did in Mexico, their impact on real incomes will be more pronounced.

To trace the impact of adjustment on living standards, some authors propose to examine the following categories of income: *earned* (pretax), *disposable* (earned income minus taxes plus transfers), *social* (value of services provided by government nontransfer expenditures), and *total* (the sum of disposable and social income).[3] A devaluation of the currency (switching policy) will change the pattern of earned income and its distribution. Under the most plausible assumptions, a devaluation will result in a fall in real earned wages.[4] The fall in real wages will be more pronounced the less responsive domestic supply is to relative price changes. A cut in the fiscal deficit (expenditure reduction policy) will result in a fall in the earned wage, the social wage, and the disposable wage, and thus in the total real wage. Several mechanisms cause this fall. First, a reduction of the fiscal deficit in the short run will result in a drop in aggregate demand and thus in output. Labor demand will be more slack, and therefore real earned wages will tend to fall. Second, the fiscal deficit will usually be reduced through a combination of tax increases and the elimination of subsidies, which reduces disposable incomes. Third, fiscal cutbacks are achieved by a reduction of nontransfer expenditures (such as social spending), which reduces both the social wage and often the earned wages because the expenditures are reduced by cutting the wages of governmental employees. In addition, public investment cutbacks might reduce future earned and social income.

Thus, adjustment will cause total real wages to fall. The fall in real wages will be higher when structural rigidities are more widespread (for example, when imported machinery or raw materials cannot easily be replaced with domestic production), and when external borrowing is limited, because this will entail a greater fall in output and aggregate expenditures in the short run and thus in total earned income.[5] In addition, the more "stubborn" inflation is, the more pronounced will be the fall in real wages in the transition from a high inflation equilibrium to a low one.[6] Switching policies may result in a rise in earned profits, but social and disposable profits could fall. However, this process refers to domestic profits alone. Profits earned by nationals will tend to rise as they receive interest or dividends on their capital invested abroad.

The adjustment process will also entail changes in domestic relative prices associated with the switching and expenditure-reducing mechanisms. A change particularly relevant for Mexico is the evolution of the terms of trade between agriculture and the rest of the economy. The reason for this is that a higher proportion of the poorest households (the bottom 20 percent) in Mexico are engaged in agricultural activities, and a higher proportion of those engaged in agriculture are concentrated among the lower income deciles (table 3-1).[7]

The available data for Mexico do not allow us to trace the effect of adjustment on the neatly defined categories mentioned above for a number of reasons. For example, no information exists on aggregate profits. National accounts pool together all the nonwage income, including the mixed incomes, in particular the wages imputed to the self-employed which should have been classified as wages. Second, there are no data on disposable income disaggregated into wage and nonwage income or on personal disposable income even at an aggregate level. Third, the evolution of real social income is measured by real social spending, that is, the nominal social spending deflated by the implicit GDP price deflator. This "real" social spending, however, may not be an accurate measure of "real" output in the social sectors.[8] Finally, the trend in real incomes captures not only the impact of market forces on factor payments but also the evolution of general consumption subsidies as captured by the consumer price index.

In addition, to obtain an accurate picture of the impact of adjustment costs on poverty and the distribution of household income, one would ideally have access to two household income and expenditure surveys (with a record of pre- and aftertax income), one before and one after adjustment. Unfortunately, such information is not available except for aggregate tabulations. The only survey available to the author with information at the household level was conducted in 1984, two years after the crisis started; a second one, conducted in 1989, had not been made public at the time this book was completed.[9] In the absence of such information, the analysis of who bore the cost of adjustment must be inferred from the behavior of other variables such

TABLE 3-1. *Demographic Characteristics of Households, Intra- and Interdecile, Third Quarter, 1984*
Percent unless otherwise specified

Household decile[a]	Average per capita income[b]	Intradecile			
		Rural	Urban	Agriculture	Non-agriculture
I	6,190.1	72.5	27.5	66.6	33.4
II	10,680.6	58.1	41.9	51.9	48.1
III	14,295.8	47.6	52.4	44.8	55.2
IV	18,651.4	35.6	64.4	31.8	68.2
V	23,573.9	37.7	62.3	29.8	70.2
VI	29,649.8	30.1	69.9	17.1	82.9
VII	38,051.9	17.4	82.6	11.7	88.3
VIII	48,753.1	18.1	81.9	13.4	86.6
IX	68,621.9	17.0	83.0	14.2	85.8
X	151,588.0	13.8	86.2	12.4	87.6
Total	41,005.6	34.8	65.2	29.4	70.6
Rural	25,451.4	...	...	...	...
Urban	49,303.5	...	...	...	...

Source: Author's calculations based on data from Instituto Nacional de Estadística, Geografía e Informática (INEGI), *Encuesta nacional de ingresos y gastos de los hogares, tercer trimestre de 1984* (Mexico City, 1989).

a. The total number of households is 14,988,551. Households are ranked by total per capita income.

as wages, nonwage income, agricultural incomes, and the known characteristics of poor households.

Data limitations notwithstanding, enough information exists to make an initial assessment of the impact of adjustment on living standards. On the basis of the available information, the following questions are addressed: What happened to real wage and nonwage incomes? How did agricultural indicators perform? What was the evolution of employment and unemployment? What was the impact of fiscal cuts on social expenditures? Were social services affected by declining resources? Which sectors of the population were most affected by declining incomes? In addition to income and unemployment, other indicators of welfare are examined. These include infant mortality rates, causes of death and disease, years of schooling, and

TABLE 3-1. *(continued)*

Interdecile				Household size (number)	Ratio of income earners to household size	Ratio of members under 12 to household size
Rural	Urban	Agriculture	Nonagriculture			
20.9	4.2	22.7	4.7	7.0	23.2	45.2
16.7	6.4	17.7	6.8	6.6	26.3	42.2
13.7	8.0	15.3	7.8	6.0	29.7	36.8
10.2	9.9	10.8	9.7	5.5	34.0	31.3
10.8	9.6	10.2	9.9	5.2	34.1	30.9
8.7	10.7	5.8	11.7	4.8	37.5	27.3
5.0	12.7	4.0	12.5	4.6	41.6	24.3
5.2	12.6	4.6	12.3	4.1	48.1	21.7
4.9	12.7	4.7	12.2	3.8	52.7	19.7
4.0	13.2	4.2	12.4	3.1	60.7	12.6
100.0	100.0	100.0	100.0	5.1	38.8	29.2
. . .	. . .	. . .	. . .	5.3	35.7	32.5
. . .	. . .	. . .	. . .	4.9	40.4	27.4

b. Pesos per quarter, June 1984 pesos. Income includes monetary and nonmonetary income. Dollar figures can be obtained by dividing the figures in pesos by the June 1984 exchange rate, which was equal to 185.19 pesos per dollar.

school dropouts. What follows is a brief description of the living conditions in Mexico before the 1982 crisis.

Living Conditions before the Crisis

The fall in living standards since 1982 occurred when large segments of the Mexican population were already living under precarious conditions. Despite remarkable growth and governmental efforts to improve living conditions in the post–World War II era, by the end of the 1970s poverty was pervasive, and the levels of education and public health were in need of substantial improvement.

According to the 1977 Income and Expenditure Survey, approximately 41 percent of sampled households had total earnings below the prevailing minimum wage in 1977 equal to U.S.$120 a month), considered at the time an acceptable poverty line.[10] Small landowners and landless peasants in the rural areas and those employed in the so-called informal sector in the urban areas, especially in commerce and personal services, seem to have made up the bulk of poor households.[11]

Although per capita supply of calories and proteins was sufficient to meet nutritional standards (had food availability been uniform), in 1979 the National Institute of Nutrition reported that almost 19 million people, 13 million of whom lived in rural areas, suffered from malnutrition.[12] The estimated rate of infant mortality in 1981 was 51.3 per 1,000.[13] Infants of low birth weight constituted 12 percent of the total—high compared with similar countries with lower per capita income levels, such as Colombia and Panama. In addition, between 1979 and 1983 Mexico's rate of low birth weight infants was higher than the estimated average of 10.1 percent for all of Latin America.[14] Avitaminosis and other nutrition-related problems were the sixth most frequent cause of infant mortality.[15]

In 1978 an estimated 45 percent of the population, a substantial proportion of which was made up of the rural poor, was not receiving health care coverage from private sources, because of cost, or from any of the institutions providing free or quasi-free care.[16] Illiteracy was approximately 17 percent in the early 1980s, a substantial improvement over the approximate 26.5 percent figure registered in 1970.[17] In the early 1980s, however, approximately 22 million Mexicans still were either illiterate or had not finished primary school,[18] and average schooling in 1980–81 was 5.4 years (table 3-11). According to the 1980 census, 50.1 percent of Mexican households had no running water, and 32 percent used the kitchen as the bedroom.[19] It was also estimated that 25 percent of Mexican households did not have electricity.[20]

Trends in Earned Real Incomes since 1982

An analysis of the broad trends in earned real incomes disaggregated into wage income, nonwage income, and incomes in agriculture is presented. For reasons mentioned previously, it was not possible to measure the evolution of pure factor returns.

Wage Income

The mechanisms involved in the adjustment process resulted in a sharp fall in real wages.[21] As shown in table 3-2, the fall of real wages per worker was between 40 and 50 percent (excluding *maquiladoras*) in the period 1983–88, with the sharpest declines occurring during the two years of deepest economic contraction, 1983 and 1986. The total wage bill also fell by a similar amount (table 3-2). The behavior of wage income is the combined result of the evolution of the real wage and employment. The available indicators show that the decline of wage income is a result of contracting real wages, not of reduced employment. According to the National Accounts, employment rose an average of 0.4 percent a year between 1983 and 1988 (table 3-3).[22]

The data on real wages show some interesting patterns (table 3-2). Between 1983 and 1988 the wage contraction in *maquiladoras* (in-bond firms, allowed to import materials duty free if output is exported) was lower than in the rest of the economy. Wages in the formal industrial sector contracted less than those in other sectors, except for the *maquiladoras*. However, employment in this sector declined (table 3-3). Note also that the minimum wage is not always a reliable indicator of wage performance; for example, in 1989 the minimum wage contracted, while all other wages increased.[23]

Given the large contraction of real wages one wonders whether some policy decisions subjected wages to an unwarranted decline, that is, a fall beyond what was required to restore equilibrium in the economy, even with the prevailing external conditions.[24] This is an important question. Such an analysis would shed light on whether some of the measures undertaken—or not undertaken—by policymakers to restore equilibrium and curb inflation placed an unnecessary burden on wage earners.[25]

One wonders, first, whether an earlier application of incomes policy would have reduced some of the wage losses linked to stabilization and adjustment. The results of the Economic Solidarity Pact (discussed in chapter 2) seem to support the idea that stabilization programs that combine fiscal and monetary restraint with incomes policy have a lower negative impact on wages, perhaps because they reduce part of the loss caused by accelerating inflation. Second, whether policies directed toward improving the relationship between business and government (that is, an early-on reprivatization of the banking system) may have resulted in higher investment levels and precluded part of the contraction in wages. Lastly, whether Mexico's labor law, by making layoffs possibly difficult or expensive, may have produced a greater contraction of the real wage than would have prevailed under

TABLE 3-2. *Evolution of Real Wages and Per Capita Private Consumption, 1981–90*
Annual percent change

Item	1981	1982	1983	1984	1985
Total wage income[b,c]	11.3	−5.4	−24.7	−2.8	2.0
Wage income per worker[d]	4.8	−5.1	−22.9	−5.0	−0.2
Wages in *maquiladoras*[b,e]	−0.4	8.5	−20.1	−2.0	−0.6
Blue collar only[b,f]	−0.6	4.6	−21.9	−3.5	−2.7
Wages as registered by IMSS[g]					
Total	n.a.	n.a.	n.a.	−1.8	0.7
With <10 workplaces	n.a.	n.a.	n.a.	3.4	−0.2
With >300 workplaces	n.a.	n.a.	n.a.	−4.3	0.4
Wages quoted by industrial survey[h]	5.0	0.1	−24.1	−6.8	1.1
Minimum wage[i]	1.0	−0.1	−21.9	−9.0	−1.2
Wages to government employees, per worker[b,j]	5.4	−2.6	−28.0	−5.8	0.3
Private consumption per capita[k]	4.9	−4.8	−7.4	1.1	1.5

n.a. Not available.

a. Preliminary figures.

b. Real figures are calculated using the CPI from the Banco de México, *Indicadores económicos; Resumen*, p. f (Mexico City, February 1990). The 1991 index was calculated using the average annual change in consumer prices as reported by Banco de México, *The Mexican Economy, 1991: Economic and Financial Developments in 1990, Policies for 1991* (Mexico City, 1990), table 28, p. 204. All price indexes are converted to base 1980=100.

c. For 1980–86, *Compendio de indicadores de empleo y salarios*, no. 2 (Mexico City: Comisión Nacional de los Salarios Mínimos, December 1989), table 4.6, p. 135. For 1987–90, Instituto Nacional de Estadística, Geografía e Informática (INEGI), unpublished document (received by fax from María Eugenia Gómez Luna, Director of National Accounts, INEGI).

d. For 1980–86, *Compendio de indicadores* (1989), table 2.6, p. 67. For 1987–90, unpublished INEGI document.

e. *Compendio de indicadores* (1989), p. 180; and *Compendio de indicadores de empleo y salarios*, no. 3 (Mexico City: Comisión Nacional de los Salarios Mínimos, September 1991), table 4.16, p. 132.

f. Nominal wage figures from Carlos Salinas de Gortari, *Tercer informe de Gobierno, 1991: Anexo* (Mexico City, 1991), p. 336.

g. IMSS (Instituto Mexicano del Seguro Social). *Compendio de indicadores* (1989), pp. 127–28; and *Compendio de indicadores* (1991), p. 122. Data on wages are averages from

TABLE 3-2 *(continued)*

1986	1987	1988	1989	1990[a]	Average, 1983–88	Cumula- tive, 1983–88	Average 1983–85	Average 1986–87
−10.7	−2.0	−8.3	5.9	3.0	−8.2	−40.0	−9.2	−6.4
−9.4	−3.0	−9.1	4.6	1.9	−8.6	−41.5	−9.9	−6.2
−2.2	1.7	−4.4	6.3	0.4	−4.9	−26.0	−8.0	−0.2
−6.2	−1.2	−5.9	16.6	−3.9	−7.2	−36.0	−9.8	−3.7
−7.5	−9.9	−5.9	6.6	−0.7	n.a.	n.a.	n.a.	−8.7
−2.4	−14.3	−9.9	3.8	−0.0	n.a.	n.a.	n.a.	−8.6
−9.2	−7.6	−4.8	4.8	−1.6	n.a.	n.a.	n.a.	−8.4
−6.9	−6.5	−0.5	8.9	n.a.	−7.7	−38.0	−10.6	−6.7
−10.5	−6.3	−12.7	−6.6	−9.1	−10.5	−48.5	−11.1	−8.4
−14.0	0.6	−8.4	7.1	n.a.	−9.8	−46.1	−12.0	−7.0
−4.6	−2.2	0.3	4.5	4.0	−1.9	−11.1	−1.7	−3.4

bimonthly observations and are deflated by the consumer price index in note b. The missing 1987 October observation is estimated as the August–December average. The 1983 yearly average, used to estimate the rate of growth for 1984, is constructed as the December 1982–December 1983 average.

h. *Compendio de indicadores* (1989), pp. 157–60; and *Compendio de indicadores* (1991), p. 122. Figures for 1989 are preliminary.

i. For 1980–86, *Salarios: Compendio estadístico* (Mexico City: Comisión Nacional de los Salarios Mínimos, December 1986), table 5A, pp. 25–27. For 1987–90, Banco de México, *Informe anual*, p. 119 (1987), p. 136 (1988), p. 138 (1989), p. 139 (1990).

j. Salinas de Gortari, *Tercer informe de gobierno, 1991*, p. 145.

k. For 1980–84, INEGI, *Sistema de cuentas nacionales de México, 1980–1986*, tomo I: *Resumen general* (Mexico City, 1988), tables 66–69, pp. 118, 120, 123, 126, 129. For 1985, INEGI, *Sistema de cuentas nacionales de México, 1985–1988*, tomo I: *Resumen general* (Mexico City, 1990), table 60, p. 80. For 1986–87, INEGI, *Sistema de cuentas nacionales de México, 1986–1989*, tomo I: *Resumen general*, (Mexico City, 1991), tables 60–63. For 1988–91, Macro Asesoría Económica, *Macro perspectivas: Diagnóstico y perspectivas de la economía mexicana* (July–September 1992), table V.1, p. 22. The population figures are calculated using growth rates from Manuel Odorica, "Las cifras preliminares del censo," *Demos: Carta demográfica sobre México*, no. 3 (1990), pp. 4–6.

TABLE 3-3. Employment and Unemployment, 1981–90

Annual percent change except unemployment (in percent)

Item	1981	1982	1983	1984	1985	1986	1987	1988	1989	1990ᵃ	1983–88	Average 1983–85	1986–87
Employment[b]	6.3	-0.3	-2.3	2.3	2.2	-1.4	1.1	0.9	1.3	1.1	0.4	0.7	-0.2
Agriculture and cattle	2.8	-3.3	4.2	1.1	2.6	-2.5	1.5	2.5	-2.1	-4.6	1.6	2.6	-0.5
Mining	7.2	5.8	0.4	4.2	4.0	-0.4	5.0	2.4	-1.6	2.8	2.6	2.9	2.3
Manufacturing	4.8	-2.0	-7.1	2.1	3.2	-1.9	1.1	0.1	2.5	0.6	-0.5	-0.7	-0.4
Construction	16.7	-2.6	-19.2	6.7	3.5	-3.3	0.4	0.3	11.8	13.1	-2.3	-3.8	-1.5
Electricity	6.2	4.7	1.1	3.3	5.3	2.0	3.0	2.5	2.1	4.2	2.9	3.2	2.5
Commerce	6.4	0.9	-2.7	1.8	0.6	-1.2	1.4	1.5	2.8	3.0	0.2	-0.1	0.1
Transport	7.5	6.7	-4.5	1.6	2.3	0.6	2.4	-2.4	-0.4	5.0	-0.1	-0.3	1.5
Financial services	9.7	10.4	2.6	6.6	0.9	0.2	1.6	1.7	0.5	1.6	2.3	3.3	0.9
Personal services	6.3	1.4	-0.1	2.3	1.8	-0.4	0.2	-0.2	0.6	1.0	0.6	1.3	-0.1
Monthly industrial survey employment[c]	5.5	-2.4	-9.6	-1.0	2.3	-4.0	-3.4	...	2.4	0.0	...	-2.9	-3.7
Urban open unemployment[d]	4.2	4.2	6.3	5.7	4.3	4.3	3.9	3.5	3.0	2.8	4.7	5.4	4.1

a. Preliminary figures.

b. For 1980–86, INEGI, *Sistema de cuentas nacionales de México, 1986–1989*. For 1987–90, Dirección de Contabilidad Nacional y Estadísticas Económicas (SICNEE), INEGI, internal document.

c. *Compendio de indicadores* (1989), table 2.8, pp. 74–77. The figures up to 1987 refer to a sample of 1,157 establishments encompassing 57 classes of economic activity. The figures for 1988 and 1989 refer to a sample of 3,218 establishments encompassing 129 classes of economic activity. Therefore, the 1988 rate cannot be calculated because the figures for 1987 and 1988 are not comparable. The rates for 1990 and 1991 are from Macro Asesoría Económica, *Macro diagnóstico y perspectivas de la economía* (April–June 1992), year 5, p. 26.

d. For 1981–88, Macro Asesoría Económica, *Realidad Económica de México, 1991* (Mexico City, 1990), table 15, p. 427. For 1989–91, GEA *Económico*, no. 12 (March 12, 1992), p. 5.

more flexible employment practices. The good side of Mexican labor laws, however, has probably meant that unemployment remained relatively low even in times of severe output contraction (table 3-3). Further research on all these subjects is no doubt needed.

At first it seems puzzling that it was possible to inflict such wage cuts without provoking widespread political or social unrest and countless strikes.[26] One possible reason is that though wages were heavily cut, the cuts did not affect household incomes to the same extent, because many households received income from other sources besides wages, and nonwage income declined substantially less. Data on real per capita consumption support this interpretation. Private consumption per capita declined cumulatively by 11.1 percent between 1983 and 1988, whereas real wage income dropped 41.5 percent during the same period (table 3-2). This seems to indicate that Mexican households must have received income from other sources besides wages, or were using their savings. The lack of resistance to wage cuts can also be explained by the government's long-standing control of the labor movement, exercised through a remarkable combination of coercion and cooptation ever since the 1930s.

Nonwage Income

In contrast to wage income, which declined on average 8.2 percent a year from 1983 to 1988, nonwage income declined only 1.2 percent a year (table 3-4). This resulted in a sharp increase in the share of nonwage income in total income (wage plus nonwage), which rose from 60 percent in 1981 to 71.5 percent in 1988. The behavior of nonwage income—in contrast to wage income—perhaps reflects the fact that prices of goods and services, excluding those produced by the public sector and those subject to price control regimes, were probably more "freely" set than wages.

Part of the better nonwage performance is accounted for by rising profits in the modern sector of the economy. Though there are no estimates of profit rates, the profit margin (as a proportion of total sales) rose in most manufacturing sectors during 1982–87.[27] It would be a mistake to believe, however, that all nonwage income is profits, rents, or interest income that accrues only to the wealthy. The non-wage category includes income of the small peasant or shop owner, as well as that of the wealthy modern businessman. Nonwage income is an important share of the total income of the poor, as well as the

TABLE 3-4. *Wage and Nonwage Income, 1981–90*
Annual percent change except shares (in percent)

Sector	1981	1982	1983	1984	1985	1986	1987	1988	1989	1990	Average, 1983–88	Cumulative, 1983–88	Average 1983–85	1986–87
All[a]														
Wage income	11.3	-5.4	-24.7	-2.8	2.0	-10.7	-2.0	-8.3	5.9	3.0	-8.2	-40.0	-9.2	-6.4
Nonwage income	4.8	2.0	1.7	0.3	-2.0	-7.5	4.6	-3.8	8.0	7.4	-1.2	-6.9	-0.0	-1.6
Share of nonwage income in total income	60.0	61.8	68.6	69.2	68.4	69.1	70.5	71.5	71.9	72.7	69.5	...	68.7	69.8
Agriculture[b]														
Wage income	10.0	-12.7	-13.2	-3.8	3.0	-2.0	-5.6	-12.6	-6.7	-8.6	-5.9	-30.5	-4.9	-3.8
Nonwage income	5.9	-8.9	-2.0	14.1	9.0	-8.0	-2.2	-15.7	8.9	13.4	-1.3	-7.6	6.8	-5.1
Share of nonwage income in total income	73.9	74.7	77.0	79.8	80.7	79.8	80.3	79.8	82.3	85.2	79.6	...	79.2	80.0
Nonagriculture[b]														
Wage income	11.4	-5.0	-25.3	-2.7	2.0	-11.2	-1.7	-8.0	6.8	3.7	-8.3	-40.5	-9.5	-6.6
Nonwage income	4.7	3.3	2.1	-1.1	-3.3	-7.4	5.5	-2.4	7.8	6.7	-1.2	-6.9	-0.8	-1.1
Share of nonwage income in total income	58.6	60.6	67.8	68.1	67.0	67.9	69.4	70.7	70.9	71.5	68.5	...	67.6	68.7

a. For 1980–84, INEGI, *Sistema de cuentas nacionales de México, 1980–1986*, table 43, p. 90. For 1985–86, INEGI, *Sistema de cuentas nacionales de México 1985–1988*, table 37, p. 63. For 1987–90, unpublished, INEGI document.

b. For 1980–84, INEGI, *Sistema de cuentas nacionales de México, 1980–86*, tables 30–37, pp. 77–84. For 1985, INEGI, *Sistema de cuentas nacionales de México, 1985–1988*, tables 24–25, p. 57. For 1986, INEGI, *Sistema de cuentas nacionales de México, 1980–86*, table 2. For 1987–90, unpublished, INEGI document. The sector categories used here from INEGI are defined as follows. Agriculture: agriculture, cattle raising, forestry, and fishing. Nonagricultural: mining; industrial manufacturing; construction; electricity; gas and water; trade, restaurants, and hotels; transportation, warehousing and communications; financial services, insurance, and real estate; and community, social, and personal services. Real figures were derived using consumer price index (1980=100), from Banco de México, *Mexican Economy, 1991*, table 28, p. 204.

TABLE 3-5. *Distribution of Total Household Income by Source, Third Quarter, 1984*

Percent unless otherwise specified

Household decile[a]	Average per capita income[b]	Non-monetary	Wages and salaries	Profits	Rents	Coopera-tives	Transfers	Other	Total
I	6,190.1	30.3	33.2	28.4	0.1	0.2	7.7	0.0	100.0
II	10,680.6	22.8	46.0	23.1	0.6	0.3	7.2	0.0	100.0
III	14,295.8	21.9	41.2	29.0	0.2	0.2	7.5	0.0	100.0
IV	18,651.4	21.1	45.0	24.8	1.1	0.1	7.8	0.0	100.0
V	23,573.9	21.3	46.5	24.5	1.2	0.1	6.5	0.0	100.0
VI	29,649.8	20.5	49.3	19.3	1.3	0.4	9.1	0.1	100.0
VII	38,051.9	22.6	52.4	16.8	1.2	0.0	7.0	0.0	100.0
VIII	48,753.1	27.0	47.2	16.7	2.3	0.0	6.6	0.2	100.0
IX	68,621.9	24.3	46.0	18.8	3.5	0.4	6.7	0.3	100.0
X	151,588.0	21.6	43.3	20.4	5.0	0.2	9.0	0.6	100.0
Total	41,005.6	23.3	45.0	22.2	1.7	0.2	7.5	0.1	100.0
Rural	25,451.4	26.9	32.3	31.1	1.0	0.3	8.1	0.1	100.0
Urban	49,303.5	21.4	51.7	17.4	2.0	0.1	7.2	0.1	100.0

Source: Author's calculations based on data from INEGI, *Encuesta nacional de ingresos y gastos de los horages, tercer trimestre de 1984.*

a. The total number of households is 14,988,551. Households are ranked by total per capita income.

b. Pesos per quarter, June 1984 pesos. Income includes monetary and nonmonetary income.

rich. It is also a part of the income of the middle sectors, though a smaller one. For example, the bottom 10 percent of Mexican households derive one-third of their income from wages, with the other two-thirds more or less equally distributed between nonmonetary income (for example, home-consumed crops and imputed housing costs) and nonwage monetary income (table 3-5). Thus part of the drastic fall in wage income must have been compensated by the relatively better performance on nonwage income for all income groups. This may explain, to some extent, why consumption per capita fell much less than wages and why there was no widespread social protest.

Incomes in Agriculture

Because most of the very poor in Mexico are engaged in agricultural activities (table 3-1), it is important to analyze the evolution of wage and nonwage income in agriculture as well as of the output and price of corn—the basic peasant crop—during the adjustment period. Table 3-6 records the evolution of specific variables for agriculture and for all sectors combined. Several things should be noted. First, agriculture seems to have a life of its own in terms of output performance; it does not follow the general pattern. For example, during the severe economywide contraction in 1983, agricultural output grew. Conversely, while the rest of the economy was set on a recovery path in 1988–89, agriculture experienced a severe setback.

During the first stabilization program, from 1983 to 1985, agricultural output and employment fared better than the overall economy. Real wages in agriculture fell less than aggregate real wages (table 3-4). Nonwage income in agriculture rose, while nonwage income in the nonagricultural sector contracted (table 3-4). Better prices for agricultural goods and unusually favorable weather conditions may explain this performance. Real devaluations and attempts to align agricultural prices with world prices contributed to an improvement in agricultural prices, and the on-farm price of corn was no exception (table 3-6). Because most poor peasants are corn growers[28] and most of the corn is grown by poor peasants,[29] poor rural households may have suffered less during this crunch than their urban counterparts.

This result is confirmed by findings of another author, who conducted interviews in mid-1985 concerning the employment conditions in rural areas.[30] In all but one of Mexico's midsection states, farmers complained of labor shortages. In several areas wages offered to rural workers were well above the minimum wage. Labor shortages apparently stemmed from migration to the United States. In addition, the author found a virtual absence of return migration from urban areas, despite cuts in urban wages.

This favorable pattern for agriculture reversed itself in 1986, when output in this sector contracted (table 3-6). In addition, from 1987 on and especially in 1988 and 1989, agriculture's performance was worse than that of the economy as a whole (table 3-6). Bad weather conditions and a deterioration in agricultural prices might explain this downturn.[31] A reduction in agricultural subsidies and credit, as well as an absence of new investment, further explains the decline.[32] During 1988–89, agricultural prices may have lagged behind as a result of the Economic Solidarity Pact, which clamped down on some prices— namely agricultural prices—more than others.[33]

The evolution of corn output and prices, as well as of wage and nonwage agricultural income, indicates that economic hardship in agriculture must have been severe for the period 1988–89 (table 3-6). This suggests that during the period of the Pact, in 1988–89, just when the rest of the economic outlook appeared promising, the poorest population suffered a deterioration in living standards. In 1990 the data show an improvement in agricultural output and prices (table 3-6) and hence the incomes of the rural poor may have also recovered. The absence of data at the household level does not allow further analysis.

Unemployment and Employment Patterns

The initial sharp deceleration in aggregate output growth in 1983 was accompanied by an approximately 50 percent increase in the open urban unemployment rate (table 3-3). However, despite lagging economic performance and continuous additions to the economically active population, estimated at close to one million a year,[34] the unemployment rate during the 1980s soon descended to levels below those during the oil boom (tables 1-5 and 3-3).

This at first surprising result might be explained by the downward flexibility of Mexican real wages, as discussed earlier. The large decline in real wages, on the one hand, allowed firms to keep labor costs in check while facing declining demand without having to reduce employment; on the other, it allowed the government to reduce total expenditures without resorting to widespread layoffs. Moreover, those who did not remain employed as wage earners in the formal sector[35] were likely to be willing to work in the informal sector for lower pay or as non-remunerated family labor.[36] In a country like Mexico with no unemployment insurance benefits, it is not surprising that people will accept working at lower quality jobs rather than be unemployed. To be unemployed is a luxury that most Mexicans cannot afford.

The urban open unemployment rates seem too low when compared with the aggregate "implicit" unemployment rate, measured by the

TABLE 3-6. *Evolution of the Agricultural Sector, 1981–90*
Annual percent change except shares (in percent)

Item	1981	1982	1983	1984	1985
Gross domestic product					
Agriculture[b]	6.1	−2.0	2.0	2.7	3.8
All sectors[c]	8.8	−0.6	−4.2	3.6	2.6
Total wage income[d]					
Agriculture	10.0	−12.7	−13.2	−3.8	3.0
All sectors	11.3	−5.4	−24.7	−2.8	2.0
Wage income per worker[d,e]					
Agriculture	7.0	−9.7	−16.7	−4.9	0.3
All sectors	4.8	−5.1	−22.9	−5.0	−0.2
Employment[f]					
Agriculture	2.8	−3.3	4.2	1.1	2.6
All sectors	6.3	−0.3	−2.3	2.3	2.2
Share of agricultural employment					
in total employment[f]	27.0	26.2	28.0	27.7	27.8
On-farm real price of corn[g]	7.7	−6.9	2.7	4.3	−4.6
Corn production[h]	17.6	−26.0	22.5	−3.0	10.3
Nonwage income[d]					
Agriculture	5.9	−8.9	−2.0	14.1	9.0
All sectors	4.8	2.4	2.0	−0.3	−0.1
Share of nonwage income[d]					
Agriculture	73.9	74.7	77.0	79.8	80.7
All sectors	59.5	61.4	68.3	68.8	68.4

n.a. Not available.

a. Preliminary figures.

b. For 1980–84, INEGI, *Sistema de cuentas nacionales de México, 1980–1986*, table 91, p. 194. For 1985–87, INEGI, *Sistema de cuentas nacionales de México, 1985–1988*, table 79, p. 118. For 1988–90, INEGI, unpublished document (March 1992).

c. For 1980–84, INEGI, *Sistema de cuentas nacionales de México, 1980–1986*, table 46, p. 93. For 1985, INEGI, *Sistema de cuentas nacionales de México, 1985–1988*, table 34, p. 62. For 1986–89, INEGI, *Sistema de cuentas nacionales de México, 1986–1989*.

d. For 1980–86, *Compendio de indicadores de empleo y salarios*, no. 2 (Mexico City: Comisión Nacional de los Salarios Mínimos, December 1989), table 4.6, p. 135. For 1987–90, Instituto Nacional de Estadística, Geografía e Informática (INEGI), unpublished document (received by fax from María Eugenia Gómez Luna, Director of National Accounts, INEGI).

TABLE 3-6 *(continued)*

1986	1987	1988	1989	1990ᵃ	Average, 1983–88	Cumula- tive, 1983–88	Average 1983–85	Average 1986–87
-2.7	1.4	-3.2	-3.3	7.4	0.6	3.8	2.8	-0.7
-3.8	1.7	1.3	3.3	4.4	0.2	1.0	0.6	-1.0
-2.0	-5.6	-12.6	-6.7	-8.6	-5.9	-30.5	-4.9	-3.8
-10.7	-2.0	-8.3	5.9	3.0	-8.2	-40.0	-9.2	-6.4
0.5	-7.0	-14.8	-4.7	-4.1	-7.3	-36.7	-7.4	-3.3
-9.4	-3.0	-9.1	4.6	1.9	-8.6	-41.5	-9.9	-6.2
-2.5	1.5	2.5	-2.1	-4.6	1.6	9.8	2.6	-0.5
-1.4	1.1	0.9	1.3	1.1	0.4	2.7	0.7	-0.2
27.5	27.6	28.1	27.1	25.6	27.8	. . .	27.8	27.5
-7.0	-9.8	-0.9	n.a.	n.a.	-2.7	-15.0	0.7	-8.4
-16.9	-1.0	-8.7	3.3	33.7	-0.3	-1.6	9.4	-9.3
-8.0	-2.2	-15.7	8.9	13.4	-1.3	-7.6	6.8	-5.1
-7.5	4.6	-3.8	8.0	7.4	-0.9	-5.5	0.5	-1.6
79.8	80.3	79.8	82.3	85.2	79.6	. . .	79.2	80.0
69.1	70.5	71.5	71.9	72.7	69.4	. . .	68.5	69.8

e. For 1980–86, *Compendio de indicadores* (1989), table 2.6, p. 67. For 1987–90, unpublished INEGI document.

f. For 1980–86, INEGI, *Sistema de cuentas nacionales de México, 1986–1989.* For 1987–90, Dirección de Contabilidad Nacional y Estadísticas Económicas (SICNEE), INEGI, internal document.

g. CONASUPO (National Commission of Popular Subsistence), cited by Kirsten Appendini, "La política alimentaria y restructuración económica en México," UNRISD/ El Colegio de México, 1991, table 9, app. K.

h. Secretaría de Agricultura y Recursos Hidráulicos, in Salinas de Gortari, *Tercer informe de gobierno,"* p. 211.

ratio of total work places divided by the economically active population. Implicit unemployment was 11.4 percent in 1980 and 20.3 percent in 1985.[37] This discrepancy arises because the two statistics measure different things. To obtain the implicit unemployment levels, the National Accounts measure the labor posts required to produce a certain amount of output (with a given technology). The urban employment statistics are calculated as the difference between the economically active population and those who were employed for at least one hour during the week of reference, including people who worked for no remuneration (among whom are family members who work for no explicit payment). Thus, the definition of employment embedded in the open unemployment statistics includes all the cases of "precarious" employment, whereas the National Accounts' definition does not. In practice, for example, one labor post can be occupied by more than one person. The difference in the performance of the two indicators perhaps can be interpreted as a rough estimate of the evolution of "underemployment."[38]

The shift in the employment structure according to occupational category shows the following pattern. The proportion of wage earners in the urban labor force fell from 83.4 percent in 1982 to 76.2 percent in 1985, whereas the number of self-employed increased from 12.1 to 15 percent and unpaid family workers from 2.1 to 4.6 percent.[39] Thereafter the proportion of wage earners continued to decline, though at a much slower rate, about 1 percentage point annually until 1989.[40] Between 1980 and 1988, employment in services (characteristic of informal employment) as a proportion of total employment increased slightly, whereas the proportion in agriculture hardly changed and in industry declined, especially in construction. The changes have been 1 percentage point or less in one direction or the other.[41] The rise in the proportion of self-employed and of employment in services is consistent with the idea that during the adjustment process informal employment rose. The income obtained from informal employment was probably able to partly compensate for the dramatic decline in wage income from formal employment within households.[42]

Social Income: The Evolution of Public Spending on Social Sectors

As discussed in chapter 2, an essential component of the Mexican stabilization programs was a reduction in the public deficit. The government's efforts in this direction were significant (table 2-1). Increasing public revenues and reducing government expenditures made the decline in the fiscal deficit possible. Such a policy meant higher prices for publicly produced goods and services and higher tax rates, as well as cuts in public investment, subsidies, and other public expenditures (see chapter 4).

Total government spending declined by 6.8 percent cumulatively from 1983 to 1988 (table 3-7).[43] However, the external debt servicing component could not be reduced because its magnitude was largely dependent on factors beyond the government's direct control. As real interest rates continued to be relatively high and the initial stock of debt was large, public expenditures allocated primarily for domestic and external debt servicing (nonprogrammable spending) rose 29.6 percent between 1983 and 1988 (table 3-7). Thus, to comply with required fiscal goals, all other noninterest expenditure categories, including social expenditures, had to be reduced. The share of all noninterest expenditures (the so-called programmable expenditures) in total government spending went from about 80 percent in 1980–81 to 54.3 percent on average from 1983 to 1988 (table 3-7).

Social spending, comprising primarily expenditures on education and health,[44] contracted by 33.1 percent between 1983 and 1988 (table 3-7). Social spending was cut more than total programmable spending; as a whole, then, at the beginning of the crisis the government did not shift programmable spending in favor of the social sectors.[45] As a result, the ratio of social spending to programmable expenditures declined from 31.2 percent in 1981 to 28 percent in 1983. The tendency began to reverse itself in 1985. However, the sharpest reversal occurred from 1989 on and in 1990 the same ratio reached 37.6 percent. The reader may recall from chapter 2 that the Mexican economy began to recover in 1989 and in 1990 domestic interest rates began to fall sharply. Coupled with the Salinas government's committment to improve social conditions this explains the absolute and relative recovery of social spending.

Education and health expenditures constitute about 85 percent of social outlays. Expenditures in both areas contracted from 1983 to 1988. Spending on education fell by 29.6 percent, and spending on health by 23.3 percent. Education and health expenditures then were reduced by less than total social spending, leaving the sharpest cuts to be made in other social programs. Whether this change in the

TABLE 3-7. *Government Spending on Social Sectors: Total, Education, and Health, 1980–90[a]*

Annual percent change except shares (in percent)

Item	1980	1981	1982	1983	1984	1985
Total government spending[b]	. . .	27.8	16.7	−10.8	−0.3	−1.7
Programmable[c]	. . .	23.4	−8.9	−15.7	5.7	−5.5
Nonprogrammable[c]	. . .	47.8	114.6	−3.0	−8.9	4.5
Share of programmable spending in total spending[b,c]	82.1	79.3	61.9	58.5	62.1	59.7
Social spending[d]	. . .	24.1	−1.3	−30.1	4.3	6.3
Per capita[d,e]	. . .	21.2	−3.5	−31.5	2.1	4.3
Share of social spending in total programmable spending[c,d]	31.0	31.2	33.8	28.0	27.6	31.1
Social spending on education[d]	. . .	25.1	3.9	−29.9	7.5	2.9
Share of educational spending in social spending[d]	38.9	39.2	41.2	41.3	42.6	41.2
Share of educational spending in GDP[d,f]	3.1	3.6	3.8	2.8	2.9	2.9
Social spending on health[d]	. . .	13.9	−0.6	−21.1	−4.2	2.8
Share of health spending in social spending[d]	43.6	40.0	40.3	45.5	41.8	40.4
Share of health spending in GDP[d,f]	3.5	3.7`	3.7	3.0	2.8	2.8

a. Real figures were calculated by using implicit GDP deflators from Banco de México, *Mexican Economy, 1991*, table 6, p. 180.

b. Salinas de Gortari, *Tercer informe de gobierno*, 1991, p. 153.

c. Programmable spending excludes revenue sharing with states, municipalities, and others, fiscal incentives and interest payments, and commissions and other expenditures associated with domestic and foreign debt. Nonprogrammable spending equals total minus programmable spending.

d. Salinas de Gortari, *Tercer informe de gobierno*, 1991, p. 157.

composition of expenditures within social spending was desirable is unclear. More detailed research is needed to determine the complete and definitive social impact of the reallocation of social expenditures. Some cuts, such as those affecting the programs implemented by COPLAMAR, probably hurt the very poor.

This discussion is subject to one important caveat. To convert expenditures into real constant pesos, expenditure categories were di-

TABLE 3-7 (continued)

1986	1987	1988	1989	1990	Average, 1983–88	Cumula- tive, 1983–88	Average 1983–85	Average 1986–87
6.9	6.9	−6.6	−13.9	−3.8	−1.2	−6.8	−4.4	6.9
−6.7	−4.7	−5.4	−6.7	6.5	−5.6	−29.2	−5.6	−5.7
26.9	19.5	−7.6	−20.4	−14.5	4.4	29.6	−2.6	23.1
52.1	46.4	47.0	51.0	56.4	54.3	. . .	60.1	49.3
−8.1	−4.9	−1.1	3.6	12.9	−6.5	−33.1	−8.2	−6.5
−9.7	−6.7	−2.7	1.8	11.1	−8.2	−40.2	−10.0	−8.2
30.7	30.6	32.0	35.5	37.6	30.0	. . .	28.9	30.6
−11.7	2.2	0.6	2.1	10.1	−5.7	−29.6	−8.1	−5.0
39.6	42.6	43.4	42.7	41.7	41.8	. . .	41.7	41.1
2.6	2.6	2.6	2.6	2.7	2.7	. . .	2.8	2.6
2.9	−7.7	3.8	9.3	13.9	−4.3	−23.3	−8.0	−2.5
45.3	44.0	46.2	48.7	49.2	43.9	. . .	42.6	44.6
3.0	2.7	2.8	3.0	3.2	2.9	. . .	2.9	2.9

e. Population: Yearly levels are calculated using growth rates from Ordorica, "Las cifras preliminares del censo." Ordorica provides yearly growth rates for the 1980–90 decade and cites the 11th population census preliminary figure for total population in 1990, estimated to be 81.1 million.

f. GDP: For 1980–84, INEGI, *Sistema de cuentas nacionales de México, 1980–1986*, table 46, p. 93. For 1985, INEGI, *Sistema de cuentas nacionales de México, 1985–1988*, table 34, p. 62. For 1986–89, INEGI, *Sistema de cuentas nacionales de México, 1986–1989*.

vided by the implicit GDP deflator rather than a sector-specific deflator because of the unavailability of the latter. But the decline in government social spending may well be a reflection of lower wage outlays in those sectors rather than a reduction in "output" of the government services.[46] To correct this bias, at least partially, I measure resource availability—physical and human—in health and education in the next section.

TABLE 3-8. *Educational Resources, Total and Primary School, Academic Years 1980–81 through 1991–92*
Percent

Item	1980– 1981	1981– 1982	1982– 1983	1983– 1984	1984– 1985	1985– 1986	1986– 1987	1987– 1988	1988– 1989	1989– 1990	1990– 1991	1991– 1992[a]	Average			
													1983– 1989	1983– 1986	1986– 1988	1988– 1991
Total																
Matriculated students (annual change)	6.6	5.6	4.5	3.3	1.2	2.0	0.7	0.0	0.0	–0.9	–0.5	2.5	1.2	2.2	0.4	–0.5
Students per teacher ratio	28.5	27.7	27.1	26.6	25.6	24.8	24.2	23.9	23.3	22.9	22.5	22.8	24.7	25.7	24.1	22.9
Students per school ratio	206.1	201.5	194.9	190.2	188.5	183.0	172.0	170.5	165.3	163.7	156.9	155.1	178.3	187.3	171.3	161.9
Primary school																
Matriculated students (annual change)	3.8	2.1	1.6	1.0	–1.0	–0.6	–0.9	–1.5	–0.8	–1.1	–0.6	1.3	–0.6	–0.2	–1.2	–0.8
Students per teacher ratio	39.1	37.5	36.6	35.9	34.8	33.6	32.8	31.9	31.3	31.1	30.5	30.6	33.4	34.8	32.4	31.0
Students per school ratio	192.9	196.4	195.4	194.9	199.8	197.2	187.3	185.3	180.2	179.7	175.0	173.8	190.8	197.3	186.3	178.3
Free textbooks per student	4.8	4.9	5.2	5.4	5.4	5.4	4.9	5.0	4.8	5.0	5.1	5.1	5.2	5.4	5.0	5.0

Source: Salinas de Gortari, *Tercer informe de gobierno, 1991*, pp. 345, 346, 349.

a. Estimated figures.

Resource Availability in Education and Health

Though spending in public education contracted significantly, some key indicators of the resources available in the sector show improvement. For example, student per teacher and student per school ratios for total and primary school decreased (table 3-8).[47] However, part of this improvement may be due to the decline in school enrollment rather than to an improvement in resources. Unfortunately this question could not be answered for lack of reliable information.

Nonetheless, even if the improvement in indicators is due partly to an enrollment below desirable levels, per capita human and physical resources were not subjected to reductions anywhere near those indicated by the drop in education expenditures. Therefore, most of the decline in expenditures must be attributable to using the "wrong" price deflator. Instead of the implicit GDP deflator, a sector-specific deflator should have been used. The reduction in education spending, then, primarily reflects the drop in real wages of education employees and investment in the sector. It also might reflect a cut in the availability of school materials and in the maintenance of existing facilities. The impact of such drops on the quality of education regrettably cannot yet be assessed. Over time the teaching profession may absorb less-qualified and less-motivated people, something that may have a lasting effect on the quality of education.

Per capita medical units, beds, and doctors per capita available in the "formal" health sector deteriorated between 1983 and 1988 (table 3-9). That is, the quality health care services provided by agencies that cover only those who contribute through the social security system probably worsened during adjustment. For example, medical units, hospital beds, and doctors per covered member of the Mexican Institute of Social Security (IMSS) declined on average since 1983 (table 3-9). The Health and Social Security Institute for State Employees (ISSSTE), a separate health organization that only covers government employees, has similarly faced declines in beds and units. Both institutions covered, respectively, 41.9 percent and 8.8 percent of the total Mexican population on average between 1983 and 1988 (table 3-9).

The deterioration of IMSS and ISSSTE per-member physical and human resources in health services may have resulted from sudden increases in the number of people who joined the social security health care system, particularly IMSS, in 1984, 1985, and 1987 (table 3-9).

TABLE 3-9. *Human and Physical Resources in the Health Sector, 1980–91*
Annual percent change except shares (in percent)

Item	1980	1981	1982	1983	1984	1985
IMSS[b,c]						
Population covered						
Thousands	24,125.0	26,916.0	26,885.0	26,977.0	29,388.0	31,529.0
Rate of change	14.9	11.6	−0.1	0.3	8.9	7.3
As a ratio of						
total population[d]	36.4	39.6	38.6	37.9	40.4	42.5
Medical units						
per thousand	0.050	0.054	0.056	0.057	0.049	0.046
Rate of change	. . .	8.5	3.9	0.8	−13.4	−7.5
Beds						
Per thousand	1.142	1.041	1.095	1.095	1.007	0.851
Rate of change	. . .	−8.8	5.1	0.0	−8.1	−15.5
Doctors						
Per thousand	0.975	0.955	0.931	1.007	0.758	0.760
Rate of change	. . .	−2.0	−2.5	8.1	−24.7	0.2
Nurses						
Per thousand	1.71	1.66	1.68	1.81	1.72	1.74
Rate of change	. . .	−2.9	1.7	7.2	−4.5	1.0
Ratio of nurses						
to doctors	1.7	1.7	1.8	1.8	2.3	2.3
ISSSTE[b,c]						
Population covered						
Thousands	4,985.0	5,319.3	5,467.8	5,611.0	6,080.4	6,447.9
Rate of change	2.2	6.7	2.8	2.6	8.4	6.0
As ratio of						
total population[d]	7.5	7.8	7.8	7.9	8.4	8.7
Medical units						
Per thousand	0.2	0.2	0.2	0.2	0.2	0.2
Rate of change	. . .	−3.8	0.3	−2.1	−3.4	−4.0
Beds						
Per thousand	1.066	0.988	1.002	1.001	1.009	0.951
Rate of change	. . .	−7.3	1.4	−0.1	0.8	−5.7
Doctors						
Per thousand	1.510	1.515	1.666	1.623	1.674	1.619
Rate of change	. . .	0.4	10.0	−2.6	3.1	−3.3
Nurses						
Per thousand	1.6	1.7	2.0	2.0	2.2	2.1
Rate of change	. . .	4.3	17.9	−1.4	11.6	−3.5
Ratio of nurses						
to doctors	1.1	1.1	1.2	1.2	1.3	1.3

a. Estimated figures.

b. IMSS: Instituto Mexicano del Seguro Social; ISSTE: Instituto de Salud y Seguridad Social de Trabajadores del Estado.

c. Salinas de Gortari, *Tercer informe de gobierno, 1991*, pp. 370–71, 376–79, 381, 386, 390. Doctors are those in direct contact with patients. Beds are the number of registered beds (censables).

TABLE 3-9 *(continued)*

| | | | | | | | Average | |
1986	1987	1988	1989	1990	1991ᵃ	1983–88	1983–85	1986–87
31,062.0	34,336.0	35,066.0	37,213.0	38,575.0	38,117.0	31,393.0	29,298.0	32,699.0
−1.5	10.5	2.1	6.1	3.7	−1.2	4.5	5.5	4.4
41.1	44.6	44.8	46.7	47.6	43.9	41.9	40.3	42.8
0.047	0.043	0.044	0.042	0.042	0.043	0.048	0.051	0.045
4.1	−8.3	0.9	−4.2	−1.1	2.5	−4.1	−6.9	−2.3
0.865	0.776	0.747	0.715	0.711	0.721	0.89	0.98	0.82
1.6	−10.2	−3.8	−4.2	−0.5	1.4	−6.2	−8.1	−4.5
0.769	0.725	0.750	0.714	0.719	0.786	0.79	0.84	0.75
1.2	−5.7	3.3	−4.7	0.6	9.3	−3.6	−6.6	−2.3
1.77	1.66	1.70	1.74	1.70	1.81	1.73	1.76	1.71
1.5	−5.9	2.2	2.5	−2.5	6.4	0.2	1.1	−2.3
2.3	2.3	2.3	2.4	2.4	2.3	2.20	2.12	2.29
6,957.3	7,356.6	7,415.1	7,844.5	8,302.4	8,509.7	6,644.7	6,046.4	7,157.0
7.9	5.7	0.8	5.8	5.8	2.5	5.2	5.6	6.8
9.2	9.6	9.5	9.8	10.2	n.a.	8.9	8.3	9.4
0.2	0.1	0.2	0.1	0.1	0.1	0.2	0.2	0.2
−5.8	−5.4	3.1	−4.9	−3.9	−1.6	−3.0	−3.2	−5.6
0.884	0.837	0.830	0.781	0.770	0.755	0.9	1.0	0.9
−7.1	−5.3	−0.8	−5.8	−1.4	−2.0	−3.1	−1.7	−6.2
1.616	1.507	1.640	1.521	1.503	1.580	1.6	1.6	1.6
−0.2	−6.7	8.8	−7.3	−1.2	5.1	−0.3	−1.0	−3.5
1.8	1.9	2.1	2.0	2.0	2.0	2.0	2.1	1.9
−13.0	2.8	9.3	−3.2	−0.9	3.9	0.6	2.0	−5.4
1.1	1.2	1.3	1.3	1.3	1.3	1.2	1.3	1.2

d. For population: Yearly levels are calculated using growth rates from Manuel Ordorica, "Las cifras preliminares del censo." Ordorica provides yearly growth rates for the 1980–90 decade and cites the 11th population census preliminary figure for total population in 1990, estimated to be 81.1 million.

Some believe this to be the result of more people who previously used private doctors and hospitals needing access to medical service through social insurance schemes because of decreasing incomes.

To estimate per capita health resources in the Ministry of Health, the institution that provides health care to the poorest sectors of the population, is unfortunately very difficult, because there are no accurate estimates of the population the Ministry serves. Nonetheless, there is no indication of a reduction in total resources. Thus if one assumes that the population served by the Ministry is the difference between the total and that covered by ISSSTE and IMSS, then the resources per capita in the Health Ministry must have improved.

Food Subsidies: From General to Targeted

To reduce public expenditures, the government began eliminating general food subsidies,[48] replacing some of them with targeted subsidies available to the consumer through the public sector's food distribution chain, CONASUPO (National Commission of Popular Subsistence). Beginning in 1984 the government eliminated the general subsidy for corn tortillas, the staple for the popular diet, and introduced a two-price system whereby CONASUPO stores would sell a cheaper tortilla.[49] In April 1986 the government launched a "Tortilla-stamp" program that distributed coupons that could be exchanged for tortillas at a discounted price.[50] In early 1991 CONASUPO introduced a card distributed among the urban poor, who are entitled to one kilo of free tortillas a day.[51] In addition, the general subsidies on beans, cooking oil, bread, and eggs were also gradually eliminated during the 1980s.

Total spending on general food subsidies distributed through the CONASUPO system declined in real terms. This decline resulted from a shift away from the generalized subsidy scheme, in which all consumers had equal access to the subsidized price, to the more targeted schemes, in which only a select number of consumers benefitted. However expenditures on targeted subsidies rose in 1988 and 1989 as a result of the stabilization Pact (described in chapter 2), but remained below the level of spending in 1983.

Although justifiable from a fiscal point of view, targeting probably meant that substantial portions of the population—whose incomes were declining, and who were far from well-to-do—no longer enjoyed access to the subsidies. Second, some of the general food subsidies were not replaced by targeted programs.[52] Poor urban households consequently may have suffered from the resulting increases in food prices. The relative cost of a basic diet for a standard four-member family helps to illustrate the impact of these price increases. As a percentage of the minimum wage, the cost of the basic food basket rose from 30 percent in 1982 to over 50 percent in 1986.[53] Moreover, this increase occurred as minimum wages declined (table 3-2).

In addition, based on the results of a study that estimated the impact of lower prices on several consumption goods,[54] it can be argued that general price subsidies on corn, corn derivatives, beans, bread, rice, noodles, cooking oil, and eggs are justified from an equity point of view—that is, a higher proportion of the subsidy accrues to the poor.[55] In practice, general price subsidies have not been replaced by targeted subsidies on a one-to-one basis, and so the transfers received by poor families in the form of food subsidies have declined. In this sense the elimination of some of the general food subsidies might have increased poverty.

Social Indicators: Nutrition and Health, Education, and Incidence of Crime

The effect of declining incomes and changes in the food subsidy program on consumption and nutritional levels has not been estimated. Surveys completed by the National Consumers Institute (INCO) in Mexico City provide information on the possible impact of declining income levels on family diet. The results of the first survey,[56] compiled between March and June 1983, demonstrated that the majority of families with incomes lower than twice the minimum wage experienced a decrease in consumption of all food products except tortillas.[57] In addition, there was clearly a substitution away from animal proteins.[58] The results of a second survey, conducted between January and August 1985, were similar except that a relatively smaller percentage of households continued to experience a decrease in food consumption.[59]

The countrywide infant mortality rate continued to decline between 1982 and 1989 (table 3-10).[60] Some indicators, however, reveal a deterioration in health standards. For instance, infant and preschool mortality caused by avitaminosis and other nutritional deficiencies increased

TABLE 3-10. *Social Indicators in Health, 1980–89*

| Year | Infant mortality rate (per 1,000 births)[a] | Death caused by nutritional deficiencies | |
		As percent of total infant mortality[b]	As percent of total preschool mortality[b]
1980	53.1	1.0	1.5
1981	51.3	1.1	1.6
1982	49.6	1.5	1.8
1983	48.0	1.5	2.4
1984	46.4	1.7	2.7
1985	44.8	2.0	2.9
1986	43.4	2.1	3.0
1987	42.0	2.9	5.3
1988	40.6	5.2	9.1
1989	39.3	n.a.	n.a.
Average			
1983–88	44.2	2.6	4.2
1983–85	46.4	1.7	2.7
1986–87	42.7	2.5	4.2

n.a. Not available.

a. Consejo Nacional de Población (CONAPO), *Proyecciones de la población de México, 1980–2025* (Mexico City, November 1989). These infant mortality figures from CONAPO are not directly comparable with those in note b, because CONAPO adjusted its statistics for underreporting.

b. Salinas de Gortari, *Tercer informe de gobierno, 1991,* pp. 367–68.

from 1982 onward after years of steady decline (table 3-10).[61] Thus it is quite possible that the infant mortality rate could have improved more rapidly had nutritional conditions not deteriorated.[62]

Other indicators confirm a pattern of worsening nutritional conditions. The ISSSTE recorded an increase in the number of infants, children from birth to age one, suffering from slow fetal growth and malnutrition both in absolute terms and in proportion to total diseases. Children suffering from these ailments represented 8.5 percent of the total number of diseased children in 1981. The percentage increased to 10.3 percent in 1982, 10.6 percent in 1983, and 11.7 percent in 1984.[63]

With regard to education, after 1982 the proportion of each level of graduates who entered the subsequent educational level declined—that is, relatively more children were either dropping out of school after completing a cycle, particularly after finishing junior high or high school, or postponing their entry into the next level, probably because they entered the work force (table 3-11, "coverage for demand" statistics).[64] This may explain why the average schooling years of the population during the 1980s improved by one year, whereas the improvement between 1970 and 1980 equaled two years (table 3-11). It may also imply a delay in the development of skills, marked by a decline in the proportion of students advancing from one educational level to the next beyond primary school.

The percentage of children enrolled in primary school as a ratio of children in the relevant age group continued to rise (table 3-11, "coverage for demand"). Dropout rates from primary school continued to decline through 1987 (table 3-11). But further disaggregation shows that dropout rates improved for urban children only; in rural zones the dropout rate rose by almost 3 percent, from 7.2 percent in 1981 to 10 percent in 1987–88.[65]

Nationwide statistics on crime are not readily available. There is, however, a fairly complete record for the Federal District. According to this record the number of reported robberies jumped from 40,800 in 1981 to 73,500 in 1983 and to 101,600 in 1987. In 1989 they were back at 71,600, still considerably above the average of the oil boom years: 38,300 a year between 1978 and 1981. Other crimes did not rise significantly.[66] It would seem that as real income in the city contracted, more people attempted to bridge the gap by taking someone else's income.

Household Survival Strategies

The discussion above shows that wages declined quite dramatically during the 1980s. However, although wages declined drastically, households' total income probably fell by a lesser amount. As shown in table 3-2, the decline in per capita consumption was considerably less than that in wages. Thus, the fall in total income for the average household was most likely less drastic than that of wages. As income from wages declined, one would expect to see that individual members of households began to work more hours in the same job; that they sought additional income-generating activities, perhaps informally as

TABLE 3-11. *Social Indicators in Education, Academic Years 1970–71,
and 1980–81 through 1991–92*
Percent unless otherwise specified

Item	1970–71	1980–81	1981–82	1982–83	1983–84	1984–85
Average schooling of the population age 15 and over[b]						
Number of years	3.4	5.4	5.6	5.7	5.8	5.9
Annual rate of change	n.a.	4.7[c]	3.7	1.8	1.8	1.7
Coverage of demand for schooling						
Total[d]	51.7	58.7	60.6	62.0	62.9	62.7
Primary school[d]	78.4	91.4	92.5	93.5	95.4	98.0
Junior high school[e]	62.2	82.0	86.8	86.2	85.4	82.9
High school[e]	69.7	68.8	69.6	66.5	65.6	66.5
Higher levels of schooling[e]	n.a.	88.6	82.1	84.6	78.5	70.0
Dropout rates[f]						
Primary school	n.a.	7.2	6.9	6.0	5.7	6.4
Junior high school	n.a.	10.5	9.6	10.3	8.9	9.8
High school	n.a.	12.4	15.5	15.7	16.2	16.3

n.a. Not available.
a. Estimated figures.
b. Salinas de Gortari, *Tercer informe de gobierno*, 1991, p. 357.
c. Average annual rate of increase over the decade 1970–80.
d. Coverage of demand refers to percentage of children enrolled in school divided by the total population of school age children for the respective category.

nonwage earners; and that more members of households joined the work force.

Though no record of such a process exists at the national level, evidence from micro-level studies of rural villages and urban households indicates that in rural and urban areas, the poor, as well as the middle-income sectors, sharpened and expanded their strategies for economic survival.[67] At the household level, families intensified their work efforts and redirected expenditure patterns. For example, male household heads contributed a larger proportion of their income to the household budget, and families could no longer use the "extra" income to improve on their physical or human capital or to have a hedge against emergencies.[68] More hours were dedicated to working and diversifying sources of income. The

TABLE 3-11. *(continued)*

							Average		
1985–86	1986–87	1987–88	1988–89	1989–90	1990–91	1991–92ᵃ	1983–89	1983–86	1986–88
6.0	6.1	6.2	6.3	6.3	6.4	6.4	6.1	5.9	6.2
1.7	1.7	1.6	1.6	0.0	1.6	0.0	1.7	1.7	1.7
62.9	62.5	61.8	61.2	60.1	59.4	59.1	62.3	62.8	62.2
98.0	98.0	98.0	98.0	98.0	98.0	98.0	97.6	97.1	98.0
84.4	83.7	83.0	83.2	82.4	82.3	82.4	83.9	84.2	83.4
64.0	59.2	59.4	59.8	60.2	61.0	61.6	62.7	65.4	59.3
77.4	63.7	63.8	57.7	62.0	64.4	66.0	69.5	75.3	63.7
5.4	5.3	5.9	5.3	5.7	5.3	5.0	5.7	5.8	5.6
7.9	9.3	9.1	9.1	10.0	9.5	9.1	9.3	8.9	9.2
16.3	18.4	15.1	16.3	18.5	16.4	16.0	16.6	16.3	16.7

e. "Coverage of demand" refers to the proportion of graduates at one level who proceed to the first year of the next level of education.

f. Salinas de Gortari, *Tercer informe de gobierno, 1991*, p. 354. The dropout rate includes those students who had registered for a year of school and had not finished that same year, or who had not registered for the next course.

hardships imposed by the crisis and adjustment process, therefore, should not be measured simply by declines in income but also in relation to changes in quality of life, such as hours available for leisure and rest and "peace of mind" with respect to the future.[69]

In addition, there is evidence that migration to the United States increased. Remittances probably continued to be an important potential source of income for some rural and urban families, and information from anthropological studies indicates that an increasing number of workers viewed migration to the North—to the United States—as their best alternative.[70] As evidence of this, the number of alien apprehensions averaged 1,260,855 a year for 1981–96, up 50 percent from the average for 1971–80.[71]

TABLE 3-12. *Income Distribution in Mexico, Selected Years, 1963–89*
Percent of total household income

| | Percentile groups of households | | | |
| | 40 | 50 | 10 | |
Year	lowest	intermediate	highest	Total
1963	10.2	47.6	42.2	100.0
1968	11.2	48.8	40.0	100.0
1977	10.4	52.8	36.8	100.0
1984	14.3	52.9	32.8	100.0
1989	12.9	49.2	37.9	100.0

Sources: For 1963, 1968, and 1977, Oscar Altimir, "La pobreza en América Latina: Un examen de conceptos y datos," *Revista de la CEPAL*, no. 13 (1981), table 8, p. 90. For 1984, INEGI, *Encuesta nacional de ingresos y gastos de los hogares, 1984*, table 4, p. 20. For 1989, INEGI, *Encuesta nacional de ingresos y gastos de los hogares, 1989: Transacciones económicas* (Mexico City, 1992), table 1.

Who Bore the Costs and to What Extent?

The question of who bore the costs of the crisis is of particular relevance in a country like Mexico where the concentration of income is high and poverty is widespread. Table 3-12 shows that income concentration at the top 10 percent of the population was high for all years studied. The data show some redistribution from the top to the middle sectors between 1963 and 1977 and a further small decrease in inequality between 1977 and 1984. However, this result should be viewed with caution; an accurate comparison is not possible because the surveys are not strictly comparable. Moreover, the 1984 survey indicates that income disparities were still striking: average per capita income at the top decile was 25 times greater than at the lowest decile (table 3-1).[72]

The incidence of poverty in Mexico has also been high, though declining over time. Based on survey data, it has been found that the incidence of "extreme" poverty was 69.5 percent in 1963, 56.7 percent in 1968, 34 percent in 1977, and 29.9 percent in 1984.[73] In another study, which selects a different poverty line, the author finds that the incidence of extreme poverty in Mexico in 1968 was 12 percent.[74] Despite the lack of consensus in determining the level of poverty at a particular point in time, the available empirical evidence suggests that between 1963 and 1977 poverty was diminishing.[75]

Using my own estimates, I find that in 1984 the proportion of extremely poor households was somewhere between 11.2 and 14.7 percent.[76] The extreme poor are predominately rural and agricultural households. But in the third and fourth deciles the majority of households still living in poverty are urban and nonagricultural. Even though most of the poorest households are rural, 27.5 percent of the lowest decile are urban (table 3-1).

Compared with the rest of the population, the households of the extreme poor have more self-employed heads of household and fewer who are wage earners.[77] In terms of income sources, the extreme poor seem to derive almost one-third of their income from "profits" (table 3-5). Nonmonetary income is more important to the extreme poor and accounts for another third of their total income. Income derived from wages constitutes the final third of income. Wage income becomes increasingly—though not monotonically—important from deciles 2 to 7, at which point its share begins to decline, albeit slightly.

The characteristics of the population by income level provide some hints about how the social costs of the crisis may have been distributed. First, because most of the extremely poor work in agriculture and derive about two-thirds of their income from nonwage sources (tables 3-1 and 3-5), the absolute and relative impact on poverty of adjustment depends on the performance of agricultural output, prices, and agricultural wages. Second, given that wages are the principal source of income for the middle ranges (table 3-5), the fate of these groups will be largely tied to changes in wages.

Because wage income contracted far more than did nonwage income during the 1980s, it would appear that the middle-income ranges suffered to a greater degree than those at either the bottom or the top. This is confirmed by the comparison of the size distribution of income between 1984 and 1989 presented in table 3-12. While the bottom 40 percent loses 1.4 percentage points of total income, the "middle" 50 percent loses 3.7 percentage points. However, because agricultural wage and nonwage income deteriorated substantially from 1986 on (table 3-6), the rural poor may have endured sharp declines in living standards between 1986 and 1989.

Although the middle ranges lost relatively more than the bottom of the population, one should be aware that even a minimal decline in the income of the poor can have devastating effects on a household's present and future welfare. Also, households located in the middle range of the distribution are far from being "middle-class" families by the standards of advanced industrial countries. Those at the bottom of the middle range include many of the poor living in urban areas (table 3-1), where prices of goods are usually higher. One result that should be underscored is the sharp rise in inequality observed in this period. This is best illustrated by the rise in the concentration of income in the top 10 percent, whose share increased by 5.1 percentage points between 1984 and 1989 (table 3-12).

Concluding Remarks

The analysis and the data presented lead to the following conclusions. Despite a drastic decline in real wages, many Mexican households were probably able to avoid comparable drops in total income and per capita consumption by working additional hours, seeking new income-generating activities, and sending more family members into the work force. In rural and urban areas, the poor and the middle-income sectors sharpened and expanded their strategies for economic survival. Families worked harder and spent more carefully, struggling to maintain their standard of living despite hardships imposed by the crisis and adjustments. Migration to the United States appears to have increased, as remittances continued to be an important source of income for some families.

The consequences of the crisis were not borne equally by all social groups. The wealthy could always protect, and even expand, their wealth far more easily than the rest of society by simply transferring their assets abroad. For example, capital flight has been estimated at between U.S.$22.1 billion and U.S.$35.7 billion between 1977 and 1987, depending on the method of calculation.[78] Those without savings—the majority of the population—did not have a similar option.

The international rules of the game give labor and capital asymmetrical treatment. Whereas capital can always find a safe-haven country, labor cannot freely enter other countries. This arrangement allowed Mexican asset owners to substantially avoid the cost of adjustment in the 1980s by protecting their wealth from the negative impact of devaluations and inflation on the real value of assets, while often earning huge capital gains. Those who possessed no wealth enjoyed no equivalent escape mechanism to avoid the adjustment cost. Becoming an illegal worker in the United States and accepting lower wages than legal workers was probably the best safety valve available.

Besides this dichotomy between the fate of the wealthy and that of the rest, the data on income distribution indicate that households in the middle range bore a higher share of the costs. The middle-range families, which include some of the urban poor and the rural and urban middle sectors, were apparently hurt by their reliance on wage income. The rural poor are likely to have been badly hurt from 1986 on, given their reliance on agricultural output and prices. The crisis and its aftermath have probably left Mexico with a relatively impoverished middle class, an increasing number of poor households, and the poor worse off than before.

Economic growth alone may be ineffective in reducing hard-core poverty. If the per capita income of the bottom 10 percent in 1984 (table 3-1) grew steadily by 3 percent a year, the average growth rate of Mexico's per capita GDP in the postwar period, it would still take this group about sixteen years to reach an income level equal to the extreme poverty line (about U.S.$50 per capita per quarter). If the income of the lowest decile were to grow at the average 1988–90 per capita GDP growth rate (table 2-4), about 1 percent a year, the waiting period would be almost 47 years. In the end, this still would only provide income roughly equal to the cost of the minimum necessary food intake.[79]

This underscores the fact that implementing equity-oriented reforms is the principal task ahead. These reforms will have to combine immediate relief with productivity-enhancing policies.[80] The Salinas administration made the alleviation of poverty a major objective—at least in its political discourse—and on December 2, 1988, the day after Salinas assumed office, launched a program called PRONASOL (Programa Nacional de Solidaridad).[81] However, more time and information are required to judge its effectiveness in reducing poverty.

Chapter Four

Public Sector Reforms

THE ROLE OF the government in economic matters has been a subject of long-standing and heated debate.[1] Those who argue in favor of governmental intervention see that the government—both as a direct investor and as a regulator—can perform a fundamental, often irreplaceable, role in promoting economic development and welfare. According to this view, the state can enhance competitiveness, curb monopoly power, stimulate private investment, and raise productivity in ways that market forces alone cannot.

On the opposite side it has been argued that state intervention in the economy has done more harm than good. It has crowded out private investment and antagonized the business sector. Trade barriers and regulations have resulted in monopoly power, corruption, and inefficiency. By this interpretation, growth would be higher with a minimalist state. As is often the case in economics, evidence in support of both views has been plentiful. Results vary from country to country, from period to period, and, of course, from author to author, even when the same period and country are under study.

This is not the place to analyze the state's contribution to Mexico's economic development. Nonetheless, it is important to note that in the postwar period Mexico enjoyed more than twenty years of close to 3 percent per capita growth rates combined with low inflation rates (table 1-4).[2] Such a record suggests that state actions did not fundamentally inhibit good economic performance. Moreover, state actions could well have been an important contributor to Mexico's successful economy. However, that situation changed in the 1970s—a period that marked the end of macroeconomic stability and sustained growth. Was this turnaround the result of the cumulative effect of past mistakes? Or was it the result of contemporaneous policies?

In chapter 1, I argued that macroeconomic mismanagement and an overexpansion of the state, rather than the "maturation" of thirty years of policy mistakes, were the causes of the 1976 and 1982 crises.

Whatever the role the state had in Mexico's good performance in the 1950s and 1960s, the 1980s required fundamental changes for several reasons. First, the 1982 crisis made it clear that macroeconomic management had to change. For example, because the government had run out of noninflationary financing sources, price stability called for a sustainable cut in the fiscal deficit. That cut in turn required a reform of the tax system, including its administration and enforcement mechanisms, as well as of public pricing practices and subsidies. It also called for a careful allocation of scarcer government expenditures.[3]

Second, given its limited resources, the government could not jump-start the economy by priming public investment or current expenditures. Limited resources also precluded the use of incentive programs that required government outlays (such as export or investment subsidies). Private investment, capital repatriation, and foreign investment had to be stimulated through other means. Measures designed to boost business confidence, open new investment opportunities, and win the political support of the private sector were critical. Lastly, given the need to have more access to external credit to restore and sustain growth, the government had to introduce market-oriented reforms pleasing to multilateral institutions and the U.S. government.

In this light, it seems that the Mexican state redefined its role in the economy because it had little choice to do otherwise. This, however, is a partial interpretation. Reform has also been the result of the government's commitment to modernize the economy, the public sector in particular. In Mexico, as in most countries with similar conditions, the 1982 debt crisis brought to the forefront the discussion of the efficacy of the state in handling economic matters. The crisis and adjustment process provided an opportunity to streamline the bureaucracy, improve the public sector's revenue-collection and expenditure mechanisms, and redefine the nature and extent of state participation in the economy. Fiscal policy reform, administrative reform, decentralization, divestiture of public enterprises, and the elimination or relaxation of ownership, price setting, and trade restrictions (that is, deregulation) became the core ingredients of public sector reform.

The following sections describe three of these processes in greater detail: fiscal policy reform, divestiture of public enterprises, and deregulation. Reforms in the foreign trade and foreign investment regimes are analyzed in chapter 5.

Fiscal Policy Reform

As discussed in chapter 2, one cause of the 1982 crisis was the rising fiscal deficit. During the 1970s and early 1980s the deficit had been financed through external borrowing. After the 1982 suspension of payments, this option was no longer available. One of two additional options, inflationary financing, was not desirable for obvious reasons. The other, domestic borrowing, was limited by the imperative to maintain confidence in the economic reform program. To restore the government's credibility and financial and price stability, the fiscal deficit had to be reduced on sustainable grounds. The problem policymakers faced was that this reduction needed to be accomplished with rising interest outlays and falling oil revenues, and it had to be accomplished quickly.

The objective to cut the fiscal deficit was achieved. The Mexican government reduced the public sector borrowing requirements and generated an increase in the primary surplus (which excludes interest payments), especially remarkable considering the halving of oil export revenues between 1983 and 1989 (table 2-1).[4] How was the increase of the primary surplus accomplished? It was achieved the old-fashioned way, by increasing tax revenues, but more important by raising public prices and reducing noninterest public expenditures.[5]

Table 4-1 shows the evolution of public sector revenues and expenditures as a percentage of GDP.[6] On the revenue side, oil-related income accounts for a large proportion of the initial rise in revenues (1983–85). In particular, note the taxes paid by PEMEX on domestic sales and the indirect taxes on gasoline, reflecting an increase of the internal prices of oil derivatives.[7] Another source of higher revenues was the increase in the value-added tax from 10 to 15 percent, along with a reduction in the number of exemptions.[8]

The tax system, however, continued to have significant shortcomings. First, it generated biases against investment and in favor of corporate debt financing; second, because of collection lags it implied a loss of real revenues for the government;[9] third, corporate rates were not competitive vis-à-vis Mexico's most important sources of capital, such as the United States. In December 1986 the government introduced a tax reform that included a change in indexation mechanisms for interest payments, depreciation, and inventories that stimulated investment and favored equity, as opposed to debt, financing; brought corporate tax rates closer in line with international standards; and reduced the real income losses derived from collection lags.[10]

New reforms were introduced in December 1988. The reforms shortened the transition period from the old to the new tax system, further reduced the maximum personal income tax, and introduced a 2 percent tax on business assets.[11] The 1986 and 1988 reforms introduced changes that tightened enforcement of tax compliance (the "crusade against tax evasion") and encouraged greater tax collection efforts by states and municipalities.[12] Table 4-2 compares the pre-1987 system and subsequent reforms.

Tax reforms resulted in an increase in tax-based revenues as a proportion of GDP. Taxes paid by firms, excluding PEMEX, which fell from 2.7 percent in 1980 to 1.5 percent in 1983 because of the recession, were raised to 2.3 percent in 1988 and 2.9 percent in 1989 (table 4-1). Direct taxes paid by individuals, which fell from 2.5 percent in 1980 to 2.0 percent in 1983, rose to 2.7 percent in 1989. The value-added tax rose from 3.0 percent in 1983 to 3.5 percent in 1988. After 1986 the "crusade" against tax evasion resulted in higher nonoil tax revenues sufficient to compensate for the loss of taxes paid by PEMEX as a result of the decline in world oil prices (table 4-1).

The public spending side of the fiscal equation on the aggregate was subject to less fortunate changes than the revenue side. To meet fiscal deficit targets noninterest government spending had to be cut sharply. (For the size of the cuts, see table 3-7.) Public investment was the major casualty. It was cut in half during this period, from about 8 percent of GDP in 1982 to close to 4 percent in 1988, and nonoil investment as a proportion of GDP reached its lowest level in the post–World War II era. Particularly hard hit were investments in fishing, tourism, industry, rural development, and energy, with cumulative declines of between 53 and 87 percent during the period 1982–91.[13]

Such deep cuts in public investment are undesirable because of their effect on the maintenance and expansion of the country's infrastructure. Smaller cuts in investment, however, would have meant

TABLE 4-1. *Federal Nonfinancial Public Sector Revenues and Expenditures, 1979–89*
Percent of GDP

Item	1979	1980	1981
Total tax revenue	10.32	12.66	12.92
Taxes paid by PEMEX on domestic sales	0.38	0.53	0.63
Taxes paid by PEMEX on exports	1.10	3.00	3.18
Direct taxes paid by other firms	2.63	2.74	2.61
Direct taxes paid by individuals	2.46	2.33	2.48
Value-added tax	2.39	2.68	2.59
Indirect taxes on gasoline	0.47	0.38	0.34
Tariff revenue	0.89	0.99	1.09
Income from public enterprises	13.25	11.62	11.42
PEMEX	4.13	3.66	3.50
Other firms under budgetary control	7.38	6.53	6.48
Other firms not under budgetary control	1.73	1.43	1.43
Other income	3.13	2.63	2.36
Total revenues	26.69	26.91	26.70
External financing	2.48	2.69	8.01
Internal financing	5.21	4.40	6.76
Total government revenues and financing	**34.38**	**33.99**	**41.47**
Current expenditures	22.22	22.06	25.86
Wages	7.69	7.02	7.27
Purchase of goods	3.65	3.58	4.45
Real investment	7.50	7.96	9.18
Interest payments on dollar-denominated debt	1.25	1.13	2.05
Interest payments on peso-denominated debt	2.13	2.38	2.92
Tax sharing	1.14	1.72	1.94
Transfers	3.40	4.07	2.93
Financial subsidies	1.35	0.97	1.13
Other spending	6.16	5.58	8.94
Difference between source of funds and disbursement accounting	0.11	−0.41	0.67
Total expenditures	**34.38**	**33.99**	**41.47**

Source: José Alberro-Semerena, "The Macroeconomics of the Public Sector Deficit

TABLE 4-1 *(continued)*

1982	1983	1984	1985	1986	1987	1988	1989
13.18	14.97	14.47	14.42	13.19	14.10	13.64	14.41
0.38	2.67	2.94	3.01	1.95	2.61	1.80	1.48
4.29	3.81	2.78	2.72	1.69	2.26	1.58	1.51
1.73	1.49	1.63	1.59	1.74	1.64	2.31	2.86
2.54	1.95	1.92	1.91	1.97	1.89	2.14	2.65
2.21	3.03	3.20	3.12	3.16	3.24	3.54	3.54
1.18	1.55	1.53	1.43	1.89	1.69	1.84	1.62
0.84	0.46	0.48	0.64	0.80	0.76	0.44	0.76
13.29	15.11	15.30	14.34	14.42	13.51	13.39	11.90
5.21	7.68	7.25	5.75	5.25	4.57	4.17	3.28
6.91	6.21	7.17	7.75	8.11	7.91	7.94	6.94
1.17	1.22	0.88	0.85	1.06	1.03	1.28	1.68
2.45	2.82	2.41	2.44	2.82	2.95	2.91	4.21
28.93	32.90	32.18	31.20	30.43	30.55	29.94	30.52
3.68	2.85	1.28	−0.13	1.43	1.15	−0.74	−0.24
14.08	6.11	7.57	9.70	14.57	14.88	13.05	5.99
46.69	**41.86**	**41.03**	**40.77**	**46.42**	**46.57**	**42.25**	**36.28**
27.76	28.98	28.20	27.94	33.03	34.92	30.79	25.91
8.02	6.68	6.50	6.63	6.48	6.40	5.98	6.09
3.76	4.60	4.75	5.18	5.37	4.48	4.33	3.55
7.77	5.33	5.04	4.65	4.63	4.29	3.77	3.26
3.30	4.63	3.94	3.67	4.42	4.38	3.58	3.44
4.91	7.73	7.96	7.82	12.13	15.36	13.13	9.58
1.72	2.11	2.18	2.13	2.11	2.21	2.24	2.42
2.93	2.76	1.75	2.20	2.40	2.05	1.86	1.84
1.31	0.48	1.35	1.53	1.11	1.00	1.58	0.64
12.07	7.18	7.19	6.96	7.39	5.74	4.25	5.77
0.90	0.34	0.35	0.00	0.39	0.66	1.54	−0.30
46.69	**41.86**	**41.03**	**40.77**	**46.42**	**46.57**	**42.25**	**36.28**

in Mexico during the 1980s," El Colegio de México, June 1991, table 2.1.

TABLE 4-2. *Summary of the 1987 and 1989 Tax Reforms*

Tax	Pre-December 1986 system	1987–88 system	1989 system
Corporate income			
Rate (percent)	42	35	37–35[a]
Depreciation deduction	Yes	Yes	Yes
Indexation	Conditioned[b]	Full	Full
Interest and foreign exchange loss deductions	Nominal	Real	Real
Capital gains taxation	Yes	Yes	Yes
Rate (percent)	42	35	35
Indexation	Yes[c]	Yes	Yes
Inventories indexation	Yes	Yes (full)	Yes (full)
Dividends, deductible	Yes	Yes	No
Assets (percent rate)	No	No	2[d]
Personal income			
Dividends (percent rate)	55[e]	50[e]	10[e,f]
Interest income (percent rate)	21[g]	21[g]	21[g]
Capital gains	Yes[h]	Yes[h]	Yes[h]
Personal income and other income (percent rate)	55	50[i]	40

Source: World Bank, *Mexico: Industrial Policy and Regulation*, Report 8165-ME, Country Operations Division I, Department II, Latin America and the Caribbean (Washington, August 15, 1990), table 4-1, p. 43.

a. In 1989 the rate would be 37 percent; in 1990, 36 percent; and from 1991 on, 35 percent.

b. Depreciation could be indexed in direct proportion to the position of an enterprise's net financial assets.

c. Gains from mergers, reductions, and liquidations were not indexed.

d. This tax may be credited against the corporate income tax.

e. The same rate applies to divided remittances from foreign subsidiaries by applying a definitive withholding tax at the source.

f. Dividends from net current profits are taxed at 10 percent; dividends from other sources at 40 percent.

g. Twenty-one percent applies to the interest income flow arising from the first 12 percentage points on deposits; additional income flow is exempted.

h. Capital gains realized through sales on the Mexican stock exchange are exempted.

i. In 1987 the personal income tax on other income was 55 percent.

higher cuts in current expenditures. The latter could be achieved through further reduction in government real wages or public employment. Faced with that choice, the government decided to cut investment and protect public employment. Lower public sector total wage payments constituted another contribution to the public expenditure cutback, though one less important than the reduction in investment.[14]

From a macroeconomic point of view the fiscal adjustment has been achieved. The fiscal deficit, or public sector borrowing requirement, in 1991 has been estimated at 1.5 percent of GDP,[15] down from the 1990 level of 4.0 percent, and the lowest in a long time (table 2-1). The reduction in the public deficit should be sustainable because it is not based on one-time-only revenues such as the sale of public enterprises. Also, fluctuations in the deficit have been reduced, and from 1986 most fluctuations are attributable to the trajectory of world oil prices.[16] Moreover, to dampen the effects of these fluctuations the Salinas government created a fund whereby windfall gains from higher oil prices and privatization receipts are accumulated to stabilize a deficit in the event of a drop in world oil prices.[17]

The reforms affecting the pubic revenue side of the budget have for the most part been accomplished. In the future the task will be fine-tuning them. On the expenditure side some important work still remains. As interest payments subside (above all because of lower domestic interest rates), resources will be freed for other purposes. Public investment in infrastructure and the social sectors, as well as wages paid to social sector employees, will have to rise to improve the quantity and quality of educational and health services. This will call for important reallocation of expenditures and will require changes in the administrative structure of the federal government.

Divestiture of Public Enterprises

The 1917 Mexican Constitution endowed the state with a considerable influence in the country's economic affairs to further and protect the public interest. An extensive legal framework and institutional base support and foster state participation in the Mexican economy.[18] The 1938 nationalization of foreign-dominated oil companies and the 1982 nationalization of the banking system are examples of the extent to which the Mexican government can exercise its constitutional powers.

During the 1920s and 1930s the government created several financial institutions to promote agricultural and industrial growth. Soon the control of energy production became another state target. The government seized control of the exploitation of oil resources, which gave rise to the powerful state-run Mexican Petroleum Company (PEMEX) in 1938. In 1937 the state-owned Federal Commission of Electricity (CFE) was created, and in 1974 it became the exclusive producer of electricity.[19]

In addition, the state expanded its direct production activities in sectors that did not attract private investment, such as shipyards, railroad cars, steel, and fertilizer plants, in which return on investment was long term or the initial outlays too large. The government also created enterprises to regulate the market, like CONASUPO, the large conglomerate in charge of regulating the grains and oilseeds markets and providing consumer subsidies on staple commodities. Later, to protect employment, the government took over firms that were previously privately owned but had gone bankrupt.[20]

Even though for the most part the key public enterprises were created before 1970,[21] their number grew rapidly during the governments of Echeverría (1970–76) and López Portillo (1976–82).[22] In 1970 there were 391 public enterprises (parastatals); by 1982 there were more than 1,000.[23] The nationalization of the banking system in 1982 was the high point of this period of increasing state intervention. From then on the process began reversing itself.[24]

In the past, the extent of state participation and intervention could be decided directly by the executive. A constitutional reform introduced in 1983 reduced this discretionary power by defining explicitly which sectors could be reserved exclusively to the state (that is, state monopolies).[25] It also provided general guidelines for state participation (but no exclusiveness) in the so-called priority sectors. In practice, this constitutional reform has legitimized subsequent governments' decisions to withdraw from almost all but the strategic sectors.[26]

Motivations to divest public entities have been varied. To raise public revenues, enhance allocative and managerial efficiency, and, above all, recover the business sector's confidence were primary objectives. The program to divest public enterprises started with de la Madrid but gained momentum under the Salinas government. From 1983 on, public enterprises were privatized, closed, merged, or trans-

TABLE 4-3. *Number of Public Enterprises, 1982–90*

Year	Decentralized agencies	Entities with a majority participation of government	Public trust funds	Entities with a minority participation of government	Total
1982	102	744	231	78	1,155
1983	97	700	199	78	1,074
1984	95	703	173	78	1,049
1985	96	629	147	69	941
1986	94	528	108	7	737
1987	94	437	83	3	617
1988	89	252	71	0	412
1989	88	229	62	0	379
1990[a]	82	147	51	0	280

Source: Banco de México, *The Mexican Economy, 1991: Economic and Financial Developments in 1990, Policies for 1991* (Mexico City, May 1991), p. 119.
a. Preliminary figures.

ferred from federal to state or regional entities.[27] From the more than 1,000 public enterprises at the end of 1982,[28] there were only 269 in mid-1991.[29] The number of divested public enterprises was larger during de la Madrid's administration (table 4-3). However, most of them were relatively small or minority-interest companies.[30] The impact of these divestitures on the share of public enterprises in GDP and total employment was not evident, at least until 1987.[31]

The pattern of privatizing firms of lesser importance first was not accidental. The government did not want to sell the larger and potentially more profitable public enterprises before their financial situation was sound and the regulatory framework made their purchase attractive. Nor did the government want to sell them during times of fiscal shortages lest they be sold at bargain prices. The government also knew that privatization was an ideologically and politically sensitive issue—with many sectors of society possibly opposing it—and wanted to get the citizenry accustomed to the idea before applying it in full. In the meantime, the collapse of centrally planned economies in Eastern Europe and the worldwide market-oriented revival has helped make the Mexican public much more amenable to privatization.[32]

TABLE 4-4. *Top Ten Privatizations during the First Two Years of the Salinas Administration*
Amounts in millions of U.S. dollars

Company	Date of sale	Buyer	Type	Amount
1. Teléfonos de México (18 entities)	Dec. 13, 1990	Grupo Carso, S.W. Bell, France Cable and Radio	Telecommunications	1,760.0
2. Cananea Mining Co.	Sept. 28, 1990	Mexicana de Cananea	Copper mining	475.0
3. Aeronaves de México	June 12, 1989	Icaro Aerotransportes	Airline	268.0[a]
4. Co. Mexicana de Aviación	Aug. 22, 1989	Grupo Xabre	Airline	140.0
5. Fomento Azucarero	Jan. 13, 1989	Grupo Beta San Miguel	Sugar refineries	89.0[a]
6. CONASUPO, Tutitlan Plant	Feb. 23, 1990	Unilever	Vegetable oil, pasta plants	74.5[a]
7. Grupo Dina	Oct. 27, 1989	Consorcio "G" (Cummins)	Trucks, buses, motors, and so on	56.0[a]
8. Sugar Refineries	Oct. 1, 1990	Corp. Indust. Sucrum	Sugar refineries	54.5[a]
9. Mexinox	Mar. 23, 1990	Ahorrinox	..[b]	47.6[a]
10. Sugar Refineries	June 19, 1989	Anermmex	Sugar refineries	42.6[a]

Source: Laura Carlsen, "Changing Hands: Mexico's Privatization Program Proceeds in the Transfer of State-owned to Private Hands," *Business Mexico*, vol. 1 (June 1991), p. 32. Numbers are originally from Unidad de Desincorporación de Entidades Paraestatales de la Secretaría de Hacienda y Crédito Público, April 1991.

a. Converted from peso figure at exchange rate at time of sale. Approximations.

b. Not indicated in source.

In December 1987 the government announced areas and activities that would continue to be owned and operated by the state. These were upstream petroleum activities, that is, exploration, extraction, and refinement of crude oil and basic petrochemicals (PEMEX); electricity (CFE); national railways (FERRONALES); and food distribution (CONASUPO). The government implicitly announced (by not mentioning them) it would relinquish telecommunications, airlines, steel production, transport equipment, chemicals and fertilizers, mining, sugar, as well as other industrial and service activities.[33]

During the first two years of the Salinas administration, 1989 and 1990, privatization of public entities accelerated. More indicative than the number of public entities sold is their net worth—the top privatizations alone were valued at more than U.S. $3 billion (table 4-4). Privatized firms include the two leading airlines, Mexicana and Aeroméxico; the copper mining company CANANEA; and the controlling stake, 20.4 percent, in the stock of TELMEX, the national telephone company.[34]

In May 1990 the government officially informed the Congress that it planned to sell the banks back to the private sector. The reprivatization of the banking system is perhaps one of the most significant moves to restore business confidence and the goodwill of the financial community in Mexico and abroad.[35] The significant capital inflows and sharp drop in domestic interest rates that followed the announcement reflected the improvement in business confidence.[36]

In addition to selling the commercial banks,[37] during 1991 the government was in the process of selling three steel mills, an insurance company, the railroad car manufacturing company, and most of the remainder of its equity stake in TELMEX, ultimately reducing its share to only 6 percent.[38] The process of divestiture of public enterprises, except in the strategic sector, will most likely be completed before Salinas's term ends in 1994.[39]

Deregulation

In this section I discuss three aspects of deregulation in Mexico: financial liberalization, the elimination of licensing schemes and other restrictions in particular industries, and price liberalization.

Financial Liberalization

Financial liberalization included two types of action: the liberalization of financial markets and the reform of the legal and institutional frameworks that regulate financial intermediaries (for example, banks, the stock exchange, and insurance companies). The liberalization of the banking system began in 1985 and went through several stages. First, banks were allowed to engage in market operations similar to those of stock brokerage houses such as money market accounts and other financial innovations. Reforms introduced in 1988 and 1989 liberalized the banks' reserve requirements and the determination of interest rates on loans and deposits. Reserve requirements were reduced from 80 or 90 percent of deposits to a "liquidity coefficient" equivalent to 30 percent of total deposits.[40] Finally, changes introduced in 1990 allowed private sector majority ownership of banks and minority ownership by foreign investors.[41] Capital requirements were updated according to risk and vulnerability considerations, and supervision of banking operations was strengthened. The new banking regulations provide the framework for "universal banking" in line with current trends allowing greater flexibility in banking services.[42]

The new rules introduced in January 1990 also included a clear separation of insurance companies from banks, as well as a new regulating authority for the insurance sector. Also, insurance companies would be allowed to set their own rates for all lines of insurance as long as the rates were based on actuarial data.[43]

Leaving the brunt of financial liberalization until later in the adjustment process was of crucial importance.[44] Despite the potential virtues of more efficiently channeling savings and investment, it is argued that premature financial liberalization can be disastrous. Successful liberalization must be based on the fulfillment of four prerequisites. First, the public sector borrowing requirements have to be small; large public deficits can result in unmanageable levels of financial volatility. Second, a government must create a well-developed market for its own securities; otherwise financial liberalization may feed only a small number of holders who can manage the market at their will. Third, the banking system must be multifaceted so that competition is adequately ensured. Finally, the banking sector must be in good financial health and have an adequate regulatory framework to protect depositors.

These prerequisites were present to some degree when financial liberalization was implemented in Mexico.

Elimination of Licensing Schemes and Other Restrictions

Between 1989 and 1990 the government introduced amendments to the laws and regulations that affected many economic activities. The goal was to reduce restrictions on ownership, exploitation, and marketing activities so that private investment could operate more freely. What follows is a summary of the most important changes.

ROAD TRANSPORT. Road transport is of particular importance to Mexico, given its relatively underdeveloped railway system. About 82 percent of freight is moved by truck. Until 1989 the trucking industry was heavily regulated. There were legal barriers to entry, and licenses to operate were given only through concessions. Initially freight centers were established to take advantage of scale economies in contracting insurance services and administrative work. Over time, however, the centers came to be controlled by a few large trucking companies that enjoyed oligopolistic profits. The firms' reluctance to let the centers authorize new concessions and permits discouraged additional entries. Shippers were adversely affected because of their inability to choose carriers. Moreover, the oligopolistic structure raised shipping costs considerably.[45]

The new trucking deregulation decree passed in July 1989 changed all that. It removed route restrictions, implemented clear and minimal requirements for receiving concessions and permits, allowed private sector entry into container services, and abolished mandatory use of cargo centers. In January 1990 the government also eliminated price restrictions.[46] Rapid deregulation was made possible by trade liberalization, which altered cargo transport demand patterns. Deregulation has resulted in greatly improved truck service, an average decline in truck transport prices of 20 percent, and an influx of new registered operators.[47]

PETROCHEMICALS. The government redefined the criteria of "basic" petrochemicals—reserved exclusively for government production—in August 1989 in an effort to reduce regulation in the industry. From an initial total of 34 "basic" petrochemicals, the government reclassified 15 as "secondary" petrochemicals. At the same time, of a total of 800 "secondary" petrochemicals, 734 were reclassified into lower categories, a change that opened up new opportunities for private investment in the production of these reclassified items. Moreover, changes to the regulations of the law governing the petroleum industry eliminated the requirement for prior permits to produce derivatives of petroleum, such as lubricants, greases, asphalt, and special paraffins. This move also opened up new opportunities for private investment.[48]

FISHING. Until December 1990 the Federal Fishing Law restricted fishing rights for reserved species only to cooperatives,[49] and obtaining a license from Mexican authorities could take three to five years. Private individuals and companies were excluded from joining the cooperatives; only authorized users of public land, such as communities and public entities, were eligible. The amendments abolished licensing requirements for breeding and aquaculture, except in waters under federal jurisdiction. Marketing barriers were also abolished and foreign investment restrictions relaxed. Foreign investment in fishing up to 49 percent was now permitted.[50]

MINING. Mexico is considered a country with vast mining potential. The mining sector, however, has declined in importance over the past fifty years. Its share in GDP has declined from 4 percent to 1.5 percent. The regulatory framework impeded the realization of the sector's full potential, in part because of restrictions on private participation and an inefficient administrative structure within the public agencies that deal with the sector.[51]

The government passed new laws designed to address the allocation system and payments for mineral rights. With these new laws at least 50 percent of existing National Mining Reserves will be opened up to private exploitation, and new reserves will be designated only for minerals that may prove scarce in the future. This will significantly increase the area with mineral potential available for exploitation by the private sector. The government introduced changes in the concessions policy, streamlining administrative practices, eliminating the requirement for prior authorization for transferring concessions, and introducing an auction mechanism for allocating concessions. These new regulations also change the mineral rights payments system to encourage production and discourage holding idle land.[52]

COMMODITIES. The 1989 deregulation of the sugar industry, besides allowing the privatization of mills still in public sector hands established new pricing criteria for cane planters and sugar mills. The government also lifted regulations affecting the marketing and production of cacao beans and products. The new rules eliminate the system of supply allocation among producers. In the case of coffee, the government eliminated the supply quotas of domestic coffee beans and provided for a gradual phasing out of the Mexican Coffee Institute's (INMECAFE) control of production and marketing.[53]

TELECOMMUNICATIONS. In addition to the privatization of TELMEX, the government issued a resolution to liberalize authorization procedures for the installation and operation of telecommunications equipment. This will encourage competition and the development of private user networks, a supply of customer premises equipment (telex, telefax, and computer equipment), information services, ground stations for the reception of television signals, and so on.[54]

Price Liberalization

Price controls have been used in Mexico throughout its industrialization. The controls imposed between the 1950s and early 1970s focused on primary goods and services to provide the country's developing industrial sector with key inputs at low and stable prices. Thereafter, controls have been used to contain inflation and protect consumers' real incomes. To some extent in 1988 and 1989 all prices were "regulated" through the cooperation mechanism imbedded in the Economic Solidarity Pact and the subsequent Pact for Economic Stability and Growth. Since then, this regulation-by-agreement was relaxed in 1990 and even more in 1991. With the exception of a few basic commodities, the government lifted price controls on many products and made price setting more flexible. It shortened the list of price-controlled items and reduced the differentials between controlled and international prices.[55] In this process, the government had to balance three conflicting goals: increase the role market forces play in determining prices, prevent the development of inflationary pressures while the results of the Pacts are fully consolidated, and provide some relief to workers suffering from drastic wage cuts by keeping the prices of staples under control.

Concluding Remarks

This chapter has offered by no means an exhaustive description of public sector reform in Mexico. For example, the public enterprises that were not divested have been subjected to extensive administrative and financial restructuring, which is still under way.[56] The central government has also undertaken administrative reform in an attempt to streamline and decentralize decisions and save resources.[57] Monitoring mechanisms of macroeconomic performance have been improved,[58] as have the mechanisms to finance the fiscal deficit, so that the so-called inflation tax has practically disappeared.[59] Monetary policy rests more on open-market operations than on direct control of interest rates by the banking system.[60] Finally, producer and consumer subsidies have been through major changes.

Undoubtedly, reforms that result in a more efficient operation of the state apparatus (the federal government and public enterprises) and in a more careful monitoring of its economic performance are always welcome. They pertain to the internal efficiency of the state. The difficulty in judging performance arises when the dichotomy state-versus-market is under scrutiny.

Which criteria should be used to establish that a completely free market is better than a regulated one or that private ownership outperforms public ownership? One criterion could be static allocative and productive efficiency. Another consideration might be the effect of alternative schemes on the distribution of income and wealth. A third approach could be to judge whether the market-oriented reforms will result in higher investment and productivity levels over time. One might also ask whether the reforms result in limiting negative externalities such as environmental degradation. Finally, another criterion could be which arrangement guarantees more steady revenues to the public sector.

A thorough analysis of the consequences of public sector reform would have to look at some, if not all, of these dimensions. Have the tax reforms left Mexico with a more efficient, more progressive tax system? Will the tax scheme maximize the growth of productivity? Will it result in a better protection of the environment? Are the privatized enterprises going to be more efficient than their public counterparts? How will the change in ownership affect equity and the environment? Does the regulatory framework that replaced state ownership enhance competition? Is the deregulation of markets going to translate into higher productivity? Will consumers enjoy goods of better quality and lower prices? These are some examples of the questions to be answered.[61]

A study that reviewed some of the issues regarding privatization based on evidence from other countries reached several interesting conclusions.[62] First, the authors found that in competitive industries private ownership is usually preferable on grounds of efficiency, but in industries with natural monopoly elements the results were mixed. In fact, regarding efficiency, the authors argued that competition may be more important than ownership—hence the importance of the regulatory framework that accompanies privatization. Moreover, to use privatization to raise revenue for the government may imply much higher transaction costs than selling bonds. However, debt-ridden developing economies may not be able to issue bonds, or may do so only at higher costs, with greater risks of default.[63]

Clearly, there is as yet no way to judge the public sector reforms in Mexico on all the counts mentioned above. More research is needed and more time has to elapse. At this point it is evident that the reforms have paid by encouraging private investment (domestic and foreign) and capital repatriation (discussed in chapter 2). Perhaps, given the set of reforms, this investment will result in greater efficiency, more equity, and higher productivity growth than under the previous institutional arrangements. However, the converse is clear. Without this upsurge in domestic and foreign investment, none of these benefits could occur.

The state has an important role to play in Mexico's future economic development. The widespread prevalence of poverty and unsatisfied social needs discussed in chapter 3 calls for active state participation in a "crusade" against destitution and in favor of social justice. Increased spending on education, health, and social infrastructure becomes essential. Improvement in living standards will depend on productivity. Investment in education and infrastructure as well as development of an appropriate incentive structure to attract high-tech industries and modern methods of production and management are areas in which an active, and efficient, state will find ample room to perform.

Chapter Five

Looking Outward: Reforms in the Foreign Trade and Investment Regimes

INDUSTRIALIZATION IN MEXICO during the post–World War II period proceeded with a combination of tariff and nontariff barriers that protected local production from foreign competition. After 1955 the tariff structure changed little, but protection increased as the number of products subject to import permits or licenses grew. In 1956, 28 percent of the value of imports required permits; by 1970 this figure had increased to 68 percent. During the balance-of-payments crisis in 1976, the value of imports requiring permits rose to 91 percent but soon fell to 60 percent in 1979 in an attempt to liberalize interrupted briefly afterward as the balance of trade began to deteriorate quickly. In the 1982 balance-of-payments crisis, import permits were reinstated on virtually all products (table 5-1).

The industries subject to protection changed over time. In the 1960s and early 1970s protection favored the production of consumer durables and capital goods as opposed to consumer nondurables, raw materials, and intermediate goods. In addition to licensing mechanisms, the government relied on domestic content requirements and other policies to stimulate domestic production.[1] Agriculture was the big loser in this policy scheme. It faced substantially lower levels of effective protection and in some cases even negative effective protection.[2]

To improve the balance of trade in the early 1970s the government sought to promote exports through selective policymaking, such as the establishment of tax and tariff rebates and the creation of new institutions in charge of credit provision.[3] Later, new sector-specific programs, like the 1977 program for automobiles and the 1981 program for microcomputers, provided import protection and fiscal incentives in return for export achievements. At the same time, compliance with

TABLE 5-1. *Import Licenses and Protection Rates, 1956–83*[a]
Percent

Year	Proportion of imports subject to permits[b]	Nominal implicit protection	Effective protection
1956	28	n.a.	n.a.
1960	38	15.1[c]	12.9[c]
1965	60	n.a.	n.a.
1970	68	13.1[c]	18.4[c]
1976	91	n.a.	n.a.
1979	60	−1[d]	−9[e]
1981	83	19[d]	1[e]
1982	100	n.a.	n.a.
1983	100	−24[d]	−33[e]

n.a. Not available.

a. A negative effective protection means that value added in domestic prices was lower than the value added measured at international prices multiplied by the exchange rate. This can happen as a result of different factors. In 1983 domestic prices had not fully adjusted to the large devaluations of 1982; hence domestic prices were much lower than the product of international prices times the exchange rate. Economists describe this as a situation in which domestic production received "exchange-rate protection."

b. Gerardo Bueno, "Policies on Exchange Rate, Foreign Trade and Capital," El Colegio de México, Mexico City, 1987, table 14.

c. Ibid., table 15.

d. Ibid., table 9.

e. Ibid., table 10.

certain industry-specific foreign exchange balances replaced domestic content requirements.[4]

The costs and benefits of protectionism in Mexico have not been fully assessed. Could Mexico have developed an industrial sector without resorting to protectionist practices? Probably not. However, was protectionism implemented with "efficiency"? Probably not, either. Industrial output increased steadily during the postwar period. Average growth rates of manufacturing output were 8.1 percent in 1960–70 and 6.3 percent in 1970–80.[5] However, studies available on sources of productivity suggest that the prevailing pattern of growth was "extensive," that is, a result of the rate of capital accumulation as opposed to higher productivity.[6]

The 1976 and 1982 balance-of-payments crises demonstrated that the extensive growth pattern needed to change. If the goal was to raise per capita consumption and reduce reliance on foreign savings, it was indispensable to switch from an extensive growth pattern to one with a rising productivity of investment. Also, the 1982 crisis in particular made evident that the economy's capacity to recover from an external shock depended on the diversity of its sources of foreign revenues and on the speed with which its productive structure adjusted to changing incentives. Exports and output had to respond more quickly to changes in relative prices than they did during the 1982 crisis and subsequent adjustment. The slower the response, the more negative the impact on output in the face of an adverse external shock. If domestic production could not replace the so-called noncompetitive imports, GDP growth rates would have to slow. Furthermore, given the constraints on access to external commercial credit, new sources of capital such as foreign investment and official bilateral and multilateral credit had to be attracted. Finally, as mentioned in chapters 2 and 4, the government could not jump-start the economy through fiscal policy without threatening price stability. It had to entice the private sector into leading the recovery by introducing confidence-building measures and opening up new investment opportunities.

These considerations were the primary basis for the outward-oriented reforms that began in mid-1985. These reforms primarily affected the prevailing trade and foreign investment regimes. Liberalizing trade, relaxing restrictions on foreign ownership, and adapting Mexican legislation to international standards have been the essential ingredients of the new policymaking. Institutional initiatives such as the decision to join the GATT have also been an intrinsic part of the strategy.

The decision to pursue a free trade agreement with the United States, announced in 1990, although congruent with the new strategy, is a different kind of initiative from the others. An FTA, for example, was never part of the structural reform menu advocated by multilateral financial institutions. It also marks a radical departure from the previous Mexico–United States relationship. The decision to pursue an FTA was probably prompted by the Mexican government's recognition that, to translate adjustment into growth, an additional big boost to the confidence of private investors was needed. As discussed in chapter 2, lower wages, abundant market-oriented reforms, and a Brady-type debt accord did not produce the expected economic turnaround quickly enough. An FTA could simultaneously open up new investment opportunities and improve the expected returns from such an investment by reducing uncertainty about market access and Mexico's domestic policy.

Trade Liberalization

Trade reform was started in mid-1985. Liberalization proceeded gradually at first and was consolidated in 1988.[7] In mid-1985 more than 90 percent of domestic production was protected by a system of import licenses, with ten tariff levels, the maximum tariff being 100 percent and the production-weighted tariff equal to 23.5 percent. After the measures introduced in December 1987 tariffs were reduced to five levels, the maximum tariff was set at 20 percent, and official reference prices were abolished. Domestic production covered by import licenses settled at about 20 percent in 1988, and the production-weighted tariff was reduced to 11 percent also in 1988 (tables 5-2 and 5-3).[8]

In early 1989 the tariff structure changed to increase government revenues and reduce dispersion (table 5-2). Most products that formerly included a zero or 5 percent tariff were subject to a 10 percent tariff.[9] As a result, the production-weighted tariff increased slightly, from 11 percent in 1988 to 12.5 percent in 1990, a rate still substantially below the 23.5 percent prevailing in 1985 (table 5-3). The maximum tariff remained at 20 percent (table 5-2), far below the 50 percent limit agreed on in Mexico's protocol to join the GATT.[10]

The removal of import licenses occurred at a rapid pace. The domestic production covered by import licensing dropped from 92.2 percent in 1985 to 19 percent in 1990 (table 5-3). In December 1989 licenses were still important to a few sectors: natural gas (100 percent), petroleum refining (86.4 percent), transportation equipment (41.0 percent), and agriculture (38.4 percent). About 20 percent of food and beverages' domestic production was covered by import licenses.[11] Clearly the Mexican government was not yet prepared to eliminate trade restrictions in these sectors. The reasons differ in each case.

There was probably great fear that in agriculture, particularly in the corn sector, rapid liberalization could cause major labor displacement.[12] In the case of petroleum refining, sovereignty considerations

TABLE 5-2. *Import Trade Liberalization Schedule in Mexico, Main Events and Characteristics, 1983–89*

| | First stage | | |
| | | | |
Concept	Financial crisis import restrictions (situation in Dec. 1982)	Gradual opening (Jan. 1, 1983, to July 24, 1985)	July 1985 reform (July 25, 1985, to Dec. 31, 1985)
Import license requirements	100% of imports brought under license requirements	Gradual liberalization begins, extended to 16.4% of imports by Dec. 1984[a]	July 25, 1985, decree: liberalization extended to 64.1% of imports
Import tariffs	Dec. 31, 1982 Mean: 27.0% Levels: 16 Range: 0–100%	Simplification of tariff schedule (June 30, 1985) Mean: 21.8% Levels: 10 Range: 0–100%	July 25, 1985, decree: tariff increases to compensate reduction of license requirements (Dec. 31, 1985) Mean: 25.2% Levels: 10 Range: 0–100%
Import official reference prices (OPRs)	. . .	ORPs for 4.7% of imports[c]	ORPs extended to 9.1% of imports

Source: USITC, *Review of Trade and Investment Liberalization Measures*, Phase I, table 4-1, p. 4-2.

a. This gradual liberalization process continued throughout the first half of 1985 (711 more items liberalized). The aim was to extend freedom from license requirement to 35–45 percent of total imports by Dec. 1985. The July 25, 1985 decree, however, abruptly changed the pace by liberalizing 3,064 items out of a total 8,068 tariff items.

b. Calculations made with import/export data for the period July–November 1988 using the Harmonized Tariff System.

were important. In the case of transportation equipment, the government wanted to honor its commitments to the automobile companies, most of which are multinational corporations. These commitments are part of the industrial program for the automobile sector discussed

TABLE 5-2 *(continued)*

	Second stage	Third stage
Deepening of reform and entrance to GATT (Jan. 1, 1986, to Dec. 14, 1987)	*Economic Solidarity Pact (Dec. 15, 1987, to Dec. 31, 1988)*	*Stability and Economic Growth Pact (Jan. 1989 to March 15, 1989)*
Liberalization extended to 73.2% of imports	Liberalization extended gradually to 78.2% of imports[b]	. . .
April 30, 1986, and March 6, 1987, decrees: GATT tariff reductions (Dec. 4, 1987) Mean: 19.0% Levels: 7 Range: 0–40%	Dec. 15, 1987, decree: Economic Solidarity Pact tariff reductions Mean: 10.4% Levels: 5 Range: 0–20%	Jan. 11, 1989 and March 9, 1989 decrees: tariff increases to diminish dispersion (March 10, 1989) Mean: 10.1% Levels: 5 Range: 0–20%
ORPs virtually eliminated. Reduced to 0.5% of imports[d]	Jan. 11, 1988, ORPs eliminated	. . .

c. Data for Dec. 31, 1984. There were no changes in ORPs from this date until April 1985.

d. Data for Dec. 31, 1987. The figure is representative for Dec. 15, 1987, because ORPs did not change between those dates. Most of the dismantling of ORPs (from 960 to 53 items) occurred between March and July 1987.

below. These companies had based their investment decisions on decrees that ensured protection in exchange for sector-specific balance-of-trade performance.[13]

Changes in trade policy also implied the elimination or reduction of direct export subsidies. To a great extent, their elimination or reduction occurred within the context of the bilateral Understanding on Subsidies and Countervailing Duties signed between Mexico and the United

TABLE 5-3. *Measures of Trade Liberalization, 1980–90*[a]
Percent

Year	Domestic product covered by import licenses	Production-weighted tariff averages	Domestic production covered by import official reference prices
1980	64.0	22.8	13.4
1985	92.2	23.5	18.7
1986	46.9	24.0	19.6
1987	35.8	22.7	13.4
1988	23.2	11.0	. . .
1989	22.1	12.8	. . .
1990	19.0	12.5	. . .

Source: Claudia Schatan, "Trade Bargaining: The Mexican Case," paper presented at SELA, Caracas, Venezuela (February 5–7, 1991), tables 1, 2, 3.

a. The information is for June of each year except for 1980 (April). From 1988 on, import official reference prices were eliminated.

States in 1985.[14] By 1991 export incentives primarily included a tariff exemption on temporary imports and a program exempting exporters from import licenses on inputs.[15]

Export restrictions have also been reduced. In early 1991 export permits applied only to commodities and goods subject to price controls or international agreements, such as coffee, sugar, steel, and textiles. These goals represented about 24 percent of nonoil exports. Export tariffs were at a maximum equal to 5.5 percent and were applied to commodities subject to export restrictions.[16]

Impact of Trade Liberalization on Economic Performance

The stated objectives of trade liberalization were to stimulate nonoil exports, curb inflation, and foster economic efficiency. Research on the effectiveness of trade liberalization in curbing inflation is inconclusive. For example, one analysis did not find strong evidence linking trade liberalization to the behavior of mark-ups.[17]

Nonoil exports grew at an impressive rate, rising threefold from U.S.$5.5 billion in 1981 to more than U.S.$16 in 1990. One econometric study has shown that a competitive exchange rate and trade liberalization contributed to this improvement in export performance.[18] The improvement was found to be considerably greater for larger firms because, the argument goes, they are able to reap the benefits from the change in trade regimes more quickly than smaller firms and because multinational corporations are better able than domestic firms to exploit international networks.[19]

However, it has also been found that the exports of manufacturing sectors not subject to trade liberalization experienced the fastest growth, particularly automobiles (which accounted for 35 percent of the increase in non-*maquiladora* exports between 1982 and 1988) and computers.[20] If these two sectors along with *maquiladoras* are excluded from the calculation, the yearly average growth rate of nonoil exports between 1983 and 1988 drops from 19.5 to 15.5 percent.[21] It should not be surprising to find that the protected sectors were doing better than the rest. First, these sectors had committed themselves to a better trade performance in exchange for protection. Second, protecting the final products of these sectors while many of their inputs were liberalized resulted in some cross-subsidization, which put them in a better position to export.

Contrary to common belief, the same study mentioned above found that export performance was not positively associated with a decline in domestic demand.[22] In fact, when economies of scale are present, a rising domestic demand may encourage exports because the firms can compete better in the world markets given their cost structure. However, a contracting domestic demand—together with a competitive exchange rate—may be the necessary triggering mechanism for producers or traders to switch from internal to external markets. The study does not address this point.

Other studies present some evidence that gains have been made in productivity in the period after the trade reform. One study found that labor productivity grew 1.2 percent between 1980 and 1985 and 1.8 percent between 1985 and 1989.[23] Another study also noticed an increase in factor productivity growth, from an annual rate of 1.1 percent between 1981 and 1985 to about 4 percent between 1986 and 1989.[24] These increases could be the result of a rise in efficiency at the level of the firm associated with greater competition from imports or a desire to penetrate export markets.[25] A third study using plant-level data found that in about half the industries analyzed productivity improved from 1984 to 1989.[26] The largest productivity gains were in food and beverages, iron and steel, transportation equipment, and metal products. Most were industries that expanded. However, more research is needed to establish the contribution of trade liberalization to the increase in productivity, because not all the "winners" were subject to the same policies. For example, automobiles, which are included in transportation equipment, were heavily protected throughout the period.

Trade liberalization did not produce massive bankruptcies and lay-offs as some had feared. The number of plants actually grew between 1985 and 1988, and the contraction of manufacturing employment was small.[27] This may be indirect evidence for something that authors and policymakers in favor of liberalization had stated all along, namely, that protectionism resulted in attractive rents for producers, many of whom had cost structures that allowed them to compete against foreign producers. However, for a two-year period following the start of trade liberalization in mid-1985, Mexican industrial production enjoyed the protection of an undervalued exchange rate and depressed real wages (tables 2-1 and 3-2). Later the exchange rate appreciated, but labor costs continued to be depressed. The question that remains is whether Mexican industry will continue to be competitive at higher levels of remuneration of the work force and the prevailing exchange rate.

The evidence shows that the geographic pattern of industrial production has been changing rapidly. For example, the total number of plants increased by 4.5 percent between 1985 and 1988, while the number of plants in the two leading industrial centers, the Federal District and Monterrey, declined by 13.8 percent and 7.9 percent, respectively. Because the plants in these two centers employed large numbers of workers, total employment in industry during this period declined by 4.1 percent.[28] The geographic pattern of employment growth also changed along with the pattern followed by the industrial plants.

Industrial Programs

Since the early 1960s the Mexican government had relied on sector- or firm-specific programs to promote industrial development. Its broad objectives were to foster greater integration with domestic manufacturers, increase manufacturing exports, and develop Mexican-owned firms in specific areas. The industrial programs consisted of providing import licenses and fiscal incentives, including access to preferential credit in exchange for a schedule of local content and export targets. About 750 programs were established between 1965 and 1970 and more than 1,200 between 1971 and 1978.[29] Of course, not all of them were of equal importance. One of the leading programs was developed for the automobile and auto parts industry in 1962.[30]

Between 1983 and 1985 the scope and number of these programs shifted, but an active industrial policy continued to be an important ingredient of Mexico's trade regime.[31] The intention was to reduce the number of programs to a few in areas identified as priority industries.[32] Three industry-level programs were established: in automotive, pharmaceutical, and capital goods. A program for microcomputers was put in practice in 1985 but not published. A fifth program, for petrochemicals, was established in 1986, but it aimed only at defining rules for entry by private sector firms (see chapter 4).[33]

The main goal of the programs was to continue import substitution and specify targets for each industry's trade balance. The pharmaceutical program's objective was to produce 98 percent of all pharmaceutical goods and 60 percent of all pharmochemicals in Mexico by 1989. Other objectives included developing fully Mexican-owned firms, promoting exports, reducing import and domestic price differentials, and improving product standards.[34]

The programs included protection and regulatory measures. Protection was awarded through nontariff barriers (quantitative restrictions, in particular), which shielded firms under the industrial programs from import competition. Government procurement provided domestic firms an advantage through a price premium. Program firms could import duty free, but the auto parts and pharmochemical industries were protected by domestic content requirements.[35]

Entry into the industries was regulated further through restrictions on direct foreign investment and licensing. The objective of these restrictions was to provide "first-mover" advantage to domestic firms. However, the regulations were not specified as temporal. Program-firms were regulated through domestic content requirements, foreign exchange balances, and investment programs. The automotive program imposed limitations on scale and product lines. The pharmaceutical industry had price controls, quality norms, and rules on research and development expenditures.[36]

From mid-1985 on, the industrial programs started to be dismantled. That is the year trade liberalization and deregulation became an integral part of economic policy (see chapters 2 and 4). Although quantitative restrictions on imports were maintained, the government reduced many of the programs' other incentives and regulations. For example, it liberalized government procurement rules, reduced energy subsidies, suspended tax credits (in December 1987), brought down domestic content requirements, and reduced restrictions on foreign investment. Exports continued to be encouraged because program-firms were cross-subsidized through domestic protection. For example, automobile terminals were protected in the domestic market by quantitative restrictions on imports, while regulations on exports have been increasingly reduced. Domestic content requirements for terminals were reduced to zero for fully exported lines, and to 30 percent for lines with 80 percent or more exports, while DCRs for terminals sold in the domestic market were 60 percent.[37] This in part explains why much of the rise in nonoil exports during 1983–88 came from some of the most protected industries, automobiles and auto parts, in particular.[38]

The industrial programs were subject to change in 1989. In the new auto industry decrees passed in December 1989, automakers were allowed to import cars and trucks of their own manufacture and brand name to supplement their domestic production. Beginning in 1990 and with model year 1991, imports would gradually open. Automakers also would no longer be restricted in the number of lines and models they can produce.[39] And domestic content requirements were liberalized.[40]

The government also announced it would introduce changes in the pharmaceutical and microcomputer programs. Among these, the government said it would end the preferential treatment given to Mexican pharmaceutical firms in purchases made through public biddings.[41] In microcomputers the government reached an agreement in 1990 with industrialists to remove the sector's quantitative restrictions and domestic content and foreign exchange requirements by 1992.[42]

As the old style of sector-specific policy fades out, new forms of policy to stimulate the development of high-tech industries will most

TABLE 5-4. *Direct Foreign Investment by Source Country, 1989*

	Accumulated		New	
Country	Millions of U.S. dollars	Percent of total	Millions of U.S. dollars	Percent of total
United States	16,740	63.0	1,783	72.0
Great Britain	1,797	6.8	n.a.	n.a.
West Germany	1,661	6.3	78	3.2
Japan	1,344	5.1	n.a.	n.a.
Switzerland	1,175	4.4	171	6.9
France	n.a.	n.a.	49	2.0
Holland	n.a.	n.a.	46	1.9
Other	3,844	14.5	349	14.1
Total	26,561	100.0	2,476	100.0

Source: United States International Trade Commission, *Review of Trade and Investment Liberalization Measures by Mexico and Prospects for Future United States—Mexican Relations, Phase I: Recent Trade and Investment Reforms Undertaken by Mexico and Implications for the United States*, Investigation 332-282, Pub. 2275 (Washington, April 1990), p. 5-4.

n.a. Not available for specific country, but included in "Other."

likely develop. Industrial policy will tend to concentrate on providing the appropriate incentive structure for firms in these industries. Investment in infrastructure to compete in global markets, such as modern telecommunication networks and transport facilities, is essential. Even more important is the task of ensuring an adequate supply of skilled labor. To compete in world markets and take advantage of the existing modern technology, Mexico must concentrate its efforts on the production of skills and the dissemination of knowledge.

The Changing Foreign Investment Regime

Foreign direct investment was never a large share of total investment in Mexico. It was about 10 percent of total gross fixed investment in the 1980s. In 1979 accumulated foreign direct investment amounted to U.S.$6.8 billion. In 1989 the accumulated foreign direct investment had risen almost fourfold to U.S.$26.6 billion.[43] Over 60 percent of the accumulated investment came from the United States. The U.S. share in new foreign direct investment in 1989 was an even higher 72 percent (table 5-4).

In the past, for a number of reasons—including protecting itself from U.S. economic dominance—Mexico had not been interested in attracting substantial foreign investment.[44] In the 1970s external financing needs were met primarily through foreign borrowing. After the debt crisis this option vanished, and the resulting credit vacuum could not be filled by official lending. As foreign investment became pivotal to Mexico's new growth strategy, changes to increase the attractiveness of investing in Mexico, including reform of the foreign investment regime, were in order.

Apart from foreign investment's important macroeconomic role in closing the external gap, the Mexican administration believed that a regime conducive to foreign investment would stimulate competition and increase access to new technology, thereby raising the productivity of investment. For this reason, reforms in the foreign investment regime were not considered concessions reluctantly given for the sake of economic survival but desirable goals in and of themselves. To a great extent, fear of foreign domination subsided because of the existence of an increasingly robust domestic entrepreneurial class.

Foreign Investment Regime before the 1989 Reform

The Mexican foreign investment regime has been characterized as an "ad-mixture of nationalism and deliberate industrial policy."[45] The nationalistic component appears in the limits imposed on foreign ownership synthesized in the 1973 Law to Promote Mexican Investment and Regulate Foreign Investment (Foreign Investment Law).[46] This law identified the areas in which foreign investment was permissible, as well as limits to such investment. Two other laws also regulate foreign investment in Mexico: the 1973 Technology Transfer Law and the 1976 Law of Inventions and Trademarks, which deals with the protection of intellectual property rights.

Formerly, the foreign investment regime was restrictive. There were essentially four types of restrictions: activities reserved for the state, activities reserved exclusively for Mexicans, activities in which foreign investment cannot exceed a certain percentage set below the maximum 49 percent, and activities in which foreign investment was allowed to be no greater than 49 percent (table 5-5). In practice, the restrictions were often circumvented. One legal way to do so was by establishing a trust (*fideicomiso*), with a Mexican bank operating as a trustee.[47] Also, restrictions were probably circumvented through

TABLE 5.5 *The 1973 Foreign Investment Law and Limits to Foreign Investment*[a]

Category	Activity
Activities reserved exclusively to the Mexican state	Extraction of petroleum and natural gas; production of basic petrochemicals; exploitation of radioactive minerals and generation of nuclear energy; certain mining activities; generation of electricity; railroads; telegraphic and radio communications; and all other activities determined by specific laws or regulations
Activities reserved exclusively to Mexicans or to corporations with an exclusion-of-foreigners clause in their articles of incorporation	Radio and television; urban and interurban automotive transportation and federal highways transport; domestic air and maritime transportation; exploitation of forestry resources; gas distribution; and other activities determined by specific laws or regulations
Activities in which foreign investment was subject to specific percentage limitations	Mining under ordinary concessions (49 percent), mining under special concessions for the exploitation of national mining reserves for such minerals as coal, iron ore, phosphoric rock, and sulfur (34 percent); production of secondary petrochemicals (40 percent); manufacture of automotive parts (40 percent); and any other activities for which percentages are indicated in specific laws
All remaining activities	Foreign investment was subject to a 49 percent limitation in all remaining activities

Source: USITC, *Review of Trade and Investment Liberalization Measures*, Phase I, p. 5-4.

a. Foreign investment is defined by the Law to Promote Mexican Investment and Regulate Foreign Investment as "investments made by (1) foreign corporations; (2) foreign individuals who are not bona fide permanent residents of Mexico, or those who, because of their activities, are tied in with or bound to entities or groups making their economic decisions abroad; (3) foreign legal entities without legal personality; and (4) Mexican enterprises in which a majority of their capital is owned by foreigners, or in which foreigners control management." Article 2 of the law, cited in source.

"namelenders" (*prestanombres*), Mexican nationals who appeared as owners of a property but were only nominally so.

It has been argued that "the level of new U.S. foreign direct investment (FDI) in Mexico depends less on Mexican regulations than on the growth prospects of the Mexican economy, since the main objective of most foreign companies is to expand their internal market in Mexico."[48] But after 1982 it was no longer possible to wait for foreign investment to follow growth. Foreign investment had become a necessary precondition for growth rather than simply its by-product, as it had been in the past. The pursuit of fiscal discipline, deregulation, and the relaxation of foreign trade and foreign ownership limitations were seen as necessary steps to attract significant amounts of foreign investment.

Beginning in 1984 the regulatory framework became gradually less restrictive. In February, the government announced new guidelines, including the endorsement of majority foreign ownership in thirty-three selected activities, a significant departure from previous policy. Subsequently the commission in charge of regulating foreign investment operations improved and expedited the application process for majority ownership foreign investment. In 1986 the opportunities for foreign investment in petrochemicals were increased by the reclassification of thirty-six products from the basic to the secondary category. The production of basic petrochemicals by the Mexican Constitution are the exclusive reserve of PEMEX; in secondary petrochemicals foreign investors are limited to a 40 percent equity share. Further revisions followed in 1988. Foreign investors were allowed to acquire up to 49 percent of the shares of an established Mexican company or expand their share to 100 percent without prior approval of the regulatory body if they already controlled more than 49 percent.[49]

The Reforms since 1989

In May 1989 a new set of rules repealed all prior regulations governing foreign investment.[50] The 1973 law was not changed, but the new regulations expanded the range of operations open to 100 percent foreign ownership and, provided certain conditions were met, did not require investors to seek approval from the regulating body. The new rules were also designed to standardize requirements and increase efficiency in the authorization process; for example, approval for any application would be automatic if the regulating body did not rule in forty-five days. In addition, the new regulations introduced a trust mechanism allowing temporary foreign investment (twenty years) in restricted sectors and the automatic renewal of thirty-year real estate trusts.[51] New mechanisms have also been introduced to allow for foreign investment through the stock exchange. Corporations, for example, can issue so-called neutral shares, which entitle the foreign investor to a share of equity, but without voting power in the corporation.[52]

In August 1989 the government again reduced the number of petrochemicals classified as basic. It reclassified fifteen petrochemicals as secondary, thus allowing foreign equity in production.[53] In December 1989 the then state banks were opened to foreign participation. In January 1990 a new insurance law lifted the prohibition on foreign participation in new investment in the industry and raised the maximum of foreign participation from 15 to 49 percent.[54] Additional restrictions on foreign ownership in financial institutions were relaxed after the decision to reprivatize banks was formally announced in May 1990. Foreign ownership of up to 30 percent was allowed in stock brokerage houses, financial groups, and banks.[55]

Intellectual Property Rights

In 1987 the 1976 Law of Inventions and Trademarks governing intellectual property protection in patents, trademarks, copyrights, and trade secrets was amended. Patent terms were extended, additional patent and trademark protection for new products was granted, and other improvements in the protection of intellectual property rights and in criminal penalties were enacted. Implementation of the law in many areas was delayed until 1997.[56]

The United States was dissatisfied with the protection awarded intellectual property. It therefore withdrew Generalized System of Preferences (GSP) treatment on some chemical products in 1987. In May 1989, because of the U.S. dissatisfaction with the level of protection, Mexico was placed on the "priority watch" list of the U.S. 1988 Omnibus Trade Act. In January 1990 the Mexican government announced its intention to introduce new legislation to protect intellectual property. In a tacit exchange the United States responded by immediately removing Mexico from the "watch" list.[57] Increased protection for intellectual property has been a fundamental demand of the U.S. business community, and the passage of this new Mexican legislation was crucial for free trade negotiations to proceed swiftly.

Mexico passed a new intellectual property rights law in June 1991, which extended patent life from fourteen years to twenty years and trademarks from five years to ten years.[58] The law also simplified administrative procedures for registering patents and trademarks and improved judicial procedures to punish violators. A new copyrights law was passed in July 1991. The law "extends to all copyright owners exclusive reproduction and distribution rights for a term of fifty years, exclusive rental rights, and significantly stiffened criminal and civil penalties for copyright infringement."[59]

Intellectual property rights protection is an area of great controversy worldwide. On the one hand, the protection of intellectual rights "pays" for the investment in research and development and—for a country that does not produce new technologies—attracts investment. On the other hand, protection provides some degree of monopoly power for the duration of the patent. The optimum level of protection that should be awarded to intellectual property is hard to estimate empirically. Mexican policymakers believed that investment in research and development on the part of local firms would be part of a modern Mexico and that it was better to start by putting in place the appropriate institutional incentives.[60] Only time will tell whether this perception was correct.

Joining the General Agreement on Tariffs and Trade

In 1979 Mexico completed negotiation of the protocols to join the GATT. In early 1980, however, the Mexican government chose to delay its entry because of the strong opposition of cabinet members, political leaders, and intellectuals. At the time GATT membership was viewed as a sign of weakness; Mexico did not need or wish to subjugate its trade policy to a multilateral body dominated by the Western industrialized countries.[61]

Some of the concerns given for postponing the decision were "legitimate" at the time, in the sense that Mexican legislation and policies contradicted or were inadequate vis-à-vis the GATT rules. For example, the Mexican Global Development Plan (1980) and the Industrial Development National Plan (1979) called for the use of sector-specific subsidies that would have violated the GATT. Also, the Mexican legal framework on unfair trade practices was not consistent with the GATT because it lacked legislation on antidumping procedures and the application of countervailing duties.[62]

These obstacles were not present the second time around. Unfair trade practice legislation was modified, and the overall policy strategy was compatible with the liberalizing principles prevalent in the GATT. Shortly before joining the GATT in 1986, the Mexican government introduced fundamental changes in its trade laws. Of particular significance is the Foreign Trade Regulatory Act and the Regulations against Unfair International Trade Practices of 1986. These include comprehensive antidumping and countervailing duty laws and procedures for carrying out investigations. The act and regulations are in conformity with the GATT, except that the act fails to explicitly require the use of a "material injury" test. Mexican officials have addressed concerns about this omission by assuring other countries that the act would be applied in accordance with the GATT.[63]

Mexico joined the GATT in 1986 after several meetings with GATT and U.S. officials to agree on the terms of Mexico's accession.[64] In practice, Mexico's trade liberalization measures went far beyond those required by the protocol signed on entry into the GATT.[65] For example, Mexico agreed to bind its tariff schedule to a maximum tariff level of 50 percent ad valorem and to reduce tariffs on the majority of its import classification headings to levels of 20 to 50 percent over a period of thirty months.[66] The current maximum tariff level established in the trade liberalization measures in December 1987 is 20 percent (table 5-2).

As a new member of the GATT, Mexico has been an active participant in the Uruguay Round. Mexico's initial position was similar to that of most developing countries in that it sought favorable treatment from the industrialized countries. But as Mexico's trade liberalization accelerated, its position changed to one of seeking recognition for Mexico's unilateral reforms in the areas of trade and investment, particularly after the Salinas government came to power. At the same time, Mexican officials have been increasingly sensitive to the topics of interest to the United States: services, intellectual property rights, and investment rights. This new sensitivity may be viewed as part of Mexico's strategy to gain the confidence of the United States as a prelude to seeking a free trade agreement. An interesting change of position occurred in agriculture, when Mexico switched from a "defensive" position as a net food importer to favoring the elimination of export subsidies for agricultural products.[67]

Overall Mexico played a moderating role in the Uruguay Round. It made several constructive proposals in the controversial areas of services, intellectual property rights, and trade-related investment measures. The developing countries were pleased with Mexico's suggestion of including labor-intensive services and labor mobility issues in the services discussion. At the same time Mexico won the praise of the United States for its willingness to discuss and contribute to the new areas favored by the United States, such as intellectual property rights. Mexico was also singled out as a role model in investment liberalization by the investment group in the Uruguay Round.[68]

Seeking Closer Ties with the United States

In March 1990 it was learned through a newspaper leak that Mexican officials were exploring with their U.S. counterparts the idea of a free trade agreement (FTA).[69] The leak triggered much activity in both administrations to prepare for the subsequent formalities. In August President Salinas made an official request to start talks on such an agreement. In September 1990 President Bush responded by notifying Congress that he would like to pursue negotiations.[70] In February 1991 Canada officially decided to join the negotiations.[71] In late May the U.S. Congress approved the extension of "fast-track" procedures for two more years beginning June 1991.[72] The extension came after several months of often bitter debate.

Only a few years ago a proponent of a free trade agreement between Mexico and the United States would have faced harsh criticism in Mexico, and indifference in the United States.[73] For decades the idea of explicitly promoting increased commercial ties with the United States and bargaining with the "imperial power" to the North was blatantly rejected in most political and intellectual circles in Mexico. U.S. administrations, acknowledging Mexico's feelings of distrust, probably did not consider a free trade agreement possible. Nor did the United States consider it necessarily a desirable goal because multilateralism was the accepted U.S. trade strategy after World War II. Bilateral initiatives tended to be viewed as a diversion of institutional efforts and counterproductive to the overall trade strategy. Circumstances certainly have changed.

News of Mexico's intentions to pursue a free trade agreement first came as a surprise. However, for the close observer it is apparent that the Mexican government's attitude toward the United States became increasingly more cooperative and pragmatic after 1983. The desire to sign an FTA with the United States is largely the result of the natural evolution of a process that began in Mexico some time after the eruption of the debt crisis in mid-1982.

As discussed earlier, from 1985 to 1989 Mexico vastly reduced the use of import licenses and harmonized tariffs by reducing their average and maximum levels (table 5-2). Between 1982 and 1989 Mexico's maximum tariff fell from 100 percent to 20 percent, while the trade-weighted average also fell from 16.4 percent to 9.8 percent. By January 1988 the government had also eliminated "import official reference prices," which had been used in some sectors to bypass liberalization.[74]

The Mexican government also undertook a series of bilateral efforts designed to improve trade relations with the United States. Between 1985 and 1989 Mexico and the United States signed a number of significant agreements.[75] In mid-1985 both countries signed the bilateral Understanding on Subsidies and Countervailing Duties. This agreement gave Mexico access to procedures that included a "material injury" test. In November 1987 they signed the U.S.-Mexico Framework of Principles and Procedures for Consultation Regarding Trade and Investment Relations, considered a landmark in bilateral economic relations. This agreement was followed by sectoral accords in steel and textiles. In 1989 another comprehensive agreement—the Understanding Regarding Trade and Investment Facilitation Talks (TIFT)—was signed.

In the past few years both countries have acquired substantial experience with each other's trade practices, institutional characteristics, and bargaining procedures. This experience constitutes a solid basis for signing a free trade agreement. Also, as one author has put it, "an important by-product of the substantial trade liberalization implemented by the de la Madrid administration since July 1985 has been the reduction or elimination of numerous, long-standing bilateral trade irritants."[76]

An example of increased goodwill in trade-related bilateral relations is the evolution of Mexico's eligibility to benefit from the GSP. In 1987 a number of products were removed from the list to show dissatisfaction with changes made to Mexico's intellectual property laws.[77] In 1989, of the 306 products Mexico wished to reincorporate, 275 were approved.[78] Besides trade matters, other areas of bilateral economic cooperation have underscored the change in U.S.-Mexican relations.[79] The Mexican government had also approached Canada in a move to intensify its trade and investment relations. In March 1990 both countries signed the Canada-Mexico Framework Agreement on bilateral trade and economic relations.[80] Although it was unclear whether Mexico was ready to include Canada in its FTA agenda, it wanted to leave the door open for such an alternative or at least make the Canadians feel included in the process.

Why an FTA?

Although seeking an FTA with the United States was congruent with the Salinas government's agenda, the decision to go ahead was not anticipated. Early in the Salinas administration it seemed that the emphasis of his government would be placed on a multilateral approach to trade.[81] The objective would be to increase trade and attract investment from the world at large. The relationship with the United States would continue to be promoted through sectoral accords to the extent these were possible. The decision to seek an FTA with the United States did not fundamentally contradict the previous strategy of the Mexican government. But it did signal an important shift in the emphasis given to formal ties with the United States. What explains this shift?

When foreign investment did not respond with the expected vigor to the Brady-type debt agreement and the far-reaching economic reforms, the government had to find new ways to entice the capital inflows required for economic recovery and sustained growth.[82] Policies able to increase the expected rate of return on investment and boost private sector confidence were essential. A free trade agreement with the United States belonged to this category for two reasons in particular. An FTA would ensure future access to the U.S. market, and ensure the durability of Mexico's open economy strategy.[83] The decision did not prevent the Mexican government from continuing to pursue various trade initiatives, both multilateral and bilateral. Mexico continued to be active in the GATT's Uruguay Round and joined the Pacific Basin Agreement. It also signed a free trade agreement with Chile in 1991 and committed itself to seeking free trade agreements with Central America, and with Colombia and Venezuela.[84] At the same time, Mexico assiduously pursued stronger ties with Europe and Japan.[85]

Trade Flows and Trade Barriers

Trade between Mexico and the United States equaled U.S.$52 billion in 1989.[86] Almost 70 percent of Mexico's exports go to the United States, with about the same proportion of its imports coming from the United States (table 5-6). For the United States, trade with Mexico has recently represented between 5 to 6 percent of total imports.[87] These figures illustrate the serious asymmetry in the bilateral relationship between Mexico and the United States—as there is between Canada and the United States. Given the relative weight of the United States as a source of imports and a market for exports, the bilateral liberalization for Mexico, strictly speaking, means liberalization in full.

Trade between Mexico and Canada is comparatively modest; it reached C.$2.3 billion in 1989. In the same year Mexico exported 1.2 percent of the total to Canada and imported 1.8 percent from Canada (table 5-6). In 1989 Mexico's share in Canada's imports equaled 1.3 percent and in Canada's exports 0.5 percent. Although Canadian imports from Mexico are small, they have been growing rapidly. In 1989, for example, they increased by 27.9 percent.[88]

It is evident then that the bilateral relationship between Canada and Mexico cannot be the sole motivation for seeking free trade between them. Both want to have free trade with the United States, and Canada wants to avoid the trade or investment diversion effects that would result from not sharing in the benefits granted to Mexico in a bilateral agreement.

Trade between Mexico and the United States is relatively free. It is certainly much freer than it was before Mexico's trade liberalization and the sectoral agreements signed between both countries. According to the estimates of the Mexican Secretariat of Commerce and Industrial Promotion, the average trade-weighted tariff on Mexican imports from the United States was 12.6 percent in March 1989, whereas Mexican exports faced an average imported-weighted tariff of between 3 and 6 percent in the United States.[89] More than 80 percent of Mexican exports enter the United States in the duty range of 0–5 percent, with about 26 percent entering either duty free under the GSP,[90] or at reduced effective rates under the *maquiladora* program.

TABLE 5-6. *Mexico's Major Trading Partners, 1989, 1990*
Percent of total trade

Country or group of countries	1989		1990[a]	
	Exports	Imports	Exports	Imports
Western hemisphere	**78.5**	**73.9**	**77.9**	**71.4**
United States	69.3	68.0	69.7	64.6
Canada	1.2	1.8	0.9	1.5
Latin-American Integration				
Association[b]	3.3	3.0	3.2	4.1
Argentina	0.5	0.6	0.4	1.3
Brazil	0.9	1.5	0.6	1.4
Venezuela	0.3	0.2	0.5	0.6
Other	1.7	0.6	1.7	0.8
Central American Common				
Market[c]	1.9	0.4	1.6	0.3
Other	2.8	1.0	2.5	0.9
Western Europe	**12.5**	**16.9**	**13.6**	**18.4**
European Community[d]	11.4	14.3	12.7	15.6
European Free Trade				
Association[e]	0.8	2.6	0.9	2.6
Asia	**8.4**	**7.4**	**7.9**	**8.6**
Japan	5.8	4.5	5.6	4.7
Other	2.6	2.8	2.3	3.9
Rest of the world	**0.6**	**1.8**	**0.6**	**1.6**
Eastern Europe	0.1	0.3	0.1	0.4
Other	0.5	1.5	0.5	1.2

Source: Banco de México, *The Mexican Economy, 1991: Economic and Financial Developments in 1990, Policies for 1991* (Mexico City, 1991), table 4.6, p. 223.

a. Preliminary.

b. Comprises Argentina, Brazil, Bolivia, Colombia, Chile, Ecuador, Paraguay, Peru, Uruguay, and Venezuela.

c. Comprises Costa Rica, El Salvador, Guatemala, Honduras, and Nicaragua.

d. Comprises West Germany, Belgium, Luxembourg, France, Italy, the Netherlands, United Kingdom, Denmark, Ireland, Greece, Spain, and Portugal.

e. Comprises Austria, Finland, Norway, Sweden, Switzerland, and Iceland.

Similarly, under the same program a share of U.S. exports to Mexico enter duty free if they are reexported.[91]

However, many Mexican products face a U.S. tariff higher than the 20 percent maximum tariff prevailing in Mexico.[92] Clearly, there is room for trade creation through further reductions on both sides. Nonetheless, the elimination of nontariff barriers may be more important to both countries. For example, about 20 percent of Mexican imports are still subject to licensing, with import licenses for agricultural products and livestock the most widespread.[93] The automotive sector is still subject to important restrictions. The United States also places important restrictions on the import of textiles, steel, and agricultural products.[94]

In the United States, protectionism often creeps in disguised, through what is called "contingent protectionism." This occurs when U.S. producers, faced with alleged unfair trade practices, such as foreign subsidies or "dumping," take or threaten to take action to limit trade or impose countervailing duties.[95] In practice, charges of unfairness presented by U.S. producers have become a common protective device. This is the kind of protectionism that the Mexican government—like its Canadian counterpart—is particularly keen on eliminating. For that reason the creation of a dispute settlement mechanism acceptable to all parties is a crucial item in the NAFTA negotiators' agenda.

Canadian imports from Mexico face low barriers. In fact, 82 percent of Mexican exports to Canada entered duty free in 1989, either under the most-favored-nation principle or the Canadian General Preference treatment. Higher duties prevail in labor-intensive sectors such as textiles and clothing.[96] Many Canadian and Mexican manufacturers compete directly in certain segments of the United States and other markets. Mexico's labor-cost advantage has thus prompted fear in Canada that as the remaining tariff barriers disappear, Canadian workers will suffer. According to one author, the risks of labor displacement, however, should not be exaggerated, because several factors, such as lower productivity and poorer infrastructure, offset Mexico's labor-cost advantage.[97]

Concluding Remarks

The benefits and costs of NAFTA will depend on the agreement's characteristics. Nonetheless, because of the relative size of the economies and the relative importance of bilateral trade, the impact will most likely be much greater for Mexico than for the United States or Canada. In the United States the 1990 GDP was U.S.$5.5 trillion, in Canada U.S.$572 billion, and in Mexico U.S.$214 billion. Mexico's per capita GDP has been about one-tenth of those in the United States and Canada.[98]

As already stated, signing an FTA with Canada and the United States is expected to produce benefits for Mexico that would not be attainable if the same objectives were pursued through sectoral accords, even if comprehensive sectoral accords were possible (which they may not be).[99] In the short run, the most important benefit for Mexico is the capital inflow resulting from an anticipation of the benefits of NAFTA. In 1991 there was an upsurge in foreign investment, especially portfolio investment, to approximately U.S.$10 billion, or almost three times the average of the previous three years.[100] In addition to solidifying market access and domestic policy reforms, a North American Free Trade Agreement (NAFTA) would have an impact on the expectations of prospective domestic and foreign investors, beyond the considerations just mentioned. The prospect of an FTA with Canada and the United States has provided an excellent chance to advertise to the world the business opportunities available in Mexico.

The benefits of capturing greater amounts of U.S. and Canadian investment largely depend on Mexico's being the "first comer" in the hemisphere with an FTA with the United States and Canada. These are the benefits derived from "exclusiveness." If no other countries sign a free trade agreement with the United States and Canada in the near future, Mexico will be able to fully exploit its geographic proximity and comparative advantage stemming from its factor endowments. Other benefits—such as those derived from economies of scale and greater competition—do not depend on exclusiveness. On the contrary, these benefits should increase with the extension of the free trade area to other countries in the region.

In the medium term Mexico, Canada, and the United States should benefit from increased efficiency due to further specialization.[101] More important than the so-called static gains in efficiency, however, is the expected impact on medium-term growth, in particular the improvement in productivity levels as economies of scale are exploited. The removal of trade barriers will encourage more efficient plant sizes and a cross-country vertical and horizontal integration of production processes. Eliminating current excess capacity in some sectors also may produce a one-shot boost to productivity.

In terms of costs, some dislocation of labor is expected during the "transition" period—the period when producers, workers, and consumers adjust to the new set of rules. The extent of the labor dislocation and its effect on wages will depend on how comprehensive the agreement is in terms of sectors, trade and nontrade barriers, and timetables for implementation. It will of course also depend on how quickly markets adapt to the new conditions.

In any event, labor dislocation in the aggregate should be relatively low in the United States, though it may be significant in some sectors and regions.[102] In Mexico, the extent of labor dislocation will depend largely on the treatment of agricultural products in the FTA, corn in particular. Depending on the length of the phasing-out period and the extent of safety nets, liberalization of corn would leave Mexican peasants vulnerable to the more efficient U.S. and Canadian producers and could dislocate a relatively large number of them.[103] Unemployment and Mexican migration to the United States would rise rapidly unless nonagricultural employment grows at sustained high rates.

In the three countries, however, the extent of labor dislocation and its effect on unemployment and real wages will be more affected by the performance of the economies than by the impact of liberalizing their mutual trade. The evolution of fiscal and monetary policies, and the exchange rate in particular, could have a far greater impact on aggregate employment and wage levels than changes caused by the removal of tariff and nontariff trade barriers. The impact of domestic macroeconomic policies, particularly those of the United States, is felt well beyond the border. If the three countries wish to turn the process of economic integration into an economic success for the entire North American region, policy consultation in areas beyond trade matters will be in order.

One commonly voiced concern is that Mexico may be "condemned" to exporting "cheap" labor goods, particularly to the United States, as a result of NAFTA. However, whether Mexico's role in the division of labor is this unpalatable specialization will not primarily be determined by NAFTA. Mexico's capacity to become a producer and exporter of higher-wage goods will depend on the portion of investment allocated to education (in particular, to technical and engineering schools) and to the development of infrastructure. A well-developed transportation system, adequate port facilities, and modern telecommunications networks are some of the crucial ingredients that, together with satisfactory educational and labor skill standards, will ensure increasing levels of productivity and higher wages.

Epilogue

On August 12, 1992, the negotiations for a North American Free Trade Agreement were concluded. The agreement now awaits deliberation and formal approval in the three countries. At the time this book went to press, the contents of NAFTA had not been made public. Nonetheless, once, and if, NAFTA is signed and ratified, prevailing restrictions on U.S. and Canadian trade with and foreign investment in Mexico will be further eliminated, and the remaking of the Mexican economy will continue at a more accelerated pace.

PART 2

The *Re*-Remaking of an Economy

Chapter Six

Slow Growth and the Peso Crisis

Following the debt crisis in the early 1980s, Mexico departed from the import- substituting policies of the past and redefined its role in the world economy. After more than a decade of an expansionary fiscal policy, the government dramatically reduced its public deficit. By the early 1990s, inflation was substantially lower and economic recovery was under way. At the time, many observers believed that Mexico was going to turn into a Latin American economic miracle. When the North American Free Trade Agreement (NAFTA) was approved in 1993, optimistic expectations became even more rampant. The optimistic view was also reinforced by the fact that the Mexican government had engaged in an antipoverty program geared to reduce the gap in health and education infrastructure,and had increased considerably the share of public spending allocated to the social sectors since 1989.[1] Mexico appeared to be on a firm path toward economic and social modernization.

However, although GDP per capita grew at positive rates from 1989 onward, it did so at a declining rate and per capita growth was negative in 1993. Also, domestic savings fell by close to 5 percentage points between 1989 and 1993.[2] The counterpart of a growing saving-investment gap was a rising current account deficit, which in 1994 reached 7.1 percent of GDP (tables 6-1 , 6-2) This gap was filled by capital inflows—largely, portfolio investments—making Mexico's economic performance increasingly more vulnerable to changes in sentiment in the international markets (table 6-2). The optimistic view—and after NAFTA's passage not necessarily unrealistic—argued that Mexico's dependence on volatile capital inflows was a transitory phenomenon. Economic reforms and the benefits of greater integration with the United States would result in higher productivity growth rates, and

TABLE 6-1. *Macroeconomic Indicators, 1989–96*
Percent unless otherwise specified

Item	1989	1990	1991
Gross domestic product[a]			
(average annual growth rate)			
(1980 base year)	3.3	4.5	3.6
(1993 base year)	4.2	5.1	4.2
Consumption (1993 base year)[b]			
Private	7.3	6.4	4.7
Public	2.2	3.3	5.4
Investment (1993 base year)[c]			
Private	5.3	13.8	14.5
Public	7.1	11.2	0.6
Primary government			
surplus (percent of GDP)[d]	8.3	8.0	5.5
Economic balance (percent of GDP)[e]	−5.0	−2.8	−0.5
Current account deficit (percent of GDP)[f]	−2.8	−3.0	−5.1
Balance of trade (percent of GDP)[g]	0.2	−0.4	−2.5
External debt (percent of GDP)[h]	46.1	42.7	40.6
Credit to private sector (percent of GDP)[i]	18.8	22.7	28.5
Inflation (annual growth rate)[j]			
Consumer prices			
Annual average	20.0	26.7	22.7
December/December	19.7	29.9	18.8
Real exchange rate index	83.6	83.2	91.2
(1980=100)[k]			
Real interest rate on	33.9	17.3	4.4
one-month CETES (percent)[l]			

Sources: Information from the Banco de México website was downloaded on July 23, 1997; for 1997 figures, downloaded May 20, 1998. The figures for 1997 are preliminary.
n.a. Not available
a. For 1980 base year, Banco de México, *The Mexican Economy 1996* (Mexico, 1996), table 7, p. 266. The 1995 figure is preliminary. For 1993 base year, for 1989 to 1995, Instituto Nacional de Estadística Geografía e Informatica (INEGI) website, "Producto interno bruto a precios constantes de 1993" (http://dgcnesyp.inegi.gob.mx/bdine/a10/a1000i.htm). For 1996 to 1997, Banco de México website, "Informe Anual 1997," cuadro 2 (http://banxico.org.mx/public_html/inveco/infors.html).
b. For 1989 to 1995, Banco de México website, *The Mexican Economy 1997*, table 8. (www.banxico.org.mx/public_html/doyai/mexecon97/t08.html). For 1996 to 1997, Banco de México website, *Informe Anual 1997*, cuadro 2 (http://banxico.org.mx/public_html/inveco/infors.html).

TABLE 6-1. *(continued)*

1992	1993	1994	1995	1996	1997	Average growth 1989–94
2.8	0.6	3.5	–6.9	n.a.	n.a.	3.0
3.6	2.0	4.5	–6.2	5.2	7.0	3.9
4.7	1.5	4.6	–9.5	2.2	6.3	4.8
1.9	2.4	2.9	–1.3	–0.7	1.8	3.0
15.0	–3.3	9.8	–31.2	15.3	25.7	9.0
–3.3	0.4	2.9	–19.8	20.3	4.3	3.0
5.9	3.3	2.1	4.7	4.4	3.5	5.5
1.6	0.7	–0.1	0.0	0.0	–0.8	–1.0
–7.4	–5.8	–7.1	–0.6	–0.6	–1.9	–5.2
–4.8	–3.3	–4.4	2.5	2.0	0.2	
35.7	32.7	33.8	59.3	50.7	38.4	38.6
36.0	41.1	52.2	41.0	n.a.	n.a.	33.2
15.5	9.8	7.0	35.0	34.4	20.6	17.0
11.9	8.0	7.1	52.0	27.7	15.7	15.9
96.9	103.2	97.2	60.0	62.2	n.a.	n.a.
1.6	7.0	6.6	4.0	9.4	5.2	11.3

c. For 1989 to 1995, Banco de México website, *The Mexican Economy 1997*, table 8. (http://banxico.org.mx/public_html/doyai/mexecon97/t08.html). For 1996 to 1997, Banco de México website, *Informe Anual 1997*, cuadro 2 (http://banxico.org.mx/public_html/inveco/infors.html).

d. For 1989 to 1992, Banco de México, *The Mexican Economy 1996*, table 31, p. 294." For 1993 to 1995, website of Banco de México, *The Mexican Economy 1997*, table 1 (www.banxico.org.mx/public_html/doyai/mexecon97/t01.html). For 1996 to 1997, Banco de México website, *Informe Anual 1997*, cuadro 17 (http://banxico.org.mx/public_html/inveco/infors.html). The primary surplus is the difference between revenues and expenditures other than interest payments of the nonfinancial sector.

e. For 1989 to 1992, Banco de México, *The Mexican Economy 1996*, table 31, p. 294. For 1993 to 1995, Banco de México website, *The Mexican Economy 1997*, table 1, (http://banxico.org.mx/public_html/doyai/mexecon97/t01.html). For 1996 to 1997,

TABLE 6-1. *(notes continued)*

Banco de México website, *Informe Anual 1997*, cuadro 17 (website address: http://banxico.org.mx/public_html/inveco/infors.html). The economic balance is the difference between revenues and expenditures of the nonfinancial public sector.

f. The figures are calculated with U.S. dollars. For 1989 to 1992, for the current account, Banco de México, *The Mexican Economy 1996*, table 5, p. 264. For GDP, Banco de México, *The Mexican Economy 1996* (Mexico, 1996), table 5, p. 264. For 1993 to 1995, for current account, Banco de México website, *The Mexican Economy 1997*, table 46, and for GDP, Banco de México website, *The Mexican Economy 1997*, table 46 (www.banxico.org.mx/public_html/doyai/mexecon97/t46.html). For 1996 to 1997, JP Morgan database, Mexico City, 1997.

g. The figures are calculated with U.S. dollars. For 1989 to 1992, for the trade balance, Banco de México, *The Mexican Economy 1996*, table 5, p. 264 and for GDP, Banco de México, *The Mexican Economy 1996*, table 5, p. 264. For 1993 to 1995, for trade balance, Banco de México website, *The Mexican Economy 1997*, website, table 46, and for GDP, Banco de México website, *The Mexican Economy 1997*, table 46, (http://banxico.org.mx/public_html/doyai/mexecon97/t46.html). For 1996 to 1997, JP Morgan database, Mexico City, 1997. In 1992, the Bank of Mexico changed its methodology for calculating the current account so that merchandise transactions now include the gross value of transactions that result from all temporary imports. The balance of trade is the difference between merchandise exports and merchandise imports.

h. The figures for 1989 to 1995 are calculated using values for the total external debt and GDP, both denominated in U.S.$. GDP for 1989 to 1992, Banco de México, *The Mexican Economy 1996*, table 5, p. 264. GDP for 1993 to 1995, Banco de México website, *The Mexican Economy 1997*, table 1. External debt for 1989 to 1992, Banco de México, *The Mexican Economy 1996*, table 53, p. 318. External debt for 1993 to 1995, Banco de México website, *The Mexican Economy 1997*, table 59. For 1996 to 1997, JP Morgan database, Mexico City, 1997.

i. World Bank, "World Development Indicators," CD-ROM (Washington, 1997).

j. Banco de México website, *Indices de Precios y Salarios* (www/banxico.org.mx/public_html/inveco/infecon/cuadros/cra4/html).

k. Banco de México website, *The Mexican Economy 1997*, table 32. (http://banxico.org.mx/public_html/doyai/mexecon97/t32.html). The 1997 estimate is from Macro Asesoría Económica. The index is estimated on the basis of consumer prices. Increases in the index mean an appreciation of the peso. The figures for 1995 and 1996 are preliminary.

l. For 1989 to 1996, information provided by Grupo de Economistas y Asociados (Mexico City).

Mexico's reliance on foreign savings would decline and sustainable growth would follow.

Events did not go as expected, however. In December 1994—scarcely a year after NAFTA's implementation—the Mexican government was cornered into a forced devaluation once again.[3] Following the devaluation, instead of the awaited prosperity, Mexico faced its worst economic crisis since the Great Depression.[4] Furthermore, instead of converging toward greater social harmony, there were manifestations of rising political violence. Striking examples were the armed uprising by the Zapatistas—the guerrillas in the state of Chiapas—in January 1994 (on the day NAFTA came into effect); the assassination of Luis Donaldo Colosio, the presidential candidate, of the ruling party, in March 1994 and its secretary general in September 1994;[5] and, the appearance of the Popular Revolutionary Army—a guerrilla movement better known by its Spanish acronym EPR—in June 1996.[6] Finally, despite the government efforts to fight extreme poverty, its incidence in the poorest states was on the rise (see chapter 8).

Slow Growth: Why Were Reforms Not Paying Off?

Which factors lie behind Mexico's disappointing economic performance? Although most of the attention of analysts and policymakers has focused on the Mexican peso crisis and its aftermath in 1995, understanding Mexico's relatively slow growth prior to the crisis is equally—or perhaps even more—challenging. The puzzle is that slow growth followed successful stabilization and far-reaching reforms and coincided with large capital inflows from abroad. There were good reasons to expect a growth dividend from reforms. Trade and financial liberalization should have led to higher productivity gains, and large capital inflows meant that foreign savings were available to accelerate capital accumulation.

Demand Side Factors: The Appreciation of the Peso

In theory, both demand and supply factors must have played a role in explaining Mexico's disappointing performance. Among the demand factors, the real appreciation of the peso probably stands out as one of the leading ones. The use of a relatively rigid exchange rate policy to stabilize the economy resulted in the peso appreciating substantially in real terms (table 6-1), and probably the tradable sector (that is, importable and exportable goods) lost competitiveness. The

TABLE 6-2. *External Sector, 1989–96*

Item	1989	1990	1991
Balance of trade			
(U.S.$ billions)[a]	0.4	–0.9	–7.3
Current account balance			
(U.S.$ billions)[b]	–5.8	–7.5	–14.6
Gross international reserves			
-end of period			
(U.S.$ billions)[c]	6.6	10.2	17.5
Direct foreign investment			
(U.S.$ billions)[d]	3.2	2.6	4.8
Portfolio investment			
(U.S.$ billions)[e]	0.4	3.4	12.8
Debt			
Total external debt[f]			
(U.S.$ billions)	95.3	104.3	116.5
Public sector external debt[g]			
(U.S.$ billions)	76.1	77.8	80.0
Interest payments			
(U.S.$ billions)[h]	9.3	9.2	9.2
Ratio of external debt			
to GDP (percent)[f,i]	46.1	42.7	40.6
Debt service			
Ratio (percent)[j]	23.5	88.1	24.0
Oil exports, interest rates and terms of trade			
Export oil prices—average			
(U.S.$/barrel)[k]	15.6	19.2	14.5
Share of oil exports in total			
exports(percent)[l]	22.4	24.8	19.1
U.S. prime rate			
nominal (percent)[m]	10.9	10.0	8.5
Terms of trade[n]	3.6	5.1	–8.5
U.S. gross domestic product[o]			
(growth rate)	3.4	1.2	–0.9

Sources: Information from the Banco de México website was downloaded on July 14, 1997 (notes d, l); on July 23, 1997 (notes, g, h, i, j); and on May 20, 1998, for 1996 and 1997 figures. The figures for 1995 and 1996 (notes h through l) and for 1997 are preliminary. The BEA website (note o) was downloaded on July 28, 1997, and on May 20, 1998, for 1996 and 1997 figures.

n.a. Not available.

a. For 1989 to 1992, Banco de México, *The Mexican Economy 1996* (Mexico, 1996), table 5, p. 264. For 1993 to 1995, Banco de México, *The Mexican Economy 1997*, table 46. (http://banxico.org.mx/public_html/doyai/mexecon97/t46.html). For 1996 to 1997,

TABLE 6-2. *(continued)*

1992	1993	1994	1995	1996	1997	Average growth 1989–94
−15.9	−13.5	−18.5	7.1	6.5	0.6	−7.4
−24.4	−23.4	−29.7	−1.6	−2.3	−7.5	−15.1
18.6	24.5	6.1	15.7	17.5	28.0	14.2
4.4	4.4	11	9.5	7.6	12.1	3.9
18	28.9	8.2	−9.7	14.1	5.0	12.7
117.5	131.7	142.2	169.9	167.5	154.7	113.1
75.8	78.7	85.4	100.9	98.3	n.a.	77.7
9.6	10.9	11.8	13.6	13.5	12.4	9.6
35.7	36.4	38.3	59.3	50.7	38.4	40.3
31.9	23.4	24.3	21.2	27.6	n.a.	38.2
14.8	13.1	13.8	15.7	19.0	n.a.	15.4
18.0	14.3	12.2	10.6	12.1	10.3	19.7
6.3	6.0	7.2	8.8	8.3	8.4	8.3
−0.9	−4.8	5.3	0.2	1.3	−1.5	n.a.
2.7	2.3	3.5	2.0	2.8	3.8	n.a.

Banco de México website, *Informe Anual 1997*, cuadro 8 (http://banxico.org.
mx/public_html/inveco/infors.html). In 1992, the Bank of Mexico changed its methodology for calculating the current account so that merchandise transactions now include
the gross value of transactions that result from all temporary imports. The balance of
trade is the difference between merchandise exports and merchandise imports.

b. For 1989 to 1992, Banco de México, *The Mexican Economy 1996* (Mexico, 1996), table 5,
p. 264. For 1993 to 1995, Banco de México website, *The Mexican Economy 1997*, table 46.
(http://banxico.org.mx/public_html/doyai/mexecon97/t46.html). For 1996 to 1997
Banco de México website, *Informe Anual 1997*, cuadro 13. (http://banxico.org.mx/

TABLE 6-2. *(notes continued)*

public_html/inveco/infors.html). In 1992, the Bank of Mexico changed its methodology for calculating the current account so that merchandise transactions now include the gross value of transactions that result from all temporary imports.

c. For 1989 to 1995, Banco de México, *The Mexican Economy 1996* (Mexico, 1996), table 43, p. 309. The 1996 and 1997 figures are from Grupo de Economistas y Asociados *GEA Economico*, no. 88 (April 1998), p. 22.

d. For 1989 to 1995, Banco de México website, "Sector Externo: Inversion Extranjera." (http://banxico.org.mx/public_html#Balanza de Pagos [nueva presentacion]). The 1996 and 1997 figures are from Grupo de Economistas y Asociados, *GEA Economico*, no. 88 (April 1998), p. 22.

e. For 1989 to 1995, Banco de México website, "Sector Externo: Inversion Extranjera" (http://banxico.org.mx/public_html#Balanza de Pagos[nueva presentacion]). The 1996 and 1997 figures are from Grupo de Economistas y Asociados, "GEA Economico," no. 88 (April 1998), p. 22.

f. For 1989 to 1994, Banco de México, *The Mexican Economy 1996* (Mexico, 1996), table 53, p. 318. For 1995 to 1995, Banco de México website, "The Mexican Economy 1997," table 59 (www.banxico.org.mx/public_html/doyai/mexecon97/t59.html). For 1996 to 1997, JP Morgan database, Mexico City, 1997.

g. For 1989 to 1994, Banco de México, *The Mexican Economy 1996*, table 53, p. 318 (Mexico, 1996). For 1995 to 1996, Banco de México website, "The Mexican Economy 1997," table 59. (http://banxico.org.mx/public_html/doyai/mexecon97/t59.html).

h. For 1989 to 1994, Banco de México, *The Mexican Economy 1996*, table 43, p. 308. For 1995 to 1995, Banco de México website, *The Mexican Economy 1997*, table 59. (http://banxico.org.mx/public_html/doyai/mexecon97/t59.html). For 1996 to 1997, JP Morgan database, Mexico City, 1997.

i. The figures are calculated using values for the total external debt and GDP, both denominated in U.S.$. For 1989 to 1992, Banco de México, "The Mexican Economy 1996" (Mexico, 1996) table 5, p. 264. For 1993 to 1995, Banco de México website, *The Mexican Economy 1997*, table 1. http://banxico.org.mx/public_html/doyai/mexecon97/t01.html). For 1996 to 1997, JP Morgan database, Mexico City, 1997.

j. For 1989 to 1994, Banco de México *The Mexican Economy 1996* (Mexico, 1995), table 43, p. 308, table 54, p. 319. For 1995 to 1996, Banco de México website, *The Mexican Economy 1997*, table 47, table 59. (http://banxico.org.mx/public_html/doyai/mexecon97/t47.html and /t59.html). The ratio is calculated as 'interest payments plus amortizations' divided by 'exports of goods and services.'

k. For 1989 to 1994, Ernesto Zedillo, "Primer Informe de Gobierno, Anexo" (Mexico, 1995), p. 107. For 1995 and 1996, Macro Asesoría Económica, "Macro Update: A Current Analysis of the Mexican Economy," year 10, no. 4 (Mexico, June 1997), p. 46, table 7. The 1997 figure is from Macro Asesoría Económica, "Macro Update," year 10, no. 5 (August 1997), p. 46. Price given is a weighted average of Mexico's oil export mix.

l. For 1989 to 1995, Banco de México website, "Sector Externo: Balanza Comercial." This series is measured in U.S. dollars (http://banxico.org.mx/public_html#Balanza de Pagos [nueva presentacion]). For 1996 to 1997 Banco de México website, *Sector Externo: Comercio Exterior.* This series is measured in U.S. dollars. (http://banxico. org.mx/public_html/inveco/infecon/cuadros/civ-2.html).

m. U.S. Federal Reserve Board website (http://bog.frb.fed.us/releases/h15/data/a/prime.txt).

n. Banco de México website. *Indices de Precios y Salarios* (http://banxico.org.mx/public_html/inveco/infecon/cuadros/cra4/html).

TABLE 6-2. *(notes continued)*

o. For 1989 to 1995, Bureau of Economic Analysis website, "Summary National Income and Product Series, 1929-1996, in "Survey of Current Business" (Washington, May 1997), table 2A, p. 14. For 1996 to 1997, BEA website, "National Accounts Data," table 1.1 (http://bea.doc.gov/bea/dn1.html).

real appreciation of the peso combined with trade liberalization contributed to shift domestic demand to foreign goods—now not only available but relatively cheap—resulting in output growing below its "potential" (that is, the growth rate that would have prevailed had the peso not been overvalued).

This hypothesis has been embraced by Rudiger Dornbusch and Alejandro Werner.[7] Using several exchange rate measures, they show that the real appreciation of the peso over the period 1989 to 1993 was nontrivial. They also show that the so-called formal employment in industry was falling and that starting in 1992 industrial production was at best flat (figure 6-1). In their view, what was happening in Mexico was the converse of a contractionary devaluation. Briefly, in countries like Mexico the devaluations are contractionary in the short run because of their depressive effect on incomes (that is, real wages) and hence aggregate demand.[8] In the medium term, devaluations are

FIGURE 6-1. *Industrial Production and Employment in Mexico, 1988–93*
Index, 1980=100[a]

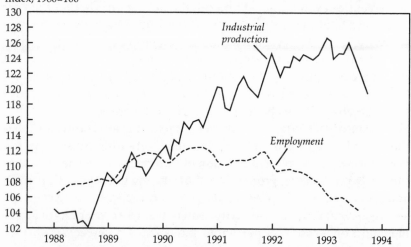

Source: Rudiger Dornbusch and Alejandro Werner, "Mexico: Stabilization, Reform and No Growth," *Brookings Papers on Economic Activity* (1994), p. 266, figure 8.
a. Indexes are constructed using three-month moving averages of the data.

expansionary as the substitution effect—the shift of demand from nontradables to tradables (importables and exportables)—dominates and output expands.[9] A real appreciation would do the converse.

Available evidence suggests that devaluations are contractionary in Mexico in the short run.[10] As for the medium run, authors differ: some find devaluations are expansionary while others do not.[11] Evidence from agriculture also indicates that the real appreciation of the peso was a contributing factor to what some authors have described as a "profitability crisis" affecting the *ejido* sector in particular.[12] Hence, the real appreciation of the peso could explain the lack of growth, at least in part. Other possible factors operating on the demand side were the recession in the United States and Mexico's austere fiscal policy in the early 1990s, particularly in 1992 and 1993 (tables 6-1, 6-2).

Supply Side Factors: Low Investment Rates and Slow Productivity Growth

Even if the demand-side story seems persuasive, factors on the supply side affected economic performance as well. In particular, slow growth in Mexico must be linked to low accumulation of capital. Although in Mexico the investment rate was around 25 percent for the period 1989–95 and even lower during the 1980s (chapter 2), in countries like Korea and the South East Asian economies it has been around 30 percent or even higher. Although the debate on whether the East Asian and South East Asian success stems from high growth in productivity versus high capital accumulation has not been settled, there are indications that the large investment (and savings) rates of that region account for a significant portion of their high growth rates.[13] As the recent Asian crisis reveals, however, these high investment (and savings) rates did not shield the countries from crisis.

Furthermore, evidence for the manufacturing sector indicates that the growth rate of productivity was relatively unimpressive in the years following the implementation of trade reforms.[14] The estimates for yearly productivity growth in manufacturing fall between 1 percent and 2.4 percent for the period 1985–90.[15] In comparison, between 1975 and 1990, total factor productivity growth was close to 4 percent a year in Hong Kong, about 3.5 percent in Taiwan, and 3 percent in Korea.[16] All of these were higher than even the highest estimates for Mexico.[17]

Why was productivity in manufacturing not growing faster?[18] Contrary to what has been argued by the critics of reform, economic openness appears to have had a positive effect on productivity growth,though not uniformly.[19] In part, slow productivity response to economic reform may be owing to factors intrinsic to the reforms. Taking advantage of the opportunities brought by reforms takes time. Even though trade liberalization brings tangible benefits to a country—by opening up new markets, stimulating demand for new goods, and introducing new technology—adapting to these factors is a gradual process.[20] Furthermore, the improvement of technology has a secondary effect of increasing the rate of depreciation of now obsolete or relatively more costly existing capital. This increased rate of depreciation dampens the productivity response, at least until the existing capital is fully replaced.[21] Finally, rigidities in the labor market such as high dismissal costs and restrictions for hiring temporary and part-time employees could have slowed down the reallocation of workers among sectors.[22] In fact, data on total factor productivity in the industrial sector seem to indicate that performance was changing for the better over time (figure 6-1).

Although the reform minded emphasize the incompleteness of reforms or the fact that their impact takes time as the cause of Mexico's lackluster performance, flaws in the reform process can be equally damaging.[23] The lack of an appropriate regulatory framework before the privatization process was started has resulted in undesirable concentration of wealth and ownership in some of the privatized areas as well. Often the bulk of the purchases and shares went to established industrial or financial groups.[24] High concentration may result in monopolistic practices detrimental to productivity growth.[25] In the short run, economic openness may not be sufficient to counter these practices. Finally, in agriculture some reforms have been the cause of institutional failures. The privatization, liquidation, or scaling down of many of the state-run institutions were only partially replaced by new institutional arrangements. The result was a reduction in the availability and a rise in the cost of access to credit, water, seeds, modern inputs, insurance, markets, and technical assistance, in particular for *ejidos*.[26] These factors combined with the appreciation of the peso hurt agriculture particularly badly as evidenced by its poor performance.[27]

The previous discussion on how demand and supply factors could have affected Mexico's growth performance can give helpful insights. However, the final answer to a puzzling slow growth still remains elusive. To some degree the slack economic performance was a conditioning factor for the oncoming crisis. As we shall see, at the root of the peso crisis lay an overextended financial system. Financial liberalization combined with optimistic expectations on Mexico's economic future led to a lending boom. When growth rates slowed down, nonperforming loans began to accumulate. A vulnerable financial sector precluded the monetary authorities from raising interest rates in 1994 to deter capital outflows and the massive conversion of short-term government securities to dollar-indexed Tesobonos. (Tesobonos are Mexican short-term public debt instruments redeemable in pesos but denominated in dollars.)

The Devaluation in December 1994

Although the performance of the Mexican economy left a lot to be desired, in the early 1990s there were no real signs that Mexico was heading toward a major financial crisis. A combination of adverse political shocks and volatile capital markets turned modest policy mistakes into a disaster at the end of 1994.

After the Brady Plan was signed in 1990 and particularly after the passage of NAFTA in 1993, there was a widespread perception that Mexico was unlikely to face a debt crisis of major proportions again. Macroeconomic policy was not repeating the mistakes that led to the previous two crises in 1976 and 1982. In particular, the main source of the previous crises, namely, the fiscal deficit, was under control: in 1992 and 1993 the government's accounts were in surplus (table 6-1). Yet, as it had occurred before, the Mexican government was cornered into a forced devaluation of the peso in December 1994.[28] The devaluation was followed by a major financial crisis in Mexico with significant spillover effects on other countries, particularly in Latin America.[29] What was originally intended as a modest correction of the exchange rate put Mexico on the verge of default in a matter of days, which was only stopped by an international financial rescue package of unprecedented magnitude.

The rapid flight of capital in early 1995, not only from Mexico but especially from other so-called emerging markets in Latin America and elsewhere, took the investor community, governments, and international financial institutions by surprise. Moreover, despite the sizable rescue package, Mexico's output fell by more than 6 percent (measured in 1993 pesos) and average real manufacturing wages fell by

12.5 percent in 1995 (table 6-1).[30] This episode leaves us with at least three sets of questions. First, what caused the devaluation in December 1994? Second, why did the devaluation turn into a financial crisis? Finally, why did output fall so sharply in 1995, the rescue package notwithstanding? This section will address the first two questions; the third one is discussed in chapter 7.

Exchange Rate Appreciation, Capital Inflows, and the Growing Current Account Deficit

As discussed in chapter 2, with the launching of the stabilization program known as the Pact,beginning in 1988 the nominal exchange rate was used as an *anchor*: that is, the dollar value of the peso was fixed.[31] The Pact was successful in bringing inflation down, but as experience shows, in other similar cases the use of the nominal exchange rate as an anchor results in a real appreciation of the local currency. Mexico was no exception. Even when the exchange rate regime passed through several modifications[32]—from a fixed to a crawling peg and, subsequently, to an adjustable band that in time had its boundaries widened—the appreciation of the peso continued, independently of the definition used.[33]

The appreciation of the peso was not only the result of the stabilization program. Starting in 1990, Mexico (like many other developing countries) received large capital inflows. The capital inflows were the combined result of a deliberate policy of attracting private capital and, more importantly, the fall in interest rates in the United States. As discussed in chapter 2, the Mexican government set out to attract foreign capital through highly visible means. Among these, two are notable: the privatization of the banks announced to Congress in May 1990 and the intention to negotiate a free trade agreement with the United States, leaked to the public in March 1990. The signing of the Brady-type agreement contributed to the rise in capital inflows as well. Changes in U.S. regulations introduced by the Securities and Exchange Commission affecting the speed and norms under which some operations could take place also explains in part the initial sharp rise in these flows.[34]

Gross capital flows toward Mexico rose tenfold from 1989 to 1993, from U.S.$3.2 billion to U.S.$32.6 billion.[35] Some of those inflows reflected the repatriation of capital that had left in previous years. But a large proportion was due to new portfolio investment. Practically nonexistent in 1989, total portfolio investment equaled 60 percent of total capital inflows—or U.S.$55.2 billion from 1990 to 1993.[36] An important portion of portfolio flows were equity investments. Following the Stock Market Law of December 1989—which among other things liberalized access to foreign investors—equity investments went from less than U.S.$1 billion annually, to almost U.S.$28 billion from 1990 to 1994.[37] In dollar terms, returns were very high, averaging 52 percent a year over the period 1990–93.[38] Bond placements also rose steadily, amounting to U.S.$24 billion from 1990 to 1993.[39] Portfolio investments came from foreign pension funds and other financial intermediaries, which with growing fervor entered Latin American markets in search of better yields.

A Victim of Its Own Success

Mexico, as did many other developing countries emerging from the trauma of the debt crisis, received the capital inflows with glee. The problem was that the Mexican economy became dependent on them. The pattern was as follows. The real exchange rate appreciation caused by the exchange-rate-based stabilization program resulted in a growing disequilibrium in the current account (table 6-1). This disequilibrium was financed by capital flows from abroad (table 6-2). With time, capital inflows caused the real exchange rate to appreciate even further and worsened the trade deficit through both their impact on the exchange rate and the savings-investment gap. Between 1989 and 1993, the trade balance as a proportion of GDP went up from a 0.2 percent surplus to a 3.3 percent deficit (table 6-1).

The widening of the savings-investment gap resulted from a fall in domestic private savings and a moderate increase in investment. Although the factors explaining the fall in savings are not yet fully understood, two appear to have contributed. As a result of the financial liberalization, a sharp rise in the availability of consumer credit occurred, fueling a consumption boom. In a country where credit for consumption had been severely restricted, the "pent-up" demand must have been extremely high. Between 1989 and 1993, consumption grew at 4.9 percent a year and consumer credit as a percentage of GDP rose from 18.8 percent to 41.1 percent.[40]

Ironically, during this period Mexico became a victim of its own success. For a while the current account deficit was "overfinanced" in the sense that so much capital was flowing into Mexico that the central bank was able to accumulate international reserves (table 6-2). The downside was that Mexico became increasingly vulnerable. The low domestic savings rate could make debt servicing very difficult in the future. In the short run, if exogenous "shocks" affected the pace of capital flows, and the large current account deficit could no longer be financed, the Mexican economy could be forced to a sudden and major adjustment.[41] This is exactly what happened.

U.S. Interest Rates, Political Shocks, and Mexican Monetary Policy in 1994

NAFTA came into effect in 1994. As a result, the hopes for promising economic performance in Mexico were high. However, sooner rather than later, the good news was matched with bad news. Because of the sustained economic recovery in the United States and fears of inflationary pressures in 1994, the Federal Reserve decided to raise the federal fund rate.[42] The result was an increase in the yields of financial instruments in the United States starting in February of that year (figure 6-2). As various studies have shown, capital flows to the developing world are very sensitive to interest rate changes in the United

FIGURE 6-2. *Nominal Interest Rates in Mexico and the United States*

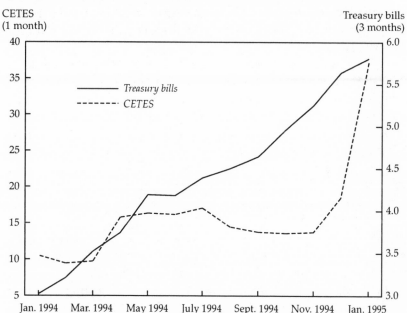

Source: IMF, *International Financial Statistics* CD-ROM, Washington, September 1997.

States.[43] Because of this, as argued by Guillermo Calvo, Leonardo Leiderman, and Carmen M. Reinhart , a rise in interest rates in the United States can bring about serious problems for countries that depend on attracting capital to finance their external deficits and to maintain exchange rate parity.[44] In particular, the problems could become worse if the period of inflows was associated with bubbles in the stock or commodity markets and an excessive expansion of domestic credit. In the latter case, the sudden flight of capital could threaten the stability of the recipient country's financial system.

Moreover, 1994 was a year of unprecedented political turmoil in Mexico. In January, a guerrilla uprising took place in the poverty-stricken state of Chiapas;[45] in March, the PRI's presidential candidate, Luis Donaldo Colosio, was assassinated; in the period running up to the elections (in particular, during June and July) tensions mounted; and, in September, the secretary general of the PRI, José Francisco Ruiz-Massieu, was killed.[46] Whatever their ultimate cause, these events changed the perception of investors about Mexico's political predictability. For the first time in decades Mexico's political stability could no longer be taken for granted. Higher returns abroad and a rise in political uncertainty slowed the pace of capital flows. International reserves reflected those changes, particularly immediately after the assassination of Colosio. Within days, reserves fell from U.S.$26 billion to U.S.$18 billion, a fall of nearly 31 percent in less than a month (figure 6-3).[47]

At this point, the government had two options. It could increase the crawl of the ceiling of the exchange rate band or even raise the ceiling of the band with a discrete shift.[48] Alternatively, the government could make no change in exchange rate policy and, instead, raise domestic interest rates, use international reserves up to a limit, and issue more dollar-indexed government debt instruments known as Tesobonos to fend off capital outflows.[49] The authorities chose the second course primarily under the presumption that expectations would turn around in the near future. As a result, interest paid on twenty-eight day Mexican Treasury bonds (CETES)[50] rose to 15.79 percent in April 1994, a modest increase, and outstanding Tesobonos began to increase quite rapidly (figure 6-2). It should be noted, however, that the increase in interest rates did not match the hike in U.S. interest rates.

Interestingly, initially the decision to stick to the existing exchange rate policy received the tacit support of the United States and Canada.

FIGURE 6-3. *International Reserves*

Billions of U.S. dollars

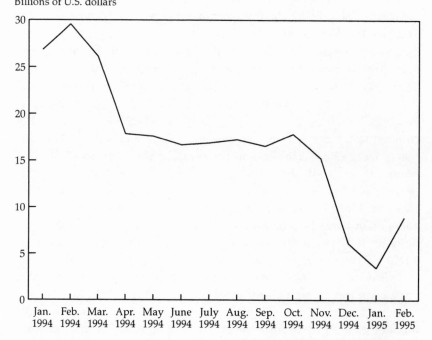

Source: Banco de México, *The Mexican Economy 1995* (Mexico, 1995), table 20, pp. 222–223, figures for end of each period.

Evidence is the fact that the two countries agreed to a "swap" arrangement for close to U.S.$7 billion[51] in the aftermath of Colosio's assassination.[52] However, Mexico did not resort to the use of this facility.

The decision not to modify exchange rate policy immediately after Colosio's assassination was heavily affected by political considerations. In particular, former President Salinas had selected as a new presidential candidate someone who was not necessarily popular within the PRI.[53] Under the new circumstances, it was ever more important to generate an upbeat economic climate in the months preceding the August elections. A devaluation of the peso could have jeopardized the economic outlook in the short run. Moreover, for the Salinas government, managing the political situation took precedence over managing the economy: in 1994, his economic cabinet met less than ten times, whereas in the previous year it had met once a week.[54]

After April 1994, the peso exchange rate (pesos/U.S.$) often was at the ceiling of the band.[55] However, the Bank of Mexico has argued that the relative stability of the international reserves—which remained at around U.S.$17 billion throughout most of the period until November—was a clear sign that the peso was not under unmanageable pressures.[56] However, the huge change in the amount of Tesobonos held by the public indicated that something anomalous was happening. Between March and June of 1994, the sum of Tesobonos increased from U.S.$3.1 billion to U.S.$ 12.6 billion; they climbed to U.S.$ 19.2 billion in September and reached U.S.$29.2 billion in December.[57] Throughout the year, the composition of the government's domestic debt changed radically. In December 1993, 76.5 percent was in CETES and Tesobonos were only 4.8 percent of the total. In December 1994, 14.2 percent of the debt was in CETES and 80.6 percent was in Tesobonos.[58] Clearly, many investors, fearing a devaluation, preferred to hold Mexican debt instruments that, although redeemable only in pesos, were indexed to the dollar.

The systematic increase in Tesobonos held by the public ought to have been interpreted as a sign of the lack of credibility of the prevailing exchange rate policy. This "dollarization" of the internal public debt probably explains the surprising stability of international reserves from April onward in the face of the rise in external interest rates and the internal political uncertainty (figure 6-3).[59] The Tesobonos, in fact, gave the Mexican government and its creditors what in the end turned out to be a false sense of security. To the investors, the Tesobonos signaled the government's commitment to the exchange rate regime since it was the government itself that was undertaking a large portion of the exchange rate risk. However, the U.S.$29 billion in outstanding Tesobonos was one of the principal causes of the financial crisis that followed the devaluation in December 1994.

The slowdown in capital inflows was accompanied by a monetary policy that in the end proved incompatible with the exchange rate policy. The monetary authorities "sterilized" the fall in international reserves by increasing net domestic credit and thus kept the monetary base approximately constant (figure 6-4).[60] This led to a fall in the domestic interest rates beginning in July, a trend contrary to the movement of U.S. interest rates (figure 6-2).[61]

These pressures continued after August, even though the presidential elections were peaceful and the PRI candidate, Ernesto Zedillo,

FIGURE 6-4. *Mexico: Monetary Base and Domestic Credit*

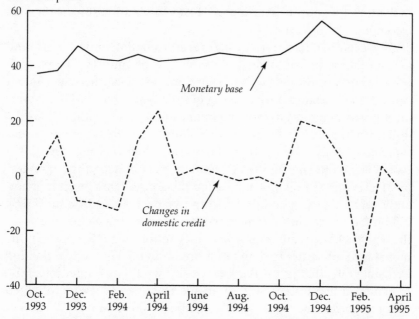

Billions of pesos

Source: Calculated from Banco de México website, Historical Economic series, downloaded September 4, 1997 (www.banxico.org.mx/public_html/inveco/serieci/ s12054.html and s06557.html).

won by a very comfortable margin. Contrary to expectations, capital inflows did not resume[62]—not even after the president-elect subscribed the Pact's commitment to the exchange rate regime in September.[63] The political uncertainty was exacerbated once again when the PRI's secretary general, José F. Ruiz-Massieu, was assassinated in late September.[64] The climate was not helped by the tensions that arose from the inevitable rivalries among prospective cabinet members in the area of finance for the incoming government. Moreover, on several occasions it was filtered to the public that some possible candidates for the post of secretariat of finance did not share the view of the incumbent secretary on exchange rate management.[65]

Confronted with the panorama of rising interest rates in the United States, the need to finance a current account deficit of close to U.S.$30 billion in 1994 and a similar deficit expected in 1995,[66] and the memory that approximately every six years since 1976 the government abandoned its vows not to devalue precisely in the last year of a presidential term, investors—in particular, Mexicans— changed their pesos into dollars at a quicker pace in late November. The pressure continued after the administration of Ernesto Zedillo took office on December 1.[67]

By December 16, international reserves had dropped to around U.S.$11 billion,the equivalent of 1.7 months of imports.[68] Faced with the situation of dwindling international reserves, the government called for an extraordinary meeting of the members of the Pact. At this meeting it was agreed to raise the ceiling of the band (within which the dollar was allowed to fluctuate) to 4 pesos to the dollar (about 15 percent above its previous ceiling). This new ceiling was announced and took effect on the morning of December 20. Following the announcement, the value of the dollar reached the 4 peso rate almost immediately, and it is estimated that within two days an additional U.S.$5 billion left the country.[69] The markets were sending a clear message: the new exchange rate ceiling was not credible. On December 21, the monetary authorities had no other option but to switch to a floating exchange rate, that is, the Bank of Mexico would no longer intervene to maintain the dollar within a prespecified band.[70] What followed was a financial "meltdown" with significant spillover effects on other countries, particularly in Latin America.[71]

One interesting feature of this forced devaluation episode is that the fiscal deficit no longer was at the root of the problem. It is true that under some measurements, the fiscal deficit was higher than the level revealed by the authorities. For example, it has been argued that net lending on the part of one of the Mexican development banks, Nacional Financiera, S.A. (NAFINSA) could have added as much as 2 percentage points to the official figures of the fiscal deficit.[72] However, even if this were the case (and there is some controversy as to whether it is conceptually correct to add this to the fiscal deficit), the fiscal deficit was much lower than it had been in 1981 and 1982 (see chapter 2). The macroeconomic disequilibria generated in the period before the 1994 episode were caused mostly by decisions taken by the private sector and, in the run-up to the crisis, by the government's decision to keep the exchange rate band unchanged (until December 1994). The Mexican experience at the end of 1994 revealed—as Chile's had twelve years earlier—that running current account deficits that are financed by volatile capital flows can result in severe crises even if the deficit is the result of market forces.

What is peculiar about Mexico's policy in 1994 is not that the outgoing government tried to avoid a devaluation at all costs. This is a typical reaction in many developing (and even developed) countries. What is more peculiar is that, once the government had decided not to change the exchange rate policy, it did not make sure that the rest of the macroeconomic measures—monetary policy in particular—was congruent with this objective in the face of lower capital inflows. In particular, it is puzzling that nominal domestic interest rates were allowed to fall, even when external rates were still rising and expectations of a devaluation were on the rise—as revealed by foreign investors intent in switching from CETES to Tesobonos almost in full.

One obvious interpretation of the policy decisions in 1994 is the determination of President Salinas to avoid (or postpone) a devaluation at any cost, in particular before the August presidential elections. Undoubtedly, allowing the massive conversion of CETES to Tesobonos and resisting a devaluation were surely driven, at least in part, by the need to have "smooth" elections.[73] Oddly, once the elections were over, the monetary policy that led to a further fall in domestic interest rates not only remained in place but was exacerbated in the latter part of the year. If the central objective was to maintain the exchange rate policy, why didn't the government take the necessary steps to make macroeconomic policy congruent with this goal? Why did the government decide not to adopt the most conservative line and assume that—given the trend in external interest rates and the nervousness generated by the political assassinations—it was advisable to follow a more restrictive monetary policy and allow the domestic interest rate to climb?

One feasible explanation is that officials were concerned with the potentially destabilizing effect that higher domestic interest rates would have on a fragile banking system.[74] Risking a banking crisis did not make sense if, in particular, as the president of the Bank of Mexico has said, the monetary authorities viewed the slowdown in capital inflows as temporary and the market was expected to return to "normalcy" once confidence was restored.[75] This perception was wrong, and erring on the optimistic side turned out to be very costly.

The Vulnerability of the Banking Sector

Between 1988 and 1992, the Mexican government undertook wide-ranging financial reforms, including the reprivatization of the banks in

1991–92.[76] The primary objective of financial reform was to increase the quantity and improve the efficiency of financial intermediation. Credit to the private sector rose very rapidly indeed from 1990 onward. But, as a result, so did the proportion of nonperforming loans. Between 1988 and September 1994, the ratio of past due loans to total loans rose from 1.3 percent to 8.3 percent.[77] As just discussed, the weakness of the banking system probably explains, in part, why the Mexican authorities tried to keep interest rates from rising during 1994. Clearly, something had gone awry.

Several factors have been mentioned to explain the expansion of nonperforming loans. The real appreciation of the peso probably resulted in a squeeze of the profits of producers of tradable goods, making it more difficult for them to sustain payments on their loans.[78] This problem must have been compounded by the relatively high real interest rates prevailing in 1992 and 1993. Second, as new banks came into the system, what some authors called a "supercompetitive" market behavior followed. In essence, bank owners stretched their capital and deposits in efforts to expand loans and capture a higher market share.[79] In the aftermath of the privatization, the banks expanded consumer credit without a commensurate increase in adequate information regarding the creditworthiness of their borrowers.[80] No well-organized credit reporting systems existed in Mexico. Third, the large capital inflows—with the consequential abundance in liquidity—probably masked risky borrowers.[81] The reader might remember that during those years Mexico was experiencing some degree of market euphoria as a result of the economic reforms and the prospects of new business opportunities created by NAFTA (which would come into effect January 1, 1994).

At the root of the problems faced by banks were some flaws in the privatization process and some important shortcomings in the regulatory framework and its enforcement. In 1982 the Mexican government nationalized the banking system.[82] Between 1991 and 1992 they were reprivatized. Eighteen banking groups were sold, generating government revenues of about U.S.$12.4 billion.[83] It caught the public's attention that in many of the operations the price was equal to or more than three times the book value (when the international average was about two).[84] Although the reprivatization of the banking system was generally well received by the multilateral institutions and governments in the industrialized world, there were areas of concern.

One issue was that the improvements in bank supervision were undertaken after the reprivatization process was under way.[85] In particular, the group ownership of banks and the creation of financial conglomerates with their potential for interlocking risks could create new risks for the banking system.

Another factor that probably did not help was that before 1990, most banking system deposits were channeled into financing the fiscal deficit, so the banks failed to develop experience and expertise in assessing the creditworthiness of the private sector. At the same time, the authorities also failed to develop experience with supervision and regulation within a market environment. It was the lack of experience both by the regulators and the banks they were regulating that made the surge of capital flows—which translated into greater liquidity in the banking sector—in the early 1990s so dangerous.

Although financial liberalization was accompanied by improvements in bank regulation and supervision, such as establishing a loan classification system, defining "stringent" provisioning policies for loans, increasing public disclosure of bank financial performance, and implementing risk-adjusted capital adequacy guidelines,bank regulation and supervision remained weak, something that would subsequently cause serious problems.[86] A universal banking system naturally contains its own class of regulatory problems, especially involving "self-lending." However, in Mexico's case, these problems were exacerbated by the fact that until 1995, Mexican accounting standards did not require consolidated reporting. This made it difficult to regulate lending within financial groups.[87] In addition, partly because on-shore and off-shore accounts were not required to be consolidated, commercial banks could engage in highly leveraged and risky currency plays involving trading derivatives that would completely escape the eyes of the regulators for whom the dollar-denominated liabilities were matched by dollar-denominated assets.[88] To that, one must add that accounting standards for financial institutions were far less demanding than those in most developed countries and that responsibilities for regulation and supervision were under several agencies with overlapping roles and little real authority.[89]

Some authors have identified another serious problem with Mexican regulations that compounds the moral hazard created by a system in which the government explicitly or implicitly guarantees deposits in full. Shareholders in Mexico were not really obliged to face the consequences of their banks' failure as fully as those in other coun-tries such as the United States. In the case of a failed bank, the share-holders were not only allowed to keep equity interest after the bank was sold, but the purchaser was given guarantees to be protected from losses on existing loans. As a result, these guarantees cushioned both depositors and the bank's stockholders from risky bank behavior.[90]

The vulnerabilities embedded in the banking system were more worrisome in the context of the surge of capital flows just described. The financial system could be subjected to sudden increases and losses of liquidity for which it was not really prepared. Following the Basle framework, the Mexican banks were not obliged to hold liquid assets or reserve requirements. As mentioned, financial liberalization trans-lated the large inflows into a domestic credit boom that did not end well. According to official figures, credit for consumption increased by 260 percent in real terms between December 1989 and June 1993, while credit for residential housing rose by 275 percent during the same period. As a result, credit for consumption purposes (including resi-dential housing) increased from 12 percent to 23 percent of total credit.[91]

The expansion of nonperforming loans was partly a result of the fact that the credit boom was subsiding and that prior assessments of creditworthiness made by the banks were wrong. Here is where the role of the regulator becomes crucial. Banking authorities should have implemented a plan to reduce the growth of deposits in and credits given by the weaker, riskier banks. Authorities should have started a restructuring program for past due loans. The banks with greatest troubles should have been subjected to very close on-site scrutiny on the part of regulators. However, no initiatives were taken in this respect. On the contrary, the authorities permitted, and even explicitly encouraged, an excessive expansion of the weakest banks. For exam-ple, in 1994, instead of putting troubled institutions under strict super-vision, the authorities actually funded their expansion.[92]

Given this panorama, when capital flows slowed down in 1994, the Bank of Mexico probably had little choice but to accommodate mone-tary policy to keep interest rates from rising too much. Under the assumption that the paucity of capital flows was of a temporary nature, the monetary authorities' main concern was to avoid a costly banking crisis. In the end, the effort was futile because the peso crisis caused a banking crisis with a cost (at present value) whose estimates

range from 7.2 percent of 1996 GDP (estimated by the Mexican government) to 12 percent of 1995 GDP (estimated by private institutions).[93] The actual cost is still unknown and may be higher yet.

The Financial Crisis

Once the peso was allowed to float on December 21, expectations
were that following a few days of market turmoil during which spec-
ulators could cash in their profits, the situation would stabilize.
Instead, the peso continued its downward trend and a financial crisis
loomed. By the first half of January 1995, Mexico seemed on a sure
path toward a financial crash.

Why did the devaluation turn into a financial crisis? Or, to put it in
other words, why did investors refuse to roll over outstanding
Tesobonos, a decision that put the Mexican authorities on the verge
of default? Although it is true that several analysts had anticipated
that sooner or later there would be a forced devaluation of the
peso, practically no one predicted the financial crisis that followed.[94]
The majority of economists from the academic world, governments,
and the multilateral lending institutions in Washington were gen-
uinely surprised by the intensity with which markets reacted to the
devaluation. Clearly, there had been a serious miscalculation.

At the time the peso was allowed to float, the Mexican government
had about U.S.$6 billion in international reserves and sizeable imme-
diate obligations in dollars. In particular, a total of U.S.$3.3 billion of
Tesobonos were to reach maturity in January 1995 and U.S.$9.9 bil-
lion were to reach maturity during the first quarter of 1995.[95] Before
the devaluation, Mexican authorities—and the markets—assumed
that outstanding Tesobonos would be rolled over without effort. After
the devaluation, however, the fact that the Mexican authorities did not
have enough foreign exchange to amortize Tesobonos coming due in
the weeks ahead suddenly became a concern in market circles. Never
mind that Mexico would not have been able to amortize its total (private and public) short-term dollar commitments in full anyway, even
before the devaluation. Or that a large number of countries would
have faced similar difficulties in the event the markets refused to roll
over all their short-term obligations. Clearly, the devaluation triggered
a panic response. The reasons are not yet fully understood, but three
factors can be identified.

First, there was great concern that the Mexican government was not really capable of managing the economy as people had believed. The way the devaluation was handled during the week of December 19 made the new government appear inexperienced and confused. This was in sharp contrast with the image of self-confidence that had characterized the cabinet during the Salinas administration.[96] Second, the fact that the government devalued the currency despite repeated promises to the contrary (made even as close as two days before the event) caused a severe loss of reputation. It did not help that the devaluation was announced as "a lifting of the ceiling of the band, " avoiding the use of straightforward language, and that the announcement was made through a public channel, without any attempt to explain the decision directly to major U.S. institutional investors. Fair or not, in the eyes of U.S. investors, the government had lost control of the situation, did not have a damage-control strategy, and had reneged on its word. On top of that, the devaluation implied that dollar-indexed obligations would exercise considerable pressure on the public finances.[97] And furthermore it didn't help that among the new investors in Mexico were pension fund administrators inexperienced in managing exchange rate risk.

Finally, as a result of this breakdown in communications, confidence, and trust, investors began to speculate that the next logical step for the Mexican government would be to impose capital controls or even default on its obligations. After all, they recollected, that is what the government had done with Mexdollar accounts in mid-1982 when they were converted into pesos at an exchange rate almost 50 percent below the market rate (see chapter 2). The fact that the head of the Central Bank was the same person during both crises probably did not help. Once the rumor circulated that capital controls or a forced debt restructuring (that is, a default) might be imposed, panic spread.[98]

One of the manifestations of this panic was the market's reluctance to roll over the Tesobonos coming due in the week immediately following the devaluation. This failed Tesobono auction triggered additional pressures on the peso through at least two channels. First, the peso went down for the simple reason that Tesobonos were being amortized and the pesos immediately changed into dollars. Second, and less known to the public, Mexican debt instruments had been used by Mexican banks in a variety of derivative market operations (many of which were designed to circumvent Mexican prudential regulations), which may have magnified the destabilizing effects of the devaluation.[99]

Although the precise mechanics vary from case to case, the case of Tesobono swaps illustrates the point.[100] About U.S.$16 billion of Tesobonos were involved in these swaps at the time of the devaluation.[101] Mexican banks used the Tesobono swaps, performed offshore, to leverage Tesobono holdings. In this type of derivative operation, the Mexican bank would receive the yield earned on Tesobonos in exchange for LIBOR plus, multiplied by a notional amount of dollars. The advantage of the swap was the avoidance of the regulations of the Comisión Nacional de Valores, which prevented the holding of financial assets on margin in Mexico.

In the days following the devaluation, Tesobono dollar market values fell. This happened primarily because the rumors that the Mexican authorities might impose capital controls affected the Tesobono auctions in the week after the devaluation. Capital controls would have hurt Tesobono holders because although the instruments' face value was indexed to the dollar, Tesobonos were redeemable in pesos. A fall in the dollar market value of Tesobonos triggered margin calls to deliver dollars to compensate for the drop in value of the collateral. The Mexican banks, then, had to acquire these dollars or else close out the position (which would have required the delivery of an even much larger amount in dollars). The purchase of dollars to cover such margin calls and position close outs played a role in the currency turmoil of January and February 1995. Certainly the large attack on the Banco de México's reserves on December 20, 1994, also stemmed from these dynamics.[102]

As the peso took the first nose dive at the end of December, the United States took the lead in arranging a rescue package of U.S.$18 billion.[103] However, this amount turned out to be insufficient to calm investor fear that the Mexican government would be forced to declare the inconvertibility of the peso. This fear surged, when through simple arithmetic calculations, investors saw that payments coming due in 1995 (which, assuming that most of the short-term debt would not be rolled over, were estimated at about U.S.$50 billion) were far greater than the estimated resources available. International reserves in the Bank of Mexico were about U.S.$6 billion and, as stated, the first international rescue package was equal to U.S.$18 billion.[104] The rescue package plus the international reserves would barely cover half of Mexico's financial obligations for 1995.

It quickly became evident that to calm the markets and stop the financial "meltdown," the rescue package had to be large enough to put the fears of default to rest. Otherwise, panic selling and the spillover into other markets would not be halted. It was essential to find a lender of last resort. The realization of this resulted in an unprecedented international financial rescue package of close to U.S.$50 billion led by the United States and the IMF, announced at the end of January 1995.[105]

As already discussed, several factors contributed to the destabilizing effect of the devaluation. In essence, the episode had many ingredients of a self-fulfilling crisis. If the initial rumors of capital controls had not hit the markets, it is possible that Tesobonos would have been rolled over and pressures on the peso because of leveraged operations would not have occurred.[106] In the economist's jargon, Mexico was in a world of multiple equilibria, and rumors of capital controls pushed the economy toward a "bad" equilibrium, that is, one in which the peso would "endlessly" fall.[107]

The role of a financial rescue package under such circumstances is to prevent individual market decisions from resulting in an outcome in which everybody is worse off. However, to be really effective, the financial facility should be in place before "rumors" make their inroads into expectations, and hence, decisions. In Mexico, the rescue package came too late for that. Its main contribution, as discussed in chapter 7, was not in preventing the peso crisis from happening but in bringing it to a halt, and avoiding the crisis from spreading and assuming global proportions. Of equal importance, the rescue package helped restore Mexico's access to international capital markets much more quickly than anticipated.

Most analysts agree that until the crisis erupted, little evidence pointed toward Mexico's insolvency.[108] So, contrary to what critics of the package said, the idea of punishing investors for making poor investment decisions was not the point. This is precisely what a self-fulfilling crisis is about: investments that initially appear to have a low sovereign risk can become bad investments because the sum of the individual actions of economic agents—each acting rationally—leads to a bad outcome for everybody. International capital markets are particularly prone to such situations.[109] Moreover, the proliferation of so-called derivatives in international capital markets "can have devastating effects on macroeconomic stability by heightening crisis dynamics, increasing miscalculations of market risks, and encouraging excessive risk-taking by investors evading prudential regulations."[110]

Some analysts identify the delay in changing the exchange rate policy as the principal cause of the peso debacle.[111] Although it will never be known for sure whether a change in exchange rate policy in January, April, September, or even on December 1, 1994, would have had less dire consequences, it is reasonable to assume that, with more international reserves and fewer outstanding Tesobonos, the government could have handled the situation with much greater ease. If for no other reason, the monetary authorities would have had more resources to give credibility to the new parity. It should be remembered that by December 1994 the international reserves had fallen from U.S.$27 billion in February 1994 to U.S.$11 billion and the outstanding Tesobonos—all of them due in 1995—had increased from less than U.S.$3 billion in January 1994 to U.S.$29 billion and had become about 81 percent of the domestic short-term government debt held by foreigners.[112] But the most salient aspect of the peso crisis does not rest with policy misjudgments. Rather, it gives the opportunity to witness the inherent volatility of international capital markets at play and how this characteristic can produce quite devastating effects. In 1997 the world was able to watch this again in Thailand, Indonesia, Malaysia, and the leading Asian "tiger" South Korea.[113]

Chapter Seven

Rescue, Recession, and Recovery

In contrast to 1982, at the time of the crisis in 1994 potential financial support from the United States was already formalized in the North American Framework Agreement (NAFA) signed by the three NAFTA countries in April 1994. In fact, a potential financial support package from the United States, Canada, and European central banks had been quietly arranged during the NAFTA vote in early November 1993. At the time there were fears that if NAFTA were not passed by the U.S Congress, the Mexican peso would be subject to a speculative attack. As a result, the industrialized governments agreed to put in place U.S.$12 billion in swaps to which the United States contributed half. These agreements remained secret and expired on December 31, 1993. No drawings were made by Mexico.[1]

Then, on March 24, 1994, U.S. Treasury Secretary Lloyd Bentsen and U.S. Federal Reserve Chairman Alan Greenspan put in place a U.S.$6 billion swap line, with each agency contributing one-half, immediately after the assassination of PRI presidential candidate Luis Donaldo Colosio.[2] This swap facility was to be available for two months while the pressure on the peso subsided. However, on April 26 the three NAFTA countries signed the North American Framework Agreement (NAFA), making permanent the U.S.$6 billion contribution from the United States in a swap arrangement with Mexico and Canada. Under this agreement, the Bank of Canada and the Bank of Mexico also expanded their existing swap arrangement from C$200 million to C$1 billion (then about U.S.$723 million), while the Federal Reserve and the Canadian central bank reaffirmed their existing U.S.$2 billion swap line.[3] By implementing this agreement, the United States and Canada were giving tacit support to Mexico's decision to keep the exchange rate policy unaltered in the aftermath of the assassination.

Non-U.S. support was called upon once again when an additional U.S.$6 billion was quietly put together by European countries and Japan, with the help of the U.S. Federal Reserve, in order to back the peso in the period running up to the August 1994 presidential elections. It was recognized that, given the uncertainties generated by the assassination of Luis Donaldo Colosio, it was an awkward time to change exchange rate policy. Under this U.S.$12 billion contingent swap facility, of which the United States would contribute up to half, Mexico "would be able to draw until September 30 for a period of 90 days [and] all drawings would have to be repaid by December 30."[4] Mexico did not make any drawings from either facility. This episode reveals that at least up until August 1994 the industrialized nations were implicitly endorsing Mexico's exchange rate policy (and economic policy more broadly).

The Unexpected Financial Debacle

The increase in the potential commitment of financial resources for Mexico was accompanied by a closer scrutiny of Mexico's economy on the part of the U.S. Treasury and the Federal Reserve. The release of a number of previously classified documents reveals that—especially during 1994—U.S. financial authorities were monitoring economic events in Mexico rather closely, with a particular concern for the exchange rate.[5] In both the U.S. Treasury and the Federal Reserve the predominant view was that the peso was overvalued, but there was no consensus on the extent of the overvaluation. Moreover, the recommended course of action was not a sudden change but a gradual one, undertaken as "part of a concerted policy rather than an emergency response to a crisis."[6]

U.S. government concern with Mexico's decision to stick to the existing exchange rate policy deepened after Mexico's August 1994 presidential elections, when capital inflows failed to materialize despite the peaceful PRI victory. The Mexican government tried to inject confidence in the markets by announcing a renewal of the Pact in September, when the exchange rate policy was ratified. To add to the credibility of this agreement, President-elect Zedillo endorsed it explicitly. U.S. financial authorities, however, remained skeptical. Larry Summers, then undersecretary for international affairs at the U.S. Treasury, commented:

The Mexican Government surprised the financial markets with the announcement of a new 'Pact' with business and labor on Saturday. Most significant for us, the agreement maintains the current pace of depreciation of the floor of the exchange rate band at four percent per year. . . . The Mexican announcement presents us with two issues. The first is the substantive question of whether they made the right decision on the exchange rates. The view of many credible independent analysts is that the peso is still significantly overvalued. The current account deficit is very high at 7 percent GNP.[7]

As the uncertainty of Mexico's economy and the sustainability of the exchange rate increased, the U.S. government became very concerned that Mexico would make a request to draw on the contingent commitment agreed under NAFA to support what was viewed as an unsustainable policy. In light of circumstances, high-level officials at Treasury recommended discouraging the consideration of such a request.[8] In a memorandum of October 1994 addressed to the Federal Reserve's chairman, Alan Greenspan, in anticipation of a meeting with Mexican officials, Charles Siegman argued:

You may want to indicate that while we understand the reasons why Mexican officials prefer operating with a relatively fixed exchange rate (against the U.S. dollar), there is some concern about the risks and costs of trying to defend an unsustainable exchange rate. It could be costly in terms of Mexico achieving its broader economic growth objectives, could be disturbing for Mexican financial markets, and could be disruptive to U.S. financial and trade relations with Mexico. Mexican officials should be aware that they should not count on the United States for financial support via the Federal Reserve and Treasury lines to sustain an inappropriate exchange rate. The swap lines are intended to deal with what are viewed as transitory market disturbances, not to buttress an unsustainable exchange rate regime.[9]

The account in the available documents leaves one with the impression that officials at the U.S. Treasury and the Federal Reserve were observing Mexican markets and policy moves closely and that they disagreed with the Mexican authorities' decision to stick to the exchange rate policy in the aftermath of the presidential elections. However, the documents also reveal that the United States was not certain about whether Mexico would be forced to devalue or, more important, aware of the potentially devastating effects that a surprise devaluation would have on market confidence.[10] Remarkably there seems to have been no discussion of the risks entailed by first the accelerating conversion of peso-denominated securities (CETES) into the dollar-denominated Tesobonos; second the fact that a large portion of the latter were in the hands of foreign investors; and third the tendency of the ratio of international reserves to Tesobonos to fall at an increasing pace. Apparently, these issues escaped the scrutiny of the IMF and the World Bank as well. This is most remarkable because the outstanding Tesobonos in the hands of foreigners became one of the fundamental causes of the financial debacle. Like their counterparts in the IMF and the World Bank, U.S. authorities were not really prepared for a worst case scenario.

Although they knew that the peso was under considerable pressure and had discussed a wide range of policy alternatives with the Mexicans at various points in the past, U.S. authorities were not warned about the Mexican government's decision to change the exchange rate policy when it finally happened. In a U.S. Treasury memo sent on December 19, the day before the announced change in the exchange rate band, a U.S. official expressed his concern at the news received from Mexico that the peso was under pressure and worried about the possibility that the "Mexicans might well make a decision to 'withdraw from the market' before or right after Christmas without consulting us."[11]

The fears candidly expressed by the cited U.S. official were well founded. On the same evening that the memo was written, the Mexican government convened an emergency meeting of the Pact and the following day, December 20, Finance Secretary Jaime Serra announced that the ceiling of the band within which the dollar was allowed to fluctuate would be raised by 15 percent. Time had run out for the Mexican government and the U.S. Treasury: the change in exchange rate policy occurred when reserves were too low, with no leeway to prepare an economic plan and U.S. financial support to cushion the impact of a devaluation. Prevention had not really worked, so the next step was damage control.

Although officials at the U.S. Treasury and Federal Reserve sensed that the change in the exchange rate policy had not been well received by the markets, neither the Mexican nor the U.S. government anticipated the scale of the shattering of financial markets that followed.[12]

It did not take long to reveal that the perceptions of Mexican and U.S. officials on the potential impact of the December 20 announcement to change the ceiling of the exchange rate band were wrong. On the day after the devaluation, reserves fell by close to U.S.$5 billion. On December 22 the Mexican authorities had no alternative but to allow their exchange rate to float. Ever since, Mexico has had a floating exchange regime, with some intervention introduced subsequently.[13]

As of December 21, the U.S. Treasury became intensely involved. In a memo prepared for incoming Secretary Rubin, Larry Summers mentions that outgoing Secretary Bentsen had authorized the activation of the swap line, that the Treasury was advising Mexicans on how to respond to the circumstances, that the New York Federal Reserve was arranging a meeting of Secretary Serra with major financial institutions for the morning of December 22, and that Summers would try to ensure favorable press coverage.[14] The swap line with Canada was also activated.

However, none of the above actions calmed the markets. Secretary Serra was not well received during the meeting in New York, and a few days later he resigned. On December 28, Serra was replaced by Guillermo Ortiz as secretary of finance.[15] Two days earlier the peso reached its 1994 low of 5.7 new pesos to the dollar, and the government had to cancel the auction of Tesobonos because there would not be any buyers at reasonable interest rates. On the same day, the Mexican government announced that it was preparing a new economic plan that would be presented on January 2, 1995.

Clearly neither the Mexican authorities, nor the U.S. government, nor the IMF and other financial institutions expected what happened, that is, foreign investors, particularly holders of Tesobonos, were not willing to roll over the government securities they held. They wanted to cash them and convert them into dollars as soon as they became due. Since Mexico's reserves plus the swap lines were considerably lower than the amounts coming due in 1995, the specter of nonconvertibility began to reach Wall Street.

The absence of a clear and well-defined economic plan at the time that the peso was first devalued added to the uncertainty. But, as has become more evident in retrospect, the problem of lack of credibility on the part of market agents was not solely associated with the hesitancies of the Mexican authorities. Had there not been the U.S.$17 billion of Tesobonos in the hands of foreigners (close to U.S.$10 billion coming due in January alone), U.S.$18 billion of foreign currency liabilities of local commercial banks all falling due in 1995, and so on, there probably would not have been a financial debacle following the devaluation.

The Rescue Package Is Increased

The realization that the source of the instability was the Mexican debt profile—and, more important, the response to this realization—took a few days. At first U.S. and Mexican authorities realized that the financial rescue provisions made under NAFA would be insufficient. This prompted the arrangement of a U.S.$18 billion package announced on January 2, 1995. The package was composed of an expansion of the U.S. swap facility set up under NAFA from U.S.$6 billion to U.S.$9 billion; U.S.$5 billion from other governments through the Bank of International Settlements; C$1.5 billion (then about U.S.$1.1 billion) from Canada, which also expanded its contribution beyond the commitments under NAFA; and a potential commitment of U.S.$3 billion from international banks.[16]

The presumption at the time of the announcement was that U.S.$18 billion would calm market agents since it covered the outstanding Tesobonos held by foreigners coming due in 1995. In the previous chapter, it was described how derivatives (such as Tesobono swaps) in combination with rumors that Mexican authorities might impose capital controls were contributing to the peso's weakening. When the U.S.$18 billion package was announced, the process of a self-fulfilling crisis was already set in motion. Now not just the Tesobono holders feared capital controls or a forced restructuring. Panic was quickly spreading to other holders of Mexican securities. The U.S.$18 billion clearly could not take care of the certificate of deposits by foreigners in Mexican banks and other short-term obligations coming due in 1995. It was assumed, or hoped, that a large portion of them would be rolled over. This assumption was not shared by Mexico's creditors, though, and the pressure on the peso continued unabated. Through simple arithmetic calculations investors estimated that payments coming due in 1995 (of about U.S.$50 billion, assuming that most of the short-term public and private debt—except interbank loans—would not be rolled over) were far greater than the estimated resources available: international reserves in the Bank of Mexico were about U.S.$6 billion and the first international rescue package was equal to U.S.$18 billion. The rescue package plus the international reserves would barely cover half of Mexico's financial obligations for 1995 of at least U.S.$50 billion.[17]

By the end of the first week of January, it became clear to Mexican Secretary of Finance Guillermo Ortiz that the problem was much more difficult than anticipated. The news on January 6 that some Mexican banks were unable to renew the certificate of deposits held by foreigners triggered another wave of flight from the peso. It became clear that there would be great difficulties in rolling over any short-term government debt coming due in the first part of 1995. At this time the Mexican authorities began to discuss the terms of an agreement with the IMF and explore other alternatives of support with the U.S. Treasury.

The sentiment of the markets is well reflected in an anecdote told by a high level IMF official who recounts that a fund manager stared at him with perplexity when told that the Mexicans had committed themselves to a balanced budget for 1995. The fund manager's reply was a daunting question: had the Mexicans included all the payments of the Tesobonos coming due in 1995 in the expense side of the budget?

The U.S.$40 Billion in Loan Guarantees

On January 9, 1995, the Mexican government drew U.S.$500 million from the U.S. swap line and C$83 million from the Canadian one. The Bank of Mexico used these resources to intervene in the exchange rate market to stop the run on the peso. However, the peso continued to slide. On January 10 the dollar closed at 5.75 pesos, and the stock market in Mexico and other places in the world were falling sharply.[18] That other markets reacted in "sympathy" with Mexico's is reflected by the evolution of the stripped yields of Brady par bonds for Argentina, Brazil, Bulgaria, Morocco, Nigeria, Poland, and the Philippines.[19]

Edwin Truman, director of the Division of International Finance of the board of governors of the U.S. Federal Reserves, notes:

> When the crisis erupted, investors panicked, not only investors in the Mexican stock market and in Mexico debt instruments but also investors in similar instruments issued by borrowers in other countries, especially countries in the same part of the world or perceived to be in similar circumstances. These contagion sales of assets were induced by at least two types of forces. First, as perceived risks rose and expected returns fell,

individual investors were induced to disinvest. Second, institutional holders such as mutual funds faced with actual or threatened redemptions were led to liquify their holdings not only of Mexican paper but also of the paper of other countries especially if they could do so while limiting their capital losses.[20]

Whether this was the prelude to a financial debacle engulfing the whole of the developing world can certainly not be proved. Nevertheless, the indications that such a scenario was possible were there. This ominous possibility and the certainty that Mexico was on the verge of financial collapse prompted President Clinton to announce on January 11 that "the United States is committed to doing what we can to help Mexico through what I believe is and should be a short-term crisis."[21] The impact of Clinton's pronouncement let itself be felt almost instantaneously in Mexico's financial markets: the Mexican stock market's index, for example, reversed its downward trend literally a minute after Clinton's speech.

On the following evening, Clinton announced his proposal to request authorization from the U.S. Congress to extend U.S.$40 billion to Mexico in loan guarantees, a package modeled on the U.S.$10 billion in loan guarantees provided to Israel in 1992.[22] The president secured the support of the congressional leaders from both parties and at least initially a relatively speedy and affirmative vote seemed feasible. This assumption turned out to be incorrect. Members of Congress from both parties felt very uncomfortable—to say the least—approving a sizable rescue package for Mexico at the same time that they advocated austerity measures in the United States. Moreover, many of the new Republican members were isolationists and unsympathetic to NAFTA and Mexico. The conditions to be requested from Mexico began to mount, and they eventually covered the entire range of bilateral issues: migration, relations with Cuba, extradition practices, narcotics trafficking, and so on. Eventually it became clear that congressional approval of a bill that would also be acceptable to the Mexican government, at least in the foreseeable future, could not be secured.[23]

The IMF Comes on Board

It may be surprising that the "NAFA plus" assistance package of U.S.$18 billion announced in early January did not involve the IMF. Officials from the IMF did go to Mexico at the end of December.

However, the Mexican authorities were reluctant to negotiate an agreement with the IMF because they thought it would send a signal of weakness. It was not that Mexican authorities disagreed fundamentally with the IMF prescriptions as had been the case of Lopez-Portillo in 1982. The main problem was the message: countries that went to the IMF had misbehaved. In the case of Mexico in early 1995 the necessary message, at least as perceived by Mexican officials, was that the Mexican government had been and would continue to be reliable. The confidence crisis, it was thought, was based on misperceptions that an agreement with the IMF could only strengthen. The resistance probably arose from the prevailing impression—in retrospect, a wrong one—that the market's reaction was temporary and the situation would soon return to normalcy: that is, that short-term obligations coming due in 1995 would be rolled over.[24]

The resistance to go to the IMF vanished when the Mexican authorities realized that the panic of the markets was in crescendo. In particular, they became convinced that an agreement was necessary when the incidents of the nonrenewal of certificates of deposits held in a Mexican bank occurred at the end of the first week of January 1995. Around that time, and shortly after the announcement of the Mexican economic plan, Michel Camdessus, the IMF's managing director, said that the Fund would begin negotiations with Mexican authorities. The announcement of an impending agreement with the IMF, however, did not do much in terms of restoring confidence in the markets.

On January 26, 1995, the IMF announced that Mexico had requested an eighteen-month standby arrangement for U.S.$7.8 billion (equivalent to 300 percent of Mexico's quota). This agreement was prepared, and the quantitative targets were set, under the assumption that the U.S.$40 billion in U.S. loan guarantees would be approved. In essence, the agreement included the same quantitative targets as the Mexican economic plan announced on January 2 in terms of fiscal cutbacks, but the Mexican government agreed to further tightening in the future if the evolution of the exchange rate and current account deficit made it necessary.[25]

The problem with the IMF agreement was that market agents were not convinced—and correctly so—that the targets in the economic program of early January were credible.[26] By the end of January the assumption of an exchange rate of 4.5 new pesos to the dollar and a predicted 19 percent yearly inflation for 1995 seemed unrealistic. The endorsement of those targets at the time probably caused more harm to IMF's credibility than helped Mexico's.

The February 1995 Rescue Package

As already mentioned, toward the end of January it became increasingly evident that the U.S. loan guarantee package was not supported in Congress and that if it were submitted to a vote any time soon, it would face a defeat. The consequence was another round of capital flight. The peso began its seemingly uncontrollable downward slide once again. This led to the two most dramatic decisions of this episode. On January 31, 1995, President Clinton announced that his administration would use executive authority to provide Mexico with up to U.S.$20 billion in loans and loan guarantees through the Exchange Stabilization Fund (ESF), the largest ever use of this facility and more than three times the size of the financial assistance to Mexico in mid-1982 if measured in real terms. At the same time, Michel Camdessus announced that the IMF would increase the eighteen-month standby arrangement to U.S.$17.8 billion, the largest ever extended by the IMF in terms of its value and as a percentage of the country's quota.[27]

In addition to the unprecedented contributions of the U.S. government and the IMF, the package would include U.S.$10 billion from other industrialized nations through the Bank of International Settlements (BIS); U.S.$1 billion from Canada; U.S.$1 billion in currency swaps from Argentina, Brazil, Chile, and Colombia, which did not materialize; and, U.S.$3 billion in new loans from commercial banks, which also did not materialize. The total came close to U.S.$53 billion. However, only the U.S.$20 billion from the United States, the U.S.$17.8 billion from the IMF, and the U.S.$1 billion from Canada became available, plus loans from the World Bank and the InterAmerican Development Bank for U.S.$3 billion in total (table 7-1). Although the BIS loan became available on paper, it was not very helpful because of the stringent restrictions on its use. In reality, other industrialized nations viewed Mexico's financial troubles as a U.S. problem and hence were not eager to help. It appears that some were even annoyed because they were asked to help.

Of the total rescue package, the U.S.$7.8 billion from the IMF standby became immediately available. One limitation of the rest of

TABLE 7-1. *Financial Rescue Package, 1995*

Item[a]	U.S.$ billions (unless otherwise noted)
Total	48.8[b]
United States	20.0[c]
Disbursements	13.5[c]
Payments by Mexico as of February 1996	3.0[d]
Payments by Mexico as of August 1996	10.0[d]
Payments by Mexico as of January 1997	13.5[e]
Outstanding Debt as of January 1997	None
International Monetary Fund	17.8[f]
Disbursements	13.0[f]
Outstanding debt as of June 1997	9.0[g]
Canada	1.0[h]
Disbursements	350 million
Outstanding debt as of February 1996	None
Bank of International Settlements	10.0[i]
Disbursements	None

a. Rescue package announced on January 31, 1995. It does not include the initial contributions that failed to materialize.

b. General Accounting Office, "Mexico's Financial Crisis: Origins, Awareness, Assistance, and Initial Efforts to Recover," GAO/GGD-96-56 (Washington, 1996), p. 109.

c. Exchange Stabilization Fund; maximum amount potentially available. Funds could be used in short-term currency swaps, medium-term loans, and security guarantees. GAO, "Mexico's Financial Crisis," p. 109.

d. The U.S.$3 billion paid by February 1996 consisted of short-term currency swaps. The remaining U.S.$10.5 billion, in medium-term swaps, was originally due between June 1997 and June 2000. Department of Treasury, *Semi-Annual Report to Congress by the Secretary of the Treasury on Behalf of the President, Pursuant to the Mexican Debt Disclosure Act of 1995* (December 1996), p. 1, and annex, "Amortization Schedule."

e. David Wessel and Craig Torres, "Mexico Will Close Out Its Debt to U.S." *Wall Street Journal*, January 16, 1997, p. A10.

f. An eighteen-month standby agreement announced on February 1, 1995. Of the total, U.S.$7.8 billion were available immediately, to be paid over five years, with three and one-quarter years of grace period. GAO, "Mexico's Financial Crisis: Origins," p. 110, 127.

g. Leslie Crawford, "Mexico to Repay Dollars 6 Bn Notes," *Financial Times*, June 18, 1997, p. 6.

h. Short-term swaps. GAO, "Mexico's Financial Crisis," p. 110, and Dow Jones, News/Retrieval, "Canada Reports Mexican Repayment of Support," March 6, 1997.

i. Terms were too short-term. Not drawn by Mexico. GAO, "Mexico's Financial Crisis," p. 110.

the funds was that they would not be available all at once but in tranches, and that their availability would depend on Mexico's strict compliance with a set of economic conditions and targets. The availability of the ESF loans would also be affected by domestic political factors in the United States. Because of the vehemence of the critics of the U.S. rescue package in Congress, the administration became increasingly more cautious in extending the ESF loans to Mexico, particularly after the objective of solving Mexico's short-term liquidity problem was on the whole achieved.[28]

The announcement of the package stopped the panic selling but did not reestablish lasting confidence, partly because the rescue package did not make all the funds immediately available. But the lack of confidence also originated in the uncertainty surrounding the economic and political situation in Mexico.[29] Surprisingly, IMF endorsement of the economic plan did not restore the confidence of the markets either. There were many questions about whether the targets of the economic program announced at the beginning of January were realistic. It was soon obvious that they were not; in particular, the exchange rate assumed in the plan of 4.5 pesos to the dollar was—short of some extraordinary event—beyond reach.

The Terms of the U.S. Assistance

The terms of the ESF-based U.S.$20 billion U.S. package were formalized in the U.S.-Mexico Framework Agreement for Mexican Economic Stabilization, signed on February 21, 1995, which governs the U.S. loan and loan guarantees package for Mexico. The terms specify that disbursements can take place for one year and can be renewed once for six months.[30] As part of this agreement and since the use of ESF money required an assured source of repayment, the Mexican government agreed to deposit the proceeds of oil export sales by PEMEX and the two export sales subsidiaries in a pass-through special account at the Federal Reserve Bank of New York (Oil Proceeds Facility Agreement, that is, annex A of the 1995 framework agreement).[31] While the package was being negotiated, Mexico drew another short-term swap from ESF, this time for U.S.$1 billion.[32]

The 1995 framework agreement also specifies that Mexico is responsible for the payment of all costs, fees, and expenses; reporting, notification, and consultation requirements; and, in the case of medium-term swaps, Mexico will pay interest charges that are sufficient to cover U.S. government credit risk cost for Mexico. Most important, under the agreement, the Mexican government committed itself to comply with the IMF program and additional requirements set by the U.S. Treasury in its Economic Policy Memorandum (annex C of the framework agreement). The latter essentially deepens the policy commitments undertaken by Mexico in the IMF accord. In particular, the Mexican government agreed not to intervene in the foreign exchange market using international reserves but to stabilize the peso through fiscal and monetary policy. In addition, the Mexican government agreed to regularly disclose information on a number of variables and policy decisions in a systematic and transparent way and proceed with structural reforms.

The announcement of the new rescue package at the end of January halted the peso's nosedive. However, the markets remained jittery until after the Mexican government announced a new economic program with more realistic and credible targets on March 9, 1995, and the first drawing on the ESF funds took place.[33]

One important element that received relatively little public attention is the economic policy conditions that the U.S. financial authorities attached to the rescue package. In particular, U.S. Treasury officials were convinced that to stabilize the peso, Mexican authorities would have to raise domestic interest rates to the point of generating positive returns even in the very short run. The Mexican government, in contrast, favored the stabilization route that had been pursued in 1983, that is, a larger depreciation of the peso and lower real domestic interest rates. The Mexicans argued that high interest rates would assess a devastating blow to an already battered banking system. U.S. authorities were concerned that further depreciation of the peso would continue to erode market confidence, cause further runs on the peso, and possibly lead to hyperinflation. For the U.S. financial authorities, the worst nightmare was one in which ESF loans to Mexico would vanish in the form of capital flight at the same time that the peso would continue on its downward slide. Ultimately, Treasury's view prevailed, but the discussion was far from smooth.[34]

In the aftermath, the U.S. Treasury has been engaging in activities of monitoring and surveillance, which in the past would have been the sole responsibility of the IMF. Since February 1995, for example, the U.S. Treasury created a Mexico Task Force whose purpose has been to monitor Mexico's economy and economic policymaking. This should come as no surprise. In 1982 the United States had lent the equivalent of U.S.$5.7 billion in 1995 dollars and the maturity of the loans was one year. In 1995 U.S. financial assistance was for up to U.S.$20 billion, and of the U.S.$13.5 billion actually disbursed, U.S.$10.5 billion were in medium-term swaps coming due between June 1997 and June 2000.[35] Given the size and the maturities of the current lending program, it is understandable that the United States would want to monitor economic events in Mexico much more closely than in earlier times.

Was the Financial Assistance Package Successful?

If renewed access to capital markets is taken as a measure of success, the financial rescue package was a coup. As early as April 1995, a Mexican development bank was able to borrow in the international market and, between mid-1995 and early 1996, Mexico was able to raise about U.S.$8 billion, with the terms and maturities of the loans improving over the period.[36] Moreover, although there have been a few additional incidents of market volatility, the peso has achieved an acceptable degree of stability, particularly since November 1995.[37] In fact, the rescue package was so successful in restoring market confidence that Mexico was able to pay back all of the U.S.$13.5 billion in loans from the United States by the end of January 1997, though the original schedule called for payment between June 1997 and June 2000.[38]

The package was also successful in the sense that the possibility of the crisis spreading to other countries in the region and other regions as well was brought to a halt.[39] In contrast to 1982, when the debt crisis engulfed much of the developing world, the liquidity and confidence crisis was really limited to two countries: Mexico and Argentina.[40]

The record is less pristine in terms of Mexico's economic performance during 1995. The almost U.S.$50 billion rescue package was not able to spare Mexico from a major recession, the worst since the Great Depression, with peak levels of unemployment and drastic falls in real wages (see chapter 8). However, the economy experienced a quick turnaround, much quicker than during the previous crisis. The recovery of output growth started in the third quarter of 1995 and GDP increased by 5.2 percent during 1996 and 7.0 percent during 1997. During the second quarter of 1997, GDP grew at a recordbreaking

8.6 percent.[41] The speed of the recovery may be a result of the trade reforms introduced a decade earlier. The now more open economy was ready for an export-led push.

Why Was the Response So Swift in 1995 Compared with 1982?

The previous account identifies one fundamental difference between the financial assistance package of 1982—the previous debt crisis—and the one in 1995. Although the 1982 crisis was followed by a decade of "living in exile" from the international capital markets, the 1995 response was successful in quickly restoring market access. The difference in the outcomes must be related to the size of the financial package and its medium-term quality. In 1995 the financial rescue package was designed to be large enough to solve Mexico's liquidity crisis; in 1982, the package was large enough to avoid a Mexican default, but for the next six years the country had to go from one rescheduling exercise to another, with the uncertainty of whether Mexico would be able to meet its obligations always looming on the horizon. The 1995 package's success must also be attributed to two other factors. First, despite the external disequilibrium in the years leading up to the crisis, the Mexican economy was in far better shape than in 1982 in its fiscal stance, the diversification of its export base, and the ability of its productive structure to respond to changes in terms of trade. Second, the external environment was much more adverse in 1982 than in 1995, with world interest rates at record high levels and oil prices falling at the same time oil exports represented 80 percent of Mexico's total exports.

To a large extent, the differences in the characteristics of the package stem from the differences in the U.S. response. In 1982 the U.S. Treasury organized a U.S.$2 billion short-term loan only when Mexico's reserves were practically down to zero despite repeated warnings from the Mexican finance ministry. In addition, in the 1982 negotiations the U.S. Treasury put the Mexican government on the spot by trying to extract a concessional price for oil sales and large fees, showing not only political insensitivity but a lack of awarenes of how much it was in the U.S. interest to avoid a Mexican default. Although the U.S. Federal Reserve was much more sympathetic to Mexico and well aware of the systemic dangers of a Mexican default, the chosen strategy did not solve the more fundamental problem of Mexico's overindebtedness.

Why was the U.S. response different in 1995? First, since de la Madrid's presidency and especially under President Salinas, the Mexican government had won the confidence and the praise of the U.S. government and the international community at large for its committment to price stability and market-oriented reforms. Mexico was constantly featured as a model reformer before other countries. Reform advocates did not want to leave the impression that despite all the effort and sacrifices, reforming countries would remain unrewarded, opening the way for the return of a populist backlash.

The difference in the response is also explained by the differences in the causes and nature of the crises. Policy errors notwithstanding, the severity of the markets' reaction that followed the December 1994 devaluation was totally disproportionate. Bad luck and market hysteria played a fundamental role in Mexico's crisis this time. This view was shared by key members of the U.S. cabinet and high levels of the multilateral institutions.

The memories of the "lost decade" following Mexico's suspension of payments in 1982 was too fresh in the key policymakers' minds. The fear of a contagion to other so-called emerging markets around the globe raised the specter of another crisis of systemic proportions, something that policymakers in the United States and multilateral institutions were not ready to risk.

The U.S. response was couched by other factors as well. The Clinton administration acted on the belief that the government can and should play an active role to correct failures of the markets; this view contrasted with the "laissez faire" ideology prevailing during the Reagan years. Moreover, a financial collapse in Mexico could result in increasing tensions between the two nations, particularly because of the effects of a protracted economic crisis on migration flows from Mexico. Furthermore, the Clinton administration had invested an important share of political capital in Mexico with its strong endorsement of NAFTA. A collapse of the Mexican peso would haunt President Clinton throughout his reelection campaign and turn the passage of NAFTA into a political embarrassment. Finally, the climate of goodwill that followed the negotiation of NAFTA signaled how much the bilateral relationship had evolved from one characterized by distrust and resentment to a more constructive and pragmatic relationship. The ties that had been forged among policymakers from both countries surely helped. The U.S. government could treat Mexico as a

TABLE 7-2. *Supply and Demand, 1989–96*
Growth rates in percent

Item	1989	1990	1991
Output and income			
Gross domestic product[a]			
1980 base year	3.3	4.5	3.6
1993 base year	4.2	5.1	4.2
Gross domestic product per capita[a,b]			
1980 base year	1.2	2.4	1.6
1993 base year	2.1	3.0	2.2
Consumption (1993 base year)[c]			
Private	7.3	6.4	4.7
Public	2.2	3.3	5.4
Investment (1993 base year)[d]			
Private	5.3	13.8	14.5
Public	7.1	11.2	0.6
Imports[e]			
1980 base year	21.3	19.7	16.8
1993 base year	18.0	19.7	15.2
Consumer (1993 base year)[f]	75.8	38.9	29.5
Intermediate (1993 base year)[f]	17.3	15.2	18.3
Capital goods (1993 base year)[f]	13.1	41.6	25.4
Exports[g]			
1980 base year	2.3	3.6	4.6
1993 base year	5.7	5.3	5.1
Maquila exports (1993 base year)[h]	9.5	10.3	5.3
Non-Oil exports (1993 base year)[i]	3.1	6.6	7.5
Manufacturing exports (1993 base year)[j]	3.1	7.0	7.4

Sources: Information from the Banco de México website was downloaded on July 23, 1997; for 1996 and 1997 figures, downloaded May 20, 1998. The 1997 figures are preliminary. The INEGI website was downloaded on July 27, 1997.

n.a. Not available.

a. For the 1980 base-year series, Banco de México, *The Mexican Economy 1996* (Mexico, 1996), table 7, p. 266. The 1995 figure is preliminary. For 1993 base year series, for 1989 to 1995, Instituto Nacional de Estadística Geografía e Informática (INEGI) *Sistema de cuentas nacionales de México: Cuentas de bienes y servicios: 1988–1995.* (Aguascalientes, 1996), tomo II, p. 67, cuadro 144, and is measured in 1993 pesos. For 1996 to 1997, Banco de México website, *Informe Anual 1997*, cuadro 2 (http://banxico.org.mx/public_html/inveco/infors.html).

b. Calculated using data from Consejo Nacional de Población (CONAPO) de México.

TABLE 7-2. *(continued)*

1992	1993	1994	1995	1996	1997	Average growth 1989–94
2.8	0.6	3.5	–6.9	n.a.	n.a.	3.0
3.6	2.0	4.5	–6.2	5.2	7.0	3.9
0.9	–1.3	1.7	–8.6	n.a.	n.a.	1.1
1.7	0.1	2.6	–7.8	3.3	n.a.	1.9
4.7	1.5	4.6	–9.5	2.2	6.3	4.8
1.9	2.4	2.9	–1.3	–0.7	1.8	3.0
15.0	–3.3	9.8	–31.2	15.3	25.7	9.0
–3.3	0.4	2.9	–19.8	20.3	4.3	3.0
20.9	–1.3	12.9	–27.5	n.a.	n.a.	14.8
19.6	1.9	20.5	–12.8	22.8	22.0	15.6
32.6	–1.1	27.0	–48.1	22.4	n.a.	31.9
19.6	1.4	18.2	–18.1	34.6	n.a.	14.8
31.8	–6.4	22.9	–36.5	26.3	n.a.	20.4
1.7	3.7	7.3	28.4	n.a.	n.a.	3.9
5.0	8.1	17.4	33.0	18.2	13.0	7.7
15.0	12.2	28.2	30.0	26.3	n.a.	13.2
1.9	10.3	18.1	47.5	16.7	n.a.	7.8
4.3	9.9	20.2	48.5	19.7	n.a.	8.5

c. For 1989 to 1995, Banco de México website, *The Mexican Economy 1997*, table 8. (http://banxico.org.mx/public_html/doyai/mexecon97/t08.html). For 1996 to 1997, Banco de México website, *Informe Anual 1997*, cuadro 2 (http://banxico.org.mx/public_html/inveco/infors.html).

d. For 1989 to 1995, Banco de México website, *The Mexican Economy 1997*, table 8. (http://banxico.org.mx/public_html/doyai/mexecon97/t08.html). For 1996 to 1997, Banco de México website, *Informe Anual 1997*, cuadro 2 (http://banxico.org.mx/public_html/inveco/infors.html).

e. For the 1980 base-year series, Instituto Nacional de Estadística Geografía e Informática (INEGI) website, *Importacion de Bienes y Servicios, a precios de 1980* (http://dgcnesyp.inegi.gob.mx/bdine/a11/a110005.htm). The 1995 figure is preliminary. For the 1993 base-year series, from 1989–95, INEGI, *Sistema de cuentas nacionales de*

TABLE 7-2. *(notes continued)*

México, (Aguascalientes, 1996), tomo II, p. 32, cuadro 111. For 1996 to 1997, Banco de México website, *Informe Anual 1997*, cuadro 2 (http://banxico.org.mx/public_html/inveco/infors.html). In 1992, the Bank of Mexico changed its methodology for calculating the current account so that merchandise transactions now include the gross from all temporary imports. The second series reflects this new methodology. Thus, these two series are not directly comparable.

 f. For 1989 to 1995, INEGI, *Sistema de cuentas nacionales de México*, (Aguascalientes, 1996), tomo II, p. 35, cuadro 114. The 1996 data are from Grupo de Economistas y Asociados (Mexico City) based on INEGI data. These series are measured in 1993 base-year pesos. After 1994, data are preliminary.

 g. For the 1980 base-year series, INEGI website, *Exportación de Bienes y Servicios, a precios de 1980.* (http://bdine/a11/a110008.htm). The 1995 figure is preliminary. For the 1993 base-year series, 1989–95, INEGI, *Sistema de cuentas nacionales de México*, tomo II, p. 64, cuadro 143 (Aguascalientes, 1996). For 1995 to 1997, Banco de México website, *Informe Anual 1997*, cuadro 2. (http://banxico.org.mx/public_html/inveco/ infors.html). In 1992, the Bank of Mexico changed its methodology for calculating the current account so that merchandise transactions now include the gross from all temporary imports. The second series reflects this new methodology.

 h. For 1989 to 1995, INEGI, *Sistema de cuentas nacionales de México*, (Aguascalientes, 1996), tomo II, p. 64, cuadro 143. The 1996 data are from Grupo de Economistas y Asociados (Mexico City) based on INEGI data. After 1994, the data are preliminary.

 i. For 1989 to 1995, INEGI, *Sistema de cuentas nacionales de México*, (Aguascalientes, 1996), tomo II, p. 64, cuadro 143. The 1996 data are from Grupo de Economistas y Asociados (Mexico City) based on INEGI data.

 j. For 1989 to 1995, INEGI, *Sistema de cuentas nacionales de México*, (Aguascalientes, 1996), tomo II, p. 64, cuadro 143. The 1996 data are from Grupo de Economistas y Asociados (Mexico City) based on INEGI data.

partner and an ally because it knew where Mexico's government stood in most areas of the bilateral agenda.

The Mexican Recession and Economic Recovery

During 1995 Mexican output fell by more than 6 percent, unemployment doubled to average over 6 percent for the year, and real manufacturing wages contracted by 13.5 percent (tables 7-2 and 7-3). Although without the financial assistance the situation would undoubtedly have been far worse, it is remarkable that a sizable financial support program did not translate into a softer landing of the Mexican economy. Why was the recession so severe?

At the onset of the peso crisis, the government had, essentially, to deal with four main issues: restructuring its short-term debt, reducing the current account deficit to a level that could be financed, restoring an acceptable level of international reserves, and, implementing the restructuring of the financial system and a financial support program for the banking system and its debtors. At the same time, it had to implement a stabilization program to prevent runaway inflation. To achieve these goals required, among other things, some combination of tight fiscal and monetary policy. The tightness of these policies hinged on the availability of capital inflows. The higher the net inflows, the lesser the needed adjustment. However, no one could really predict the way markets would react even with the rescue package in place.

Clearly, the Mexican government, at least up until the end of January, was not pessimistic. This is apparent in the policies imbedded in the economic program announced on January 3, which assumed that the current account deficit would be cut in half to $14 billion in 1995,[42] said the dollar would average 4.5 new pesos in 1995, and proposed a primary surplus for the fiscal accounts of 2.2 percent of GDP—not really different from the surplus recorded in 1994.[43] Moreover, monetary policy was such that the short-run real interest rates were negative.

However, to judge from the evolution of the peso value of the dollar (figure 7-1) and the statements made by Wall Street investors,[44] capital flows would not resume, and capital flight could continue as long as it was not clear how the Mexican government would pay its short-term obligations, in particular, the Tesobonos. Hence the need for the financial rescue package. If investors were sure that Mexico would not be cornered into a default, they would eventually come back (or at least not leave). Even more, the sole assurance that Mexico would have the resources to comply with its short-term payments might have been sufficient to bring about a rollover of the short-term debt by the private markets themselves. This, however, was the more optimistic scenario. It required, at a minimum, a sufficiently large rescue package available immediately or as needed, and a sound economic program to be pursued by the Mexican government. None of these conditions was really fulfilled, and that is one set of reasons why the recession in 1995 was so sharp.

There are other reasons. The rescue package was not as sizable in reality as it seemed on paper. Ultimately, the only loans that were available were the $17.8 billion program of the IMF and the U.S. Treasury's program of up to U.S.$20 billion. So, instead of almost

TABLE 7-3. *Real Wages and Unemployment, 1989–96*
Growth rates for the average of the period, in percent unless otherwise specified

Item	1989	1990	1991
Wages			
Real minimum wage[a]	–6.5	–9.2	–4.4
Real manufacturing wage[b]	9.1	2.8	6.6
Real average remuneration[c]	6.0	1.5	6.2
Real average remuneration			
in manufacturing[d]	8.4	–0.3	3.3
Open unemployment[e]			
Annual	3.0	2.8	2.6
Quarterly			
First	3.2	2.5	2.7
Second	3.0	2.8	2.3
Third	3.3	3.1	2.9
Fourth	2.5	2.6	2.6

Sources: The Banco de México website was downloaded on September 10, 1997, for 1996–97 figures downloaded, May 29, 1998. The INEGI website was downloaded May 20, 1998. The 1997 figures are preliminary.

n.a. Not available

a. Banco de México website, *The Mexican Economy 1997*, table 20. (http://banxico. org.mx/public_html/doyai/mexecon97/t20.html). For the 1997 figure, Grupo de Economistas y Asociados, *GEA Economico*, no. 88 (April 1998), cuadro 4.

b. Ibid.

c. INEGI, *Sistema de cuentas nacionales de México: Cuentas de bienes y servicios 1988–1995* (Aguascalientes, 1996), tomo I, cuadro 89, p. 182.

d. For 1989 to 1993, INEGI, *Sistema de cuentas nacionales de México*, tomo I, cuadro 89, p. 182. For 1994 to 1996, Macro Asesória Económica, *Macro Update* (August 1996), table 9, p. 35, and *Macro Update* (August 1997), table 9, p.35, based on data from INEGI. For 1997, Grupo de Economistas y Asociados, *GEA Económico*, no. 88 (April 1998), cuadro 4."

U.S.$50 billion, the rescue package was—potentially—equal to U.S.$37.8 billion. More important, the Treasury monies were not made available at once. Following a disbursement of U.S.$1 billion under a short-term swap on February 2, 1995, the first substantial disbursement took place as late as March 14, 1995, and for U.S.$3 billion, or less than a sixth of the total.[45]

Although the delay in making the first sizable disbursement was partly because the Mexican government was able to approve the new economic program only on March 9, 1995, the availability of the funds

TABLE 7-3. *(continued)*

1992	1993	1994	1995	1996	1997	Average growth 1989–94
–4.7	–1.5	0.0	–12.3	–8.3	–1.1	–4.4
8.9	7.2	3.7	–13.5	–11.1	n.a.	6.4
7.6	6.9	4.3	–13.2	n.a.	n.a.	5.4
5.3	1.2	4.2	–12.5	–10.9	–0.4	3.6
2.8	3.4	3.7	6.3	5.5	3.8	3.0
2.9	3.5	3.7	5.1	6.2	4.3	3.1
2.8	3.2	3.6	6.3	5.6	3.9	2.9
2.9	3.7	3.9	7.4	5.5	3.7	3.3
2.7	3.3	3.6	6.1	4.7	3.1	2.9

e. Reported figures are those based on the National Survey of Urban Employment, which classifies as employed all persons aged 12 years old or more who worked at least one hour in the week previous to the survey; did some work as an unpaid family or nonfamily worker; were temporarily absent from work owing to illness, leave, and so on; did not work or receive pay but were expected to begin a new job in the upcoming month. For 1989–95 annual figures, Enrique Rafael Davila Capalleja, "Evolution and Reform of the Mexican Labor Market," in Sebastian Edwards and Nora Lustig, eds., Labor Markets in Latin America: Combining Social Protection with Market Flexibility (Brookings, 1997), table 1. For 1996 to 1997 annual figures, Banco de México website, *Informe Anual 1997*, cuadro 7 (http://banxico.org.mx/public_html/inveco/infors.html). Quarterly figures for 1989 to 1995, INEGI website, *Empleo y desempleo* (http://dgcnesyp.inegi.gob.mx/BDINE/I10/I100016.html). For 1996 to 1997, Banco de México website, *Informe Anual 1997*, cuadro 7 (http://banxico.org.mx/public_html/inveco/infors.html).

was surrounded by political uncertainty because of pressure from the U.S. Congress. Prominent members of the U.S. Congress made efforts to block the disbursement of ESF monies and pass legislation to make disbursements subject to congressional approval.[46] The latter did not happen in the end, but the congressional pressure hurt the effectiveness of the package for two reasons.[47] First, it prevented a larger disbursement up front. Obviously, the effectiveness of the package would have been much greater if the United States would have disbursed U.S.$10 billion shortly after the rescue plan was assembled. Second, because of the delay, the United States did not have a chance to estab-

FIGURE 7-1. *Peso Exchange Rate, December 1994 to November 1995*

Peso/dollar

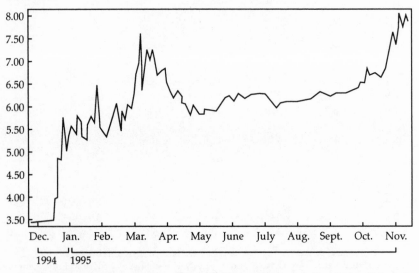

Source: Federal Reserve Board as cited in U.S. General Accounting Office, "Mexico's Financial Crisis: Origins, Awareness, Assistance, and Initial Efforts to Recover," Report GAO/GGD-96-56 (February 1996), p. 138.

lish the credibility that it would come through with its commitments. This made the capital markets feel very uneasy, an uneasiness that lasted until March, when the peso value of the dollar finally began to stabilize around 6.3 pesos (figure 7-1).

The implementation of a more aggressive stabilization program was delayed partly because of differences of opinion between the U.S. Treasury and the Mexican government and partly because it was hard to sell domestically within the framework of the Pact. With the peso value of the dollar already at 5.7 pesos in early February and still rising, and the anti-Mexican sentiment prevailing on Wall Street, it was not at all clear where the funds would come from to finance the projected current account deficit. When the U.S. Treasury put together the rescue package using ESF moneys, it wanted to minimize—understandably—the risks of a failure.

As already mentioned, one hotly debated point between the Treasury and the Mexican government was how tight monetary policy should be. Or, to put it in other words, whether to favor high real interests or a weaker peso. The Treasury endorsed the former very

strongly. In its view, this would be the only way to deter further capital flight and avoid the possibility of another bout of devaluations
with all its ominous consequences. It was feared that if the peso was
not stabilized the situation would get out of control, as happened in
late December and early January, and the rescue package prove pretty
much useless. The U.S. Treasury could not afford to allow the use of
the ESF funds to defend the peso from the market's overreaction. The
funds were there to assure the markets that Mexico would be able to
honor its short-term obligations.

In the end, the Treasury's view prevailed and, starting in February,
nominal interest rates rose and reached a maximum of over 80 percent in March (figures 7-2 and 7-3). Besides tighter monetary policy,
the Mexican government also agreed to increase its primary fiscal surplus to 3.4 percent of GDP, 1.2 percentage points above the initial budget.[48] Part of this tighter budget would result from a very unpopular
increase of the value-added tax rate from 10 to 15 percent effective as
of April 1, 1995.[49] Mexican labor did not support the new program,
and the government decided to implement it outside the Pact. The
program was formally announced on March 9, 1995.[50]

Needless to say, higher interest rates and the devaluation compounded the problems of balance-sheet quality in the Mexican banks.
The government had to implement several financial support programs
for the banking system and its debtors whose cost, as mentioned in
chapter 6, is estimated between 7 percent and 12 percent of GDP,

FIGURE 7-2. *Nominal Interest Rates, 1995*

Percent

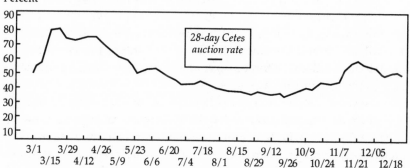

Source: U.S. Department of Treasury, *Semi-Annual Report to Congress by the Secretary of
the Treasury on Behalf of the President, Pursuant to the Mexican Debt Disclosure Act of 1995*
(December 1995).

FIGURE 7-3. *Real Interest Rates, 1995*

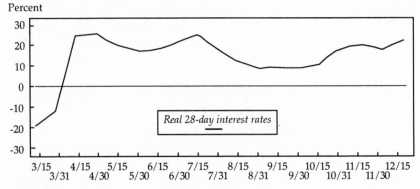

Source: U.S. Department of Treasury, *Semi-Annual Report to Congress by the Secretary of the Treasury on Behalf of the President, Pursuant to the Mexican Debt Disclosure Act of 1995* (December 1995).

depending on the source.[51] For many observers, the weak situation of the banking sector continued to be an area of concern even two and a half years after the peso crisis started.[52]

During 1995 several of the objectives just mentioned were accomplished. First, and thanks primarily to the international rescue package, Mexico was able to reconfigure its domestic debt profile (figure 7-4), and the maturities of external debt were extended (figure 7-5). While amortizing a significant portion of its debt, the government was able to rebuild international reserves from U.S.$6.1 billion to U.S.$14.6 billion.[53] After peaking in April 1995, inflation moderated (figure 7-6). Real interest rates fell between July and November 1995, while the peso/dollar rate remained stable. However, in November markets became uneasy once more, and the peso weakened; the monetary authorities responded immediately by raising interest rates. Although this helped stabilize the foreign exchange market, it was no good news for the recovery or the banking sector.

Nevertheless, a recovery was firmly under way (figure 7-7). The recovery was primarily export led. During 1995 real exports grew by 33 percent while private consumption and private investment contracted by 9.5 and 31.2 percent, respectively (table 7-2). As a result of the devaluation and fall in real incomes, imports fell sharply: by 12.8 percent (table 7-2). The combination of higher exports and lower imports caused the trade account to go from a deficit of 18.5 billion

FIGURE 7-4. *Profile of Domestic Debt*[a]

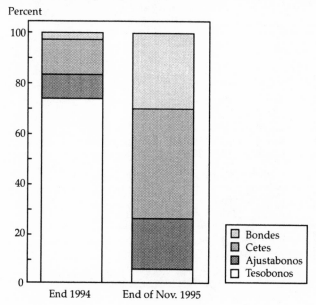

Source: U.S. Department of Treasury, *Semi-Annual Report to Congress by the Secretary of the Treasury on Behalf of the President, Purusant to the Mexican Debt Disclosure Act of 1995* (December 1995).

a. Debt held by public.

dollars (4.4 percent of GDP) in 1994 to a surplus of 7.1 billion dollars (2.5 percent of GDP) in 1995. The large current account deficit of 29.7 billion (7.1 percent of GDP) in 1994, practically vanished: it equaled 1.6 billion (0.6 percent of GDP) in 1995 (tables 6-1, 6-3).

It is important to point out that this export-led recovery is quite different from what was observed in the previous crisis in 1982. Although real export growth was roughly the same in both episodes, this time the momentum came from trade in manufactures, constituting 77 percent of total exports in 1995.[54] In the previous crisis oil exports predominated. Second , although in the previous adjustment the contraction of imports played a very important role (see chapter 2), this time although imports contracted too, there was a decisive export boom. GDP grew by 5.2 percent in 1996 and 7.0 percent in 1997.[55] Private investment began to recover starting in the second quarter of 1996,[56] and it grew by 15.3 percent for all of 1996 and 25.7 percent in

FIGURE 7-5. *Maturities of External Debt* [a]

U.S. $ billions

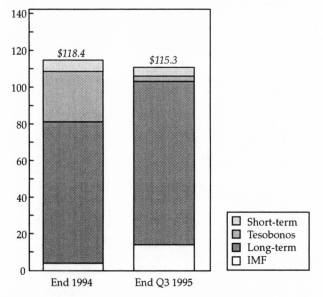

Source: U.S. Department of Treasury, *Semi-Annual Report to Congress by the Secretary of the Treasury on Behalf of the President, Purusant to the Mexican Debt Disclosure Act of 1995* (December 1995).

a. All external public sector debt plus tesobonos, owed by GOM, plus IMF and U.S. liabilities of the Bank of Mexico.

FIGURE 7-6. *Inflation, November 1994–November 1995*

Changes from previous month
Percent

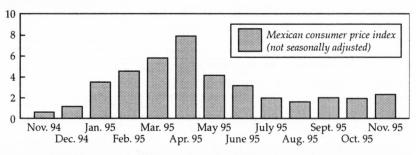

Source: U.S. Department of Treasury, *Semi-Annual Report to Congress by the Secretary of the Treasury on Behalf of the President, Purusant to the Mexican Debt Disclosure Act of 1995* (December 1995).

FIGURE 7-7. *Evolution of GDP, 1991–96*

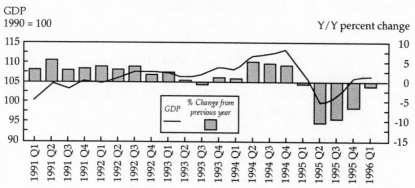

Source: U.S. Department of Treasury, *Monthly Report by the Secretary of the Treasury* (May 1996). Quarterly figures seasonally adjusted by J.P. Morgan.

1997. Private consumption has responded more slowly: it grew at 2.2 percent in 1996 and 6.3 percent in 1997 (table 7-2). Altogether, the swiftness of the Mexican recovery appears to favor the interpretation that the crisis was primarily one of a short-run liquidity crunch rather than deep-seated structural problems.

In the meantime, Mexico has been able to attract sizable portfolio flows from abroad to the tune of U.S.$14.1 billion during 1996. Foreign direct investment has also been strong, underscoring NAFTA's impact on its performance. On average, between 1994 and 1996 foreign direct investment is almost double (close to U.S.$8 billion a year) what it was in the three years before NAFTA's implementation. Moreover, in 1995, when portfolio flows became highly negative, foreign direct investment was 75 percent above the level in the three years before NAFTA.[57] A comparison with the previous crisis may be telling. During 1983, foreign direct investment fell to one-fifth of what it had been in the previous years. Clearly, the business opportunities brought by NAFTA have had a positive impact on foreign direct investment decisions, the peso crisis notwithstanding.

Nevertheless, renewed capital inflows, while a blessing in one respect, have revived concerns around the value of the peso. Although the Bank of Mexico has sterilized part of the inflows (as indicated by the rise in reserves),they have caused a real appreciation of the peso.[58] For example, between January 1996 and August 1997, the peso appreciated 19 percent.[59] As in the past, this makes some investors nervous about the pace of recovery, even in the absence of another crisis. An indication of Mexico's diminished vulnerability, however, was its performance during the shock waves sent by the Asian financial crisis in late 1997. Following a brief moment of instability, the peso emerged from the episode with a relatively small depreciation received by exporters and portfolio investors with relief. Paradoxically, the Asian crisis induced a correction in the exchange rate that many observers were expecting or wishing for.

Chapter Eight

The Unhappy End: Poverty and Inequality

The change in Mexico's economic strategy had ultimately one main objective: to improve the living standards of the majority of the Mexican population. However, more than ten years later, it largely remains an unfulfilled promise. At the same time, the distance between the haves and the have-nots has increased. Why should this be a matter of concern? First, because in Mexico economic inequality and the incidence of poverty—particularly in some areas of the country—have been traditionally high. Second, because frustrated expectations could trigger a backlash, undoing several years of prudent macroeconomic policies and market-oriented reforms. Even if reforms are not rolled back, unfulfilled expectations could obstruct any further reforms. This problem may be especially evident in labor legislation, which still keeps many restrictions that affect labor mobility.

Finally, in the last few years, rural violence has been on the rise, particularly in the southern part of Mexico. Poverty, and the feeling of being left behind by an economic modernization with no or negative payoffs for many inhabitants in the backward areas of Mexico, lies at the heart of these armed conflicts that pose a threat to the country's social cohesion.

The Evolution and the Profile of Poverty and Inequality

In the aftermath of the debt crisis, poverty and inequality increased.[1] Between 1984 and 1989, moderate poverty rose from 28.5 percent to 32.6 percent and extreme poverty from 13.9 percent to 17 percent (table 8-1).[2] Income inequality as measured by the Gini coefficient increased substantially, and the share of income going to the top

10 percent of the population increased from 42.9 percent to 49.5 percent (table 8-2).

What happened since? Between 1989 and 1994, with the incipient economic recovery in the early 1990s, both extreme and moderate poverty fell from 17.1 percent to 15.5 percent, and from 32.6 percent to 31.8 percent, respectively, while income distribution improved (tables 8-1, 8-2).

A differentiated pattern emerges if the households are classified into subcategories according to criteria such as location, occupation, and activity. Rural poverty is between seven and ten times higher than

TABLE 8-1. *Poverty Measurements*
Percent unless otherwise specified

Poverty index[a]	1984	1989	1992	1994
Extreme poverty (U.S.$1 per day)				
Headcount (H)	13.9	17.1	16.1	15.5
Poverty gap (HI)	4.5	6.3	6.1	5.6
FGT (P2)	2.1	3.3	3.1	2.8
Number (millions of persons)	9.9	13.5	13.6	13.8
Moderate poverty (U.S.$2 per day)				
Headcount (H)	28.5	32.6	31.3	31.8
Poverty gap (HI)	12.8	15.6	14.8	14.4
FGT (P2)	7.2	9.3	8.9	8.4
Number (millions of persons)	20.4	25.6	26.3	28.4

Source: Nora Lustig and Miguel Szekely, "La evolucion de la pobreza y la desigualdad en Mexico," prepared for project, The Determinants of Poverty in Latin America, sponsored by the UN Development Program, Inter-American Development Bank, and UN Economic Commission for Latin America and the Caribbean, December 1997. Estimations measured using Income-Expenditure Survey data from INEGI (Instituto Nacional de Estadística, Geografía e Informatica).

a. The headcount measurement is the proportion of individuals living below the specified poverty line divided by the total population. The poverty gap measures the amount of money necessary to raise the income of all poor individuals to the level of the poverty line as a proportion of the poverty line. The FGT (Foster-Greer-Thorbecke) (or P2) index weights individuals by their degree of poverty. For the properties of the various estimates, see Martin Ravallion, "Poverty Comparisons: A Guide to Concepts and Methods," Living Standards Measurement Study, Working Paper 88 (Washington: World Bank, 1992). The poverty lines (extreme, moderate) are expressed in U.S. dollars reflecting purchasing power parity.

TABLE 8-2. *Income Distribution*

	Percentage of total income			
Decile	*1984*	*1989*	*1992*	*1994*
I	0.69	0.68	0.73	0.79
II	1.28	1.36	1.42	1.53
III	1.95	2.08	2.20	2.35
IV	2.99	2.99	3.23	3.31
V	4.53	4.06	4.54	4.52
VI	6.51	5.46	6.19	6.03
VII	8.78	7.35	8.36	8.12
VIII	12.37	10.48	11.30	11.26
IX	18.04	16.02	16.47	16.64
X	42.86	49.53	45.56	45.46
Gini coefficient	58.23	62.05	58.96	58.61

Source: Lustig and Szekely, "La evolucion de la pobreza y la desigualdad en México." The Gini coefficient is an inequality index that increases as the distribution of income becomes more skewed. The data have been corrected for underreporting. Wage and nonwage income for each household is multiplied by an adjustment factor.

urban poverty as shown in table 8-3, which classifies households according to their geographical location and characteristics of the head.[3] Furthermore, although the incidence of urban poverty fell between 1989 and 1994, rural poverty practically did not change. Moreover, poverty increased sharply for rural workers but fell for industrial workers, white-collar workers, workers in domestic services, and street vendors. Consistent with this finding, poverty rose in the agricultural and mining sectors, while it fell in the manufacturing sector, and commerce and services.

Evidence also points to strong regional differentiation between the southern and central regions and the northern part of the country. Table 8-3 highlights these differences. The incidence of poverty is highest in the Southeast (composed of the states of Chiapas, Guerrero, and Oaxaca) followed by the South (composed of Tabasco and Veracruz) and the Central Region (including Hidalgo, Querétaro, Tlaxcala, Mexico, Morelos, and Puebla). Poverty in the Southeast is more than five times higher than in the Northeast and close to forty times higher than in the Federal District. More important, while in some of the regions poverty fell and in others it rose very slightly, between 1989 and 1994 poverty in the South and the Southeast rose.

TABLE 8-3. *Extreme Poverty by Subcategories*

Subgroup	Proportion of poor			
	1984	*1989*	*1992*	*1994*
Location				
Rural	29.4	35.1	35.0	34.4
Urban	4.8	5.9	3.0	1.7
Education				
No education	28.7	34.1	35.3	31.5
Incomplete primary	18.2	23.5	22.5	23.2
Complete primary	2.8	8.6	9.3	8.9
Some secondary	0.3	4.6	3.1	2.3
Some high school	0.0	1.2	0.6	0.6
University or more	0.0	0.4	0.0	1.6
Region				
Northwest	6.4	6.4	6.5	7.7
Northeast	6.6	6.8	4.8	2.8
North	18.5	18.8	14.8	16.1
Central West	16.6	22.4	11.0	13.8
Central	19.8	14.9	16.8	14.4
South	16.7	25.1	19.8	29.0
Southeast	15.6	34.0	47.4	37.2
Southwest	14.4	14.2	14.0	12.9
Mexico City, federal district	0.2	2.1	0.8	0.7
Occupation of head				
Unclassified	10.1	10.8	9.7	11.8
Professional and technical	1.1	5.9	1.0	1.9
Rural workers	37.9	48.7	53.0	51.0
Industrial workers	1.9	10.0	8.2	6.5
Middle level workers	0.0	1.5	1.0	1.7
Dom. workers and street vendors	0.0	6.8	4.5	3.9
Sector of activity				
Primary	37.5	46.1	51.7	50.0
Manufacturing	0.5	1.0	0.6	1.8
Electricity and construction	2.4	21.4	17.7	10.9
Commerce, restaurants	0.5	1.0	0.8	0.6
Services	0.9	4.2	2.2	4.1
Occupational position				
Owner-employee	8.7	12.2	12.2	12.0
Employer	18.6	14.7	15.9	10.4
Self-employed	22.1	28.0	25.5	24.0
Without remuneration	35.5	11.0	36.1	26.5

Source: Lustig and Szekely, "La evolucion de la pobreza y la desigualdad en Mexico." Estimations measured with income data from INEGI. The extreme poverty line equals NS$197.3 new pesos per person per month in 1994.

Moreover, while the index sensitive to the distribution of income among the poor (that is, the FGT index) shows that the poorest of the poor both in rural and urban areas fared better in 1994 than in 1989, this was not the case of the poorest in these two regions. The results are particularly significant because those states were among the main target of antipoverty efforts supported by the multilateral development banks during the period under consideration.[4] These are regions with a large concentration of indigenous communities, with 46 percent of the indigenous population residing in the regions here defined as South and Southeast.[5] Furthermore, rural violence has been particularly conspicuous in the three southeastern states. Chiapas is the cradle of the Zapatista Army's uprising, while Guerrero and Oaxaca are the two states where another guerrilla group, the EPR (Ejército Popular Revolucionario or Popular Revolutionary Army), has targeted most of its actions.

These trends suggest that a process of rising economic differentiation among regions is under way. The rise in regional economic differentiation is not well captured by the conventional measure of economic inequality. As reported, the Gini coefficient fell between 1989 and 1994 because the rise in poverty in the southern part of the country is compensated by falling poverty levels in other regions where the poor fared better (for example, parts of the Center—the region called *Centro Occidente*—and the Southwest).

Poverty in The Primary Sector: Why Did It Rise?

As already noted, between 1989 and 1994 extreme and moderate poverty in the primary sector rose and rural poverty remained unchanged (table 8-3). Geographically, poverty rose in the southern and southeastern regions, while it fell or remained constant in the rest over the same period. These results are disturbing because the incidence of poverty is much higher in the primary sector and poverty is highest in the South and the Southeast. This means that while the poor in relatively richer states and the urban areas were able to benefit from the mild economic recovery observed in the early 1990s, the benefits did not reach an important subset of the poorest of the poor.

Several factors explain this trend. One of them is the appreciation of the peso, discussed in chapter 6. The real exchange rate appreciated considerably between 1989 and 1994 (up until the devaluation in December) (table 6-1). This hurt the profitability in the tradeable goods sectors, notably agriculture. See table 8-4 which disaggregates income by sectors. Clearly, households whose main source of income came from agriculture were hit relatively harder. The appreciation of the peso was one factor that explained the rise in rural poverty. However, it is not the only one.

The decline of the prices of the most important cash crops cultivated by the poor in the regions under consideration is another factor. In particular, between 1984 and 1992, international coffee and cocoa prices declined by more than 70 percent. It has been estimated that the incomes of subsistence and small farmers of the Pacific South must have fallen by an average amount of 15 percent.[6] The states of Chiapas, Veracruz, and Oaxaca are the three most important coffee-growing states.[7] In the early 1990s, particularly as a result of the dis-

TABLE 8-4. *Wage and Nonwage Income*
Annual percent change except shares (in percent)

Item	1989	1990	1991	1992	1993	1994	1995	Average growth 1989–94
All sectors[a]								
Wage income	9.0	6.4	9.4	9.4	7.5	7.5	–15.7	8.2
Nonwage income	10.0	5.9	2.1	–0.9	–0.7	4.9	2.3	3.5
Share of nonwage income in total income	67.7	67.6	66.0	63.8	62.0	61.4	65.8	64.7
Agriculture[b]								
Wage income	–4.2	–8.8	–0.1	–2.8	0.1	0.1	–15.2	–2.7
Nonwage income	10.9	11.2	0.3	–10.0	–4.5	–4.4	–7.8	0.3
Share of nonwage income in total income	81.3	84.1	84.1	83.1	82.4	81.7	82.9	82.8
Nonagricultural[b]								
Wage income	9.8	7.1	9.8	9.8	7.7	7.7	–15.7	8.6
Nonwage income	9.9	5.4	2.3	0.0	–0.3	5.7	3.1	3.8
Share of nonwage income in total income	66.5	66.2	64.6	62.4	60.6	60.1	64.8	63.4

a. INEGI, *Sistema de cuentas nacionales de México: 1988–1995*, tomo I (Mexico, 1996), table 3, pp. 40–41. The real figures for growth rates are calculated using the consumer price index from Banco de México, *The Mexican Economy 1996* (Mexico, 1996), table 24, p. 286.

b. INEGI, *Sistema de cuentas nacionales de México*, table 65, p. 132, table 77, p. 156. The real figures for growth rates are calculated using the consumer price index from Banco de México, *The Mexican Economy 1996*, table 24, p. 286.

mantling of the International Coffee Agreement, coffee prices in the international markets plummeted from an average of U.S.$1.32 a pound in 1986—to $0.53 a pound in 1992.[8] Although no direct calculations are available, it seems reasonable to attribute, if not all at least in part, the rise in poverty in the Southeast and the South to the behavior of coffee and cocoa prices. Among the hardest hit were producers in indigenous communities, who constitute 65 percent of all of Mexico's coffee producers and who produce one-third of Mexico's coffee output.[9]

Also hard hit was the *ejido* sector in agriculture.[10] At the same time that the appreciation of the peso was hurting revenues to *ejidatarios*, the real support price of the main staple crops was falling, interest rates were increasing, and subsidies to the sector were being cut.[11] Structural factors were also affecting the *ejido*. Historically, the *ejido* sector (also known as the "social sector" because of the special treatment of land property rights that used to characterize it before the 1992 constitutional reform of article 27) was constituted by a peasant economy characterized by strong state intervention. State controls were accompanied by a variety of subsidies.[12] Over time, this system of controls and subsidies eroded, and the *ejido* sector entered a period of crisis that lasted more than two decades. The elimination of these controls and supports became an inherent part of the modernization program of the Salinas government. The most salient feature was the reform of article 27 of the Constitution in 1992, which changed the legal statute regulating the use and ownership of *ejido* land, essentially legalizing the rental and private ownership of *ejido* land.[13]

As part of the effort to modernize agriculture, many of the public institutions supporting the sector have been privatized, reduced, or eliminated.[14] The decline in the role of the state in agriculture has left an institutional vacuum. There has been "only a very partial reconstruction of alternative institutions to support the ejido sector. In general, this reduced availability and raised the cost of access to credit, insurance, markets, modern inputs, seeds, water, and technical assistance."[15] Against this background of relaxed state controls, adverse macroeconomic conditions, and institutional gaps, a process of social differentiation is emerging, with a small group of producers turning into successful entrepreneurs while others are lagging behind or even abandoning their land.[16] The successful entrepreneurs tend to be those who either have more land or more access to credit and irrigation, that is, the relatively better off. On the other end of the spectrum are the small farmers and indigenous community members who find it difficult to modernize and diversify because of the limited access to investable funds and institutional services. The latter, in fact, might be worse off as a result of the reforms introduced in agriculture, which dismantled much of the state support.

Economic Openness and Inequality

Trade liberalization was perhaps the most important and far reaching of the reforms. Although there is no assessment of the effect of trade liberalization on overall poverty and inequality, some studies have looked at its effect on the wage gap in manufacturing between the skilled and unskilled. Given that at least on the surface Mexico's abundant factor is unskilled labor, trade theory predicts that the removal of trade restrictions should result in a relative improvement of unskilled wages. That is not what has happened. As shown in figure 8-1, the skilled-unskilled wage gap widened substantially after 1985. Such a trend is consistent with the finding of other studies that have observed that the return to schooling increased during the 1980s.[17]

One study finds that the reduction in tariffs and the elimination in import-license requirements can account for 23 percent of the increase in the relative wage of skilled labor over the period 1986–90.[18] As an explanation for this result—which runs contrary to theoretical predictions—the authors argue that Mexico offered relatively high protection to the unskilled-intensive industries during the inward-looking period and, hence, those were the hardest hit sectors by the removal of barriers. Although Mexico is intensive in unskilled labor when compared with, for example, the United States, Mexico may have an intermediate abundance in skilled labor vis-à-vis other developing countries. For example, greater exposure to competition from China could have contributed to a decrease in the relative wage of unskilled workers.[19]

The same study finds that "foreign plants and exporters paid relatively higher returns to skilled workers."[20] Since these plants are better situated to compete in the world economy, they are likely to expand their output and their number as the economic integration process deepens particularly with NAFTA. As a result, the demand and earnings for skilled labor are likely to continue to rise, further widening the skilled-unskilled wage gap.

FIGURE 8-1. *Skilled versus Unskilled Wages*

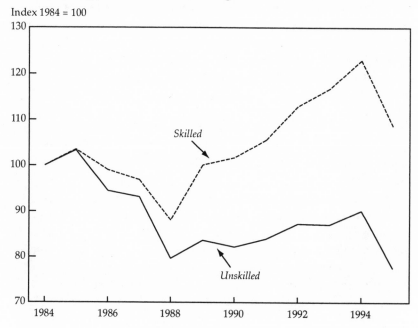

Index 1984 = 100

Source: For 1984 to 1988, author's calculations with data from Gordon H. Hanson and Anne Harrison, "Trade, Technology and Wage Inequality," NBER Working Paper 5110 (Cambridge, Mass.: National Bureau of Economic Research, 1995); for 1988 to 1995, Instituto Nacional de Estadística Geografía e Informática (INEGI), *Sistema de cuentas nacionales de México: 1988–1995*, Tomo I (Aguascalientes, 1996); The INEGI source uses salary in manufacturing industry (table 93, pp. 190–91) as proxy for skilled wages and wages in manufacturing industry (table 91, pp. 186–87) as proxy for unskilled wages. Real figures are calculated with CPI from Banco de México, *The Mexican Economy 1996* (México, 1996), table 24, p. 286.

Overall, these results suggest that unless Mexico engages in a serious effort to upgrade the skills of its working population, the process of economic modernization is likely to be accompanied by a rise in income inequality among wage earners even if overall inequality declines.

Living Standards and the Peso Crisis

Although there is no direct information (that is, obtained from household surveys) on the impact of the peso crisis and the recession that followed on households' living standards, several indicators suggest that it must have been quite strong. Private consumption declined by 9.5 percent in 1995 (table 7-2). Open unemployment rose from the 3.7 percent average in 1994 to a peak of 7.3 percent in September 1995.[21] During 1995 more than 1 million jobs were lost in the formal sector, and average real wages declined by 12.5 percent (table 7-3).[22] In addition, anecdotal evidence suggests that many families lost their homes and household items because the double squeeze of very high interest rates and lower wages forced them to default on their loans. Although the open unemployment rate fell during 1996 to 5.5 percent on average, real average wages continued their decline. Cumulatively, between the onset of the crisis and July 1997, real wages in manufacturing fell by 39 percent.[23]

Because wage earners seem to be among the hardest hit during the crisis, one would expect urban poverty to have risen. As to the rural sector, areas producing tradable goods should have benefited from the real devaluation of the peso. However, wage and nonwage income in agriculture fell sharply, hence rural poverty must have also risen (table 8-4).[24] Furthermore, given that nonwage income in the nonagricultural sectors rose, it should be expected that the crisis was also accompanied by a rise in income inequality.[25]

Because the 1995 recession—particularly its magnitude—was largely unexpected, there were no effective safety nets in place. There was an effort on the part of the government to limit the impact of austerity on the publicly funded social services. As a proportion of programmable expenditures, social spending actually rose slightly from 51 percent in 1994 to 52 percent in 1995. Nevertheless, because the government had to simultaneously reduce fiscal spending while devoting a larger share to debt servicing, social spending contracted by 12 percent in real terms (table 8-5).[26] As in the previous crisis, a large portion of this contraction happened by allowing real wages for staff working in the social sectors to fall.

The 1995 recession resulted in a sharper rise in unemployment than the recession in 1983. Mexico, however, has no unemployment insurance, and there were no employment programs like the ones that existed in Chile during its economic downturns. For lack of a better solution, the government decided in effect to use the program designed for retraining unemployed workers as an income-maintenance program.[27] As a result, the number of beneficiaries rose from 198,000 in 1994 to 350,000 in 1995, nothing near the amount of workers

TABLE 8-5. *Social Spending according to Growth and GDP, 1989–96*

Item	1989	1990	1991	1992	1993	1994	1995	1996
Growth rates								
Total public spending	–6.0	3.4	3.2	4.7	6.0	11.3	–13.5	2.9
Social spending	4.4	10.5	22.6	14.9	11.1	10.9	–12.0	–15.0
Education spending	2.8	6.9	19.6	16.1	16.0	13.4	–9.7	0.7
Health and labor spending	10.3	10.8	17.3	8.5	9.3	6.8	–11.6	–5.0
Percent of GDP								
Total public spending	16.1	15.9	15.7	15.8	16.5	17.6	15.8	15.9
Social spending	5.7	6.0	7.0	7.8	8.5	9.0	8.2	6.8
Education spending	2.4	2.5	2.9	3.2	3.7	3.9	3.7	3.6
Health and labor spending	2.8	2.9	3.3	3.4	3.7	3.8	3.4	3.2

Source: Grupo de Economistas y Asociados, Mexico, September 1997.

that were laid off in the first months of 1995.[28] According to some estimates, nearly 1 million jobs were lost in the formal sector during that year.[29] The duration of the courses offered by the program are limited, participants must have some minimum qualifications (which leave out many of the poor), and any one individual can only participate once in a lifetime. Its objective is to upgrade workers' skills. The program was ill-designed to act as an effective social safety net.

The government, shifting resources from other poverty-focused programs, instituted a short-term employment program in 1995.[30] The program resulted in the creation of more than half a million short-term jobs, 70 percent of which were in rural areas. Because workers received 80 percent of the going minimum wage, the program was largely self-targeted. One of the difficulties of the program is that it had mixed objectives, that is, it was not clear whether it was there to help the chronically poor or provide a source of income to those who became unemployed as a result of the recession. Although addressing chronic poverty is extremely important in Mexico, it is still true that this program might not have been the safety net needed to deal with the sharp rise in open unemployment observed in the first part of 1995.

The economic recovery has not yet reached the pockets of the average Mexican. Between the outbreak of the peso crisis in January 1995 and July 1997, average remuneration in manufacturing fell by almost 40 percent.[31] If current economic trends continue, real wages should start growing once more. It could take several years for Mexican wages to reach pre-crisis levels.

Could Mexico grow its way out of poverty? If the distribution of income were to remain unchanged, GDP grew at 5 percent a year, and population growth continued to decline at the same pace as in the 1980–95 period, it would take until 2033 to eradicate extreme poverty and until 2050 to eradicate moderate poverty.

Consider the outcome if it were possible to perfectly transfer resources to the poor. Eradicating extreme poverty would require appropriating 1.96 percent of the income of the top decile (or 0.87 percent of GDP) and giving it to households living in extreme poverty.[32] To rely on "trickle down," would keep extreme poverty around for a long time. However, a small, well-targeted, and sustained redistribution effort could eliminate extreme poverty in a very short time.

The Mexican government has started to work toward this end with the launching of the antipoverty program PROGRESA (Programa de Educacion, Salud y Alimentacion; Program of Education, Health and Nutrition) in mid-1997. The program's goal is to reach 2 million of extremely poor families by mid-1998 (about 10 million individuals), of which 2.7 million are rural. These beneficiary families of PROGRESA receive an income transfer designed to increase the amount of food intake and visits to the health posts of infants and small children, and fellowships designed to increase school attendance for children between the third grade of primary and the third year of secondary school. On average, it has been estimated that beneficiary families receive close to U.S.$30 a month, equivalent to raising the average income of a beneficiary family by close to 30 percent.[33] Given the short period lapsed since PROGRESA began to operate, it is premature to assess the program's impact. However, it is worth underscoring the attractiveness of this program. While it increases the current income of the poor, PROGRESA stimulates investment in the "human capital" of the children of the poor—thereby raising their potential income in the future.

Chapter Nine

Conclusion

Since the early 1990s, Mexico has experienced a series of dramatic events on the economic and political fronts. This book focuses on the economic dimension. At the time NAFTA was approved, Mexico was perceived to be on a firm path to economic prosperity. Events turned out differently. Confidence in Mexico's prospects, and its highly qualified economic team, was shattered when, at the end of 1994, Mexico faced a serious financial crisis. Even before the crisis, a closer look at its performance revealed that Mexico's output growth was slow, especially considering the important reforms introduced since the mid-1980s and its achievements in macroeconomic stability.

Understanding what went wrong in a country that was a darling of international investors and multilateral lending institutions is of particular importance for other reforming nations and the international community more broadly. Even if we still do not have final answers as to why Mexico did not grow faster and the ultimate causes of the peso crisis, a close analysis of the period sheds light on some fundamental questions about economic reforms. Are the same market-oriented reforms that received so much praise from the international community to be blamed for Mexico's disappointing economic performance? Should other countries interpret Mexico's experience as a warning and interrupt or even undo some of the reforms?

Chapter six reveals that the short answer to both questions is no, but with some qualifications. Slow growth should be primarily attributed to the slowdown in domestic demand caused by the appreciation of the peso. This was the price paid for stabilization based on the exchange rate. In addition, slow growth occurs because the payoff from reforms is likely to take time. Mexico is no exception to this rule.

After all, it also took Chile more than ten years and a severe financial crisis to reap the benefits of reform.[1] Now, for more than twelve years, Chile has enjoyed the highest sustained growth rate in the region.[2] The relocation of factors of production, the adoption of new technologies, and the upgrading of the labor force are not instantaneous processes. The fact that in Mexico some sectors, such as the labor market, have not been reformed yet may contribute to the delay.

Having said this, events in Mexico do suggest that flaws in the reform process can produce undesirable outcomes. The leading example is the banking sector. Some of the characteristics of the privatization process and the lack of adequate prudential regulation resulted in a very weak banking system.[3] A weak banking system was an indirect cause of the financial crisis because of the constraints it imposed on monetary policy during 1994. Inadequate prudential regulation also contributed indirectly to the crisis through the fast expansion of consumer credit, whose counterpart was a fall in private savings and a rise in the current account deficit. One clear lesson is that the institutions that guarantee a well-functioning financial system have to be given the highest priority before large-scale financial liberalization is undertaken. Chile in the early 1980s and Mexico in the mid-1990s learned this lesson the hard way. Maybe others will learn from the example.[4]

The Mexican experience also suggests market-oriented reforms damaged performance directly in some areas. This appears to be true in agriculture, where the elimination of state interventions left an institutional vacuum and many producers with less access to credit and technical assistance. In the presence of market failures, the answer to enhance productivity will often not be market-oriented reform as it is commonly understood but efficient forms of state intervention.

The Mexican crisis and the lackluster growth that preceded it highlight the difficulties posed by exchange rate policy. Because the authorities' goal was to lower inflation to the level of Mexico's major trade partners in a rather short period of time, the peso-dollar exchange rate was pegged (or rather quasi-pegged). Although this action helped bring inflation down effectively, it caused two big problems. Because inflation did not fall fast enough, foreign goods became relatively cheap. This result shifted demand from the internal to the external markets and hurt domestic output. The real appreciation of the exchange rate was one of the major factors contributing to the slow growth in the early 1990s. Furthermore, another mechanism by which the real appreciation hurt growth was through its effect on private consumption. The appreciation not only made the trade liberalization measures less credible but also encouraged a consumption spree of imported goods, thereby lowering private savings. It should be noted, however, that the real appreciation of the peso was not the result of the exchange rate regime throughout the entire period. During at least part of it, the peso appreciated because of large capital inflows.

A second problem arose in the wake of the Mexican peso crisis. The exchange rate rule turned out to be too restrictive when capital flows began to leave the country. Under a floating exchange rate regime, the peso would have depreciated significantly in April 1994. However, the authorities resisted changing it because they knew it would affect Mexico's reputation with the investor community, as well as weaken the economy in the wake of a difficult presidential election. Hoping for the best, the authorities decided to wait it out. When a forced devaluation finally occurred in December 1994, the loss of reputation was devastating. One important lesson appears to be, then, that fixed or quasi-fixed exchange rate regimes—although helpful to stabilize prices—can impose severe costs when capital markets change their mind. A more flexible regime, especially one in which the government's reputation is not so linked to an unanticipated change in the exchange rate owing to *external* shocks, would be preferable as a rule.

A key question about the Mexican peso crisis is whether it was the result of policy mistakes or bad luck. As discussed in chapter 6, both these factors were at work. One important lesson is that the peso crisis occurred without fiscal excesses. This underscores the need to focus on other dimensions of policymaking in the process of monitoring a country that is in a vulnerable position: in particular, monetary policy and debt management. Once the decision to stick to the exchange rule was made, the mistake from a policy stance was to sterilize capital outflows by increasing domestic credit and switching most of the peso-denominated short-term government debt to debt indexed to the dollar. Now it is known that the main reason to sterilize outflows was to keep interest rates from rising and avoid a banking crisis. However, the whole strategy was based on the presumption that bad news (political shocks) was temporary and that good news (NAFTA) was permanent and that capital flows would resume. Interestingly, optimistic expectations—about the evolution of oil prices and access to international credit—were also behind the decision to postpone policy actions in the wake of the crisis in 1982.

That the crisis also resulted from factors that were beyond the Mexican government's control is undeniable. During 1994 Mexico confronted a number of political shocks as well as the rise in U.S. interest rates and felt the merciless character of international capital markets. Mexico's experience highlights the difficulties posed by volatile capital flows. When euphoria was rampant, capital inflows contributed to the real appreciation of the exchange rate. If Mexico had been under a flexible exchange rate regime, the appreciation might have been worse. When real returns were higher in the United States and Mexico's political future became uncertain following the Colosio assassination, capital simply left.

This unwieldy character of (portfolio) capital flows has led to debates on what is the best way to handle them. Some recommend the use of some form of capital controls like Chile's as one solution.[5] The IMF, however, is much more cautious about recommending their use.[6] In practice, this decision will have to be taken by governments on a case-by-case basis. Certainly, capital controls are a very bad idea when a government is trying to reestablish its reputation with international investors and attract foreign capital. But it may work as a shock absorber for bad times if they are introduced in periods of capital inflow bonanza. Ultimately, reducing capital market volatility or shielding an economy from its impact will rest on a credible exchange rate policy, a sound financial system, and high domestic savings. Of all three, perhaps the sound financial system is the more crucial. The Mexican peso crisis, and the more recent crises in Asia, underscore the danger of lending booms by a not well- scrutinized banking sector facing high illiquidity risks.

An analysis of the financial crisis that followed the devaluation revealed another perilous characteristic of today's international capital markets: that is, the destabilizing role of financial derivatives. As discussed in chapter six, the Tesobono-derivatives appear to be one of the factors that transformed the devaluation into a self-fulfilling financial crisis. Rumors of a default or capital controls were enough to send the markets into panic. Tesobonos could not be rolled over and hence their prices fell, leading to margin calls to Mexican banks that had to go out and buy dollars. With that, the price of the peso fell further, the fear of default increased, and so on. This perverse process had

to be stopped, and the only way to do so was by offering Mexico financial resources large enough to put the default fears to rest. This is precisely why the financial rescue package assembled by the United
States and the IMF was needed. It did stop the peso from collapsing
and prevented the crisis from spreading to other countries. Its success can also be seen in how rapidly Mexico recovered its access to
international capital markets and in the fact that the Mexican government fully repaid its loans to the United States several years ahead of
schedule.

The Mexican peso crisis was a wake-up call to the international
community. It showed that major crises could occur even in the face
of relatively small policy mistakes or as a consequence of external
shocks. Not everything depended on a country's domestic policies.
Financial rescues could not be left to bilateral decisions either. As suggested in chapter seven, political turmoil in the United States almost
jeopardized the implementation of the package. Internationally
assembled financial rescue packages had to be orchestrated in a relatively depoliticized environment. The institution best suited for that
role is the IMF's New Arrangements to Borrow (NAB), an agreement
adopted in January 1997, which will provide resources in emergency
situations. Up to U.S.$48 billion will be available under this facility.
Although the NAB does not replace the General Arrangements to
Borrow, it will be the first credit source to which member countries
will turn when they need supplementary resources.[7] That the United
States came out so forcefully to assemble a rescue package was a
reflection of the U.S.-Mexico special relationship, a result of geographical proximity and, more recently, the implementation of
NAFTA. In fact, had it not been for the U.S. role during this period,
Mexico's output would have contracted much more drastically. The
NAB is necessary if only because such U.S. responses cannot be
assumed in the future, even should there be another Mexico crisis. In
fact, the Asian financial crisis has revealed that even the NAB may
not be enough of a resource to address financial crises in large countries if they happen—as they could—simultaneously. During the transition to fully globalized capital markets, when risks are likely to be
highly diversified, the international monetary system will continue
to require a sizable safety net.

One issue that has haunted Mexico for many decades is high levels
of inequality and poverty. The findings presented in chapter eight sug-

gest that matters did not improve much even during the incipient recovery of the early 1990s. Although urban poverty declined at an even pace with the rise in average real wages, poverty in the agricultural sector and poverty in the poorest states rose. Two important factors explain this rise in poverty in the poorest regions of the country during a period when presumably the government was making an extra effort to reduce it. The real exchange rate appreciation hurt incomes in agriculture, and the fall in coffee prices following the dismantling of the International Coffee Agreement hit such areas as Chiapas, particularly hard.

Although the Mexican government had developed an antipoverty program that focused primarily in the building and refurbishing of infrastructure for the poor (the Programa Nacional de Solidaridad/ National Solidarity Program, or PRONASOL), there were no real safety nets available to deal with external shocks. The very large fall in coffee prices in the early 1990s (a decline of about 60 percent from their average price in the late 1980s)[8] undoubtedly affected the poor in the states of Chiapas, Veracruz, and Oaxaca. However, there were no attempts to compensate workers for their income losses, at least in part. An analogous situation emerged during the sharp recession of 1995. Open unemployment rose very quickly. This was a new phenomenon in Mexico, a country that additionally does not have unemployment insurance. An ideal response would have been to put in place a temporary emergency employment program. Although it is hard to implement such programs quickly, precious time was lost during the first couple of months after the crisis started.

Although measures of overall inequality do not show much change, other measures of income disparities are troubling. For instance, the gap in the wages of unskilled and skilled workers has been steadily rising. At least one study finds that one important factor explaining the rise in the wage gap was trade liberalization. Another study finds that the dismantling of the state intervention in the agricultural sector—the *ejidos*, in particular—has been accompanied by rising social differentiation among producers. There are reasons to believe, then, that in its initial phases, economic modernization in Mexico may produce higher levels of inequality, at least in some areas. This should come as no surprise. Those who stand to benefit from greater access to jobs in the export sector, for example, tend to have higher education and skills. In agriculture, those who do survive and do well in a less

protected environment are likely to have inherent entrepreneurial abilities. Both education and skills, including entrepreneurial abilities,
are unequally distributed in Mexico. The answer is not to roll back on
trade liberalization or go back to old forms of state intervention.
Rather, to reduce inequality in the medium term, people need the education and training necessary to have access to the better jobs.

As discussed in chapter seven, Mexico's economy recovered in
1996. Growth for 1997 is expected to be close to around 7.5 percent,
while in the coming three years it is anticipated to lie between 5 percent and 6 percent a year.[9] Is this recovery for real? Will Mexico finally
reached sustained high growth? One would like to venture an
unequivocal yes. As modern growth theory and empirical analysis
reveals, openness helps growth. In particular, openness vis-à-vis a
technologically advanced country, such as the United States, should
help Mexico grow faster and steadily. One key role for the United
States in this process is to make its contribution toward the fulfillment and consolidation of NAFTA's objectives. The United States can
also help by maintaining a cooperative approach to deal with the ever
present bilateral irritants such as drug trafficking and undocumented
migration. Mexico cannot modernize its police and judicial system
overnight. Excessive pressure in this area can backfire. Furthermore,
international investors get nervous whenever the United States
appears to be on the verge of acting against Mexico. And Mexico will
have to rely on foreign savings, that is, capital inflows, to grow for
some time to come.

Ideally, Mexico should generate enough domestic savings to
finance its investment, but this is not likely to occur in the immediate
future. The truth is that nobody really knows what can make private
savings rise. And public savings are not likely to increase by any significant amount. In fact, they may even decline given the new political
landscape (as of September 1997) in which opposition parties control
the lower chamber of the Mexican Congress.[10] However, although
Mexico will continue to rely on capital flows to finance its growth for
several years, it should avoid relying on volatile flows. For 1997 the
news is encouraging in this respect: according to official figures, of the
U.S.$15 billion capital inflows expected to arrive in Mexico, 70 per-
cent are in the form of direct investment.[11]

The skies are not completely clear yet. During 1997 large capital
inflows resulted in a real appreciation of the peso. Although a crisis

of the magnitude observed in 1995 is very unlikely, the road could be rockier than hoped for, should there be sudden adjustments in the value of the peso becauses of changes in market sentiment. Furthermore, as happened before, if productivity growth does not accelerate, the expected trends in the exchange rate and domestic savings could stifle growth. It is hoped that Mexico's increased economic integration with world markets will prevent this dire outcome from occurring. The relative ease with which Mexico withstood the shock waves sent by the Asian financial crisis in late 1997 and the orderly fiscal adjustment that followed the sharp decline in international oil prices are good omens.

Appendix

Agreement Signed by Mexico and Its Commercial Banks on Debt and Debt Service Reduction

IN JULY 1989 the government of Mexico and the Bank Advisory Committee announced an agreement in principle to deal with Mexico's eligible long- and medium-term debt equal to approximately U.S.$48 billion.[1] The agreement presented the banks with three options: (1) exchange debt at a 35 percent discount for a single maturity, thirty-year bond carrying an interest rate of 0.81 percent over LIBOR, (2) exchange debt for a thirty-year par bond carrying a fixed 6.25 percent interest rate, or (3) provide new lending over the next four years equivalent to 25 percent of the bank's outstanding debt not assigned to option 1 or 2. The terms for these new loans are a spread of 0.81 percent over LIBOR for interest payments and a fifteen-year maturity with a seven-year grace period.

The final agreement was signed on February 4, 1990. The banks chose the following option mix: almost 43 percent of the eligible debt was committed to discounted bonds, the principal reduction option; approximately 47 percent went to par bonds, the interest reduction option; and slightly more than 9 percent served as a base for additional lending, the new money option.[2] The agreement also includes a clause that allows the banks, beginning in 1996, to increase the yield on their bonds, up to a specified maximum, if the price of petroleum were to exceed U.S.$14 a barrel in real terms. If the price of oil were to fall below U.S.$10, Mexico will receive U.S.$1 billion in new lending.[3] The banks were also entitled to limited and specific types of debt-equity swaps equivalent to U.S.$1 billion a year over the three and a half years following completion of the agreement.[4] Finally, the terms of the agreement, including its benefits, were retroactive from July 1, 1989.[5]

Available Credit Enhancements

All discount and par bonds were secured by the pledge of zero coupon U.S. Treasury obligations or comparable securities in other currencies. Interest payments on discount and par bonds were secured for an amount equivalent to eighteen months of interest payments due. If not used, these guarantees would be rolled over. A total of U.S.$7.1 billion was needed to secure the debt and debt service reduction instruments. The U.S.$7.1 billion in enhancements came from the following sources: $2.0 billion from the World Bank, $1.3 billion from the IMF, $1.4 billion from Japan, $1.4 billion from Mexico itself, and $1.1 billion in a letter of credit from commercial banks.[6]

Estimates of Debt Relief Implied by the Agreement

Several analysts have estimated the amount of debt relief implied by the agreement. Assuming the mix noted above, the total nominal debt will undergo almost no change. The amount reduced through the discount bond option (approximately U.S.$7 billion)[7] is roughly equal to the sum of the loans required for collateral plus the loans provided by the commercial banks that chose this option (approximately U.S.$5.7 and U.S.$1.4 billion each). Arguably the agreement will reduce the increment in total debt that would have accumulated under the previous conditions had Mexico continued punctual service of the debt and maintained its growth goals.[8] Of greater importance than the changes in the nominal debt are the implicit rate of return on the enhancements, if they are viewed as investment capital, and the impact of the agreement on more immediate cash flows.

One study estimates the real rate of return on enhancements to be 36 percent, well above both the cost at which Mexico is borrowing the funds and the rate of return Mexico itself could expect on the reserves it has pledged to the agreement.[9] When the agreement was concluded, initial estimates of cash-flow savings over the first five years ranged from more than U.S.$3.8 billion to about U.S.$1 billion a year. The lower estimate excluded (a) foregone amortizations, assuming that these would have been rescheduled as in the past;[10] (b) the Mexican collateral of U.S.$1.4 billion that the country had to generate by drawing on its own reserves; and (c) the funds "deviated" from the official loans to finance the guarantees, assuming that these loans would have been available anyway and could have been used by Mexico for balance-of-payments purposes.[11] All these estimates were sensitive to the assumed interest rate, which at the time was about 9 percent. Given the subsequent decline in interest rates, actual cash-flow savings have been lower.

To put cash-flow savings in perspective, it is useful to note that from 1983 to 1988 the average annual total interest payments for Mexico were approximately U.S.$9.5 billion (table 2-2). Thus, the net cash-flow savings are disappointing when compared with Mexico's total interest obligations.

The key question, however, is whether the relief is enough to cover the financing gap associated with the country's growth goals. By themselves the savings derived from the agreement were not enough. Nominal domestic interest rates, which fell sharply the month after the agreement—which in principle was signed in July 1989—rebounded almost to their pre-agreement level by March 1990.[12] This is the reason why the government pursued other avenues to attract foreign investment and capital repatriation. Two initiatives turned out to be particularly important in this respect: the reprivatization of banks and the pursuit of a free trade agreement with the United States, both announced in the first half of 1990 (see chapter 2).

Nonetheless, a better agreement—that is, one with more debt reduction—was probably not realistic, given the amount of funds available for credit enhancement, the amount of political leverage that would, or could, be exercised by creditor governments, and the existing institutional framework for handling the debt problem. A larger reduction would have required considerably more political pressure from creditor governments on the commercial banks; an increase in the amount of funds available for credit enhancements so that banks would face a much lower "Mexican risk" on their discounted debt;[13] or suspension of payments by Mexico, which would have lowered the price of debt in the secondary market even further.

The disadvantage of a suspension of payments was that though it would have imposed high costs on the creditor banks, the costs could have been even higher for Mexico itself. Mexican government officials believed a suspension of payments would send the wrong signal to domestic and foreign private investors. We will never know whether this perception was accurate, but it did lead the government of Mexico to refrain from using the suspension of payments for bargaining purposes.

Therefore, to obtain a larger discount and thus increase Mexico's debt relief, the creditor governments had only two other alternatives: exercise more political pressure on the banks, or increase funding available for debt and debt service reduction operations. The extent to which increased political pressure from creditor governments on the banks was feasible is not apparent. But more funding could have been made available for credit enhancements. Moreover, the enhancements should have been generated with funds that were clearly additional and, of course, earmarked for the debt and debt service reduction operations. Part of the funds used to finance the enhancements came from loans that Mexico would have received anyway from the IMF and the World Bank, and part came from Mexico's own reserves—the approximately U.S.$1.4 billion pledged by Mexico itself. The latter especially should not have been required, considering Mexico's short-run foreign exchange needs. Moreover, the funds used for credit enhancements are not transfers from creditor to debtor countries, because their use is contingent. If the country services the discounted debt in full, the funds need not be used. It is not entirely clear why, with the exception of Japan, the rich industrialized countries—the United States, in particular—were reluctant to pledge funds for the enhancements.

Notes

Introduction

1. During Mexican President Carlos Salinas de Gortari's visit to Washington in June 1990, he and President Bush announced their interest in free trade negotiations. See Larry Rohter, "U.S. and Mexicans Cautiously Back Free-Trade Idea," *New York Times*, June 12, 1990, p. A1; Peter Truell, "Bush, Salinas to Seek Pact on Free Trade," *Wall Street Journal*, June 12, 1990, p. A2; and Stuart Auerbach, "U.S.-Mexico Trade Pact Promised," *Washington Post*, June 12, 1990, p. D1. Salinas formally requested negotiations in August, and Bush notified the U.S. Congress of his intention to seek a free trade agreement with Mexico under "fast track" procedures in September. See chapter 5 for more details.

2. *Ejido* is the land unit in which the *ejidatarios* are given the right to exploit the land but do not "own" it; that is, they cannot sell or rent it or borrow against it. The reform of constitutional article 27, ratified by the Mexican Congress on December 5, 1991, potentially opens the way for *ejidatarios* to privatize their *ejido* if they so desire. This reform states that (a) there will be no further land distribution; (b) commercial companies will be able to own rural land within defined limits; and (c) the productive portion of *ejidos* can be divided among members of the same *ejido*, and *ejidatarios* can also enter into associations with each other or outsiders to exploit, rent, or sell their holdings. "Mexico: Changes to Constitution Concerning Land Ownership," *LDC Debt Report*, January 27, 1992, p. 9; and John Watling, "Opposition to Ejido Reforms Continues Despite Congressional Approval," *El Financiero International*, December 16, 1991, p. 3.

3. Wages fell even more, social expenditures contracted, and poverty most likely rose (see chapter 3). It will take many years of equity-oriented policy-making to undo the damage to living standards that occurred during the 1980s.

4. See Macro Asesoría Económica, *Realidad económica de México, 1991* (Mexico City, 1990), pp. 14–15.

5. NAFTA negotiations began in Toronto on June 12, 1991. See "U.S., Canada and Mexico Begin Free Trade Talks," *New York Times*, June 13, 1991, p.

D8; and Bernard Simon, "Work Starts on Free Zone from Arctic to Acapulco," *Financial Times*, June 12, 1991, p. 2.

6. In my view the inefficiency associated with state-led industrialization would have been reflected in slower growth rates, not an economic collapse.

7. Banco de México, *The Mexican Economy in 1983* (Mexico City, May 1983), pp. 4–5.

8. For example, the devaluation was followed by a recommendation to raise nominal wages, thereby signaling that inflation would continue to rise.

9. The last loan given to Mexico was U.S.$2.5 billion in May–June 1982. Only 75 of 650 banks subscribed, despite attractive terms. See Ernesto Zedillo Ponce de León, "The Mexican External Debt: The Last Decade," in Miguel S. Wionczek in collaboration with Luciano Tomassini, eds., *Politics and Economics of External Debt Crisis: The Latin American Experience* (Boulder, Colo.: Westview Press, 1985), p. 316. For an account of the events of August 1982, see Joseph Kraft, *The Mexican Rescue* (New York: Group of Thirty, 1984).

10. Banco de México, *Mexican Economy in 1983*, p. 5.

11. For an econometric testing of the three hypotheses, see Darryl McLeod and Edmund Sheehey, "Exchange Rate Policy, Debt and Growth: Explaining Mexico's 'Lost Decade,'" Fordham University, Economics Department, New York, August 1990.

12. See, for example, Rudiger Dornbusch, "Mexico: Stabilization, Debt and Growth," *Economic Policy: A European Forum*, vol. 3 (October 1988); McLeod and Sheehey, "Exchange Rate Policy"; José Córdoba, "El progama mexicano de reordenación económica, 1983–1984," in *El FMI, el Banco Mundial y la crisis latinoamericana* (Mexico City: Siglo Veintiuno Editores, 1986); and Guillermo Ortiz, "Mexico beyond the Debt Crisis: Toward Sustainable Growth with Price Stability," in Michael Bruno and others, eds., *Lessons of Economic Stabilization and Its Aftermath* (MIT Press, 1991), pp. 283–313.

13. See, for example, José L. Alberro and Jorge E. Cambiaso, "Características del ajuste de la economía mexicana," paper prepared for a project, Políticas Macroeconómicas de Ajuste en América Latina, HOL/85/543 (Mexico City, December 1986).

14. See, for example, Vladimiro Brailovsky, Roland Clarke, and Natán Warman, *La política económica del desperdicio: México en el período 1982–1988* (Mexico City: Universidad Nacional Autónoma de México [UNAM], 1989).

15. For instance, in 1986 the price of oil had declined 64 percent below its 1981 level, and oil exports were about 70 percent of total exports at the beginning of the 1980s. See table 2-2.

16. *Net resource transfers* to the rest of the world are defined as the sum of gross amortizations, interest payments, and other net outflows (that is, capital flight) minus the sum of gross external credit, direct foreign investment, and net remittances. Large resource transfers to the rest of the world present problems because, for example, real domestic interest rates have to be high in order to attract capital inflows and deter capital flight, but high interest rates negatively affect the fiscal balance and domestic investment. Second, and more important, large resource transfers of this type place the sustainability of

fiscal discipline in doubt, thereby fueling inflationary expectations and capital flight. For a discussion of these issues, see, for example, Dornbusch, "Mexico: Stabilization, Debt, and Growth."

17. A two-year adjustment period was initially visualized by the Mexican government and the IMF when they signed an extended fund facility (EFF) in December 1982. See Banco de México, *Informe anual, 1982* (Mexico City, April 1983), p. 60.

18. For a discussion of the mechanisms by which a relatively large external debt, or "debt overhang," can impede growth, see Michael P. Dooley, "An Analysis of the Debt Crisis," IMF Working Paper WP/86/14 (International Monetary Fund, December 4, 1986); Paul Krugman, "Financing vs. Forgiving a Debt Overhang," *Journal of Development Economics*, vol. 29 (November 1988), pp. 253–68; Jeffrey D. Sachs, "Conditionality, Debt Relief, and the Developing Country Debt Crisis," NBER Working Ppaper 2644 (July 1988); and Jeffrey D. Sachs, "New Approaches to the Latin American Debt Crisis," Essays in International Finance 174 (Princeton University, July 1989).

19. McLeod and Sheehey estimate that the devaluation of the peso explains about one-fifth of the fall in average growth during 1981–88. See "Exchange Rate Policy," p. 7.

20. For an analytical discussion of these mechanisms, for example, see Lance Taylor, *Structuralist Macroeconomics: Applicable Models for the Third World* (Basic Books, 1983); and Paul Krugman and Lance Taylor, "Contractionary Effects of Devaluation," *Journal of International Economics*, vol. 8 (August 1978), pp. 445–56.

21. The negative impact of devaluation on investment in the Mexican case is analyzed by William R. Easterly, "Devaluation in a Dollarized Economy: Some Theoretical Models in the Context of the Mexican Experience," prepared for Seminario ITAM-COLMEX, February 10, 1984.

22. For a discussion of the relationship between external shocks and inflation in the case of Mexico, see Eliana A. Cardoso, "Deficit Finance and Monetary Dynamics in Brazil and Mexico," *Journal of Development Economics*, vol. 37 (1992), pp. 173–97.

23. This is the case because in Mexico currency devaluations are translated almost immediately into price increases.

24. *Incomes policy* is the name given to a set of policies designed to control or regulate prices and wages. In practice, its implementation and scope vary from case to case. Often it implies a freeze on wages and prices.

25. See, for example, Alberro and Cambiaso, "Características del ajuste."

26. This interpretation of structural reforms could be à la Hirschman.

27. For a discussion of moratoria in Latin America, see Oscar Altimir and Robert Devlin, eds., *La moratoria en América Latina: Experiencia de los países* (Mexico City: Fondo de Cultura Económica, forthcoming).

28. Part of the explanation may be that the relationship between the government and the most powerful segments of the private sector were, to say the least, strained, because of the bank nationalization in September 1982. Perhaps one reason relations continued to be strained was that de la Madrid

did not reprivatize the banks when he took power at the end of 1982. The Mexican and U.S. governments were not on good terms, particularly because the Reagan administration was annoyed by Mexico's "friendliness" toward the Sandinistas in Nicaragua. In a way, Costa Rica's successful moratorium may be explained on two counts: the relative smallness of its foreign debt, and the fact that the U.S. government considered Costa Rica of particular strategic importance in Central America.

29. For a discussion of this, see Córdoba, "El programa mexicano," p. 380. On the role of stabilization loans, see Rudiger Dornbusch, "Policies to Move from Stabilization to Growth," *Proceedings of the World Bank Annual Conference on Development Economics, 1990* (Washington: World Bank, 1991), pp. 19–48.

30. Sachs, "Conditionality, Debt Relief"; Sachs, "New Approaches to the Latin American Debt Crisis"; Krugman, "Financing vs. Forgiving a Debt Overhang"; and UN Economic Commission for Latin America and the Caribbean (CEPAL), *The Evolution of the External Debt Problem in Latin America and the Caribbean*, Estudios e Informes de la CEPAL 72 (Santiago, 1988). Krugman notes that there is a trade-off between the "financing" option and the "debt forgiving" one. With financing, if countries do well, then "creditors will not have written down their claims unnecessarily" (p. 253). This is perhaps the reason that banks and creditor governments supported the debt strategy that prevailed.

31. CEPAL, "América Latina y el Caribe: Opciones para reducir el peso de la deuda," (March 19, 1990).

32. CEPAL, *Evolution of the External Debt Problem.*

33. Robert Devlin, *Debt and Crisis in Latin America: The Supply Side of the Story* (Princeton University Press, 1989).

34. In the 1942 agreement, total Mexican debt (principal plus interest) was reduced from U.S.$509,516,222 to $49,560,750; that is, more than 90 percent. However, before this settlement Mexico's moratoria made it difficult for the country to acquire international credit. See Jan Bazant, *Historia de la deuda exterior de México (1823–1946)* (Mexico City: El Colegio de México, 1968), p. 221.

35. For a description of the rules established to govern bank reprivatization, see Banco de México, *The Mexican Economy, 1991: Economic and Financial Development in 1990, Policies for 1991* (Mexico City, May 1991), pp. 24–28. The new banking law was announced on May 2 and approved on July 1, 1990. In March 1990 the *Wall Street Journal* first reported that private meetings to discuss the idea of a free trade agreement between Mexico and the United States had taken place in late February in Washington. See Peter Truell, "U.S. and Mexico Agree to Seek Free-Trade Pact," *Wall Street Journal*, March 27, 1990, p. A3. The trade talks signaled a significant change in the bilateral relationship. The United States was no longer seen as an inevitable burden north of the border but rather as a market for Mexico's exports and a source of foreign investment and modern technology.

36. Foreign investment equaled roughly U.S.$10 billion in 1991, almost three times the average of the previous three years. See Secretaría de Comercio

y Fomento Industrial (SECOFI), "Evolución de la inversión extranjera directa en 1991," Mexico City, January 1992, table 1.

37. For the sake of price stability, officials will also have to avoid an adjustment of the exchange rate.

38. Although authoritarianism is not a necessary condition for successful adjustment, the authoritarian and corporatist character of the Mexican state made economic adjustment policy easier. Fortunately, the politics of consensus is a viable alternative to authoritarianism. It has been applied effectively, for example, in Spain and Costa Rica to generate support for economic change.

Chapter One

1. Mexico was seen as an exception in Latin America, where in many countries inflation had become endemic as early as the 1950s.

2. For a discussion of Mexico's economic development in the pre- and post–World War II period, see, for example, Roger D. Hansen, *The Politics of Mexican Development* (Johns Hopkins Press, 1971); Enrique Cárdenas, *La industrialización mexicana durante la gran depresión* (Mexico City: El Colegio de México, 1987); Leopoldo Solís, *La realidad económica mexicana: Retrovisión y perspectivas* (Mexico City: Siglo Veintiuno, 1975); and Raymond Vernon, *The Dilemma of Mexico's Development: The Roles of the Private and Public Sectors* (Harvard University Press, 1963).

3. Gerardo Bueno, "Policies on Exchange Rate, Foreign Trade and Capital," El Colegio de México, 1987, table 14. For further discussion of protection and Mexico's industrialization process, see, for example, Timothy King, *Mexico: Industrialization and Trade Policies since 1940* (London: Oxford University Press, 1970); Bela Balassa, "La política de comercio exterior de México," *Comercio Exterior*, vol. 33 (March 1983), pp. 210–22; Nora Claudia Lustig, "Distribution of Income, Structure of Consumption and Economic Growth: The Case of Mexico," Ph.D. dissertation, University of California, Berkeley, 1979; and René Villarreal, *El desequilibrio externo en la industrialización de México (1929–1975): Un enfoque estructuralista* (Mexico City: Fondo de Cultura Económica, 1976).

4. Instituto Nacional de Estadística, Geografía e Informática (INEGI), *Estadísticas históricas de México, tomo 1* (Mexico City, August 1985), table 1.5, p. 33.

5. Coordinación General de los Servicios Nacionales de Estadística, Geografía e Informática, *México; Información sobre aspectos geográficos, sociales y económicos: Aspectos sociales*, vol. 2: (Mexico City, September 1982), table 1.2, p. 9.

6. For a discussion of this "stabilizing development" period, see, for example, Solís, *La realidad económica mexicana*. "Stabilizing development" refers to the period when economic growth was effectively combined with macroeconomic stability (with low inflation rates, in particular).

7. By "prudent" macroeconomic policy I understand first and foremost the avoidance of large and rising fiscal deficits that eventually need to be financed

by money creation. Even though economic information before 1965 is not readily available, the ratio of the public deficit to GDP was an average of 2.5 percent between 1965 and 1972 (table 1-4). Another source estimates this ratio at nearly 2 percent. See Francisco Gil Díaz, "Mexico's Path from Stability to Inflation," in Arnold C. Harberger, ed., *World Economic Growth: Case Studies of Developed and Developing Nations* (San Francisco: Institute for Contemporary Studies, 1984), table A-6, p. 374.

8. Fixed exchange rate policies were strongly advocated by the Bretton Woods institutions. Of course, over time the combination of a fixed dollar-peso rate plus an inflation rate (though very low) that was higher in Mexico than in the United States caused a steady appreciation of the peso that in the mid-1970s was not sustainable.

9. Luis Echeverría Álvarez was president of Mexico from December 1, 1970, to November 30, 1976.

10. By the beginning of the 1970s, the growth rate of overall productivity had clearly declined. For further discussion of the evolution of productivity in Mexico, see Enrique Hernández Laos, *Evolución de la productividad de los factores en México, 1950–1967* (Mexico City: Centro Nacional de Productividad, 1973); Alain Ize and Javier Salas, "El comportamiento macroeconómico de la economía mexicana entre 1961 y 1981: Especificaciones alternativas y pruebas de hipótesis," in Alain Ize and Gabriel Vera, eds., *La inflación en México* (Mexico City: El Colegio de México, 1984), pp. 171–230; and Robert E. Looney, *Economic Policymaking in Mexico: Factors Underlying the 1982 Crisis* (Duke University Press, 1985), table 1.2, p. 7. However, productivity in manufacturing was not lagging by international standards. See Ricardo Samaniego Breach, "The Evolution of Total Factor Productivity in the Manufacturing Sector in Mexico, 1963–1981," Seminario ITAM-COLMEX, December 7, 1984. Perhaps Mexico's problems with protectionism stemmed from its implementation. Firms were not subject to performance criteria, and rents derived from protection were considered a permanent bonus, unlike, for example, in Korea. See Alice H. Amsden, *Asia's Next Giant: South Korea and Late Industrialization* (Oxford University Press, 1989), pp. 25–155. Also, protected industries resulted in an implicitly overtaxed agriculture, locking rural population in poverty and causing a decline in agricultural exports.

11. The killings of Tlatelolco in 1968 and some subsequent repressive incidents were viewed as the result of a state that had become too much an instrument of the economically powerful. This is argued in Carlos Bazdresch, "La economía mexicana: Cuatro ensayos," CIDE, Mexico City, 1989.

12. For a discussion of the underlying political motivations for Echeverría's policies, see Carlos Bazdresch and Santiago Levy, "Populism and Economic Policy in Mexico, 1970–1982," in Rudiger Dornbusch and Sebastian Edwards, eds., *The Macroeconomics of Populism in Latin America* (University of Chicago Press, 1991), pp. 223–62.

13. See Ernesto Zedillo Ponce de León, "Mexico's Recent Balance-of-Payments Experience and Prospects for Growth," *World Development*, vol. 14 (August 1986), table 4, p. 968.

14. Data from the Banco de México, cited in Macro Asesoría Económica, *Realidad económica de México* (Mexico City, 1990) table 21.5, p. 562.

15. Ernesto Zedillo Ponce de León, "The Mexican External Debt: The Last Decade," in Miguel S. Wionczek and Luciano Tomassini, eds., *Politics and Economics of External Debt Crisis: The Latin American Experience* (Boulder, Colo.: Westview Press, 1985), table II.2, p. 298.

16. These are yearly averages. Data from Macro Asesoría Económica, *Realidad económica de México*, table 16.1, p. 433.

17. By the end of 1976 the public sector foreign debt rose to U.S.$21 billion. See Zedillo, "Mexico's Recent Balance-of-Payments Experience," table 3, p. 967.

18. The peso went from a value of 8 cents to the dollar to about 5 cents. See Bueno, "Policies on Exchange Rate," table 17.

19. See Zedillo, "Mexico's Recent Balance-of-Payments Experience," table 1, p. 965.

20. To his credit, Echeverría opened up the political debate by allowing substantial freedom of the press. In addition, the increase in social spending must explain (at least in part) the improvement in social indicators observed in the 1970s, as programs in health, education, and rural infrastructure were expanded. Unfortunately, these improvements occurred at the expense of efficiency and macroeconomic balance.

21. Proven reserves rose from about 6 billion barrels in 1975 to 40 billion in 1978. By 1982 proven reserves were estimated to be slightly more than 70 billion. See Pascual García Alba and Jaime Serra Puche, *Causas y efectos de la crisis económica en México*, Jornadas 104 (Mexico City: El Colegio de México, 1984), table 13, p. 54.

22. The average price of crude oil, which had been U.S.$13.34 per barrel on average from early 1977 to early 1979, was equal to U.S.$22 per barrel by mid-1979 and was more than U.S.$30 per barrel by February 1980. See García-Alba and Serra-Puche, "Causas y efectos de la crisis," table 16, p. 58.

23. See Zedillo, "Mexico's Recent Balance-of-Payments Experience," pp. 974–77.

24. Data on employment comes from the National Accounts reproduced in *Compendio de indicadores de empleo y salarios* (Mexico City: Comisión Nacional de los Salarios Mínimos, December 1989), table 2.7, p. 68.

25. In principle, Mexico's economic policy for 1977–79 was framed within the limits established in its agreement with the IMF (signed in late 1976). However, given Mexico's new and rising oil revenues, IMF funding was no longer needed and the IMF-approved program was not followed.

26. According to some estimates, the margin of overvaluation was equal to 25 percent in 1980 (assuming that the exchange rate for 1977, was the equilibrium exchange rate). See Macro Asesoría Económica, *Realidad económica de México 1991*, table 20.1, p. 539.

27. The price of oil for the Mexican blend went from U.S.$19.6 per barrel in 1979, to U.S.$31.3 in 1980, and to U.S.$33.2 in 1981. See table 2-2, and Macro Asesoría Económica, *Realidad económica de México 1991*, table 21.2, p. 555.

28. *World Bank Development Report, 1980* (Oxford University Press, 1980), table 2.4, p. 8.

29. *World Bank Development Report, 1981* (Oxford University Press, 1981), p. 13.

30. See Zedillo, "Mexico's Recent Balance-of-Payments Experience," table 6, p. 971.

31. The net increment of aggregate public debt averaged U.S.$3.3 billion in the period from 1978 to 1980, which was considered a reasonable amount given Mexico's prospects as a major oil exporter. See Zedillo, "Mexico's Recent Balance-of-Payments Experience," p. 971.

32. Ibid., table 6, p. 972. Private debt includes debt of commercial banks and excludes direct suppliers' credits.

33. In economic literature the negative effects that accompany this kind of boom are known as the "Dutch disease," owing to an experience endured by Holland. For further discussion of the phenomenon, see W. Max Corden and J. Peter Neary, "Booming Sector and De-Industrialization in a Small Open Economy," *Economic Journal*, vol. 92 (December 1982), pp. 825–48.

34. In 1981 the peso was overvalued by 34.7 percent on average (using September 1977 as a base). See Macro Asesoría Económica, *Macro perspectivas 2do trimestre, 1991* (Mexico City, 1991), table III.1, p. 14.

35. In retrospect, the initial decline in the world oil price seems small compared with the sharp fall from an average of U.S.$25.5 per barrel in 1985 to U.S.$12.0 in 1986 (see table 2-2). The difference is that in 1986 the economy was so "cooled down" that the required turnaround was less dramatic than in 1981.

36. The "debt overhang" is the portion of the total debt that is extremely difficult to serve because of fiscal shortfall, the drop in foreign exchange revenues, or both.

37. Macro Asesoría Económica, *Realidad económica de México 1991*, table 3.1, p. 54.

38. See Zedillo, "Mexico's Recent Balance-of-Payments Experience," pp. 977–79. This unwise shift in policy from an economic point of view may be a reflection of López Portillo's political shift. López Portillo felt betrayed by the private sector, which he believed took advantage of the many subsidies provided during the oil boom and yet did not respond to his call for cooperation, but rather engaged in continuous and massive capital flight. As an alternative he turned to the labor sector and to the members of his cabinet who were more on the left and pro-state, a move that also explains his subsequent decision to nationalize the banking sector.

39. Nora Lustig and Jaime Ros, *Mexico*, WIDER Country Study 7 (Helsinki: World Institute for Development Economics Research of the United Nations University, March 1987), p. 13.

40. After mid-1981 Mexico had to resort to short-term commercial loans to finance about two-thirds of its borrowing requirements. In the following twelve months short-term debt rose up to U.S.$10.8 billion. This continuous search for short-term credit sources increasingly eroded commercial banks'

confidence. After early 1982 banks became more reluctant to extend new loans, first individually and then as a group. In mid-1982 many banks stopped giving out new loans, and some were even reluctant to roll over their debt in an attempt to lower their exposure. Ángel Gurría Treviño, "La reestructuración de la deuda: El caso de México," in Stephany Griffith-Jones, ed., *Deuda externa, renegociación y ajuste en la América Latina*, Lecturas 61 (Mexico City: Fondo de Cultura Económica, 1988), pp. 77–78.

41. Mexico's involuntary moratorium was initially considered a cash flow problem. The creditor banks agreed, but not without pressure from their governments and multilaterial financial institutions to continue their lending and to reschedule payments. Over time this interpretation would prove faulty. See, for example, Joseph Kraft, *The Mexican Rescue* (New York: Group of Thirty, 1984).

42. Banco de México, *Informe anual, 1982* (Mexico City, 1983), pp. 140–80.

43. See, for example, Jose L. Alberro and Jorge E. Cambiaso, "Características del ajuste de la economía mexicana," paper prepared for a project, Políticas macroeconómicas de ajuste en América Latina (HOL/85/543), Mexico City, December 1986; Terry Barker and Vladimiro Brailovsky, "La política económica entre 1976 y 1982 y el plan nacional de desarrollo industrial," *Investigación Económica*, vol. 42 (October–December, 1983) pp. 273–317; Carlos Bazdresch P., "Las causas de la crisis," paper presented at the seminar on the Mexican economy, El Colegio de México, Mexico City, August 1983; José Córdoba, "El programa mexicano de reordenación económica, 1983–1984," in *El FMI, el Banco Mundial y la crisis latinoamericana* (Mexico City: Siglo Veintiuno Editores, 1986); Rudiger Dornbusch, "Mexico: Stabilization, Debt and Growth," *Economic Policy: A European Forum*, vol. 3 (October 1988), pp. 233–83; García Alba and Serra Puche, *Causas y efectos de la crisis*; Alain Ize and Guillermo Ortiz, "Fiscal Rigidities, Public Debt, and Capital Flight," *International Monetary Fund Staff Papers*, vol. 34 (June 1987), pp. 311–32; Alain Ize, "Savings, Investment, and Growth in Mexico: Five Years after the Crisis," IMF Working Paper WP/9 (International Monetary Fund, February 21, 1989); Jaime Ros, "Mexico from the Oil Boom to the Debt Crisis: An Analysis of Policy Responses to External Shocks, 1978–85," in Rosemary Thorp and Laurence Whitehead, eds., *Latin American Debt and the Adjustment Crisis* (University of Pittsburgh Press, 1987), pp. 68–116; Lance Taylor, "The Crisis and Thereafter: Macroeconomic Policy Problems in Mexico," in Peggy B. Musgrave, ed., *Mexico and the United States: Studies in Economic Interaction* (Boulder, Colo.: Westview Press, 1985), pp. 147–70; and Zedillo, "Mexico's Recent Balance-of-Payments Experience."

44. See, for example, García Alba and Serra Puche, *Causas y efectos de la crisis*.

45. See, for example, Barker and Brailovsky, "La política económica 1976 y 1982."

46. It is estimated that capital flight could have been between U.S.$17.3 and $23.4 billion from 1980 to 1982. See Dornbusch, "Mexico: Stabilization, Debt and Growth," table 6.

47. See the simulation result of a model used at the Ministry of Budget

and Programming presented in Córdoba, "El programa mexicano," tables 1 and 2, p. 325.

Chapter Two

1. José Córdoba, President Salinas's chief of staff, has emphasized the contribution of this consensus to the success of Mexico's adjustment program in a recent article on the lessons to be learned from Mexico's reform. José Córdoba, "Diez lecciones de la reforma económica mexicana," Nexos, vol. 14 (February 1991), pp. 31–48.

2. For a description of the PIRE, see José Córdoba, "El programa mexicano de reordenación económica, 1983–84," in Sistema Económico Latinoamericano (SELA), El FMI, el Banco Mundial y la crisis latinoamericana (Mexico City: Siglo Veintiuno Editores, 1986).

3. In addition, making the dollar particularly expensive by devaluing the peso would allow for temporary negative domestic interest rates, thus ameliorating the fiscal impact of servicing the internal debt without fear of capital flight. This occurred, especially in 1983.

4. The EFF was announced on December 23, 1982. See "Mexico to Use Resources from Fund to Support Major Adjustment Effort," IMF Survey, January 10, 1983, pp. 1–3.

5. Expressed in special drawing rights (SDR), the EFF was equal to 3,410.6 million.

6. The dual exchange rate was implemented by López Portillo's administration on September 1, 1982, when the banks were nationalized and generalized exchange controls were implemented. This two-tier rate was kept in place by de la Madrid's team, IMF objections notwithstanding; the exchange controls, however, were eliminated. The controlled exchange rate was set by the government and was applicable to all the transactions of trade and nonfactor payments. Capital outflows had to be financed at the "free" exchange rate. Initially the gap between the two was large, but after December 1982 the controlled exchange rate would be depreciated daily by a fixed amount so that it would converge to the free rate. The free exchange rate was the price paid for the dollar in the market, and in principle people could purchase as many dollars as they wanted at the free rate. The rate of depreciation of the free exchange rate, however, has also been set by the authorities. In practice, the rate must have reflected prevailing demand and supply because no black market developed. See Macro Asesoría Económica, Realidad económica de México, 1991 (Mexico City, 1990), table 3.1, p. 54.

7. "Mexico to Use Resources from Fund," p. 2.

8. Payments of the principal were stretched over eight years, with a four-year grace period. The interest rate premium was set at 1 7/8 points over the London interbank offered rate (LIBOR), and 1 3/4 over the U.S. prime rate. On debt rescheduling, see José Angel Gurría T., "La política de deuda externa de México, 1982–1990," Mexico City, January 1991 (forthcoming in Carlos

Bazdresch, Nisso Bucay, and Nora Lustig, eds., *Mexico: Auge, crisis y ajuste* [Mexico City: Fondo de Cultura Económica]).

9. The program, known as FICORCA (Trust Fund for the Coverage of Exchange Rate Risks), was launched in April 1983. Enterprises that had been able to restructure their debt for an eight-year period were allowed to enter the FICORCA system. Participation in the system implied that payments would be constant in real terms and that they could be made at the controlled exchange rate. This avoided the lumpiness of payments in the first years, which for many enterprises would have meant bankruptcy. At times the savings to enterprises were considerable, given the difference between the controlled and free exchange rates. See ibid., pp. 4–5.

10. See José Angel Gurría Treviño, "La reestructuración de la deuda: El caso de México," in Stephany Griffith-Jones, ed., *Deuda externa, renegociación y ajuste en la América Latina*, Lecturas 61 (Mexico City: Fondo de Cultura Económica, 1988), graph 1, p. 81.

11. This outcome could be characterized as a typical case of overkill because the adjustment in the current account went beyond what was required by the external conditions. That is, there was room for a smaller current account surplus and, thus, a higher level of output.

12. Jaime Ros, "Mexico from the Oil Boom to the Debt Crisis: An Analysis of Policy Responses to External Shocks, 1978-85," in Rosemary Thorp and Laurence Whitehead, eds., *Latin American Debt and the Adjustment Crisis* (University of Pittsburgh Press, 1987), p. 101.

13. Imports increased 17.8 percent and nonoil exports increased 20.7 percent in constant pesos in 1984, compared with a contraction of imports of 33.8 percent and a rise in nonoil exports of 32.5 percent in 1983 (table 2-4).

14. Prices of other raw materials exported by Mexico also fell in the world market. See Banco de México, *The Mexican Economy: Economic and Financial Developments in 1985, Policies for 1986* (Mexico City, June 1986), p. 99.

15. From a peak of 117.2 percent in April 1983 to 59.2 percent in November and December 1984. Macro Asesoría Económica, *Realidad económica de México, 1991*, table 2-1, p. 22.

16. Ibid.

17. See Nora Lustig and Jaime Ros, *Mexico*, WIDER Country Study 7 (Helsinki: World Institute for Development Economics Research of the United Nations University, 1987); and Vladimiro Brailovsky, Roland Clarke, and Natán Warman, *La política económica del desperdicio: México en el período 1982–1988* (Mexico City: Universidad Nacional Autónoma de México, 1989).

18. See for example, José L. Alberro and Jorge E. Cambiaso, "Características del ajuste de la economía mexicana," paper prepared for a project, Políticas Macroeconómicas de Ajuste en América Latina, HOL/85/543 (Mexico City, December 1986).

19. Nominal fiscal deficit is measured as the percent of the nominal public sector borrowing requirement to GDP.

20. This contractionary effect occurs primarily through two mechanisms. First, in economies like Mexico's a devaluation results in a reduction of the

real wage (see chapter 3). Second, devaluation may deter private investment because of its impact on the financial conditions of firms with dollar-denominated debt. Without an explicit model it is not easy to see which policy combination would have reduced the overkill. One could argue that a smaller initial nominal devaluation may have resulted in lower inflation and a higher output. The question is whether a lower devaluation may have been sufficient to stop capital flight.

21. Córdoba, "El programa mexicano de reordenación económica," pp. 372–73. As Córdoba points out, three "choices" are available to a particular government to deal with a sizable permanent external shock: to repudiate past external (and internal) debt, to smooth out government revenues and expenditures so that the new intertemporal budget constraint is satisfied, or to overadjust in the short run to satisfy the present budget constraint. The last option puts all the burden of adjustment on the current generation. The first option seriously damages government credibility. The second, undoubtedly the best option of the three, requires adequate external financing to allow for a smooth transition.

22. Guillermo Ortiz, "Mexico beyond the Debt Crisis: Toward Sustainable Growth with Price Stability," in Michael Bruno and others, eds., *Lessons of Economic Stabilization and Its Aftermath* (MIT Press, 1991), p. 286.

23. López Portillo's bank nationalization in 1982 angered the financial and business communities, which included the reprivatization of the banks among their key "demands." See Roberto Newell G. and Luis Rubio F., *Mexico's Dilemma: The Political Origins of Economic Crisis* (Boulder, Colo: Westview Press, 1984), pp. 263–66.

24. For a discussion of the split within the ruling party and of the bankers' demands, see Sylvia Maxfield, *Governing Capital: International Finance and Mexican Politics* (Cornell University Press, 1990), pp. 149–53.

25. Nora Lustig, "Políticas de estabilización, nivel de actividad, salarios reales y empleo: Argentina, Brasil, México y Perú, 1980-1988," Instituto Latinoamericano de Estudios Transnacionales (ILET), June 1990.

26. During the 1980s Argentina and Brazil accumulated a large sum of arrears with the commercial banks.

27. United States International Trade Commission (USITC), *Review of Trade and Investment Liberalization Measures by Mexico and Prospects for Future United States–Mexican Relations, Phase 1: Recent Trade and Investment Reforms Undertaken by Mexico and Implications for the United States*, Investigation 332-282, Publication 2275 (Washington, April 1990), p. 4-3.

28. The reforms in the trade regime are discussed in chapter 5.

29. By an unfortunate coincidence of events, the suspension of IMF disbursements was made known to the public through a newspaper article that appeared the day after the earthquake. Gurría, "La reestructuración de la deuda," p. 93.

30. The Mexican government had anticipated some decline in oil prices but not anywhere near the actual drop. In late 1985 the 1986 budget was

prepared assuming a price of U.S.$23 a barrel. The price for the Mexican blend fell from U.S.$24.7 a barrel in December 1985 to U.S.$19.7 in January 1986. The price continued to decline to its lowest level in 12 years (in nominal terms), when it reached U.S.$8.6, in July 1986. See Banco de México, *Informe anual, 1986* (México City, April 1987), p. 17; and Macro Asesoría Económica, *Realidad económica de México, 1991*, table 8.8, p. 247.

31. Banco de México, *Informe anual, 1986*, p. 17.

32. Ibid.; and Ortiz, "Mexico beyond the Debt Crisis," p. 289.

33. Gurría, "La reestructuración de la deuda, p. 94.

34. An initial agreement was completed in February 1986, but it was decided to postpone a final agreement until the course of oil prices became clearer. Ibid., pp. 95–96, 106–07.

35. IBRD, "Statement of Loans," Latin American and the Caribbean, March 1992, p. 438.

36. It has been suggested that differences of opinion in this area lay behind the resignation of Jesús Silva Herzog, who until then had been the star in de la Madrid's cabinet. Gurría, "La reestructuración de la deuda," pp. 95–96.

37. Ibid., p. 96.

38. In 1985 the government and the commercial banks signed another restructuring agreement, which covered the U.S.$48 billion of medium- and long-run debt. Amortizations were rescheduled, and the U.S. prime rate was replaced by the LIBOR; the surcharges were also reduced. Gurría, "La política de deuda externa," p. 5.

39. Macro Asesoría Económica, *Realidad económica de México, 1991*, table 3-1, p. 55.

40. Net reserves, however, declined by U.S.$1 million. Ibid., p. 575.

41. Banco de México, *Informe anual, 1986*, p. 22.

42. Lustig and Ros, *Mexico*, p. 49.

43. Gurría, "La política de deuda externa," p. 5.

44. Gurría, "La reestructuración de la deuda," graph 2, p. 89.

45. This was the name given to the U.S.-led "Program for Sustained Growth" when James Baker was Secretary of the Treasury. The plan, announced in September 1985, signaled a shift in the emphasis of creditor countries' official management of the debt problem from austerity to growth. Secretary Baker promised to raise U.S.$29 billion of new credit over a three-year period for the fifteen so-called problem debtors. Mexico was one of them. U.N. Economic Commission for Latin American and the Caribbean (CEPAL), *The Evolution of the External Debt Problem in Latin America and the Caribbean*, Estudios e Informes de la CEPAL 72 (Santiago, 1988), pp. 25–27.

46. Gurría, "La política de deuda externa," pp. 6–7.

47. In August 1986 Mexico had negotiated a bridge loan of U.S.$1.6 billion. Of this total, some U.S.$1.1 billion came from OECD (and a few Latin American) countries and U.S.$500 million from commercial banks. The first were paid back in February 1987 with disbursements from the IMF and the World Bank. Gurría, "La reestructuración de la deuda," p. 100. Once again Gurría

provides a detailed account of the difficulties involved in generating this bridge loan.

48. Gurría, "La política de deuda externa," pp. 6–7.

49. Ibid., p. 6.

50. Gurría, "La reestructuración de la deuda," pp. 98–99.

51. The inflationary consequences of a crawling peg are by now widely acknowledged in the economic literature.

52. Pacto de Solidaridad Económica, known as PSE, PASE, or simply "el Pacto." See Nora Lustig, "México, El 'Pacto de Solidaridad, Económica': La heterodoxia puesta en marcha en México," in Guillermo Rozenwurcel, ed., *Elecciones y política económica en América Latina* (Buenos Aires: Grupo Editorial Norma, 1991).

53. The primary surplus of the public sector was to increase by 3 percentage points in 1988. Private credit would be restricted by setting lending ceilings equal to 90 percent, and later 85 percent, of the commercial banks' outstanding average balance in December 1987. Ortiz, "Mexico beyond the Debt Crisis," pp. 291–92.

54. Workers, businessmen, and the government would agree on a "basic commodity" basket. After February they would jointly project inflation based on this basic commodity basket and agree to increase wages and prices according to this projection. The "Pact" included a trigger clause should inflation exceed the projected rate by a cumulative five percentage points. Under these circumstances the minimum wages would be fully adjusted to past inflation. Pedro Aspe, "Estabilización macroeconómica y cambio estructural: La experiencia de México (1982–1988)," in Carlos Bazdresch, Nisso Bucay, and Nora Lustig, eds., *México: Auge, crisis y ajuste* (Mexico City: Fondo de Cultura Económica, forthcoming).

55. It is not clear whether this policy change was not known in December or whether it was kept secret to avoid negative reactions from the public and business sectors.

56. This 3 percent increase in minimum wages was far lower than the cumulative loss of purchasing power during January and February. Inflation (CPI) was at its highest rate, 15.5 percent, in January but began to slide in February and reached 8.3 percent. Aspe, "Estabilización macroeconómica"; and Macro Asesoría Económica, *Realidad económica de México, 1991*, table 2.1, p. 23.

57. Ortiz, "Mexico Beyond the Debt Crisis," pp. 291–93.

58. Macro Asesoría Económica, *Realidad económica de México, 1991*, table 2-1, pp. 22–23.

59. Ibid., table 14.2, pp. 412–13.

60. See Daniela Gressani, "The Effects of the Mexican Stabilization Program on Inflation: Simulation Results with a Model for Wage and Price Determination," World Bank, October 1989.

61. Aspe, in "Estabilización macroeconómica," underscores the conspicuous lack of external support from either the IMF or commercial banks. Also, see table 2-5.

62. Though some would argue that the November 1987 devaluation may have been unwarranted, it became one of the factors that set the stage for implementation of the Pact. The acceleration in inflation to unprecedented levels encouraged Mexican policymakers to explore unchartered waters in stabilization policy in Mexico.

63. Ortiz, "Mexico beyond the Debt Crisis," p. 292. For a more detailed description of trade liberalization, see chapter 5.

64. The yearly real domestic interest rate reached was 30 percent on average during 1989. Sweder van Wijnbergen, "Debt Relief and Economic Growth in Mexico," *World Bank Economic Review*, vol. 5, no. 3 (1991), pp. 452–53. During January through June of 1989, the implicit annual real return on treasury bonds was 38 percent. Banco de México, *The Mexican Economy, 1990: Economic and Financial Developments in 1989, Policies for 1990* (Mexico City, May 1990), p. 77.

65. Ortiz, "Mexico beyond the Debt Crisis," p. 294; and Banco de México, *The Mexican Economy, 1989: Economic and Financial Developments in 1988, Policies for 1989* (Mexico City, May 1989), p. 120.

66. For further discussion of the relationship among the quasi-fixed exchange rate policy, interest rates, and fiscal accounts during the Pact, see Daniel F. Oks, "Stabilization and Growth Recovery in Mexico: Lessons and Dilemmas," Working Paper WPS833 (World Bank, January 1992).

67. The appreciation is inevitable because the nominal value of the peso is kept fixed while inflation, though lower, continues.

68. See Alain Ize, "Trade Liberalization, Stabilization and Growth: Some Notes on the Mexican Experience," IMF Working Paper WP/90/15 (Washington, March 1990).

69. See Rudiger Dornbusch, "Policies to Move from Stabilization to Growth," *Proceedings of the World Bank Annual Conference on Development Economics, 1990* (Washington: World Bank, 1991), pp. 19–48.

70. A priori it is not clear what causes domestic interest rates to be high. Is it because the demand for money rises as a consequence of the fall in inflation and the supply of money does not accommodate to the rise? Or is it because the fixed exchange rate rule is not credible and high interest rates are just a premium for risk of holding pesos? As Aspe points out, this poses a serious dilemma regarding which monetary policy to follow; in the case of Mexico lack of credibility seems to have been the cause of high domestic interest rates. Aspe, "Estabilización macroeconómica."

71. Córdoba, "Diez lecciones de la reforma económica," p. 35.

72. For an analysis of the political economy of the Pact, see Robert Kaufman, Carlos Bazdresch, and Blanca Heredia, "The Politics of the Economic Solidarity Pact in Mexico: December 1987 to December 1988," paper presented at the Conference on the Political Economy of Democratic Transitions, World Bank, Washington, D.C., May 4–5, 1992.

73. However, these periodic revisions also introduced greater uncertainty on the sustainability of the Pact, which translated into the very high domestic interest rates.

74. Córdoba, "Diez lecciones de la reforma económica," p. 35, argues that the Pact was successful because it also conveyed a sense of "justice." However, given the evolution of real wages and real interest rates this is questionable.

75. Rojas-Suárez argues that "economic agents' concerns about the sustainability of the fiscal and monetary efforts were also a major factor preventing the success of the adjustment programs conducted throughout the period 1983–87." Liliana Rojas-Suárez, "From the Debt Crisis toward Economic Stability: An Analysis of the Consistency of Macroeconomic Policies in Mexico," IMF Working Paper WP/92/17 (Washington, March 1992), p. 28.

76. Salinas's influence on economic policy had been strong, especially from 1986 to 1988, during de la Madrid's administration. As secretary of budget and programing, Salinas proposed many of the reforms that were implemented and played a role in coordinating them.

77. Net resource transfers are defined as the sum of gross amortizations, interest payments, and other net outflows (that is, capital flight) minus the sum of gross external credit, direct foreign investment, and net remittances. For a discussion of how net resource transfers to the outside world limit stabilization policies and economic recovery, see, for example, Ortiz, "Mexico beyond the Debt Crisis"; and Rudiger Dornbusch, "Mexico: Stabilization, Debt and Growth," *Economic Policy: A European Forum*, vol. 3 (October 1988), pp. 262–67.

78. Brailovsky, Clarke, and Warman, *La política económica del desperdicio*, p. 364. Figures are measured in 1970 prices.

79. Gurría, "La política de deuda externa."

80. Named after U.S. Secretary of the Treasury Nicholas Brady, during whose term the plan was announced.

81. For a description of the agreement, see the appendix.

82. With 1992 interest rates, the savings in cash flow were even lower. Initial estimates were calculated at a LIBOR equal to about 9 percent a year. Two years later LIBOR rates fell to almost half that level, so the savings in cash flow due to interest rate reduction were almost halved.

83. See, for example, the analysis by van Wijnbergen, "Debt Relief and Economic Growth," pp. 437–55.

84. Banco de México, *The Mexican Economy, 1991: Economic and Financial Developments in 1990, Policies for 1991* (Mexico City, May 1991), p. 80.

85. Interest rates fell immediately after the agreement in principle with the commercial banks was reached in July 1989 but rose again thereafter. Banco de México, *Mexican Economy, 1990*, p. 79; and Macro Asesoría Económica, *Realidad económica de México, 1991*, table 9.9, p. 325.

86. Banco de México, *Mexican Economy, 1991*, p. 81.

87. This number includes U.S.$2.9 billion that was registered under a new fiscal amnesty scheme known as the Fiscal Stamp. Secretaría de Hacienda y Crédito Público, "Mexico: A New Economic Profile," Mexico City, January 1991, p. 23.

88. *GEA Económico* (Grupo de Economistas y Asociados), Mexico City,

December 12, 1991, p. 19. The figures are based on data from the Bank of Mexico.

89. Secretaría de Comercio y Fomento Industrial (SECOFI), "Evolución de la inversión extranjera directa en 1991," Mexico City, January 1992, tables 1 and 3.

90. Gurría, "La política de deuda externa," pp. 13–14. In early 1992 Mexico's total World Bank lending reached U.S.$20 billion. Thus Mexico became the main receiver of overall World Bank lending. IMF, "Morning Press," May 13, 1992.

91. The current account deterioration cannot be ascribed to the public sector because "nominal public saving rose more than enough to finance increased investment implying that the entire current account deterioration could be ascribed to declining private saving." Patricio Arrau and Daniel F. Oks, "Private Saving in Mexico, 1980–90," WPS 861, (World Bank, February 1992), p. 3. Conventional measures of private saving showed a sharp decline in 1990; however, the picture is somewhat changed when data are corrected (ibid., pp. 3–4). A corrected measure of private saving shows a decline, albeit smaller. For some observers, this decline of private saving "could put at risk Mexico's economic recovery as the accumulation of external liabilities is not backed by additional resources to service them in the future." Daniel F. Oks, "Stabilization and Growth Recovery in Mexico," p. 17.

92. Banco de México, *Informe anual, 1991* (Mexico City, 1992), p. 5.

93. The Mexican situation has some similarities to the private sector boom experienced in Chile before the crash of 1982. This causes some concern. However, in Mexico, compared with Chile in that period, there is much more control over the banking and financial sector, there is no automatic wage indexation mechanism, and there is the prospect of a NAFTA. For an analysis of alternative scenarios, see, for example, Jaime Ros, "Mexico: Constraints on Medium-term Economic Growth," paper prepared for the WIDER project on Medium-Term Development Strategy, rev. version, January 1990.

94. If trade liberalization occurs with an undervalued exchange rate, and as a result of liberalization the share of imported goods increases, internal prices could actually go up instead of down during the first stage of liberalization.

Chapter Three

1. For an exposition of these mechanisms, see, for example, W. M. Corden, *Inflation, Exchange Rates and the World Economy: Lectures on International Monetary Economics* (University of Chicago Press, 1977), chaps. 1, 2; and François Bourguignon, Jaime de Melo, and Christian Morrisson, "Poverty and Income Distribution during Adjustment: Issues and Evidence from the OECD Project," *World Development*, vol. 19 (November 1991), pp. 1485–1508.

2. In general, real life situations lie somewhere in between, because gov-

ernments may be unable to produce a smooth adjustment even with carefully engineered policies.

3. See, for example, Corden, *Inflation, Exchange Rates and the World Economy*, pp. 28–29.

4. See, for example, ibid., pp. 26–28; Rudiger Dornbusch, *Open Economy Macroeconomics* (Basic Books, 1980), pp. 73–74; and Lance Taylor, *Structuralist Macroeconomics: Applicable Models for the Third World* (Basic Books, 1983), pp. 25–27.

5. For an analytical discussion of these issues, see Joshua Aizenman and Marcelo Selowsky, "Costly Adjustment and Limited Borrowing," *International Economic Journal*, vol. 5 (Summer 1991), pp. 17–38.

6. Real wages can be flexible in the downward direction even if money wages are not, so long as the rise in money wages falls below that of the general price level.

7. Instituto Nacional de Estadística, Geografía e Informática (INEGI), *Encuesta nacional de ingresos y gastos de los hogares, tercer trimestre de 1984* (Mexico City, 1989).

8. One way out of this is to analyze the evolution of physical and human resources per capita in the health and education sectors, something that is done later in the chapter.

9. See INEGI, *Encuesta nacional de ingresos y gastos, 1984*; and INEGI, *Encuesta nacional de ingresos y gastos de los hogares 1989: Transacciones económicas* (Mexico City, 1992).

10. Coordinación General del Sistema Nacional de Información, *Encuesta nacional de ingresos y gastos de los hogares 1977: Primera observación* (Mexico City, Secretaría de Programación y Presupuesto, August 1979), table P2.3, p. 79. For a compilation of these data, see Nora Lustig, "Distribución del ingreso y consumo de alimentos: Estructura, tendencias y requerimientos redistributivos a nivel regional," *Demografía y Economía*, vol. 16, no. 2 (1982), table 2, p. 111. For the minimum wage in pesos, see Lustig, ibid., table 3, p. 112. For the dollar exchange rate, see Macro Asesoría, *Realidad económica de México, 1991* (Mexico City, 1990), p. 445.

11. Nora Lustig, "Distribución del ingreso y consumo de alimentos," table 5, p. 115.

12. Poder Ejecutivo Federal, *Plan global de desarrollo, 1980–82* (Mexico City), p. 199. Mexico's total population was 66.9 million in 1980. See INEGI, *Estadísticas históricas de México*, tomo 1 (Mexico City, August 1985), p. 33.

13. See table 3-11. Mexico's rate is higher than those of other countries with lower per capita income levels (such as Malaysia and Paraguay). UNICEF, *Estado mundial de la infancia* (Madrid: Siglo Veintiuno de España, 1984, 1986).

14. UNICEF, *Estado mundial de la infancia*, 1986, pp. 120, 135. Low birth weight is one indication of the prevalence of malnutrition.

15. Miguel de la Madrid, *Cuarto informe de gobierno: Anexo* (Mexico City, 1986), p. 316.

16. COPLAMAR, *Necesidades esenciales en México: Situación actual y perspectivas al año 2000*, vol. 4 (Mexico City: Siglo Veintiuno, 1982), pp. 172–75.

17. UNICEF, *Estado mundial de la infancia*, 1986, p. 139.

18. Jorge Padua, *Educación, industrialización y progreso técnico en México* (Mexico City: El Colegio de México, 1984), p. 105 and table 3-10.

19. Centro de Investigación para el Desarollo (CIDAC), *Vivienda y estabilidad política* (Mexico City: Editorial Diana, 1991), p. 16.

20. COPLAMAR, *Necesidades esenciales en México*, vol. 3 (Mexico City: Siglo Veintiuno, 1982), p. 57.

21. There was *no* decline in nominal wages. Real wages declined as nominal wages rose at a slower pace than the general price level.

22. The definition of *employment* used by the National Accounts is of work-posts, that is, the number of laborers needed to produce a certain level of output given some labor-to-output coefficients. It is an indirect estimate of employment.

23. The other wages included in table 3-2 measure actual wage performance, whereas the minimum wage is a legal convention.

24. One author, for example, suggests that other paths are possible though perhaps difficult to implement. See Raúl Ramos Tercero, "La caída de los salarios reales y las transferencias al exterior: Una interpretación inspirada por la experiencia mexicana, 1982–1987," Mexico City, n.d.

25. Some authors go as far as to state that real wages did not need to decline at all if a different policy direction had been taken. For example, David Barkin suggests that crisis management in Mexico should have been equivalent to managing a "war economy." His recommended solution was for Mexico to substantially raise grain prices and pass "a decree to double the 1990 minimum wage." Barkin, *Distorted Development: Mexico in the World Economy* (Boulder, Colo.: Westview Press, 1990), pp. 115–23. In another study, using a computable general equilibrium (CGE) model of the Mexican economy, Irma Adelman and J. Edward Taylor find that abandoning what they call the "wage-repression strategy" would result in higher growth rates, a more equal distribution of income, a lower fiscal deficit, and a just slightly worsened trade balance. Adelman and Taylor, "Is Structural Adjustment with a Human Face Possible? The Case of Mexico," *Journal of Developmental Studies*, vol. 26 (April 1990), pp. 387–407. For all their humanitarian appeal, the recommendations of these authors may not be based on solid analytical ground. If the decision is to absorb external shocks internally, a rise in nominal wages would result in higher inflation, increased capital flight, and a deeper economic decline. If the decision is *not* to absorb shocks internally, then keeping real wages from falling would depend on the impact of a debt moratorium on private investors' behavior and the availability of other sources of foreign exchange. Adelman and Taylor's results probably follow from their assumptions about the determinants of output (primarily demand-driven) and the behavior of expectations. In real life, countries that tried to apply policies analogous to those recommended by them found themselves in deep trouble. Take as examples the consequences of the 1986 "heterodox shock" in Peru, and Brazil after the "Crusado Plan."

26. The number of strikes did rise compared with prior years, but the

increase seems modest when compared with the size of wage cuts. In 1982 the number of strikes rose by over sixfold to 675. However, the number fell in 1983 to 230, even though real wages declined by 25 percent in that year alone; there was an upsurge with the 1986 oil shock, when the number reached 312. Thereafter the numbers fell to precrisis levels. Carlos Salinas de Gortari, *Segundo informe de gobierno: Anexo* (Mexico City, 1990), p. 334.

27. Alain Ize, "Trade Liberalization, Stabilization, and Growth: Some Notes on the Mexican Experience," Working Paper 90/15 (International Monetary Fund, March 1990), table 1, p. 6.

28. CEPAL, *Economía campesina y agricultura empresarial: Tipología de productores del agro mexicano* (Mexico City: Siglo Veintiuno, 1982), table 17, p. 152.

29. Kirsten Appendini, "De la milpa a los tortibonos: La reestructuración de la política alimentaria en México," Instituto de Investigaciones de las Naciones Unidas para el Desarrollo Social (UNRISD), June 1991, pp. 69–70.

30. Peter Gregory, "The Mexican Labor Market in the Economic Crisis and Lessons of the Past," in William E. Cole, ed., *Mexico's Economic Policy: Past, Present and Future*, Socioeconomic Research Series (Knoxville, Tenn.: Center for Business and Economic Research, November 1987), p. 57.

31. Appendini, "De la milpa a los tortibonos," pp. 64–66.

32. Ibid., pp. 75–76.

33. Ibid., pp. 84–85.

34. *Compendio de indicadores de empleo y salarios* (Mexico City: Comisión Nacional de los Salarios Mínimos, 1989), p. 27.

35. There is evidence that formal sector employment declined. Gregory, "Mexican Labor Market," p. 56.

36. The percentage of wage earners in total employment fell between 1982 and 1989. The percentage of family workers without remuneration in three major urban centers increased between 1982 and 1985, then held steady afterward. Of the three urban centers, only in Mexico City was there an increase in the percentage of self-employed workers between 1982 and 1985. Between 1985 and 1989, the average percentage of self-employed workers in sixteen urban areas rose. See Nora Lustig, "Economic Crisis and Living Standards," table 9, p. 56; and *Compendio de indicadores*, pp. 99–100.

37. The implicit unemployment rate was calculated as the ratio between total employment and the economically active population (EAP). Figures for total employment are from *Compendio de indicadores*, table 1.1, p. 27. The figure for EAP is a linear extrapolation from figures in ibid., table 2.6, p. 67.

38. The concept of underemployment is always difficult to define. It refers to the fact that people are employed in activities with very low productivity levels and pay.

39. Gregory, "Mexican Labor Market," p. 55.

40. *Compendio de indicadores*, pp. 99–100.

41. Ibid., p. 67.

42. An indirect indicator of this is that real private consumption per capita declined by substantially less than real wages (table 3-2).

43. Total government spending here refers to the sum of the so-called

programmable plus nonprogrammable expenditures. For a definition, see table 3-7.

44. Social expenditures also include spending on two other categories known as "solidarity" and "urban development."

45. This was not the case every year, but it was particularly true in 1983.

46. This means that actual changes in government services may differ from those reflected by the numbers in the text, and also that, strictly speaking, trends among the various expenditure categories cannot be compared. In particular, sector-specific deflators for programmable and nonprogrammable expenditures are probably different.

47. Some of the yearly changes in the student per school ratios cannot easily be explained. See, for example, the sharp decline between 1985–86 and 1986–87, a shift that may be more indicative of the poor quality of education statistics in Mexico than of any actual changes.

48. The general food subsidies covered bread, tortillas, beans, eggs, milk, and cooking oil. Their final price was set by the government, and the producer was provided with subsidized inputs. For a description of the subsidy schemes and how they changed, see Antonio Martín del Campo and Rosendo Calderón Tinoco, "Restructuración de los subsidios a productos básicos y la modernización de CONASUPO," in Carlos Bazdresch, Nisso Bucay, and Nora Lustig, eds., *Mexico: Auge, crisis y ajuste* (Mexico City: Fondo de Cultura Económica, forthcoming).

49. Ibid., p. 43.

50. Ibid., p. 44.

51. Author's interview with CONASUPO official, December 1991.

52. Martín del Campo and Calderón Tincoco, "Restructuración de los subsidios."

53. For a description of the author's methodology in this calculation, see Lustig, "Economic Crisis and Living Standards," p. 38.

54. Pascual García Alba and Jaime Serra Puche, *Causas y efectos de la crisis económica en México* (Mexico City: El Colegio de México, 1983), table 23, pp. 104–07.

55. This is so because the consumption of these items is more concentrated at the lower level of the income scale. In contrast, the general subsidy on gasoline is strikingly regressive.

56. Instituto Nacional del Consumidor (INCO), "100 días en el consumo familiar," Mexico City, 1983.

57. Jacobo Schatan, "Nutrición y crisis en México," paper presented at the Fifth Seminar on Third World Agricultural Economics, UNAM, Mexico City, Nov. 11–15, 1985, p. 47.

58. Ibid., p. 51.

59. Ibid., p. 52.

60. It has been observed that the impact of an economic crisis is usually not reflected in average indicators and that its effect on health becomes obvious only over the long run. See, for example, a classic study on the effects of the Great Depression on health: G. St. J. Perrott and Selwyn D. Collins, "Sickness

among the Depression Poor," *American Journal of Public Health*, vol. 24 (February 1934), pp. 101–07.

61. Carlos Salinas de Gortari, *Tercer informe de gobierno: Anexo* (Mexico City, 1991), pp. 367–68.

62. To establish this would require a more careful analysis, though. An increase in the death rate due to nutritional deficiencies may be a consequence of a decrease in a substitute cause, such as intestinal diseases. Nonetheless, data show that deaths associated with both causes declined steadily through the 1970s. However, in the 1980s deaths caused by intestinal diseases fell, while those caused by nutritional deficiencies rose in both absolute and relative terms. See ibid. Even so, the statistics on causes of death may be subject to large measurement errors, and thus one should read the trends presented in table 3-10 with caution.

63. Miguel de la Madrid, *Tercer informe de gobierno: Salud y seguridad social*, vol. 16 (Mexico City, 1985), pp. 417–18.

64. These trends should be treated cautiously. There are some oscillations in the yearly figures that are difficult to explain and may be the result of measurement errors.

65. Fernando Valerio, "Fiscal Shock, Wage Compression and Structural Reform: Mexican Adjustment and Educational Policy in the 1980s," Innocenti Occasional Paper 17, Economic Policy Series, Fiscal Policy and the Poor (UNICEF, June 1991), p. 26.

66. Salinas de Gortari, *Segundo informe de gobierno*, p. 118.

67. Merilee S. Grindle, "The Response to Austerity: Political and Economic Strategies of Mexico's Rural Poor," in William L. Canek, ed., *Lost Promises: Debt, Austerity, and Development in Latin America* (Boulder, Colo.: Westview Press, 1989), pp. 190–215; and Mercedes González de la Rocha, "Economic Crisis, Domestic Reorganisation and Women's Work in Guadalajara, Mexico," *Bulletin of Latin American Research*, vol. 7, no. 2 (1988), pp. 207–23.

68. González de la Rocha, "Economic Crisis," pp. 219–20.

69. González de la Rocha mentions that the people she interviewed were more tired, worked more, and were more anxious about their future. Ibid., p. 220.

70. This was recorded by Grindle in her study of three rural Mexican villages. "Response to Austerity," pp. 199–205. For a discussion of undocumented migration to the United States, see Frank D. Bean, Barry Edmonston, and Jeffrey S. Passel, eds., *Undocumented Migration to the United States: IRCA and the Experience of the 1980s* (Washington: Urban Institute Press, 1990).

71. Apprehensions peaked in 1986 at 1,767,400 and slowed to 1,099,165 on average for 1987–88, probably as a result of the Immigration Reform and Control Act of 1986 (IRCA). Georges Vernez and David Ronfeldt, "The Current Situation in Mexican Immigration," *Science*, vol. 251 (March 8, 1991), p. 1190.

72. The Gini coefficient for households was estimated at .4384 and for individuals at .4881. See table 15 in Nora Lustig, "The Incidence of Poverty in Mexico, 1984: An Empirical Analysis," Brookings, October 1990.

73. Enrique Hernández-Laos, "Medición de la intensidad de la pobreza y

de la pobreza extrema en México," *Investigación Económica*, vol. 49, no. 191 (1990), p. 282. According to Hernández-Laos the extremely poor were those households or individuals whose income fell below a minimum consumption basket, which includes food and nonfood items.

74. Oscar Altimir, "The Extent of Poverty in Latin America," Working Paper 522 (World Bank, 1982), p. 82. Poor households are those whose income falls below a minimum food consumption basket.

75. In addition to Hernández-Laos, Joel Bergsman has presented evidence of diminishing poverty during this period. See Bergsman, "La distribución del ingreso y la pobreza en México," in *Distribución del ingreso en México: Ensayos*, vol. 1 (Mexico City: Banco de México, 1982), table 5, p. 224.

76. The poverty lines used to calculate the proportion of extremely poor households were U.S.$50.6 and U.S.$56.5 per quarter, respectively. The first poverty line is proposed in Santiago Levy, "Poverty Alleviation in Mexico," Policy, Research, and External Affairs Working Paper 679 (World Bank, May 1991), n. 42, p. 28, and table 2, pp. 24A–24B. The second poverty line is proposed by CEPAL, "Magnitud de la pobreza en América Latina en los años ochenta," no. 533 (May 31, 1990), table 9, p. 24. For a description of my method of poverty estimation, see Lustig, "Incidence of Poverty," pp. 18–20. I converted the peso-dominated lines of Levy and CEPAL to June 1984 U.S. dollars.

77. Lustig, "Incidence of Poverty," table 21. Of those who are wage earners, a large proportion work in agriculture. It is interesting to note that the fraction of employers, especially small employers, does not differ greatly between the lowest deciles and the ninth decile. The poor employers are probably peasants or small shopkeepers who may hire workers, also poor, to help with tasks. Most of the heads of household that are agricultural workers belong to the lowest deciles: 78 percent of them are in the lower 50 percent of households. Ibid., table 27.

78. The lower estimate excludes interest earned on foreign assets from capital-flight estimates. For more details, see Nora Lustig, "Dollar Waves: Mexico's Experience with Capital Flight and Repatriation," *International Economy*, vol. 5 (November–December 1991), pp. 67–71.

79. By the definitions used here, the extreme poverty line is the total cost of a food basket required to cover minimum caloric and protein needs.

80. For a discussion of policy options and their advantages and disadvantages, see Levy, "Poverty Alleviation in Mexico," pp. 45–71.

81. *Programa nacional de solidaridad: La solidaridad en el desarrollo nacional* (Mexico City: Secretaría de Programación y Presupuesto, September 1991), p. 3.

Chapter Four

1. For review articles on this debate, see Helen Shapiro and Lance Taylor, "The State and Industrial Strategy," *World Development*, vol. 18, no. 6 (1990),

pp. 861–78; and Albert Fishlow, "The Latin American State," *Journal of Economic Perspectives*, vol. 4 (Summer 1990), pp. 61–74. Throughout this chapter I use the terms *government* and *state* interchangeably.

2. To derive the per capita growth rate, I subtracted the average annual population growth rate—about 3 percent in the postwar era—from the average GDP growth rate in table 1-4. For the population growth statistics, see Instituto Nacional de Estadística, Geografía e Informática (INEGI), *Estadísticas históricas de México*, tomo 1 (Mexico City, August 1985), p. 10.

3. As discussed later, the government made more progress in increasing revenues and cutting expenditures than in reallocating the latter.

4. For oil exports, see World Bank, *Mexico in Transition: Towards a New Role for the Public Sector* (Washington, May 1991), p. 140. A "truer" measure of fiscal effort must exclude interest payments because they are not the direct result of fiscal policy. For more discussion of this issue, see chapter 2.

5. José Lusis Alberro-Semerena, "The Macroeconomics of the Public Sector Deficit in Mexico during the 1980s," El Colegio de México, June 1991, p. 67.

6. The public sector includes the federal government and public enterprises.

7. Prices of oil derivatives including gasoline had been kept low (below U.S. prices) during the oil-boom years. Jaime Mario Willars, "El papel del petróleo durante los ochenta: Elementos de política y perspectivas," paper presented at a conference, El Seminario sobre la Economía Mexicana: Situación Actual y Perspectivas Macroeconómicas, El Colegio de México, August 1983, p. 19.

8. Alvaro Baillet, "La evolución de los ingresos del sector público, 1983–1988," El Colegio de México, November 1988, pp. 58–59.

9. The loss of revenues because of collection lags is known as the Olivera-Tanzi effect. Baillet estimated that lags caused the Mexican government to lose 26 percent of potential income tax revenues in 1986. Ibid., p. 29.

10. For a discussion of the pre-1986 system's flaws and the reforms, see World Bank, *Mexico: Industrial Policy and Regulation*, Report 8165-ME (Washington, August 1990), pp. 42–46. Provisional tax payments were changed from quarterly to monthly, thereby reducing the Olivera-Tanzi effect.

11. Ibid, pp. 47–48.

12. For a description of the "crusade," see Baillet, "La evolución de los ingresos," p. 80.

13. World Bank, *Mexico in Transition*, pp. 120, 219.

14. Ibid., p. 145.

15. *GEA Económico* (Grupo de Economistas y Asociados), December 12, 1991, p. 28.

16. Alberro, "Macroeconomics of the Public Sector Deficit," pp. 66–67.

17. Ted Bardacke, "It Was Nice While It Lasted," *El Financiero International*, October 14, 1992, p. 3.

18. For detailed discussions of the constitutional basis of state intervention, see Berta Ulloa, *Historia de la Revolución Mexicana, 1914–1917: La Constitución de 1917* (Mexico City: El Colegio de México, 1983), chaps. 3–7; and Félix Vélez

Fernández Varela, "Condicionamientos estructurales del derecho económico en México," in Francisco Gil Díaz y Arturo M. Fernández, eds., *El efecto de la regulación en algunos sectores de la economía mexicana*, Lecturas 70 (Mexico City: Fondo de Cultura Económica, 1991), pp. 23–40.

19. For CFE's creation, see William Patton Glade, Jr., "Las empresas gubernamentales descentralizadas," *Problemas agrícolas e industriales de México*, vol. 11 (January–March 1959), p. 123. For the decision to convert CFE into a state-owned monopoly, see World Bank, "Public Enterprise Reform in Mexico" (Washington, May 1990), p. 6.

20. For a discussion of Mexican *parastatals'* history, see Glade, "Las empresas gubernamentales," pp. 35–182; and María Amparo Casar and Wilson Peres, *El estado empresario en México: ¿Agotamiento o renovación?* (Mexico City: Siglo Veintiuno, 1988), pp. 27–42.

21. Casar and Peres, *El estado empresario en México*, p. 29.

22. Recall that presidential terms begin on December 1 of the first calendar year in office.

23. United States International Trade Commission (USITC), *Review of Trade and Investment Liberalization Measures by Mexico and Prospects for Future United States—Mexican Relations*, Phase I: *Recent Trade and Investment Reforms Undertaken by Mexico and Implications for the United States*, Investigation 332-282, Pub. 2275 (Washington, April 1990), p. 3-7.

24. World Bank, "Public Enterprise Reform," tables II.3.1, II.3.4, II.3.7. The share of public enterprises (output) in GDP rose from 6.2 percent in 1975 to a peak of 16.1 percent in 1983. Excluding oil the share went from 3.9 percent in 1975 to 6.0 percent in 1983. Public enterprise employment in total employment rose from 3.5 percent in 1975 to 5.1 percent in 1983. The share of public enterprise investment in total investment fell from 38.2 percent in 1975 to 34.6 percent in 1979, rising again to around 38 percent in 1983.

25. In 1986 the government passed the Federal Law of Public Enterprises to establish the legal framework governing the relationship between public enterprises and regulatory agencies. Regulations and by-laws of this law were published in January 1990. They spell out methods and procedures for managing, operating, supervising, and privatizing public enterprises. See Antonio Martín del Campo and Donald Winckler, "State-Owned Enterprise Reform in Latin America," LATPS Occasional Paper 2, World Bank (Washington, July 25, 1991), p. 9.

26. The "strategic" sectors are minting of coins, mail service, telegraphs, radio and satellite communications, money emission, oil extraction, basic petrochemicals, radioactive materials, nuclear energy, electricity, and railways. Ibid. Agriculture is considered an example of a "priority" sector.

27. For a detailed analysis of this process, see ibid., pp. 23, 25–26.

28. In a special magazine section, the Secretariat of Finance and Public Credit (Secretaría de Hacienda y Crédito Público) states that there were 1,228 public enterprises in 1982. "El proceso de enajenación de entidades paraestatales," *Nexos*, vol. 14 (June 1990), graph 1, p. III. The Secretariat of Programming and Budget (Secretaría de Programación y Presupuesto) states that there

were 1,155 in 1982 (table 4-3). Estimates on the number of public enterprises have differed, but all are about 1,000. See Oscar Humberto Vera Ferrer, "The Political Economy of Privatization in Mexico," in William Glade, ed., *Privatization of Public Enterprises in Latin America* (San Francisco: Institute for Contemporary Studies, 1991), p. 45.

29. "El proceso de enajenación," graph 1, p. III. The definition of public enterprise here includes those enterprises in which the state has a majority or a minority of the shares.

30. The most important divested public enterprises during this period are Renault de México (automobiles) in 1983, Nacional Hotelera (hotels) in 1985, Cementos Anáhuac del Golfo (cement) in 1986, Finacril (synthetic fibers) and Grupo Atenquique (textiles) in 1987, and Ingenio El Potrero (sugar) and Tereftalatos Mexicanos (petrochemicals) in 1988. Banco de México, *The Mexican Economy, 1991: Economic and Financial Developments in 1990, Policies for 1991,* (Mexico City, May 1991), p. 119. The primary method of privatization was direct sale to private companies or, in some cases, labor unions.

31. Excluding PEMEX, the public enterprises' output share in GDP rose from 4.8 percent in 1982 to 6.4 percent in 1987. The rise does not reflect an expansion of the public sector; its output merely contracted by less than that of the private sector. Public enterprise employment (with PEMEX) in total employment hardly changed during 1983–87 (it equaled about 5 percent). See World Bank, "Public Enterprise Reform," tables II.3.1, II.3.7.

32. Poll results show that 39 percent of those questioned thought that privatization would help them and 29 percent thought it would harm them. *Este país: Tendencias y opiniones,* no. 9 (December 1991), p. 16.

33. Jaime Ros, "Apertura comercial y reestructuración económica en México," paper presented at the Seminar on Structural Reform in Latin America, Cartagena, Colombia, April 1991, p. 23.

34. The two airlines (Aeroméxico and Mexicana) and the copper mining company (CANANEA), however, had been put on sale during de la Madrid's administration. Apparently, in these three cases, the process of privatization was far from smooth. The contract of sale for Aeroméxico was signed at the end of de la Madrid's administration, but the deal was not concluded until June 1989. See Enrique Quintana, "Empresas privatizadas: Divorcios y conflictos," *Este país,* no. 9, (December 1991), pp. 12–13; "El proceso de enajenación," p. xii; and Banco de México, *Mexican Economy, 1991,* p. 119.

35. When the banks were nationalized by López Portillo in 1982, the financial community viewed it as an act of extreme arbitrariness on the part of the government. Early in his term de la Madrid had announced that the private sector could own up to one-third of the banks. This partial reversal may have pleased neither those who opposed the reprivatization nor those who were against the nationalization in the first place. In that sense it failed to have the confidence-building effect hoped for with the formal announcement made in May 1990. However, given the political and economic conditions of that period, a full reprivatization of the banks may not have been advisable. For a discussion of the privatization decision, see Banco de México, *Mexican*

Economy, 1991, pp. 92–96. For analysis of de la Madrid's policy approach, see Sylvia Maxfield, *Governing Capital: International Finance and Mexican Politics* (Cornell University Press, 1990), pp. 149–53.

36. Banco de México, *Mexican Economy, 1991*, pp. 79–80; and chapter 2.

37. By the end of 1991 the government had sold nine of eighteen state-owned banks, including the two most important, Banamex and Bancomer, for a total of U.S. $7.12 billion. See Mike Zellner, "Banks Are Selling Well—Maybe Too Well," *El Financiero International*, December 30, 1991, p. 9.

38. Banco de México, *Mexican Economy, 1991*, p. 119.

39. "Government Privatizations Near End," *El Financiero International*, January 6, 1992, p. 3.

40. José Córdoba, "Diez lecciones de la reforma económica en México," *Nexos*, no. 158 (February 1991), p. 39. In mid-1991 the "liquidity coefficient" rule was subject to another change. Its impact is controversial. See Fundación CEDEAL, *Situación Latinoamericana* [Madrid], no. 5 (October 1991), pp. 124–25.

41. See Centro de Análisis e Investigación Económica (CAIE), "The Liberalization of Financial Services in Mexico," *The Mexican Economy: A Monthly Report*, vol. 8 (February 1991), p. 19; and USITC, *Review of Trade and Investment Liberalization Measures*, Phase I, p. 3-1.

42. Córdoba, "Diez lecciones," p. 39.

43. USITC, *Review of Trade and Investment Liberalization Measures*, Phase I, p. 3-1.

44. See Córdoba, "Diez lecciones," p. 39.

45. Ros, "Apertura comercial," pp. 20–21.

46. Ibid., p. 21. The decree did not eliminate the prohibition of foreign carriers from operating in Mexico. However, officials of Mexico and the United States expect this to change as a result of negotiations for a North American Free Trade Agreement. The Mexican government announced it will formulate a new regulatory framework for tourism, which would include lifting current restrictions on the movement of U.S. passenger bus lines and chartered U.S. buses on Mexican highways. See USITC, *Review of Trade and Investment Liberalization Measures*, Phase I, pp. 3-4, 3-5.

47. World Bank, *Mexico: Industrial Policy and Regulation*, p. ix.

48. USITC, *Review of Trade and Investment Liberalization Measures*, Phase I, pp. 3-5, 3-6, and 5-10.

49. Reserved species include abalone, clams, cabarilla, shrimp, lobsters, oysters, sea turtles, and totoabas. USITC, *Review of Trade and Investment Liberalization Measures*, Phase I, p. 3-2.

50. Ibid.

51. World Bank, *Mining Sector Restructuring Project*, Staff Appraisal Report 9428-ME (Washington, May 30, 1991), p. 8. According to this study, 50 percent of the 12 million hectares of discovered mineral land are currently reserved for the state.

52. Ibid., pp. 10–11.

53. USITC, *Review of Trade and Investment Liberalization Measures*, Phase I, pp. 3-6, 3-7.

54. Ibid., p. 3-6.

55. World Bank, *Mexico: Industrial Policy and Regulation*, pp. 20–23; and *GEA Económico*, September 12, 1991, p. 4.

56. For a description, see Martín del Campo and Winckler, "State-Owned Enterprise Reform," pp. 9, 13–14, 15, 19–22.

57. John J. Bailey, *Governing Mexico: The Statecraft of Crisis Management* (St. Martin's Press, 1988), pp. 83–86.

58. For example, inflation is announced bimonthly instead of once a month, and foreign reserves, stock exchange, and interest rate movements are followed closely.

59. Alberro, "Macroeconomics of the Public Sector Deficit," table 2.4, pp. 18, 21. The inflation tax is defined as the amount of revenue the government implicitly collects by paying negative rates of return on government debt or reducing the purchasing capacity of money in the hands of the public.

60. CAIE, *The Mexican Economy: A Monthly Report*, vol. 7 (March 1989), pp. 7–8. Open-market operations are compatible with the fixed exchange rate system that Mexico is striving to achieve, and with the free mobility of capital already in place.

61. Alain de Janvry and Elisabeth Sadoulet, for example, argue that the response to the debt crisis may have led to too much of a reduction of the state's role in the economy. This reduction is likely to be reversed in the future as the costs of "overderegulation" become patent or new needs for government intervention arise. See de Janvry and Sadoulet, "State, Market, and Civil Institutions in Latin America Beyond the Debt Crisis: The Context for Rural Development," University of California at Berkeley, n.d.

62. John Vickers and George Yarrow, "Economic Perspectives on Privatization," *Journal of Economic Perspectives*, vol. 5 (Spring 1991), pp. 116–18.

63. Ibid., pp. 118–19.

Chapter Five

1. In addition to the licensing system, the government introduced domestic content requirements in the automobile sector in 1962 and so-called manufacturing programs designed to enhance the production of heavy intermediate products and capital goods. See Jaime Ros, "Mexico's Trade and Industrialization Experience since 1960: A Reconsideration of Past Policies and Assessment of Current Reforms," paper presented to the UNU/WIDER Conference on Trade and Industrialization (Paris, June 1991), pp. 3–4.

2. Adriaan Ten Kate, Robert Bruce Wallace, and others, *La política de protección en el desarrollo económico de México* (Mexico City: Fondo de Cultura Económica, 1979), pp. 128–29, 139–55.

3. Ros, "Mexico's Trade and Industrialization," pp. 4–7. For background on Mexico's industrial and trade policy, see, for example, René Villarreal, *El desequilibrio externo en la industrialización de México, 1929–1975: Un enfoque estructuralista* (Mexico City: Fondo de Cultura Económica, 1976); Gerardo

Bueno, "The Structure of Protection in Mexico," in Bela Balassa and Associates, *The Structure of Protection in Developing Countries* (Johns Hopkins Press, 1971); and Ten Kate, Wallace, and others, *La política de protección.*

4. Ros, "Mexico's Trade and Industrialization," pp. 6–7.

5. Ibid., p. 11.

6. Ibid., pp. 15–19.

7. For a detailed discussion of trade liberalization, see Adriaan Ten Kate, "Trade Liberalization and Economic Stabilization in Mexico: Lessons of Experience," *World Development*, vol. 20 (May 1992), pp. 659–72; Jaime Zabludovsky and Florencio López-de-Silanes, "Trade and Industrial Policy for Structural Adjustment in Mexico," Mexico City, July 1989, pp. 13–22; and United States International Trade Commission (USITC), *Review of Trade and Investment Liberalization Measures by Mexico and Prospects for Future United States-Mexican Relations*, Phase I: *Recent Trade and Investment Reforms Undertaken by Mexico and Implications for the United States*, Investigation 332-282, Pub. 2275 (Washington, April 1990), chapter 4; and Ros, "Mexico's Trade and Industrialization," pp. 31–41.

8. In chapter 2, I discussed the rationale the government gave for intensifying the liberalization process in December 1987. The idea was that external prices would work as "ceilings" for domestic prices in the tradables sector. That was seen as important for ensuring the success of the Economic Solidarity Pact.

9. USITC, *Review of Trade and Investment Liberalization Measures*, Phase I, p. 4-4.

10. Ibid.

11. Ten Kate, "Trade Liberalization and Economic Stabilization," table 3, p. 664.

12. Available modeling exercises support this. See, for example, Raúl Hinojosa-Ojeda and Sherman Robinson, "Alternative Scenarios of U.S.-Mexico Integration: A Computable General Equilibrium Approach," Working Paper 609 (University of California at Berkeley, Department of Agricultural and Resource Economics, April 1991); and Santiago Levy and Sweder van Wijnbergen, "Maize and the Mexico—United States Free Trade Agreement," World Bank, Washington, December 1990. For a summary of the results, see Raúl Hinojosa-Ojeda and Sherman Robinson, "Labor Issues in a North American Free Trade Area," in Nora Lustig, Barry Bosworth, and Robert Z. Lawrence, eds., *North American Free Trade: Assessing the Impact* (Brookings, 1992).

13. USITC, *Review of Trade and Investment Liberalization Measures*, Phase I, pp. 4-9, 4-10.

14. Ibid., p. 4-17.

15. Ros, "Mexico's Trade and Industrialization," p. 34.

16. Ibid.

17. Alain Ize, "Trade Liberalization, Stabilization, and Growth: Some Notes on the Mexican Experience," Working Paper 90/15 (Washington: International Monetary Fund, March 1990).

18. Aslan Cohen, "Effects of Trade Liberalization on Exports," University of California at Berkeley, June 1989, pp. 14–27.

19. Cohen, "Effects of Trade Liberalization," pp. 17–18.

20. Ros, "Mexico's Trade and Industrialization," p. 44; Nora Lustig, "Tipo de cambio, protección efectiva y exportaciones manufactureras: México, 1983–1987," in James W. Wilkie and Jesús Reyes Heroles González Garza, eds., *Industria y trabajo en México* (Mexico City: Universidad Autónoma Metropolitana Azcapotzalco, 1990), pp. 209, 217–21; and José I. Casar Pérez, *Transformación en el patrón de especialización y comercio exterior del sector manufacturero mexicano, 1978–1987* (Mexico City: Nacional Financiera, 1989), pp. 89–101.

21. Ros, "Mexico's Trade and Industrialization," table 2.5, p. 45. The extent to which growth of automotive and computer exports is explained by the foreign exchange requirements demanded from these sectors as a result of the respective industrial programs—regardless of the exchange rate and the status of trade liberalization—is a question that merits further research.

22. Cohen, "Effects of Trade Liberalization," pp. 16–17.

23. Ros, "Mexico's Trade and Industrialization," pp. 50–53.

24. Georgina Kessell and Ricardo Samaniego, "Apertura comercial, productividad y desarrollo tecnológico: El caso de México," Documento de Trabajo 112 (Banco Interamericano de Desarrollo, March 1992), p. 63.

25. The link between trade reform and efficiency at the level of the firm is another area that deserves further analysis.

26. James R. Tybout and M. Daniel Westbrook, "Trade Liberalization and the Structure of Production in Mexican Manufacturing Industries," paper funded by Mexico's Secretary of Commerce and Industrial Development (SECOFI), Office of Trade Negotiations, October 9, 1991, p. 37.

27. Ros, "Mexico's Trade and Industrialization," pp. 42–43.

28. Ibid., table 2.4, p. 43.

29. Ibid., p. 35.

30. World Bank, *Mexico: Industrial Policy and Regulation*, Report 8165-ME, (Washington, August 1990), p. 111.

31. For a summary of the policy objectives in this period see, for example, Wilson Peres Nuñez, *Foreign Direct Investment and Industrial Development in Mexico* (Paris: OECD, 1990), pp. 41–46; Ros, "Mexico's Trade and Industrialization," p. 36; and World Bank, *Mexico: Industrial Policy and Regulation*, pp. 12–16.

32. These priority industries included automobiles and autoparts, pharmaceuticals, capital goods, microcomputers, petrochemicals, consumer appliances, food products, textiles, shoes, furniture, cellulose and paper, iron and steel, cement, basic chemicals, and transport. See World Bank, *Mexico: Industrial Policy and Regulation*, p. 15.

33. Ibid., p. 12. Firms in priority industries without broad programs continued receiving many of the industrial incentives of the firm-specific programs, especially credits and energy subsidies.

34. World Bank, *Mexico: Industrial Policy and Regulation*, p. 12.

35. Ibid.

36. Ibid., p. 14.

37. Ibid., p. 112.

38. Ibid., p. 14; and Ros, "Mexico's Trade and Industrialization," table 2.5, p. 45.

39. In the past this restriction had been removed for terminals exported. See World Bank, *Mexico: Industrial Policy and Regulation*, p. 14.

40. For more details, see USITC, *Review of Trade and Investment Liberalization Measures*, Phase I, p. 4-10.

41. For more details, see ibid., pp. 4-8, 4-9.

42. Ros, "Mexico's Trade and Industrialization," pp. 39–40.

43. USITC, *Review of Trade and Investment Liberation Measures*, Phase I, p. 5-1.

44. For an overview of foreign direct investment in Mexico, see Peres Nuñez, *Foreign Direct Investment*.

45. Sidney Weintraub, *A Marriage of Convenience: Relations between Mexico and the United States* (Oxford University Press, 1990), p. 101.

46. Restrictions on capital flows have irritated potential investors and policymakers, especially in the United States. However, the limitations on foreign ownership in some countries are analogous to limitations imposed on labor entry in others. In both cases governments set out to protect something that belongs to the nation by its sovereign right. In the case of restrictions on migration, governments protect the resources available per unit of labor, thereby protecting the level of wages. In the case of foreign investment limitations and local participation in firms, the government may want to protect its ownership structure for reasons of national security, to protect the right of its nationals to develop an indigenous entrepreneurial class, or to generate mechanisms that guarantee their nationals' exposure to new technologies.

47. USITC, *Review of Trade and Investment Liberalization Measures*, Phase I, pp. 5-4 to 5-5.

48. Weintraub, *Marriage of Convenience*, p. 101.

49. For detailed analysis of all these reforms, see USITC, *Review of Trade and Investment Liberalization Measures*, Phase I, pp. 5-6, 5-7.

50. Ibid., p. 5-7.

51. Ibid., pp. 5-7 to 5-9. The trust fund mechanism, for example, was extended to permit investment in mining. See World Bank, *Mexico: Mining Sector Restructuring Project*, Staff Appraisal Report 9428-ME (Washington, May 1991), p. 12.

52. Centro de Análisis e Investigación Económica (CAIE), *Informe mensual sobre la economía mexicana*, vol. 7 (May 1989), pp. 18–19. These "neutral" shares are, in legal terms, class C shares. Class B shares, by contrast, which are also open to foreign participation, guarantee all investors full voting rights. Class A shares, the most restrictive form, are open only to Mexican investors, unless the issuing corporation places them in a trust with Mexico's development bank, NAFINSA. The trust issues foreign investors certificates of ownership stripped of any voting rights.

53. USITC, *Review of Trade and Investment Liberalization Measures*, Phase I, pp. 3-5, 3-6, and 5-10.

54. Ibid., pp. 5-10, 5-11.

55. CAIE, *The Mexican Economy: A Monthly Report*, vol. 8 (February 1991), p. 18. If current tendencies continue, a change should be expected in the Foreign Investment Law (FIL) that will remove restrictions on foreign ownership further. How soon that will happen will depend on the pace at which foreign investment continues to come to Mexico and to what extent changing the FIL becomes a pressing issue in the free trade negotiations with the United States and Canada.

56. USITC, *Review of Trade and Investment Liberalization Measures*, Phase I, p. 6-1.

57. Ibid., pp. 6-1 to 6-2.

58. Press release, Mexican Investment Board, July 1, 1991.

59. "New Mexican Copyright Law Praised by U.S. Music Industry," *U.S.–Mexico Free Trade Reporter*, July 22, 1991, p. 1.

60. Roberto Villarreal Gonda, "La nueva ley mexicana en materia de propiedad industrial," July 1991, pp. 1–2, 21–22. The author is director general of technology development in the Secretariat of Commerce and Industrial Promotion in Mexico.

61. USITC, *Review of Trade and Investment Liberalization Measures*, Phase I, p. 2-1. Before joining the GATT, Mexico was the largest market economy that was not a member.

62. Claudia Schatan, "Trade Bargaining: The Mexican Case," paper presented at a workshop sponsored by the Industrial Development Research Council, SELA (Caracas, February 5–7, 1991), p. 9.

63. In addition, Mexico has given the GATT Antidumping Code treaty status, meaning that the code is equal in authority to the act under Mexican law. See USITC, *Review of Trade and Investment Liberalization Measures*, Phase I, pp. 4-12 to 4-15.

64. Schatan, "Trade Bargaining," p. 10. To accept a country's request of accession, the GATT consults with that country's major trading partners, which in the case of Mexico is the United States.

65. The new protocol was not substantially different from that prepared in 1979. The 1986 protocol gave Mexico the possibility of attaching some conditions, the most important of which recognizes Mexico's sovereignty over its natural resources. In most respects, however, the 1986 protocol was more stringent than that of 1979. The maximum acceptable tariff was lower, the number of import permits to be eliminated was higher, and the period granted for the removal of the permits was shorter. In addition, Mexico agreed to sign several codes of conduct in the months following its accession to GATT. Ibid., pp. 10–12.

66. USITC, *Review of Trade and Investment Liberalization Measures*, Phase I, p. 2-2.

67. Schatan, "Trade Bargaining," pp. 12–13.

68. USITC, *Review of Trade and Investment Liberalization Measures*, Phase I, pp. 2-8 to 2-11.

69. *Wall Street Journal*, "U.S. and Mexico Agree to Seek Free-Trade Pact," March 27, 1990, pp. A3, A22.

70. For a timetable, see USITC, *The Likely Impact on the United States of a Free Trade Agreement with Mexico*, Pub. 2353 (Washington, February 1991), pp. 1-8 to 1-9.

71. Stuart Auerbach, "Talks Begin on Three-Nation Trade Pact," *Washington Post*, February 6, 1991, p. B1. The incorporation of Canada into the negotiations should not be surprising. Once it was clear that a U.S.-Mexico FTA was likely, the Canadian government felt it was better to be a full partner in the negotiations. Given Canada's interest, the United States could not deny its neighbor and partner from participating. Consequently, the Mexican government had to accept trilateral negotiations. Though Mexico never made its reluctance explicit, officials were wary that the inclusion of Canada would complicate the achievements of its main target: free trade with the United States.

72. Michael S. Lelyveld, "Bush Praises Bipartisanship of 'Fast-Track' Extension Vote," *Journal of Commerce*, May 28, 1991, p. 2A. Under "fast-track" procedures, Congress can give only a "yea or nay" vote on the final agreement, thus giving trade negotiators wider authority during the bargaining process.

73. For an insightful explanation of both countries' past reaction to the prospects of an agreement on free trade, see Sidney Weintraub, *Free Trade between Mexico and the United States* (Brookings, 1984), chap. 2.

74. In several cases the official price was set at a higher level than the product's fair market value, thereby introducing a form of "hidden" protectionism. See USITC, *Review of Trade and Investment Liberalization Measures*, Phase I, p. 4-6.

75. For a more detailed discussion of these agreements, see USTIC, *Review of Trade and Investment Liberalization Measures*, Phase I, pp. 2-3 to 2-8, 4-17 to 4-19; and B. Timothy Bennett "A U.S.-Mexico Free Trade Agreement: Its Evolution, Likely Content, and Related Issues," report submitted to the World Bank, Washington, November 9, 1990, pp. 2–33.

76. Bennett, "U.S.-Mexico Free Trade Agreement," p. 3.

77. Ibid., p. 22.

78. Schatan, "Trade Bargaining," p. 22.

79. Bennett, "U.S.-Mexico Free Trade Agreement," p. 33. Examples include the implementation of the largest U.S. bilateral cooperative program in agriculture, joint agreements on investment and tourism promotion, agreements on environmental problems, agreements on management of television signals and radio spectrums along the border, agreements on the exchange of tax information, and the negotiation of a bilateral income tax treaty.

80. Michael Hart, *A North American Free Trade Agreement: The Strategic Implications for Canada* (Institute for Research on Public Policy, 1990), p. 680.

81. For a discussion of this, see Pedro Noyola, "El surgimiento de espacios económicos multinacionales y las relaciones de México con Europa, la Cuenca

del Pacífico y América Latina y el Caribe," in Jaime Serra Puche, ed., *Hacia un tratado de libre comercio en América del Norte* (Mexico City: Miguel Angel Porrua, 1991), pp. 117–46.

82. The government's expectations were that after the agreement in principle was signed with commercial banks in mid-1989, Mexico's creditworthiness would rise, and capital repatriation and foreign direct investment would follow. See chapter 2 and the appendix.

83. Also, the fears and uncertainties produced by the initial failures of the Uruguay Round and by the "fortress" Europe 92 may have influenced the decision to seek an FTA with the United States.

84. The commitment to form a regional free trade zone by December 1996 is part of the "Tuxtla Declaration," signed by Mexico and the five Central American nations in January 1991. Colombia, Mexico, and Venezuela also signed a commitment in 1991 to negotiate an FTA. See Noyola, "El surgimiento de espacios económicos," p. 143.

85. For example, Mexico signed a "framework agreement" with the European Community in 1991, and it has established links with the OECD and hopes to become a full member in the future. See ibid., pp. 135–39; and letter from Mexican Secretary of Foreign Relations Fernando Solana to OECD Secretary General Jean Claude Paye, April 5, 1991.

86. Aslan Cohen, "United States-Mexico Trade Relations," Inter-American Dialogue, Washington, 1990, p. 3.

87. Weintraub, *Marriage of Convenience*, p. 75.

88. Hart, *North American Free Trade Agreement*, pp. 66–69.

89. USITC, *Review of Trade and Investment Liberalization Measures*, Phase I, table 4-2, p. 4-3; and Weintraub, *Marriage of Convenience*, p. 80.

90. USITC, *Review of Trade and Investment Liberalization Measures by Mexico and Prospects for Future United States-Mexican Relations*, Phase II: *Summary of Views and Prospects for Future United States-Mexican Relations*, Investigation 332-282, Pub. 2326 (Washington, October 1990), table D-1, p. D-6.

91. Bennett, "U.S.-Mexico Free Trade Agreement," pp. 31–32. For a discussion of the *maquiladora* program, see USITC, *Review of Trade and Investment Liberalization Measures*, Phase I, pp. 5-13 to 5-18.

92. For example, brooms (38.6 percent), glass (38 percent), footwear (37.5 percent), and melons (35 percent). U.S. duties exceed 20 percent on 117 items. See Cohen, "United States-Mexico Trade Relations," pp. 9, 12.

93. Ibid., p. 12. Agriculture, livestock, and forestry account for 66 percent of all imports subject to licensing; oil and derivatives for 27 percent; and automobiles and parts for 6 percent.

94. The following are the specific goods subject to restrictions: wool tailored suits, trousers, skirts, shirts, acrylic fibers, and cotton webs in the textile category; tubes, wires, metal sheets, and special steels in the steel category; and avocados, potatoes, milk products, and sugar products in the agricultural category. Ibid., p. 12.

95. Weintraub, *Marriage of Convenience*, p. 81.

96. Michael Hart, "Elementos de un acuerdo de libre comercio en América

del Norte," in Gustavo Vega Cánovas, ed., *México ante el libre comercio con América del Norte* (Mexico City: El Colegio de Mexico, 1991), pp. 339–40.

97. Hart, *North American Free Trade Agreement*, pp. 71–75.

98. Nora C. Lustig, Barry P. Bosworth, and Robert Z. Lawrence, eds., *North American Free Trade: Assessing the Impact* (Brookings, 1992) table 1. This volume presents a comprehensive synthesis of the current research on the impact of NAFTA.

99. Pursuit of bilateral trade liberalization through sectoral accords may be difficult because of domestic U.S. politics and compliance with GATT regulations.

100. Secretaría de Comercio y Fomento Industrial (SECOFI), "Evolución de la inversión extranjera directa en 1991," Mexico City, January 1992, table 1.

101. A free trade agreement between any pair of countries would increase economic efficiency when the trade created by the agreement exceeds the trade diverted from more efficient third countries. It is reasonable to expect that more trade will be created than diverted if tariffs and nontariff barriers continue to be at least as low as they are now in both countries vis-à-vis other partners.

102 A number of empirical analyses are available that address this question. For a review, see Hinojosa and Robinson, "Labor Issues."

103. For estimates on the impact on migration and intercountry wages, see Levy and van Wijnbergen, "Maize and the Mexico–United States Free Trade Agreement;" and Hinojosa and Robinson, "Alternative Scenarios of U.S.–Mexico Integration."

Chapter Six

1. The National Solidarity Program (or, PRONASOL, its acronym in Spanish). PRONASOL's achievements have been recognized even by the international lending organizations, according to "Salt of the Earth," *Economist*, October 9, 1991, p. 48. For a discussion of this program, see the essays in Wayne A. Cornelius, Ann L. Craig, and Jonathan Fox, eds., *Transforming State-Society Relations in Mexico: The National Solidarity Strategy* (University of California, San Diego, Center for U.S.-Mexican Studies, 1994); and see table 8-5.

2. According to Barry Bosworth's estimates (memo to author, February 23, 1988), net domestic savings as a proportion of net national product fell from around 12 percent in 1989–90 to 6.7 percent in 1994.

3. NAFTA came into effect on January 1, 1994 . World Bank, "Mexico Country Economic Memorandum: Fostering Private Sector Development in the 1990s," vol. 1, Report 11823-ME, Washington, May 16, 1994, pp. 10–11.

4. Instituto Nacional de Estadistica Geografia e Informatica, *Estadísticas históricas de México*, Tomo I (Mexico City, 1985), pp. 311–12, table 9-1; and INEGI website, "Producto interno bruto trimestral, A precios de1980" (http://dgcnesyp.inegi.gob.mx/BDINE/A10/A100016.htm) downloaded July 31, 1997.

5. David Folkerts-Laundau and others, *International Capital Markets: Developments, Prospects, and Policy Issues* (Washington: International Monetary Fund, August 1995), pp. 53–55.

6. Anthony DePalma, "Mexico Sends Troops to Hunt New Rebel Group in South," *New York Times*, July 2, 1996, p. A3.

7. Rudiger Dornbusch and Alejandro Werner, "Mexico: Stabilization, Reform and No Growth," *Brookings Papers on Economic Activity*, I:1994, pp. 253–315. (Hereafter *BPEA*.)

8. See chapter 3 for a discussion of the mechanisms which bring this about.

9. Sebastian Edwards, *Real Exchange Rates, Devaluation, and Adjustment: Exchange Rate Policy in Developing Countries* (MIT Press, 1989).

10. Steven B. Kamin and John H. Rogers, "Output and the Real Exchange Rate in Developing Countries: An Application to Mexico," International Finance Discussion Papers 580 (Washington: Board of Governors of the Federal Reserve System, May 1997), p. 27; and Edwards, *Real Exchange Rates, Devaluation, and Adjustment*, table 8-2, pp. 322–23. Edwards's results show that GDP fell the year of the 1982 depreciation as well as the following year (–.6 percent and –5.3 percent, respectively). Three years after, GDP grew by 2.7 percent.

11. Ibid.

12. Alain de Janvry, Gustavo Gordillo, and Elisabeth Sadoulet, *Mexico's Second Agrarian Reform: Household and Community Responses, 1990–1994* (University of California, San Diego, Center for U.S.-Mexican Studies, 1997), p. 201. The *ejido* is a land unit in which the *ejidatarios* are given the right to exploit the land but do not "own" it, that is, they cannot sell, rent, or borrow against it.

13. See, for example, Susan Collins and Barry Bosworth, "Economic Growth in East Asia: Accumulation versus Assimilation," *BPEA* 2 (1996), pp. 135–203.

14. By productivity I mean what economists call total factor productivity, that is, what is left over when one subtracts from output growth the contributions of factor accumulation: capital (including human capital) and labor.

15. For example, the World Bank estimates that productivity grew on average 1.1 percent a year. World Bank, "Mexico. Reform and Productivity Growth," Report 12605-ME (Washington, June 1994), chap. 2, p. 15, par. 2.33. Fernando Clavijo and others estimated a growth rate of 2.4 percent a year. See Clavijo and others, *La eficiencia productiva del sector manufactero mexicano, 1985–1990* (Mexico City, Office of Advisors to the President of Mexico, 1992), cited in World Bank, "Mexico: Reform and Productivity Growth." James Tybout and Daniel Westbrook find that over the period 1984–90, the cumulative growth of productivity was 11.17 percent (slightly below 2 percent per year). James Tybout and Daniel Westbrook, "Trade Liberalization and the Dimensions of Efficiency Change in Mexican Manufacturing Industries," *Journal of International Economics*, vol. 39 (August 1995), p. 70, table 2. Other studies available, cited in World Bank, "Mexico: Reform and Productivity Growth," include Enriquie Hernández-Laos, *Evolución de la productividad total*

de los factores en la economía Mexicana, mimeo (1990) ; Anthony J. Venables and Sweder van Wijnbergen, *Trade Liberalization, Productivity and Competition: The Mexican Experience,* mimeo, 1993, and Georgina Kessell and Ricardo Samaniego, "Apertura Comercial, Productividad y Desarrollo Tecnológico: El Caso de México," Documento de Trabajo 112 (Banco Interamericano de Desarrollo, March 1992). The estimates of productivity growth vary greatly across studies. The results are very sensitive to the definition of variables, the choice of price deflators, the way the data are cleaned for outsiders, and the methodological approach used.

16. Michael Sarel, *Growth in East Asia: What We Can and Cannot Infer* (Washington: International Monetary Fund, 1996), p. 9, figure 4.

17. When the sources of productivity growth are disaggregated in the standard scale effects (pertaining to plant size), allocative efficiency effects (relocation of output from the less efficient to the most efficient firms either within a sector or between sectors), and the "residual" (sometimes called the technical efficiency effect), both the World Bank, "Mexico: Reform, and Productivity Growth," p. 16, par. 2.37, and Tybout and Westbrook, "Trade Liberalization," find that the gains in productivity owing to scale effects were rather small. The two studies differ, however, on the weight of the allocative-efficiency effect. The World Bank finds that "of the sources of TFP [total factor productivity] growth, the most important was growth in allocative efficiency *within* sectors, that is, an increasing share of labor and capital being in the more efficient firms" (p. 14, par. 2.29) (emphasis added). Tybout and Westbrook, however, find that "most sectors showed improvements in productivity and average cost during the sample period, mainly because of significant gains in the 'residual' effects " (p. 76).

18. The studies discussed above cover only the five years immediately following the date when the first measures of trade liberalization were introduced. Most of the rest of the reforms were introduced later. See chapters 4 and 5.

19. Tybout and Westbrook, "Trade Liberalization and the Dimensions of Efficiency Change," pp. 75–76. Performance in sectors involved with metals, machinery, equipment, or the processing of food, beverages, and tobacco did relatively well between 1985 and 1990; those involved with fibers, textiles, wood products, furniture, paper, cardboard, or printing did relatively poorly. World Bank, "Mexico Reform and Productivity Growth," p. 16, par. 2.38.

20. World Bank, "Mexico Reform and Productivity Growth," p. 2.

21. Ibid.

22. Enrique Dávila, "Mexico: The Evolution and Reform of the Labor Market," in Sebastian Edwards and Nora Claudia Lustig, eds., *Labor Markets in Latin America: Combining Social Protection with Market Flexibility* (Brookings, 1997). As of the time of this writing, labor reforms had not yet been passed.

23. See, for example, Sebastian Edwards, "The Disturbing Underperformance of Latin American Economies," Inter-American Dialogue (Inter-American Development Bank, January 1997), pp. 3–4. For a critique of neoliberal reforms in Mexico, see Manuel Pastor and Carol Wise, "State Policy,

Distribution, and Neoliberal Reform in Mexico," *Journal of Latin American Studies*, vol. 29 (May 1997), pp. 419–56.

24. For example, privatization in one of the areas consolidated control of almost all of Mexico's chloric acid production. As a result of the sale of the two largest copper companies to one owner, 96 percent of Mexico's copper production is under the control of one company. The privatized cement company controlled two-thirds of the Mexican cement market. In paper and paper products, four firms produce more than 60 percent of total output. World Bank, "Mexico Country Economic Memorandum: Fostering Private Sector Development in the 1990s," p. 59.

25. To make things worse, the Mexican press has printed numerous accusations of favoritism and of public officials benefiting from the privatization process. The Mexican press cites numerous cases of businessmen connected in particular with Raúl Salinas, the brother of former President Carlos Salinas. Raúl Salinas was arrested in 1995, accused of masterminding the assassination of Francisco Ruiz Massieu, the secretary general of the PRI who was murdered in 1994. During investigations it was discovered that Raúl Salinas held more than U.S.$100 million dollars in bank accounts, especially in Swiss banks. The origin of these millions is unclear, and Raúl Salinas has also been accused of "illicit enrichment" as a result. See Leslie Crawford, "Salinas Embrace Taints Corporate Mexico," *Financial Times*, July 6, 1996, p. 3. To help Raúl Salinas, several businessmen, some owners of newly privatized firms, declared the money in the bank accounts was theirs. Presumably, they were loans given to Salinas to start new business ventures. Loans of millions of dollars without any written records, however, sounded suspicious. Instead of helping Salinas, they left those businessmen's images tainted. The public imagines all sorts of complicities involving corruption, which has led to many an embarrasing public statement. In one case, a prominent businessman, Carlos Peralta Quintero, head of the telecommunications company Iusacell, who was recently handed down a prison sentence for fraud, was involved in allegedly shaky deals with the expresident's brother. Norma Jiménez, "Dictan formal prisión a Peralta," *La Reforma*, March 11, 1997. These dealings have not gone unnoticed in the U.S. press either. For example, a recent article by Tim Golden in the *New York Times* cites a CIA document, dated December 27, 1995, that said, "An informant of 'undetermined reliability' had reported that before the sale of Government-owned banks by Mr. Salinas's administration in 1990, Raul Salinas and other members of the President's family used inside information to invest heavily in financial instruments that later jumped in value." See Tim Golden, "Salinas: Plenty of Smoke; No Smoking Gun," *New York Times*, July 11, 1997, p. A10. From an economic point of view (leaving aside moral considerations), the problem is that reforms were implemented in some key sectors, such as the banking sector, in a way that may have produced the "wrong" kind of entrepreneurship.

26. de Janvry and others, *Mexico's Second Agrarian Reform*, p. 200.

27. See table 8-5.

28. Banco de México, *The Mexican Economy, 1995: Economic and Financial Developments in 1994, Policies for 1995* (Mexico City, 1995), p. 36.

29. Edwin M. Truman, "The Risks and Implications of External Financial Shocks: Lessons from Mexico," International Finance Discussion Paper 535 (Washington: Board of Governors of the Federal Reserve System, January 1996), p. 8.

30. See also table 7-3.

31. The Pact of Economic Solidarity, better known as the Pact, was signed simultaneously by the government and representatives of workers, agricultural producers, and the business sector in December of 1987. Its basic components included a commitment to further reductions of the fiscal deficit, tighten monetary policy, liberalize trade and, for the first time since the crisis of 1982, implement an incomes policy that would cover wages, prices, and the exchange rate (Pedro Aspe, "Estabilización macroeconómica y cambio estructural: La experiencia de México, 1982–1988," in Carlos Bazdresch and others, eds., *México. Auge, Crisis, y Ajuste* (El Trimestre Económico, Lecturas, Fondo de Cultura Económica, Mexico, 1992), pp. 67–104, and chapter 2 in this book. Later, the Pact changed its name but continued to be used as the mechanism to set macroeconomic policy until the plan of March 9, 1995, the first in recent years designed outside the Pact.

32. The policy based on a fixed exchange rate, designed to fight inflationary pressures, was implemented at the end of February 1988. Beginning in 1989, the fixed exchange regime was replaced by a crawling peg. Originally, the crawl was fixed at one peso per day (equivalent to the annual depreciation rate of 16 percent), in 1990 this was reduced to 80 centavos daily (11 percent annual depreciation) and, in 1991, the crawl was fixed at 40 centavos daily (5 percent annual depreciation). In November 1991, the crawling peg was replaced by a band within which the exchange rate was allowed to fluctuate. The ceiling of the band was adjusted daily by 0.0002 new pesos (or 20 cents of the old pesos). This adjustment was increased in October 1992 to 0.0004 new pesos daily while the floor was maintained at 3.0512 new pesos a dollar. On December 20, 1994, the ceiling of the band was increased by 15 percent while its subsequent daily increase of 0.0004 new pesos was maintained. This policy proved unsustainable and was abandoned two days later when the Mexican authorities were forced to adopt a floating exchange rate regime because they had practically run out of international reserves. Banco de México, *The Mexican Economy, 1995: Economic and Financial Developments in 1994, Policies for 1995* (Mexico City, 1995), pp. 36–38; and Banco de México, *The Mexican Economy, 1994: Economic and Financial Developments in 1993, Policies for 1994* (Mexico City, 1994), pp. 96–99.

33. Leonardo Leiderman, Nissan Liviatan, and Alfredo Thorne, "Shifting Nominal Anchors: The Experience of Mexico," *Economía Mexicana, Nueva Epoca*, vol. 4 (2), 2d semester (1995); and Dornbusch and Werner, "Mexico: Stabilization, Reform and No Growth."

34. In particular, rule 144A and regulation "S." Portfolio flows undergo a *stepwise* increase starting in 1990, which warrants some explanation beyond interest rate differentials.

35. Banco de México, *The Mexican Economy 1995*, p. 252, table 44.

36. International Monetary Fund, "Mexico: Recent Economic Developments" (Washington, Western Hemisphere Department, June 23, 1995), p. 55, table 15.

37. Ibid., p. 28.

38. Ibid., p. 29.

39. Ibid.

40. Consumption figure from Banco de México website, table 8 (www. banxico.org.mx/public_html/doyai/mexceon97/to8.html). Consumer credit data from World Bank, "World Development Indicators," CD-ROM, Washington, 1997. The results of an econometric analysis suggest that the real exchange rate appreciation has been associated with the fall in domestic private savings. The explanation is as follows: initially, trade liberalization was not a fully credible policy, so people set out to buy imported consumer goods (consumer durables, in particular) while they could, reducing their savings rate. Daniel Oks, "Stabilization and Growth Recovery in Mexico: Lessons and Dilemmas, " Washington, World Bank, Latin America and the Caribbean Regional Office, January 1992.

41. See, among others; Jaime Ros, "Financial Markets and Capital Flows in Mexico," in José A. Ocampo and Roberto Steiner, eds., *Foreign Capital in Latin America* (Fedesarrollo and Inter-American Development Bank, 1994), pp. 193–239 ; Darryl McLeod and John Welch, "El Libre Comercio y el Peso," *Economía Mexicana*, vol. 1 (January-June 1992), pp. 193–235; Daniel Oks, "Stabilization and Growth Recovery in Mexico: Lessons and Dilemmas " (Washington, World Bank, Latin America and the Caribbean Regional Office, January 1992); and Daniel Oks and Sweder Van Wijnbergen, "Mexico after the Debt Crisis: Is Growth Sustainable?" *Journal of Development Economics*, vol. 47 (June 1995), pp. 155–78; and Dornbusch and Werner, "Mexico: Stabilization, Reform and No Growth."

42. The first interest rate hike was announced in February 1994 when the Federal Funds rate rose from 3.0 percent to 3.25 percent. The Federal Funds rate increased six times during the year. Folkerts-Landau, *International Capital Markets* (Washington, August 1995), p. 53.

43. Guillermo Calvo, Leonardo Leiderman, and Carmen M. Reinhart, "Capital Inflows and Real Exchange Rate Appreciation in Latin America," *IMF Staff Papers*, vol. 40 (March1993), pp. 108–51. See also Ros, "Financial Markets and Capital Flows in Mexico."

44. Calvo, Leiderman, and Reinhart, "Capital Inflows and Real Exchange Rate Appreciation."

45. The Zapatista Army of National Liberation—named after the famous peasant leader of the Mexican Revolution—took the government by surprise. After ten days of fighting, both parties agreed to seek a political solution.

Although by mid-1997 no peace agreement had been reached, a military outcome seemed remote.

46. Folkerts-Landau, *International Capital Markets*, pp. 53–55.

47. U.S. General Accounting Office, "Mexico's Financial Crisis: Origins, Awareness, Assistance, and Initial Efforts to Recover," Report GAO/GGD-96-56 (Washington, February 1996), pp. 50–53.

48. This was advised, for example, in Dornbusch and Werner, "Mexico: Stabilization, Reform and No Growth."

49. By covering investors against the risks of a devaluation, the Tesobonos were meant to deter capital outflows. Folkerts-Landau, *International Capital Markets*, pp. 55–56.

50. CETES is the abbreviation for Certificados de Tesorería, Mexican Treasury bonds. Ibid., p 56.

51. The U.S. contribution was equal to U.S. $6 billion and the Canadians offered $1 billion of Canadian dollars. U.S. General Accounting Office, "Mexico's Financial Crisis," pp. 9–10.

52. This point is elaborated in the following paragraphs.

53. The candidate was Ernesto Zedillo, subsequently elected president of Mexico.

54. Information provided by one of the members of the cabinet.

55. The ceiling of the band in this period was equal to a little more than 3.4 new pesos to the dollar. The movement experienced by the peso within the band implied a 10 percent increase in its value during 1994 (before the devaluation announced on December 20). U.S. General Accounting Office, "Mexico's Financial Crisis," pp. 90–91.

56. Stability prevailed with the exception of a fall of around U.S.$2 billion in mid-1997, which was quickly recovered. Banco de México, *Informe Anual 1994* (Mexico City, 1995), pp. 192–99. As the annual report of the Bank of Mexico reported, "The stability shown by the level of international reserves . . . was indicative that: the exchange rate and interest rate policy effected from the end of April to mid-November kept the balance of payments in equilibrium, underlying concerns notwithstanding . . . These conditions did not warrant a devaluation." (Author's translation, pp. 58–59).

57. Jorge Mariscal, "The Mexico Peso Crisis: In Search for Value in Latin American Equities" (New York: Goldman Sachs, March 1995).

58. Calculated from Banco de México website (English), Economic Information, Historical Economic Series (www.banxico.org.mx/public_html/inveco/serieci/csecomen.html).

59. For example, the great fear that the elections of August could be accompanied by spurts of violence.

60. For an analysis of the problems with monetary policy in 1994 see Guillermo A. Calvo and Enrique G. Mendoza, "Mexico's Balance-of-Payments Crisis: A Chronicle of Death Foretold," *Journal of International Economics*, vol. 41 (November 1996), pp.235–64; Jeffrey Sachs, Aarón Tornell, and Andrés Velasco, "The Mexican Peso Crisis: Sudden Death or Death Foretold?" *Journal*

of International Economics, vol. 41 (November 1996), pp. 265–83; and Steven B. Kamin and John H. Rogers, "Monetary Policy in the End-Game to Exchange-Rate Based Stabilizations: The Case of Mexico," *Journal of International Economics*, vol. 41 (November 1996), pp. 285–307.

61. According to the analysis of Carstens and Gil-Diaz, the fall in interest rates was a compensatory move for the increase in interests triggered by the assassination of Colosio in March 1994. Francisco Gil-Diaz and Agustin Carstens, "Some Hypotheses Related to the Mexican 1994–1995 Crisis," Documento de Investigacion 9601, paper presented at annual ASSA meeting, 1996.

62. U.S. General Accounting Office, "Mexico's Financial Crisis," pp. 67–68.

63. Banco de México, *Informe Anual 1994* (Mexico, 1995).

64. U.S. General Accounting Office, "Mexico's Financial Crisis," p. 68.

65. Version of these tensions appeared in a letter by then Secretary of Finance Pedro Aspe. See "The Americas: Mexico's Ex-Finance Minister Sets the Record Straight," *Wall Street Journal*, July 14, 1995, p. A13.

66. U.S. General Accounting Office, "Mexico's Financial Crisis," p. 42.

67. Ibid., p. 69.

68. The figure 1.7 months is calculated from figures in Banco de México, *Informe Anual 1994* (Mexico City, 1995), pp. 199, 294.

69. U. S.General Accounting Office, "Mexico's Financial Crisis," pp. 71–72.

70. Ibid., p. 72.

71. For more details, see chapter 7.

72. See Leonardo Leiderman and Alfredo Thorne, "Mexico's 1994 Crisis and Its Aftermath: Is the Worst Over?" paper presented at Private Capital Flows to Emerging Markets after the Mexican Crisis, a conference jointly sponsored by the Institute for International Economics and the Oesterreichische Nationalbank, Vienna, 1995.

73. The desire of Salinas to leave his post "invicto," that is, without a devaluation, without a crisis, particularly in light of his candidacy as head of the World Trade Organization, probably added restrictions to economic policy.

74. Kamin and Rogers, "Monetary Policy in the End-Game to Exchange-Rate Based Stabilizations," p. 304, argue that "raising interest rates sufficiently to have prevented a devaluation would have required a concerted shift in the monetary authorities' reaction function at a time when the authorities were deeply concerned about the health of the banking system and, at least in the early part of the year, the weak level of economic activity."

75. See Miguel Mancera, "Don't Blame Monetary Policy," *Wall Street Journal* (January 31, 1995), p. A-18.

76. The author is very grateful to David Cole, Zia Qureshi and Liliana Rojas-Suarez for their valuable insights in this section.The main reforms included: (a) the elimination in 1989 of most interest rates and quantitative credit controls and of the minimum reserve requirement (and forced financing of the government); (b) the enactment in 1990 of the Credit Institutions Act which established a clear legal and regulatory framework for the provision of banking services by the private sector; and (c) the enactment, also in 1990,

of the Financial Groups Law which allowed for the establishment of a conglomerate financial regime permitting separate commercial banking, brokerage houses, insurance and bonding companies, investment companies, and auxiliary credit organizations to be controlled by a single holding company. International Monetary Fund, "Mexico: Recent Economic Developments," Western Hemisphere Department (June 23, 1995), p. 10. These reforms were the legal basis for the eventual divestiture of the state owned commercial banks.

77. Figure for 1988 from Guillermo Ortiz, *La reforma financiera y la desincorporación bancaria* (Mexico: Fondo de Cultura Económica, 1994), p. 209. For 1994, from International Monetary Fund, "Mexico: Recent Economic Developments," p. 11. One should be aware that the ratio of past due loans to total loans may in fact underestimate the fragility of the bank system. From a methodological point of veiw, past due loans, consisting of unpaid installments of principal plus interest, do not include the total amount of problem loans. Also excluded in the calculation of past due loans are loans that have been restructured without having paid any interest. Ibid.

78. William C. Gruben and Robert P. McComb, "Liberalization, Privatization, and Crash: Mexico's Banking System in the 1990s," *Economic Review of the Federal Reserve Bank of Dallas* (First Quarter, 1997), p. 24.

79. Sherrill Shaffer, "A Test of Competition in Canadian Banking," *Journal of Money, Credit and Banking*, vol. 25 (February 1993), cited in Gruben and McComb, "Liberalization."

80. Gruben and McComb, "Liberalization," p. 25.

81. Ricardo Hausmann and Michael Gavin, "The Roots of Banking Crises: The Macroeconomic Context," paper presented at the Conference on Banking Crises in Latin America, Inter-American Development Bank, 1995, cited in Gruben and McComb, "Liberalization."

82. This action led to a fall in commercial bank credit extended to the private sector. During part of the period, most bank lending was extended to the government for deficit financing purposes through very high reserve requirements. The credit to the government was often at negative real lending rates. The deposit and lending rates were fixed by the Ministry of Finance and with high and variable inflation rates, the real and nominal interest rates were very volatile. In sum, this was a period characterized by financial disintermediation. A measure of this is the fall in M4—the broadest measure of money—as a ratio of GDP from 45 percent at the onset of the 1982 crisis to about 35 percent in 1988. World Bank, "Mexico Country Economic Memorandum," pp.16, 17.

83. Ibid., p 19.

84. Ibid.

85. Diana McNaughton, "Comment" in Gerard Caprio, David Folkerts-Landau, and Timothy D. Lane, eds. *Building Sound Finance in Emerging Market Economies* (Washington: International Monetary Fund, 1994), p. 253.

86. See World Bank, "Mexico Country Economic Memorandum," p. 22.

87. Gruben and McComb, "Liberalization," p. 24.

88. Peter M. Garber, "Managing Risks to Financial Markets from Volatile Capital Flows: The Role of Prudential Regulation," mimeo (Brown University, 1996), cited in Gruben and McComb, "Liberalization."

89. McNaughton, "Comment," p. 254.

90. Gruben and McComb, "Liberalization," p. 26.

91. Ortiz, *La reforma financiera y la desincorporación bancaria*, pp. 195–96.

92. Liliana Rojas-Suárez and Steven R. Weisbrod, "Financial Fragilities in Latin America: The 1980s and 1990s," Occasional Paper 132 (Washington: International Monetary Fund, October 1995), p. 38.

93. "Mexican Banks: The 12% Solution," *Standard and Poor's Credit Week*, August 7, 1996, p.10, table 1. The source of the difference between the two estimates is carefully explained in this document.

94. For example, Dornbusch and Werner, "Mexico: Stabilization, Reform and No Growth." Guillermo Calvo was a notable exception in his warning of the destabilizing effects that a devaluation might bring. See his "Comment," to Dornbusch and Werner's article.

95. Folkerts-Landau, *International Capital Markets*, pp. 60–61.

96. Interestingly, there was a large overlap between the outgoing and incoming cabinet, but leaving out Salinas's secretary of finance, Pedro Aspe, from the new team apparently had left investors on Wall Street uneasy and prone to overreacting.

97. U.S. General Accounting Office, "Mexico's Financial Crisis," pp. 72–73.

98. I received calls from New York–based news services, asking me whether the government would impose capital controls or default on its obligations a week after the devaluation.

99. David Folkerts-Landau and Peter M. Garber, "Derivative Markets and Financial System Soundness," paper prepared for the MAE and IMF Institute Program on Banking Soundness and Monetary Policy in a World of Global Capital Markets, 1997, p. 6. These operations involved Tesobonos swaps and repurchase agreements, CETES swaps, Brady bond swaps, equity swaps and repurchase agreements, and structured notes.

100. Ibid., pp 6–9.

101. Ibid., pp. 6–7.

102. Ibid., p. 9.

103. The history of the rescue package is discussed in detail in chapter 7.

104. Folkerts-Landau, *International Capital Markets*, p. 61.

105. See chapter 7.

106. Although margin calls would still have affected the operations that used peso investments.

107. For a discussion of the Mexican crisis in multiple equilibrium models see Calvo and Mendoza, "Mexico's Balance-of-Payments Crisis"; Harold L. Cole and Timothy J. Kehoe, "A Self-Fufilling Model of Mexico's 1994–1995 Debt Crisis," *Journal of International Economics*, vol. 41 (November 1996), pp. 309–30; and Sachs, Tornell, and Velasco, "The Mexican Peso Crisis."

108. Guillermo A. Calvo and others, "Foreword," *Journal of International Economics*, vol. 41 (November 1996), p. 220.

109. See Guillermo A. Calvo, "Varieties of Capital Market Crisis," in Guillermo A. Calvo and M. King, eds., *Debt Burden and Its Consequences for Monetary Policy*, forthcoming.

110. Folkerts-Landau and Garber, "Derivative Markets and Financial System Soundness," p. 2.

111. See, for example, Dornbusch and Werner, "Mexico: Stabilization, Reform, and No Growth."

112. See Banco de México, *Informe Anual 1994*, pp. 192–99; and data from Banco de México website (English), "Economic Information, Historical Economic Series," (www.banxico.org.mx/public_html/inveco/serieci/csecomen.html).

113. "Asia Pledges $16 Billion for Thai Bailout," *Wall Street Journal*, August 12, 1997, p. A10.

Chapter Seven

1. Patricia A. Wertman, "The Mexican Support Package: A Survey and Analysis," CRS Report for Congress, 95-1006 E (Washington: Congressional Research Service, 1995), p. 6.

2. U. S. General Accounting Office, "Mexico's Financial Crisis: Origins, Awareness, Assistance, and Initial Efforts to Recover," Report GAO/GGD-96-56 (Washington, 1996), p. 82. This swap facility is subject to annual review.

3. Patricia A. Wertman, "Mexico: Chronology of a Financial Crisis," CRS Report for Congress, 95-1007 E (Washington: Congressional Research Service, 1995), pp. 3, 7. Under NAFA Mexico could make multilateral or bilateral drawings; bilateral drawings with the U.S. Treasury would be governed by the Exchange Stabilization Agreement signed on the same day.

4. U.S. GAO, "Mexico's Financial Crisis," p. 88.

5. These documents were declassified in response to requests by Senator Alfonse D'Amato, a fierce critic of the U.S. rescue package and the Clinton administration's policy toward Mexico. For more on this matter see ibid., chap.3.

6. Board of Governors of the Federal Reserve System, "Mexican Exchange Rate Options," restricted internal memorandum, Washington, August 17, 1994, p. 6.

7. U.S. Treasury, "Mexico maintains current exchange rate policy in renewal of 'Pacto'" internal memorandum from Lawrence H. Summers to Secretary Bentsen September 27, 1994, in D'Amato, Annexes: "Report on the Mexican Economic Crisis" and "Chronology of the Mexican Economic Crisis: Documents," presented by Senator Alfonse D'Amato, June 29, 1995, p. 364. The views of another U.S. Treasury official also illustrate U.S. concerns at the time: "The uncertain economic prospect of Mexico is of critical interest and of some concern to the U.S. It is possible, but unlikely, that Mexico could request activation of the swap before President Salinas' November 1 State of the Union address. Hopes for a stable post-election period and a resumption of capital inflows have not materialized. The announcement of a new PACTO did not

have the desired effect of strengthening the peso and was soon offset by renewed concerns over political stability as a result of the Ruiz [Massieu] assassination . . . Although the immediate financial situation could improve, we remain concerned that the current exchange rate system could inhibit economic growth and widen the already substantial current account deficit." U.S. Treasury, internal memorandum from Timothy Geithner to Secretary Lloyd Bentsen, October 2, 1994, in D'Amato, Annexes: "Report on the Mexican Economic Crisis" and "Chronology of the Mexican Economic Crisis: Documents," pp. 335–39.

8. See, for example, Lawrence Summers's memo to Lloyd Bentsen, October 14, 1994, in D'Amato "Report on the Mexican Economic Crisis," p. 301.

9. Board of Governors of the Federal Reserve System, "Background Material for October 20 Visit by President-elect Zedillo's Adviser Luis Tellez," internal memorandum from Charles J. Siegman to Chairman Greenspan, October 19, 1994, in D'Amato, Annexes: "Report on the Mexican Economic Crisis" and "Chronology of the Mexican Economic Crisis: Documents," pp. 383–84.

10. On the uncertainty about Mexico having to devalue, for example, in a memo prepared for Summers, someone remarks that "there is no obvious event on the immediate horizon likely to concentrate pressure or to force a decision [to devalue]." "Mexico: Planning for the Next Stage," U.S. Treasury Memorandum, December 5, 1994, in D'Amato, Annexes: "Report on the Mexican Economic Crisis" and "Chronology of the Mexican Economic Crisis: Documents," p. 417.

11. The author of the memo then says, "We will not look good if Mexico makes a move without consulting us. . . . I fear that a devaluation will have a negative impact on Congressional support for our trade policy initiatives, particularly if it is done unilaterally. The downside of initiating contact is that it could lead to a request for activation of the swap. This does not seem appropriate now. There is no visible pay-out. Investors, it appears, are not worried about the size of the current account deficit or a devaluation. [!] They worry about Chiapas and political unrest spreading. Thus, a devaluation may not bring about a resumption of capital inflows." Indeed not. U.S. Treasury,"Contact with Mexicans Before They Do Something," memo to Tim Geithner, December 19, 1994, in D'Amato, Annexes: "Report on the Mexican Economic Crisis" and "Chronology of the Mexican Economic Crisis: Documents," p. 428.

12. To give an example, in the wake of the devaluation, an official at the U.S. Treasury based in Mexico wrote the following: " We believe the markets have been waiting for the government to take action on the exchange rate and that capital inflows are likely to pick up. There probably will be considerable volatility in the foreign exchange markets for a short period of time, followed by some strengthening of the peso. . . . When all the smoke clears, probably by early next year, we expect the peso will settle about 8–12 percent below what it was trading at prior to the new policy. . . . Our best guess is that the devaluation will not affect Mexico's basic macroeconomic course or fundamentally alter the country's brighter economic prospects in 1995.

Furthermore, the devaluation has not really caught most sophisticated investors by surprise. In spite of the fact that over the next few days many Mexicans will say we told you so and that this is deja vu, the new policy is likely to have a salutary effect, unlike the traumatic effects of past devaluations." U.S. Treasury, "Bi-Weekly Report on Mexico," December 20, 1994, in D'Amato, Annexes: "Report on the Mexican Economic Crisis" and "Chronology of the Mexican Economic Crisis: Documents," pp. 432, 434.

13. On December 22, 1994, the Foreign Exchange Commission adopted the floating exchange rate system. Banco de Mexico, *The Mexican Economy, 1995: Economic and Financial Developments in 1994, Policies for 1995* (Mexico City, 1995), p. 43. Starting in 1990, the Bank of Mexico limited the annual growth of its credit, which became the main way that the central bank influences the monetary base. Thus the Bank of Mexico only affects interest rates, and by implication, exchange rates and aggregate demand, through the management of domestic credit. See Banco de Mexico, *The Mexican Economy, 1996: Economic and Financial Developments in 1995, Policies for 1996* (Mexico City, 1996), pp. 35–36.

14. Lawrence Summers, "Mexican Devaluation," memo to Robert Rubin, December 21, 1994, in D'Amato, Annexes: "Report on the Mexican Economic Crisis" and "Chronology of the Mexican Economic Crisis: Documents," pp. 438–39.

15. U.S. GAO, "Mexico's Financial Crisis," p. 74.

16. Half of the additional U.S.$3 billion for the swap facility increase came from the U.S. Treasury under the "Temporary Exchange Stabilization Agreement" (TESA), signed on January 4, 1995, and set to expire on April 3, 1995. The remaining U.S.$1.5 billion came from the Federal Reserve. See U.S. GAO, "Mexico's Financial Crisis," p. 75.

17. The estimates of total dollar-denominated short-term obligations coming due in 1995 include the following: U.S.$6.3 billion in amortization of short-term public external debt; U.S.$1 billion payments due to the IMF; approximately U.S.$6 billion in amortization of long-term external public debt; U.S.$6.1 billion of nonbank private sector debt due to banks; U.S.$2.1 billion of nonbank private sector debt due to nonbanks; and, U.S.$29 billion of Tesobonos (not classified as external debt but instruments were denominated in dollars). Adding all these figures up yields a total of U.S.$50.5 billion dollars coming due in 1995, assuming that the U.S.$24.1 billion of interbank loans would be rolled over.

18. The Mexican stock exchange closed down 6.26 percent on January 10, 1995 (*Newsday* Marketline).

19. Edwin M. Truman, "The Risks and Implications of External Financial Shocks: Lessons from Mexico," International Finance Discussion Paper 535 (Washington: Board of Governors of the Federal Reserve System, January 1996), charts 1 and 2.

20. Ibid., p. 10.

21. Following preliminary consultations with the congressional leadership on the evening of January 10, 1995. Clay Chandler and Tod Robberson,

"Clinton Pledges More Financial Help for Mexico," *Washington Post,* January 12, 1995, p. A19. On January 13, Mexico drew a short-term swap for $280 million from the Exchange Stabilization Fund.

22. Clay Chandler and Martha Hamilton, "U.S. Plan to Aid Mexico Calms Financial Markets: Loan Guarantees Get Cautious Hill Backing," *Washington Post,* January 14, 1995, p. D1.

23. For more details see the account in Jorge Montaño, "El congreso de los Estados Unidos y su política hacia México," in Rafael Fernandez de Castro, *Nueva agenda bilateral en la relación México-Estados Unidos* (Mexico: Fondo de Cultura Económica, forthcoming).

24. This perception was shared by many analysts in Mexico. I recall vividly how at the end of January I had several arguments with various colleagues when I was trying to convince them that Mexico was facing a very serious economic crisis, perhaps the most serious one in its postrevolutionary era.

25. U.S. GAO, "Mexico's Financial Crisis," p. 128.

26. In reality, the IMF agreement included contingent provisions for tightening the fiscal adjustment, for example, in the event that the outcomes for the stability of the peso and inflation were not achieved. However, the terms of these agreements are always secret and, in this case, given the confidence crisis it was considered inappropriate for the IMF to come out questioning the Mexican program from its start.

27. Current rules state that an IMF member can borrow an amount equal to 100 percent of its quota a year and with a cumulative limit of 300 percent. The February 1, 1995, agreement was equivalent to the unprecedented 688.4 percent of Mexico's quota.

28. The attack on the administration was spearheaded by Senator Alfonse D'Amato, chair of the Senate Banking Committee, who was virulently opposed to the rescue package. D'Amato held several hearings in which the majority of the nongovernment witnesses were very negative about the package and Mexico. He also launched several bouts of attacks in the press on the major players from the U.S. side.

29. See, for example, Jeffrey Frieden, "Political Sources and Political Lessons of the 1994–1995 Mexican Crisis," prepared for presentation at the Carnegie Endowment-World Bank meeting on the Mexican Crisis, mimeo (Washington, October 1995).

30. U. S. GAO, "Mexico's Financial Crisis," pp. 118–20. At the end of the first year the six-month extension was granted. The agreement expired on August 21, 1996. U.S. Department of Treasury, *Semi-Annual Report to Congress by the Secretary of the Treasury on Behalf of the President, Pursuant to the Mexican Debt Disclosure Act of 1995* (Washington, December 1996), August summary.

31. The pass-through quality of the account means that the proceeds do not accumulate as a stock. For more details on the terms of the U.S. rescue package see U.S. GAO, "Mexico's Financial Crisis," chap. 4.

32. U.S. Department of Treasury, *Semi-Annual Report to Congress by the Secretary of the Treasury on Behalf of the President,* p.28.

33. Because the Mexican government wanted to obtain the endorsement of the members of the old Pact for the new program, it was not possible to announce the Mexican program concomitant with the Framework Agreement. This of course did not help confidence building. In the end, the government was not able to secure the endorsement of the members of the Pact because they disagreed with the austerity measures, and the program was announced unilaterally by the government.

34. Whether this was the least costly stabilization path is a discussion that goes beyond the objectives of this analysis.

35. The U.S.$3 billion dollars in short-term swaps were repaid by Mexico in full. U.S. Department of the Treasury, "Monthly Report by the Secretary of the Treasury" (Washington, February 1996). See table 7-1 for complete details of the payments schedule for the medium-term swaps.

36. U.S. GAO, "Mexico's Financial Crisis," p. 140, and U.S. Department of the Treasury, "Monthly Report by the Secretary of the Treasury" (February 1996).

37. Whether this stability in the exchange rate market will continue depends on several factors, some economic and some political.

38. David Wessel and Craig Torres, "Mexico Will Close Out Its Debt to U.S." *Wall Street Journal*, January 16, 1997, p. A10.

39. Although Argentina had a sharp recession in 1995, it was able to avoid a major confidence crisis. The rest of the countries weathered the so-called tequila effect with relative ease.

40. See Barry Eichengreen and Albert Fishlow, *Contending with Capital Flows. What is Different about the 1990s?* (New York:Council on Foreign Relations, 1996).

41. Grupo de Economistas y Asociados, "GEA Economico," no. 88 (April 1988).

42. Craig Torres and Paul B. Carroll, "Zedillo Outlines His Peso-Rescue Plan, but Mexican Currency's Slide Continues," *Wall Street Journal*, January 4, 1995, p. A3.

43. Organization for Economic Cooperation and Development, *OECD Economic Surveys: Mexico 1995* (OECD, 1995), p. 46. The plan also put limits on wage increases, outlined a short-term financial bailout package, and liberalized the banking sector. See Torres and Carroll, "Zedillo Outlines his Peso-Rescue Plan," p. A3.

44. Even in May 1995, when the economy was perceived as stabilizing, the *Financial Times* reported that experts were still cautioning investors that "Mexico is not out of the woods yet." Philip Coggan, "Weekend Money: Mexican Memories Keep Analysists Wary," *Financial Times*, May 20, 1995, p. II.

45. U.S. Department of the Treasury, "Monthly Report by the Secretary of the Treasury, Pursuant to the Mexican Debt Disclosure Act of 1995" (Washington, August 1995), pp. 30, 31.

46. The critics were led by Senator Alfonse D'Amato. See D'Amato, Annexes: "Report on the Mexican Economic Crisis" and "Chronology of the

Mexican Economic Crisis: Documents." See also Clay Chandler, "Republicans Try to Block Mexican Rescue Package," *Washington Post*, March 31, 1995, p. F1.

47. The final outcome of this process was a bill passed in April 1995, which settled for a reporting requirement, from both the U.S. Treasury as well as the president, on the evolution of the Mexican economy, the use of U.S. funds, and the degree of consultation between both governments. In addition, the president would have to present a written report to Congress justifying any additional disbursements. See Mike Mills, "Treasury Says Congress Given Papers on Mexico," *Washington Post*, April 7, 1995, p. F1. See also "Gingrich Assails Clinton on Mexican Bailout," *New York Times*, May 5, 1995, p. D3, in which Gingrich reprimands Clinton for not writing a report but nonetheless giving additional disbursements. And see Senate bill, "Mexican Debt Disclosure Act of 1995," S 384, April 4, 1995.

48. *OECD Economic Surveys: Mexico 1995*, p.47.

49. Ibid.

50. Paul B. Carroll and Craig Torres, "Mexico Unveils Program of Harsh Fiscal Medicine," *Wall Street Journal*, March 10, 1995, p. A3. For formal details of the program, see "Programa de Acción para Reforzar el Acuerdo de Unidad para Superar la Emergencia Económica," Secretaria de Hacienda y Crédito Público (Mexico City, March 1995).

51. For a discussion of the programs see Banco de México, *The Mexican Economy, 1996: Economic and Financial Developments in 1995, Policies for 1996* (Mexico City, 1996), pp. 161–72.

52. In an otherwise sanguine report about the state of the Mexican economy, a report by First Boston states, "The only minor cloud on the horizon is the ever-going banking saga." Credit Suisse First Boston, "Mexico: Too Much of a Good Thing," August 5, 1997, p. 4.

53. U.S. Department of the Treasury, "Monthly Report by the Secretary of the Treasury Pursuant to the Mexican Debt Disclosure Act of 1995 (May 1996), p. 13. Figures are from the end of period.

54. Measured in 1993 pesos. See Instituto Nacional de Estadística Geografía e Informática (INEGI), *Sistema de cuentas nacionales de México: cuentas de bienes y servicios*, 1988-1995 (Aguascalientes, 1996), p. 63, tomo II, cuadro 142.

55. INEGI website, "Indicadores Económicos de Coyuntura, Producto Interno Bruto Trimestral" (http://dgcnesyp.iegi.gob.mx/pubcoy/economia/acteco/pibdiv.htm), downloaded September 18, 1997.

56. Macro Asesoría Económica, "Macro Update," Year 10, Number 5 (August 1997), p. 36, table 10.

57. See table 6-2.

58. For example, international reserves rose by U.S.$2,492 billion between January 1996 and March 1997 (Grupo de Economistas y Asociados, *GEA Económico*, July 15, 1997), p. 23.

59. Real exchange rate data from World Bank computed using the U.S. and Mexican consumer price indexes.

Chapter Eight

1. In chapter 3, I discussed the social costs imposed by the adjustment process during the 1980s. At the time of the publication of the first edition of this book, the data to analyze the evolution of poverty were not available. The information on real wages and incomes in agriculture indicated that poverty must have risen. This is confirmed by the numbers in table 8-1.

2. Poverty here refers to the headcount ratio, that is, the proportion of individuals with incomes below a prespecified poverty line. The ratios reported in all these tables use income per capita as the indicator of welfare. The data have been corrected for underreporting. Separate poverty lines have been used for rural and urban households. For extreme poverty measures, the poverty line is equal to 197 new pesos a person a month and for moderate poverty to 378 new pesos a person a month. For more details on the data sources and methodology see Nora Lustig and Miguel Szekely, "La evolución de la pobreza y la desigualdad en México," prepared for project, The Determinants of Poverty in Latin America, sponsored by the UN Development Programme, Inter-American Development Bank, and UN Economic Commission for Latin America and the Caribbean (December 1997).

3. Households are classified as urban if they live in municipalities that fulfill at least one of the following: the municipality includes at least one township of 15,000 inhabitants or more; the population total in the municipality is equal to or above 100,000 inhabitants; the municipality includes the capital of the state or is one of the twelve metropolitan areas of the country (Mexico, Guadalajara, Monterey, Leon, Merida, Chihuahua, San Luis Potosi, Puebla, Veracruz, Orizaba, Torreon, and Tampico). Households are classified as rural if they do not belong to the above with the exception of the rural areas of nineteen municipalities, which include townships of less than 2,500 inhabitants or where land is used for forestry, agriculture, or cattle raising.

4. The World Bank, for example, launched a new antipoverty strategy in 1989. The initial project included the four most disadvantaged states: Chiapas, Guerrero, Hidalgo, and Oaxaca. The project was expanded in 1994 to include Michoacan, Puebla, Veracruz, and Zacatecas. See World Bank, "Mexico: Strategy Proposal for Regional/Rural Develoment in the Disadvantaged States," vol. 1, Report 7786-ME (Washington, May 1989); and World Bank, "Mexico: Second Decentralization and Regional Development Project," Report 13032-ME (Washington, May 1994).

5. World Bank, "Mexico, Rural Poverty," Report 15058-ME (Washington, September 1996), p. 4.

6. Ibid., p. 22.

7. Consejo Mexicano del Café, website (www.inetcorp.net.mx/client/cafe/cafe.html), "Principales estados productores de café en México," downloaded September 8, 1997.

8. The International Coffee Agreement, in which members agreed to restrict their exports of coffee in order to boost prices, was dismantled in July

1989. It was readopted in March 1994. Report of the Secretary General of the United Nations, "Operational Activities for Development. Economic and Technical Cooperation among Developing Countries: State of South-South Cooperation," September 11, 1995 (from UN website, gopher://gopher.un.org/oo/ga/doc/50/plenary/340); and UN Food and Agriculture Organization, *Commodity Review and Outlook 1991-1992* (Rome, 1992), p. 37, and *Commodity Review and Outlook 1993-1994* (Rome, 1994), p. 49.

9. World Bank, "Mexico: Rural Poverty," p. 22.

10. *Ejido* is the land unit in which the *ejidatarios* are given the right to exploit the land but do not "own" it, that is, they cannot sell, rent. or borrow against it. The reform of constitutional article 27, ratified by the Mexican Congress on December 5, 1991, potentially opens the way for *ejidatarios* to privatize their *ejido* if they so desire. This reform states that (a) there will be no further land distribution; (b) commercial companies will be able to own rural land within defined limits; and (c) the productive portion of *ejidos* can be divided among members of the same *ejido*, and *ejidatarios* can also enter into associations with one another or outsiders to exploit, rent, or sell their holdings. "Mexico: Changes to Constitution concerning Land Ownership," *LDC Debt Report*, January 27, 1992, p. 9; and John Watling, "Opposition to Ejido Reforms Continues despite Congressional Approval," *El Financiero Internacional*, December 16, 1991, p. 3.

11. Alain de Janvry, Gustavo Gordillo, and Elisabeth Sadoulet, *Mexico's Second Agrarian Reform, Household and Community Responses, 1990–1994* (University of California, San Diego, Center for U.S.-Mexican Studies, 1997), p. 200.

12. Ibid., p. 199.

13. For a description and analysis of the reform of article 27, ibid., chap. 2.

14. Ibid., p. 200.

15. Ibid., p. 200.

16. Ibid., chaps. 13–16.

17. Zadia Maria Feliciano, "Workers and Trade Liberalization: The Impact of Trade Reforms in Mexico on Wages and Employment," mimeo (Harvard University, 1993); Michael Ian Cragg and Mario Epelbaum, "Why Has Wage Dispersion Grown in Mexico?" *Journal of Development Economics*, vol. 51 (October 1996), pp. 99-116; and Gordon H. Hanson and Anne Harrison, "Trade, Technology and Wage Inequality," NBER Working Paper 5110 (Cambridge, Mass.: National Bureau of Economic Research, May 1995).

18. Hanson and Harrison "Trade, Technology and Wage Inequality."

19. Results found by Ana Revenga, "Employment and Wage Effects of Trade Liberalization: The Case of Mexican Manufacturing," mimeo (Washington, World Bank, March 1995), are also consistent with this possibility. Another possible explanation for such results would be the following: although a more open economy in Mexico (or for that matter, other developing countries) leads it to specialize in more unskilled-labor intensive sectors,

this labor may be "unskilled" in developed country terms but not so in comparison to the skill distribution in Mexico.

20. Hanson and Harrison, "Trade, Technology and Wage Inequality," p. 20.

21. See table 7-3. September 1997 data are from Macro Asesoría Económica, "Macro Update," year 9, no. 5 (August 1996), table 9, p. 35.

22. World Bank, "Mexico, Poverty Reduction: The Unfinished Agenda," Report 15692 ME (Washington, December 1996), p. 22.

23. Macro Asesoría Económica, "Macro Update," year 10, no. 5 (August 1997), p. 35, table 9; and calculated from figures provided in Macro Asesoría Económica, "Macro Update," year 9, no. 5 (August 1996), p. 35, table 9.

24. Nonwage income in agriculture includes the income of peasant farmers.

25. Although completely anecdotal, *Forbes* magazine reported that one of Mexico's billionaires rose to fifth place in its 1996 list with a fortune estimated at U.S.$6.6 billion, U.S.$500 million more than in 1995. The businessman is Carlos Slim Helu, owner of Grupo Carso and Telmex. Roberto González Amador, "Slim, quinto hombre más rico del mundo," *La Jornada*, Internet edition, July 12, 1997.

26. Data from Grupo de Economistas y Asociados.

27. The PROBECAT (Programa de Becas de Capacitacion para Trabajadores, or Program of Scholarships for Training for Workers). World Bank, "Mexico: Poverty Reduction," p. 33, par. 74.

28. Ibid., p. 33.

29. Ibid., p. 22, par. 42.

30. The program is "Programa de Empleo Especial" (or Special Employment Program). Ibid., p.33, par 75.

31. Calculated from figures provided in Macro Asesoría Económica, "Macro Update," year 10, no. 5 (August 1997), table 9, p. 35; and Macro Asesoría Económica, "Macro Update," year 9, no. 5 (August 1996), table 9, p. 35.

32. For eradicating moderate poverty, 9.62 percent of the income of the top decile (or 4.29 percent of GDP) would need to be redistributed. Lustig and Szekely, "La evolución de la pobreza y la desigualdad en México."

33. José Gomez de León, director of PROGRESA, oral presentation, December 10, 1997, Inter-American Development Bank, Washington, D.C.

Chapter Nine

1. See, for example, Barry Bosworth, Rudiger Dornbusch, and Raúl Labán, eds., *The Chilean Economy: Policy Lessons and Challenges* (Brookings, 1994); and Sebastian Edwards and Alejandra Cox Edwards, *Monetarism and Liberalization: The Chilean Experiment* (University of Chicago Press, 1991).

2. Jonathan Friedland, "Chile Is Relaxed on NAFTA as Chief Begins U.S. Visit," *Wall Street Journal*, February 24, 1997, p. A18.

3. See the declarations by Francisco Gil Diaz, one of the Bank of Mexico's vice governors on this matter. According to the daily *La Jornada*, Gil Diaz, in

reference to the nationalization of the banks in 1982, said that the "banking crisis is the product of the expropriation and a privatization—undertaken by the government of Carlos Salinas de Gortari—*without control*, which took place before an impotent National Banking and Securities Commission to supervise it." (Emphasis added.) Humbeto Ortiz Moreno and Antonio Castellanos Martínez, "BdeM: 'sin control,' la privatización bancaria," *La Jornada*, September 9, 1997 (http://serpiente.dgsca.unam.mx/jornada/sincontrol/html), downloaded from INTERNET version.

4. Since the crisis, the Mexican authorities have introduced a number of changes to make the banking system less prone to crises in the future. Before the crisis of 1994, financial sector legislation restricted the participation of foreigners—and hence competition—in the banking sector. These restrictions were relaxed by legislation passed in February 1995, only after the dire state in which Mexican banks found themselves became fully evident (especially after the peso crisis of December 1994). In sum, the new legislation allowed much greater participation of foreigners. It raised the maximum percentage of foreign individuals and companies as a group to hold voting capital of (Mexican-controlled) banks from 30 percent to 49 percent, lowered the percentage of the share capital of its subsidiary that a foreign financial institution required to hold control from 99 percent to 51 percent, and it authorized the Ministry of Finance to increase, on a case-by-case basis, the market limit for foreign investment in the financial sector provided for in NAFTA. For example, under NAFTA, a single foreign-controlled bank could represent up to 1.5 percent of total capital of the banking system; the new legislation increased that percentage to 6 percent. Although NAFTA restricted the amount of all foreign-controlled banks together to 8 percent of total capital, the new arrangements raise that limit to 25 percent. International Monetary Fund, "Mexico: Recent Economic Developments" (Washington, Western Hemisphere Department, June 1995).

5. John Williamson, "Mexican Policy toward Foreign Borrowing," in Barry P. Bosworth, Susan M. Collins, and Nora Claudia Lustig, eds., *Coming Together? Mexican-United States Relations* (Brookings, 1997), pp. 59–90.

6. David Folkerts-Landau and others, *International Capital Markets: Developments, Prospects, and Policy Issues* (Washington: International Monetary Fund, August 1995), pp. 11–14.

7. International Monetary Fund, "IMF Adopts a Decision on New Arrangements to Borrow," press release 97/5, January 27, 1997 (www.imf.org/external/np/sec/pr/1997/PR9705.htm), downloaded from IMF website on September 24, 1997.

8. UN Food and Agriculture Organization, *Commodity Review and Outlook 1991–1992* (Rome, 1992), p. 37, and *Commodity Review and Outlook 1993-1994* (Rome, 1994), p. 49.

9. See, for example, the growth forecasts of Merrill Lynch "Mexico: Strongest Prospects in Latin America in 1998," New York, Global Securities, Research and Economic Group, December 25, 1997, p.1; and The Weston Group "Latin American Market Report," New York, December 19, 1997.

10. *Carta de Nexos*, vol. 2 (August 7–20, 1997).

11. Antonio Castellanos y Humberto Ortiz Moreno, "La política económica, ni partidista ni neoliberal, indica Guillermo Ortiz," *La Jornada,* September 9, 1997.

Appendix

1. For a detailed description, see José Angel Gurría T., "La política de deuda externa de México, 1982–1990," Secretaría de Hacienda y Crédito Público, Mexico City, January 1991; Sweder van Wijnbergen, "Mexico's External Debt Restructuring in 1989–90: An Economic Analysis," World Bank, March 4, 1990; and Nora Lustig, "Agreement Signed by Mexico and its Commercial Banks," prepared testimony before the Subcommittee on International Development, Finance, Trade and Monetary Policy of the Committee on Banking, Finance and Urban Affairs, U.S. House of Representatives, February 7, 1990.

2. The remainder, just over 1 percent of the total, corresponded to Facilities 2 and 3 of the 1986–87 Multi-Facility Agreement between Mexico and its commercial creditors. Gurría, "La política de deuda externa," p. 18.

3. Ibid., p. 16.

4. See van Wijnbergen, "Mexico's External Debt," p. 16. The Mexican government unexpectedly decided to complete all the debt-equity actions early, and the entire U.S.$3.5 billion in debt was swapped by October 1990. See "Debt-Equity Proves to Be a Smash Hit for Mexico," *LDC Debt Report,* October 15, 1990, p. 3.

5. See van Wijnbergen, "Mexico's External Debt," p. 15.

6. The letter of credit from commercial banks was given because funds from Japan would come between 1990 and 1992. The total credit provided by Japan in the end would equal U.S.$2.1 billion. See Gurría, "La política de deuda externa," p. 18.

7. Ibid., p. 19.

8. Some authors include the implicit reduction in total debt associated with the portion of the debt that will be subject to the 6.25 percent (below market) interest rate. See, for example, ibid., p. 19.

9. van Wijnbergen, "Mexico's External Debt," p. 23.

10. Some observers may consider that amortization of the principal should be excluded from the calculation because the principal would have been rescheduled without the need of enhancements, as in the past. The savings associated with the postponement of servicing the principal were estimated to be about U.S.$2 billion a year. It should be noted that after the fifth year the effect on amortizations must be netted out of the payments that Mexico has to make on the principal of the official loans used for the collateral.

11. Some analysts included as a cash flow benefit the interest saved on the loans that would have been made to cover the interest payments, and among the costs the interest paid on the zero coupon used to collateralize the principal.

12. Macro Asesoría Económica, *Realidad económica de México, 1991* (Mexico City, 1990), p. 325.

13. Given the amount of credit enhancements available, the discount obtained by Mexico, either through discount bonds or below-market interest rates on par bonds, is probably the largest that could have been obtained in a semi-voluntary, market-based setting such as the operation that took place. Since only eighteen months of interest payments enjoy guarantees, from the banks' perspective twenty-eight and a half years out of thirty of interest payments are still pure Mexican risk. Thus the actual market valuation of the new instruments, discount and par bonds, has an implicit discount that is higher than the nominal discount of 35 percent.

Index